DEFENSORIUM OBEDIENTIAE APOSTOLICAE
APOSTOLICAE
ET ALIA DOCUMENTA

DEFENSORIUM OBEDIENTIAE APOSTOLICAE ET ALIA DOCUMENTA

Edited and Translated by Heiko A. Oberman,
Daniel E. Zerfoss, and William J. Courtenay

THE BELKNAP PRESS OF
HARVARD UNIVERSITY PRESS CAMBRIDGE, MASSACHUSETTS
1968

PREFACE

This volume, in which we present the first modern edition of Gabriel Biel's *Defensorium obedientiae apostolicae*, is intended to make a contribution to several areas of late-medieval history. In the *Defensorium*, Biel, a major theologian of the postconciliar era, actively opposes an assault upon the papal see by Diether von Isenburg, the Archbishop-elect of Mainz. This treatise and the other documents included here serve as an excellent introduction to the ideological issues of a vicious political struggle, as viewed by contemporaries and participants. The documents likewise provide a kind of weathervane for the ecclesiological winds of the postconciliar era. The reader cannot fail to note the pronounced passion that pervades these writings. From the viewpoint of the present, the polemical overtones only underscore the issues themselves. These writers advance many arguments that are carefully expounded and developed in later treatises on canon and civil law. Thus the reader may wish to consult five closely argued legal opinions on the Mainz Stiftsfehde published recently by the Frankfurt legal historian, Adalbert Erler (*Mittelalterliche Rechtsgutachten zur Mainzer Stiftsfehde, 1459–1463*, Wiesbaden, 1964). It is hoped that our volume will prove an indispensable complement to Erler's edition.

We would like to express our gratitude to all those who offered assistance in our labors. We are especially indebted to the Mainz Stadtbibliothek and the Vatican Archives for their generosity in making the manuscripts of the *Defensorium* available to us.

PREFACE

The assistance of the librarians of both these libraries and of the Andover-Newton Library of the Harvard Divinity School is warmly acknowledged.

HEIKO A. OBERMAN
Tübingen   DANIEL E. ZERFOSS
April 1967   WILLIAM J. COURTENAY

CONTENTS

vii

INTRODUCTION
THE TWILIGHT OF THE CONCILIAR ERA

INTRODUCTION

THE TWILIGHT OF THE CONCILIAR ERA

> And we lay down that from now on, no one should dare, regardless of his pretext, to make such an appeal from our decisions, be they legal or theological, or from any commands at all from us or our successors, to heed such an appeal made by another, or to make use of these in any fashion whatsoever. But if anyone—regardless of his status, rank, order, or condition, even if he be distinguished by imperial, regal, or pontifical dignity—should violate this command when two months have expired from the day this bull has been published in the papal chancery, he, by this fact alone, incurs excommunication from which he cannot be absolved except through the pope and at the time of death.
>
> *Execrabilis*, 18 January 1460[1]

I. *EXECRABILIS* AND ITS ECHO

These words are generally regarded as sounding the death knell of conciliarism and sealing the victory of the papal monarchy. Later events seem to give strong support to this verdict. Never again did a council threaten papal ascendancy; even the strongest subsequent conciliar attempt, the Council of Pisa, convoked by Louis XII in 1511, proved a dismal failure. The heroic age of the councils was past. Pope Pius II singularly personified this decisive shift in church polity—the former secretary of the antipope Felix V and orator at the Council of Basel lived to author *Execrabilis*. In April 1463, following the model of Augustine's *Retractations*, Pius addressed to the University of Cologne a bull, *In minoribus agentes*, in which he sought pardon for his youthful conciliar "errors." He summarized his argument pithily: "Aeneam rejicite, Pium recipite." [2] Near the end of the bull, the papal monarchial assertion against the conciliar position is most clearly stated: "We

---

[1] See p. 227.
[2] *Bullarium diplomatum et privilegiorum sanctorum Romanorum pontificum*, ed. S. Franco and A. Dalmazzo, vol. V (Turin, 1860), p. 175.

3

INTRODUCTION

have never heard of an approved council that assembled without papal authority when there was an unquestioned Roman pontiff; the body of the Church is not without a head and all power flows from the head into the members." [3]

Although the strictures of *Execrabilis* are seemingly quite clear, the nature of the promulgation and application of the bull is strangely obscure. [4] Despite Pius's solemn assurances in the bull that he had consulted with the cardinals, prelates, and canonists present at the Congress of Mantua, it is notable that the daily reports of the orators of Milan and Siena at Mantua include no mention whatsoever of *Execrabilis*. [5] In addition to three copies of the bull in the Vatican Library, G. B. Picotti reports only three other known manuscripts of the text. These texts are located in Innsbruck, Dresden, and Lucca; all are copies. [6] The Innsbruck text is inserted in *Infructuosos palmites*, the bull of excommunication issued against Duke Sigismund of Tyrol on 2 November 1460. [7] Other contemporary evidence also suggests that *Execrabilis* was not widely circulated. On 13 August 1460, Duke Sigismund appealed to a future council in his dispute with Cardinal Cusa; he was apparently unaware of the Mantuan constitution. [8] Pius, at loggerheads with King Charles VII of France over Charles's continued adherence to the Pragmatic Sanction of Bourges, avoided any reference to a council or *Execrabilis* in his letters to the king. [9]

Pius drew *Execrabilis* from the papal arsenal only twice: once in *Infructuosos palmites*, [10] and again on 21 August 1461 in the bull of deposition promulgated against Archbishop Diether von Isenburg of

---

[3] *Ibid.*, p. 180; see p. 365.
[4] The writer is heavily indebted for these remarks to an article by G. B. Picotti, "La Pubblicazione e i primi effetti della 'Execrabilis' di Pio II," *Archivio della R. Società di Storia Patria* (Rome, 1914), pp. 5–56.
[5] Picotti, p. 14.
[6] Picotti, p. 19.
[7] Picotti, p. 19.
[8] Picotti, p. 30.
[9] Picotti, p. 34.
[10] *Infructuosos palmites* is reprinted in Picotti, pp. 50–56.

Mainz.[11] But three years later, a few days after the death of Cusa and Pius, Sigismund was absolved without any confession that he had fallen into heresy. Events suggest that the army of his rival, Adolf von Nassau, and not the pressure of papal censure, wrested the see of Mainz from Diether.

Execrabilis was apparently almost forgotten by the successors of Pius II. After years of tortuous diplomatic maneuver, Louis XI in 1476 effected his repeated threat to appeal to a general council by convoking a synod of the French clergy at Orleans to draft an appeal which he solemnly dispatched to Rome. Sixtus IV received the French king's embassy with a calm statement of the papal position: "The authority to will or not to will a council is fixed solely in the Roman pontiff."[12] *Execrabilis* was not invoked. The appeal of Louis XI proved to be a diplomatic feint which miscarried. The quixotic attempt of Andrea Zamometič, the Archbishop of Gran, to reopen the Council of Basel in the spring of 1482 met with fiery protests from Sixtus IV and firm reassertions of the sole right of the Pope to convoke a general council. No reference was made to the Mantuan prohibition of 1460.[13] A professor of theology at the University of Basel who wrote a moderate defense of papal primacy against Zamometič based his argument upon Boniface VIII's *Unam sanctam* and included not a word concerning *Execrabilis*.[14]

The war between Sixtus IV and Venice over Ferrara elicited a Venetian appeal to a general council. The appeal was even posted upon the doors of St. Peter's, Sant' Angelo, and the Pantheon in Rome. On 15 July 1483 the Pope responded with *Qui monitis* which declared the appeal null, sacrilegious, and detestable, and excommunicated the

---

[11] See p. 229 f.

[12] Quoted in Picotti, p. 44.

[13] Picotti, p. 42. Hubert Jedin observes that Picotti does not note that Zamometič demanded a council rather than issuing an appeal to a future council; thus he asserts that *Execrabilis* did not apply to this case. See Hubert Jedin, *A History of the Council of Trent* (New York: Thomas Nelson & Sons, 1957), I, 67n4.

[14] Picotti, p. 42.

Doge and his adherents. The bull resoundingly asserted papal primacy and vaguely referred to the constitution of Pius II as possessing validity in perpetuity.[15] However the content of *Execrabilis* was altered and amplified to permit the Venetians a year's respite before their appeal was termed heresy and schism. Indeed the peace included no demand for a revocation of the appeal; the Venetians received absolution for merely disobeying the papal precept upon the Ferrarese question.[16]

In response to a renewed Venetian appeal, Julius II in 1509 published the only careful citation of *Execrabilis* before the Reformation. *Suscepti regiminis*, dated 1 July 1509, insisted that *Execrabilis* possessed enduring validity and declared schismatic any support or approval of an appeal to a future council.[17] However in 1511 Giovanni Gozzadini, an eminent Bolognese canonist at the court of Julius II, contested the validity of *Execrabilis* in a study of papal elections. He argued that the bull was not binding because it deprived the accused of a basic right in natural law.[18] A contemporary jurist, Matthias Ugonius, concurred in his treatise, *De conciliis*: "Pius II's bull is no obstacle to an appeal to a Council, since it is at variance with natural law."[19]

As late as March 1518 the University of Paris, to protest the Concordat of Bologna, appealed counter to *Execrabilis* to a general council.[20] But the period of ambiguity ended with the celebrated *Exsurge, domine* promulgated against Luther on 15 June 1520. The rejection of the conciliar theory in thesis 28 of this bull is founded expressly upon *Execrabilis* and *Suscepti regiminis*.[21] This condemnation, however, continued to meet decided opposition in Germany. A memorial of German

---

[15] Picotti, pp. 46–47.
[16] Picotti, p. 47.
[17] Picotti, pp. 49–50; Jedin, I, 67.
[18] Jedin, I, 67.
[19] Quoted in Jedin, I, 68.
[20] Jedin, I, 172.
[21] Jedin, I, 174; the text of *Exsurge, domine* is found in *Magnum Bullarium Romanum*, 748–757.

princes at the Diet of Worms in the spring of 1521 protested: "A council alone is in a position to ascertain whether Dr. Martinus has written against the faith; he has appealed to a council and thereby tied the Pope's hands. Pius II's and Julius II's prohibitions are invalid because they are at variance with natural and divine law, as well as with the decrees of Constance, and they have not been recognized by the University of Paris." [22]

II. GERMANY'S RELUCTANT RECONCILIATION WITH THE PAPACY: THE CONCORDAT OF VIENNA AND ITS AFTERMATH

The realization that the Conciliar Era was decisively closed dawned very slowly, as is suggested by the uncertain application of *Execrabilis* in the decades before the Reformation. Yet it is quite evident that church polity in 1460 had shifted radically since the promulgation of *Sacrosancta* (6 April 1415) and *Frequens* (9 October 1417), which proved to be the high watermarks of the conciliar movement. The forty years of strife between the conciliarists and the curialists from the Council of Pisa (1409) to the surrender of the remnant of the Council of Basel (1449) sapped the energies of the Church and left a heavy residue of bitterness and disappointment. Hope aroused by the original promise of a "reformatio ecclesiae in capite et in membris" [23] expressed at Pisa and Constance faded into despair as the discovery was made that the discordant conciliar elements could not agree even upon an effective minimal program of church reform. Frustrated efforts to remove abuses fostered gnawing mistrust within the Church. This frustration echoed decades later in the words of the great cathedral preacher, Geiler von Kaysersberg: "The whole Council of Basel was not sufficiently powerful

---

[22] *Deutsche Reichstagakten unter Kaiser Karl V*, ed. Adolf Wrede (Gotha, 1896), II, 534–535; cited in Jedin, I, 201.

[23] This conciliar reform ideal was first expressed by the fourteenth-century canonist Guillaumus Durandus in his treatise, *De modo concilii generalis celebrandi;* see Jedin, I, 8.

to reform a convent of nuns when the city took their side . . . How then can a Council reform the whole of Christendom?"[24]

Against an exhausted Church powerful secular forces were straining for autonomy and new channels of expression. Perhaps most ominous for a united Christendom was the momentous growth of jealously defensive national senses of identity, most openly manifested in the Gallican Church and the enduring Bohemian schism. In the consolidation of territorial authority, rulers throughout Europe quite willingly supported ecclesiastical particularism. Aeneas Sylvius Piccolomini, the future Pius II, sensed this development dimly in a letter written in 1454: "Christianity has no head whom all wish to obey. Neither the Pope nor the Emperor is rendered his due. There is no reverence, no obedience. Thus we regard the Pope and Emperor as if they bore false titles and were mere painted objects. Each city has its own king. There are as many princes as there are households."[25] The outcries of prelates and the lower clergy against the fiscal rapacity and moral corruption of the Curia became inextricably enmeshed in national and regional issues.

Nowhere in Europe was particularism in the political and spiritual realms more apparent than in the decaying Holy Roman Empire. The Emperor had become a mere regional magnate; Germans living outside the Hapsburg domains during the long, dismal reign of Frederick III (1440–1493) were scarcely aware of the Emperor's existence. Particularist advantage lured the shadow Emperor, as it did many other German princes, to return to papal allegiance in 1446. Frederick's reward for submission was noteworthy: the lifelong privilege of nominating six bishops (Gurk, Trieste, Piben, Chur, Trent, and Brixen), three Cistercian abbots, and the visitors of all Austin convents in his lands; the lifelong prerogative of bestowing 100 benefices within the

---

[24] Quoted in Ludwig Pastor, *History of the Popes* (St. Louis, 1910), II, 49.
[25] Quoted in Joachim Johann Müller, *Des Heiligen Römischen Reichs Teutscher Nation Reichstag Theatrum* . . . (Jena, 1713), I, 484; and Viktor von Kraus, *Deutsche Geschichte zur Zeit Albrechts II and Friedrichs III, 1438–1486* (Stuttgart and Berlin, 1905), p. 314.

Hapsburg domains; the privilege of levying a tithe upon all the benefices within the Empire; and a papal grant of at least 100,000 Rhenish
gulden for the forthcoming expedition of Frederick to Rome for the
imperial coronation.[26] The hollow pomp of the coronation staged by
Pope Nicholas V in 1452 made the enfeebled dignity of the Emperor
poignantly tangible; Frederick III, who lacked the resources for his
own coronation, offered a wretched contrast to the two great Hohen-
staufen Fredericks.[27] Frederick's utter indifference to German concerns
and his readiness to support the Pope for his own dubious advantage
made it almost certain that the German territorial princes and prelates,
discontented with lawless chaos in the secular realm and with
arbitrary exploitation in the spiritual, would oppose both Pope and
Emperor.

The great feudal churchmen of Germany, led by the Spiritual Electors
of Mainz, Cologne, and Trier, were peculiarly preoccupied with defending vested ecclesiastical and secular interests. The extensive princi-
palities and feudal prominence of the most important German prelates
made neutrality almost impossible in the savage regional conflicts that
devastated the countryside. It is therefore not surprising that spirituality
was not a primary consideration in episcopal and abbatial elections,
and that the greatest ecclesiastics were more comfortable when clad in
armor than when attired in clerical vestments. A fifteenth-century
Rhenish chronicler lamented, "Alas, how many bishops abandon the
cross for the sword! One only seeks bishoprics now to arrive at temporal
power, and the religious has become an exceptional phenomenon
upon our episcopal thrones."[28] Such bishops, immersed in regional
concerns, could offer only equivocal allegiance to the universal claims
of Pope or Emperor.

---

[26] Kraus, pp. 178, 180.
[27] Kraus, pp. 291–294.
[28] Quoted in Roger Aubenas and Robert Ricard, *L'Eglise et la Renaissance: 1449–1517*,
vol. XV of *Histoire de l'Eglise depuis les origines jusqu'à nos jours*, ed. Augustin
Fliche and Victor Martin (Paris, 1951), p. 314.

INTRODUCTION

The political division of the Empire was largely responsible for the failure of the Germans during the Council of Basel to achieve the position of the Gallican Church. After Pope Eugenius IV transferred the Council from Basel to Ferrara (18 September 1437), and the intransigent remnant of the Council of Basel suspended Eugenius and forbade all Christian rulers to remain obedient to him (24 January 1438), the German imperial Electors adopted a declaration of neutrality between Basel and Eugenius (17 March 1438).[29] This declaration, intended as a temporary expedient, was repeatedly renewed in the next nine years. Seeking to emulate the French Pragmatic Sanction of 1438 and to define the position of the German Church more affirmatively, the Mainz imperial Diet of March 1439 accepted certain of the reform pronouncements of the Council of Basel.[30] The German princes did recognize conciliar supremacy implicitly, although they urged the adjournment of the Council of Basel pending the convocation of a more truly ecumenical council. The *Acceptatio*, sometimes inaccurately termed the Pragmatic Sanction of Mainz, revealed how strongly German churchmen resented the heavy fiscal exactions of the Roman Curia and Roman infringement on their jurisdiction, authority, and possessions. Annates were abolished; the practice of reservations and expectative graces was sharply curtailed, and the traditional canonical safegrounds of capitular electoral privileges asserted; frivolous judicial appeals to the Curia were forbidden; provision was made for diocesan and provincial synods; and no financial exaction of the Curia in Germany was to be sanctioned without the consent of the German rulers.[31]

---

[29] Kraus, pp. 39–40.

[30] The document which contains these proceedings has become known in German history as the *Acceptatio* of Mainz.

[31] For a fuller discussion of the Mainz Diet of 1439 and the *Acceptatio*, see Kraus, pp. 41–42; Bruno Gebhardt, *Die Gravamina der Deutschen Nation gegen den römischen Hof: ein Beitrag zur Vorgeschichte der Reformation*, 2 ed. (Breslau, 1895), pp. 114–125; and George Voigt, *Enea Silvio de' Piccolomini als Papst Pius der Zweite und sein Zeitalter* (Berlin, 1863), I, 162–166.

10

THE TWILIGHT OF THE CONCILIAR ERA

The divided Empire found itself unable to defend this stated position effectively. The resolve of the German princes to present a united front against Basel and Rome flagged, and it became increasingly apparent that neutrality was a mask for the individual ambitions of the princes. Archbishop Jacob of Trier came to an understanding with antipope Felix V in exchange for the tithes of Saxony and the provinces of Magdeburg and Bremen.[32] Under the pretext of opposing heresy and the Hussites, Felix granted the Duke of Saxony the right to fill three bishoprics and seven other Saxon benefices.[33] Delegates of the imperial cities at the Diet of Nuremberg in 1443 justifiably attacked neutrality as a selfish scheme of the German hierarchy "for the oppression of poor priests and the laity."[34]

As the fortunes of both Basel and Felix steadily declined, shrewd papal diplomats such as Carvajal and Aeneas Sylvius Piccolomini, Felix's former secretary, uttered vague recognition of conciliar principles and tempted the princes with the concrete personal advantages of individual settlement with Eugenius. With smooth evasions and intentional silences, Cusa and Carvajal represented Eugenius at the Frankfurt Diet in September 1446. They made ambiguous promises that they would attempt to satisfy the grievances expressed at Mainz in 1439, to recognize the declarations of Basel on conciliar authority for the period Eugenius had extended recognition to Basel, and even to convoke a council at a time and place acceptable to the other princes of Christendom.[35] The lure of tangible benefit, now attainable only in Rome, and the papacy's willingness to concede the ecclesiastical status quo in Germany, and to refrain from reprisals against lukewarm supporters of the Church, attracted back to the papal fold the realistic princes and even such cynical supporters of Basel as Archbishop Jacob of Trier and Archbishop Dietrich of Cologne.

---

[32] Kraus, p. 109.
[33] Kraus, p. 109.
[34] Kraus, pp. 94–95.
[35] Kraus, pp. 186–187.

INTRODUCTION

Eugenius achieved tentative accord with the most important German rulers upon his deathbed in February 1447. All benefices, confirmations, and dispensations issued by Basel before its suspension by Eugenius, and all administrative activity of the German Church during the protracted period of neutrality, received papal confirmation conditional upon return to papal obedience within six months. On the same basis, penalties against German neutrals and supporters of Basel were retracted, and all fiscal obligations such as annates and tithes incurred during the long separation were set aside. A provisional pledge was given to seek the support of the other princes of Europe within ten months for a council to be convened within the following eighteen months.[36] The conciliar principle was treated with studied ambiguity: "We accept, embrace, and venerate the General Council of Constance, *Frequens* and its other decrees, as we do other councils representing the universal Church militant and their power, authority, honor, and eminence [the conciliar term "preeminence" was carefully avoided]. Thus we follow our predecessors from whose footsteps we intend never to stray."[37] Although the terms were extraordinarily favorable to Rome, Eugenius drew up a secret document in which he attested that his concessions were due to grave illness and were void if the rights of the Apostolic See were infringed in any fashion.[38] Three weeks later Eugenius was dead and the validity of the accord was in question.

The conciliatory spirit of Eugenius' successor, Nicholas V, and the deeply felt German desire for a definitive solution led at last to the Concordat of Vienna, 17 February 1448, which confirmed the status quo but settled little else. The concordat was much briefer and more moderate than the *Acceptatio* of 1439; the considerable endeavor of the *Acceptatio* to place checks upon the Pope and the Curia by specifying the number of cardinals in the Sacred College, outlining minimal qualifications for the cardinalate, and setting standards for their

---

[36] Kraus, pp. 192–194; Müller, I, 347–351.
[37] Müller, I, 351.
[38] Kraus, p. 194; Müller, I, 352–353.

12

conduct was completely abandoned in the concordat. The concordat did attempt to set broad limits to the papal collation of benefices and to maintain the integrity of capitular elections in cathedral churches and monasteries. However, the unpopular annates abolished by the Council of Basel and the *Acceptatio* were recognized by the concordat for all cathedral churches and benefices yielding an annual income of more than 24 gulden. The limitations upon the Curia's collection of the annates were slight: provision was made for payment across a period of two years; only one levy of the annates was granted in the event of a repeated vacancy within one year; and a commission was advocated to investigate the income of the German Church and to adjust papal taxes accordingly. The omissions of the concordat were eloquent. Gone were the affirmations of the *Acceptatio* upon the authority of general councils, the regular convocation of diocesan and provincial synods, acceptance of the mild disciplinary and liturgical reforms adopted by Basel, and the *Acceptatio's* protests against the infringement of the judicial jurisdiction of the German Church.[39] The concordat exposed the weaknesses of the German Church. However, it must be noted that Rome did make significant sacrifices to territorial princes such as Frederick III, Margrave Albert of Brandenburg, and the Elector Frederick of Saxony.[40]

The clearsighted recognized that the papacy had not decisively defeated the conciliar opposition. In late 1448 Aeneas Sylvius wrote to Nicholas V: "The waves of Basel are not yet calmed, the winds are still struggling beneath the water and rushing through secret channels . . . We have a truce, not a peace. 'We have yielded to force,' say our opponents, 'not to conviction; what we have once taken into our heads we still hold fast.' So we must look forward to another battlefield and a

---

[39] The best exposition of the Concordat of Vienna is found in Gebhardt, pp. 114–125; for the text, see Müller, I, 359–362. See also Kraus, pp. 199–200, and Voigt, I, 417–423.

[40] Kraus, p. 199.

fresh struggle for the supremacy."[41] Ten years later he still reported that all Germans, "paululum docti," supported the conciliar position. Granted that this is an overstatement, the German universities of Cologne, Erfurt, Leipzig, and Vienna did remain loyal to conciliar doctrine and continued to regard the decrees of Constance and Basel as binding.[42]

The conciliar idea remained especially attractive within the circles of practical and mystical piety that were most concerned with reform. The most articulate German clerical defender of conciliarism was the aloof and austere Carthusian, Jacob of Jüterbog, who taught theology at the University of Erfurt. In an *Advisamentum* written in 1449 to Pope Nicholas V upon the subject of the reform of the Church, Jacob deplored the manner in which the statutes of the councils were ignored and abused, and contended that the Church could only be regenerated by a general council to which the Pope would submit in all matters concerned with faith and general reform. Jacob found comfort in the assurance that there were "many good men everywhere" who would not surrender the conciliar position and insisted that he would not retract what he had written unless convinced of his error by the Church or one of better insight.[43]

The voices of the opponents of the papacy at the German courts grew increasingly strident in the decade following the Concordat of Vienna. The momentary calm in Christendom, achieved by the search of Nicholas V for reconciliation and the Jubilee of 1450, passed very rapidly. A tract urging the prompt convocation of a general council and the grave need for reform of the excesses and extravagance of the Roman Curia was nailed to the door of the papal legate, Cardinal Cusa, in Mainz in late 1451. The author contended that large Jubilee indul-

---

[41] From a letter dated 25 November 1448 quoted in Pastor, II, 60–61. This passage is also found in Voigt, II, 50.

[42] Jedin, I, 32, 34; Kraus, p. 201.

[43] Karl Ullmann, *Reformers before the Reformation*, trans. as vol. VI of *Clark's Foreign Theological Library* (Edinburgh, 1855), pp. 210–216.

gences had shaken the faith of the people and had been expended for dubious purposes.[44] Repeated papal appeals for a crusade and extraordinary fiscal measures such as indulgences and general tithes to confront the increasingly dangerous Turkish threat aroused a chorus of accusations of fiscal exploitation in Germany. Disgruntled cries were heard that the Emperor and the Pope wished only to exhaust the wealth of the Germans and that the Turkish crusade was merely a pretext to conceal naked self-interest.[45]

In 1455 the Electors attempted to convince the Emperor to refuse obedience to the newly elected Calixtus III until concessions comparable to France's Pragmatic Sanction were made, but they met with no response.[46] The dogged determination of this aging pope to levy a crusading tithe in Germany fanned the German princes to fury. In August 1456 a large assemblage of princes, prelates, and representatives of cathedral chapters and imperial cities gathered in Frankfurt to organize united opposition to excessive Roman taxes and to the worst infringements of the decrees of Basel and the concordat. The Electors sharply enjoined the Emperor to attend a Reichstag at Nuremberg near the end of the year to join the German princes in the formulation of a German Pragmatic; in the event that Frederick refused the proffered invitation, as he had numerous previous ones, the Electors and princes threatened to act unilaterally and to search for a new candidate for the imperial crown.[47] Frederick refused and the Electors convened to effect their threat. The imperial reform movement was doomed to failure, however, because the Electors and princes found agreement upon a new imperial candidate impossible; moreover, the thrust for church reform was swiftly engulfed in this quagmire of German political strife.[48] Nevertheless Calixtus III was forced to recognize the strength

---

[44] Gebhardt, pp. 6–7; Pastor, II, 133.
[45] Aubenas and Ricard, p. 43; Gebhardt, p. 12; Kraus, p. 309.
[46] Müller, I, 595–596.
[47] Kraus, pp. 323–324; Pastor, II, 414–416.
[48] Kraus, pp. 325–327.

of German resistance and resentment. In a lengthy letter to Frederick III in late 1457, the Pope stoutly denied the charges formulated at the Frankfurt Diet of 1456 and protested his innocence of infringing the concordat.[49] His tardy recognition of the concordat must have seemed reluctant and arbitrary to the German opposition: "Although the authority of the Apostolic See is completely unrestrained and ought not to be confined with the bonds of covenants, nevertheless solely from our magnanimity, the zeal which we bear for peace, and the affection which we bestow upon you and your nation, we accept the concordat; nor will we permit it to be rashly violated while we are ruler of the Roman See."[50] A direct clash between the Pope and the German opposition had not yet taken place when the aged Calixtus died in August 1458.

III. THE MAINZ STIFTSFEHDE

This confrontation was the lot of the next pope, Pius II. The curialist and conciliarist forces were squarely pitted against one another in the struggle between Pius II and Diether von Isenburg, the refractory Archbishop of Mainz, from Diether's election in 1459 until his abdication in 1463. Diether, as leader of the anti-imperial and antipapal party within the Holy Roman Empire, appealed his case to a future general council. Pius II responded by deposing and excommunicating Diether as a rebel against the Apostolic See. These years also saw the culmination of the long conflict between Cardinal Cusa and Duke Sigismund of Tyrol over the bishopric of Brixen. The issues and events of this conflict cast a shadow upon the Mainz Stiftsfehde and increased the weight of the German opposition to Rome.

In the factional polemic provoked by the Mainz Stiftsfehde and by Duke Sigismund's bitter clash with the papacy are revealed the ecclesiological issues that remained matters of fundamental concern for over a

---

[49] A portion of this letter is published in Müller, I, 608–610.
[50] Müller, I, 610.

decade after the ill-fated end of the Council of Basel in 1449. The archbishop and Duke Sigismund enjoyed the services of the vitriolic pen of
Gregor Heimburg. The hot-tempered jurist composed numerous tracts
defending the conciliarist position and attacking *Execrabilis* as an
affront against divine and natural law. Heimburg assuredly inspired
Archbishop Diether's *Defense* of October 1461. The Pope's case was
espoused with equal violence by the curial favorite, Teodoro Laelio,
Bishop of Feltre, in his *Replica* addressed to Heimburg.

The most important tract that appeared during the dispute, however,
was the *Defensorium obedientiae apostolicae* of Gabriel Biel. Biel, a
stout supporter of the papal cause, had been cathedral preacher and
vicar in Mainz for several years when the struggle between Diether and
Adolf von Nassau for the archiepiscopal throne broke out in 1461. The
Defensorium summarizes the doctrinal content of the sermons he preached in the Rheingau after his flight from Mainz. In this treatise he defends himself as "the least among orthodox preachers"[51] with undue
modesty—as the most important fifteenth-century German representative of the *Via Moderna*, Biel's claim in this work to define orthodox
doctrine is striking and significant. As late as the Council of Trent he
remained a highly respected theologian whose orthodoxy was never
impugned. His view that the formulations contained in the *Defensorium*
were removed from the realm of theological controversy found echo
in the grateful reception and approval accorded this work by Pius
II.[52]

The immediate origin of the Mainz Stiftsfehde lay in the election of
Diether von Isenburg as Archbishop of Mainz on 18 June 1459. Because
documentary evidence of the official election has not been discovered,
we are forced to balance conflicting assertions made after the fact.
Diether declared repeatedly that he had received all seven votes of the

---

[51] See p. 71.
[52] The Mainz Stiftsfehde is carefully examined in a wider context in a doctoral dis-
sertation (Harvard University) by Daniel E. Zerfoss, "Gravamina Germaniae: The
Archbishops of Mainz and the Papacy, 1448–1484."

electors of the Mainz cathedral chapter.[53] Pius II contended on the contrary that Diether was strongly opposed by Graf Adolf of Nassau. According to the account of Pius, Diether and Adolf each commanded three chapter electors; the fourth and decisive vote was wooed and won by Diether for the handsome bribe of 3,000 gulden.[54] However, the allegation of the pope was made two years after the event and after papal confirmation of the election. No other contemporary called the validity of the election into question—indeed it should be noted that Biel in the *Defensorium* refers to Diether as "quondam electus."[55] Most persuasive is the absence of any charge by Diether's future opponent, Adolf, that his election was tainted by simony; in fact, Adolf recognized Diether as Archbishop-elect and continued to administer the archiepiscopal lands in Thuringia for the next two years.[56]

As the second son of Graf Diether von Isenburg-Büdingen, lord of considerable lands in the diocese of Mainz, Diether had been destined to a career in the Church from an early age. In 1429, as a youth of seventeen, he became a cathedral canon of Mainz. In the following years he accumulated other important benefices in the Rhineland, including canonries in the cathedral chapters of Cologne and Trier. Diether harbored strong ecclesiastical ambitions. By 1453 he had become *custos* of the Mainz cathedral chapter, an important official in the administration of the diocese. In 1456 he attempted unsuccessfully to be elected Archbishop of Trier.[57]

---

[53] See Diether's *Defense* of 1 October 1461, p. 253; see also his *Manifesto* of April 1462 in Müller, II, 113–117.

[54] See the bull of deposition, p. 231; this version is also related in the *Commentaries* of Pius II found in *Memoirs of a Renaissance Pope: The Commentaries of Pius II*, Leona C. Gabel, ed. (New York: G. P. Putnam's Sons, 1959), pp. 123–124, 200.

[55] See p. 122.

[56] Nicolai Serarius and Georg Christian Joannis, *Rerum Moguntiacarum* (Frankfurt am Main, 1722), I, 773.

[57] For a sketch of Diether's early life see Karl Menzel, *Diether von Isenburg, Erzbischof von Mainz, 1459–1463* (Erlangen, 1868), pp. 19–20; R. Glaser, "Diether von Isenburg–Budingen: Erzbischof und Kurfürst von Mainz (1459–1463) und die kirchlichen und politischen Reformbestrebung im fünfzehnten Jahrhundert," *Sammlung Wissenschaftlichen Vorträge*, XII (1898), pp. 763–764; and Kraus, p. 352.

THE TWILIGHT OF THE CONCILIAR ERA

Like many other German lords who pursued clerical careers, Diether apparently preferred hawking and jousting to the fulfillment of his pastoral obligations. Indeed Biel declares that it is generally known that Diether had never taken sacerdotal or any other sacred orders and sought no dispensation when elected archbishop.[58] No other source completely confirms this serious allegation. The bull of deposition promulgated against Diether on 21 August 1461 includes only the ambiguous charge that Diether had not been promoted to the episcopate within the period allotted in canon law. The bull echoes Biel's contention that the headstrong Diether persisted in celebrating mass while under the sentence of excommunication.[59]

The widening rift between Diether and the papacy in the two years following Diether's election was produced largely by more secular considerations. The death of wily Archbishop Jacob of Trier in May 1456 removed an inveterate foe of the papacy; the young Margrave Johann of Baden, a member of the imperial and papal faction in Germany, was elected his successor, thus assuring the Pope valuable new support. Archbishop Dietrich of Cologne, old and in ill health, nearing the end of a long reign stained by violence and almost exclusive concern for familial aggrandizement, had all but abandoned imperial politics. In these years, therefore, the leadership of the opposition to the Pope in the German Church fell upon the aged Archbishop Dietrich of Mainz. Upon his death, consequently, the new Archbishop, Diether von Isenburg, known to be on close terms with the Pfalzgraf Frederick, the most formidable foe of the Emperor within the Empire, became the most probable candidate to head the opposition.[60]

The Archbishop of Mainz could prove to be a redoubtable foe for the papacy; not without justification did Pius II refer to the archbishop as "a second Pope north of the Alps."[61] The archbishop, as

---

[58] See p. 129.
[59] See p. 157.
[60] For the best brief outline of German ecclesiastical politics at this time, see Gebhardt, pp. 13–15.
[61] Cf. Gabel, *Comm. of Pius II*, p. 372.

INTRODUCTION

Primate of Germany, ruled over a province comprised of twelve suffragan bishoprics which extended from Verden near the mouth of the Elbe southward through the heartland of modern Germany to Chur in the Swiss Alps. As Archchancellor of Germany and Imperial Elector, the archbishop commanded vast influence within the Holy Roman Empire. Extensive lands along the Rhine and the Main rivers and in Thuringia made the archbishop an important territorial prince as well. He was also the Chancellor of the University of Erfurt, a stronghold of conciliarist theory in the Conciliar Era.

Following his election, Diether immediately dispatched an embassy to the Pope to secure confirmation and conferral of the archiepiscopal pallium. The envoys found Pius II at Mantua still awaiting the arrival of the princes of Christendom whom he had summoned to discuss preparations for a crusade against the Turks. The Pope's bitter chagrin at the general indifference of the European rulers to the Mantuan Congress found vent in the harsh conditions which he laid down for Diether's confirmation: he must come to Mantua in person to seek confirmation; he must give his consent to a crusade tithe upon all income of the German Church; and he must promise never to seek a general council or to assemble the German Electors or his suffragan bishops without papal permission.[62]

The desire of the Pope to exploit the situation for political ends was quite evident—he hoped that the dwindling prestige of the congress might be bolstered by the presence and support of the Primate of Germany. The papal conditions were quite audacious. The Pope's contention that Diether was obligated to appear at Mantua, because it was the canonical duty of a bishop to respond to a summons to a synod, rested upon the dubious assumption that Mantua was indeed a synod.[63] The attempt to prevent Diether from convoking the bishops of his

---

[62] For one account by Pius II, see the bull of deposition of 21 August 1461, pp. 233–299; for Diether's version, see his *Defense* of 1 October 1461, pp. 255–259.

[63] This is the account of Pius II of the address of his nuncio Rudolf von Rüdesheim at the Mainz Diet of June, 1461; see Gabel, *Comm. of Pius II*, pp. 196–200.

province and the German Electors called into question Diether's
prerogatives as Archbishop of Mainz and Archchancellor of Germany.[64]
The envoys of the archbishop insisted that they had been granted no
authorization to deal with such matters, and argued that Diether could
not come due to sickness and the strain such a journey would impose
upon the straitened fiscal resources of the diocese. When Diether's
agents returned and reported the Pope's conditions, he adamantly
refused to accept them.[65]

A second legation headed by the cathedral teacher Volprecht von
Ders discovered a friendlier welcome in Mantua. In an election capitu-
lation Diether had sworn to support the Mainz cathedral chapter in its
jurisdictional wrangling with Pfalzgraf Frederick. To implement this
oath Diether was compelled to seek allies among the Pfalzgraf's
enemies in the imperial faction.[66] When Margrave Albert of Brandenburg visited Mantua in December 1459, he informed the Pope that
Diether had allied himself to the imperial faction.[67] The Pope, omitting
his earlier demands, promised to grant a bull of confirmation and the
pallium to Diether upon the condition that he appear at the papal
court within one year and pay annates assessed at 20,550 Rhenish
gulden. The figure was an astounding one. The envoys briefly considered
refusal, but finally decided to accept, and they entered into a contract
with the papal bankers for a loan of 20,000 gulden. The terms of the
loan were conventional: payment within one year under pain of minor
excommunication.[68]

The validity of this assessment, which the Curia insisted was based
upon the traditional tax, is very difficult to determine. Diether claimed
that the annates demanded were almost three times the traditional

[64] See Diether's protest, p. 257.
[65] Gebhardt, p. 39; Menzel, pp. 23–26; for Diether's version, see pp. 255–257.
[66] Kraus, p. 352.
[67] Kraus, p. 353; Menzel, p. 27.
[68] For Diether's second legation and the terms of the papal confirmation, see Glaser,
p. 769; Kraus, p. 353; Menzel, pp. 28–30; Voigt, III, 270.

sum;[69] most German contemporaries concurred.[70] The significant issue for our purposes, however, is Diether's adamant refusal to pay the annates and to appear before the Pope to swear obedience; for thus he denied the binding force of the oath that his envoys had sworn to the curial bankers and defied a papal mandate.

During the year following the return of Diether's second legation from Mantua in February 1460, Diether's influence rose markedly within the Empire, and Pius II was confronted with increasing frustration. The sound defeat of Diether and his imperial allies at Pfedersheim by the Pfalzgraf Frederick (4 July 1460) quickly led to a settlement and a twenty-year alliance between the two Electors. Archbishop Diether surrendered certain villages to the Pfalzgraf, and in return won the Pfalzgraf's support in his difficulties with the Curia.[71] This alliance became the fulcrum of the antipapal and anti-imperial faction in Germany. By the end of the year, a number of factors—the endemic warfare of skirmishes, raids, and pillaging that had been raging for months across southern Germany, gnawing discontent with imperial misrule, and anger at the Emperor's open endorsement of the fiscal exactions of the Curia—had aroused wide support among the German princes for the election of a new King of the Romans.

Papal efforts to secure support for an expedition against the Turks encountered stiff opposition in Germany. At the Vienna Reichstag (September 1460) the papal legate, Cardinal Bessarion, insisted peremptorily that a tithe should be levied upon all the Germans and that a crusade indulgence should be preached throughout the Empire. Bessarion threatened the recalcitrant with deposition, imprisonment, and excommunication. Speaking for the princes, Heinrich Luebing, the representative of Archbishop Diether, responded stiffly that such a levy

---

[69] See Diether's *Defense*, p. 261.
[70] The most complete discussion of this rather complicated issue is in an article by Fritz Hermann, "Die Mainzer Servitien-Zahlungen," *Archiv für Hessische Kirchengeschichte* (Cassel, 1905), II, 136–140.
[71] Glaser, pp. 770–772; Menzel, pp. 62–66.

could only be approved by the princes of the Empire in a new Reichstag. When his eloquence and pleas proved of no avail, Bessarion lapsed into further threats and broke off discussions.[72]

Opposition to the Emperor and the Pope grew rapidly in the ensuing weeks. By December 1460 the German Electors achieved a shaky consensus upon a candidate to assume the German crown—George Podiebrad, King of Bohemia. Podiebrad offered suitable inducements to the individual Electors and paid lip service to projected imperial reform and a crusade against the Turks. Antipapal resentments were widely aired. The Electors stated flatly that no tithe might be levied by the Pope without their consent. They also proposed a general council to be convoked in a German city upon the Rhine to reaffirm the decrees of Basel, particularly upon the matters of confirmations, annates, and infringements of jurisdiction by the Curia.[73] Events were pressing toward a decisive confrontation.

Archbishop Diether assumed leadership in the convocation of the great Reichstag which opened at Nuremberg on 23 February 1461. Diether attended in person, along with the Pfalzgraf, the Elector of Brandenburg, and many of the more important rulers of the Empire; the other Electors and princes dispatched envoys. Since December the enthusiasm of Diether and the Pfalzgraf Frederick for King George had cooled greatly, because the astute Bohemian monarch, searching as always for a religious equilibrium between his Hussite and orthodox subjects, had shifted back to a policy more friendly to Rome. The flickering candidacy of King George drastically changed the character of the Reichstag. The electors were content to send an ultimatum to Frederick III to attend a Reichstag to be convened at Frankfurt in late May; if the Emperor refused to appear, the Electors would act independently to reform the Empire and the German Church.[74]

---

[72] Glaser, pp. 777–778; Kraus, pp. 365–366; and Menzel, pp. 68–74. See also the views of the Vienna Reichstag expressed by Pius II and Diether, pp. 235 and 259–261.
[73] Glaser, p. 778; Kraus, p. 370; Menzel, pp. 95–101.
[74] Kraus, pp. 371–373; Menzel, pp. 103–104, 120–127.

INTRODUCTION

At Nuremberg Archbishop Diether published a dramatic document appealing his case to a future council upon the basis of the decrees of the councils of Basel and Constance. In this appeal Diether reviewed the heavy demands the Pope had exacted for his confirmation. He emphasized his willingness to pay the annates that his predecessors had paid; again he insisted that the annates assessed at Mantua were oppressive. He argued that an appeal to a council had become necessary because an equitable and impartial judgment of his case had become impossible at the Curia. Diether bitterly assailed the bull *Execrabilis* as a barely disguised instrument of oppression.[75]

A second appeal received the support of the Pfalzgraf Frederick, the Margraves of Brandenburg, and other princes. The princes stressed their indignation at Bessarion's arrogant demand for a tithe to be levied upon a Germany already ravaged by war and overburdened by the fiscal exactions of Rome. With more moderation, the princes appealed "to the present and future Pope" for redress; a decision upon an appeal to a general council was postponed to the Reichstag to be convoked in May. A union of princes was created to protest fiscal abuse and infringement of the decrees of Basel and Constance.[76]

Both appeals were probably penned by Gregor Heimburg, the representative of Duke Sigismund of Tyrol at Nuremberg. Heimburg had been an eloquent champion of imperial reform and conciliar ideas at German courts and diets for almost thirty years. The skilled practitioner of the stinging epithet, bitter irony, and satiric scorn entered the service of the archbishop on the day before the opening of the Nuremberg Reichstag.[77] The irascible jurist had played a crucial role in the clash

---

[75] Glaser, p. 782; Menzel, pp. 104–105. Diether declared in his *Defense* of 1 October 1461 that "should it come to pass that no one should appeal from the oppression of a Pope to a future general council, a Pope could deal with everyone according to his whim and no one could defend himself or resist. This could neither be endured nor tolerated; all would experience what burdensome oppression this would bring to anyone who had been wronged." See p. 265.

[76] Gebhardt, pp. 46–47; Glaser, pp. 782–784; Kraus, pp. 373–375; Menzel, pp. 112–120.

[77] Gebhardt, p. 43; Menzel, p. 105.

of Sigismund and Cardinal Cusa, which had entered its most critical phase in the previous year; for his composition of Sigismund's increasingly outraged appeals, Heimburg, "this son of the Devil, the father of lies,"[78] had incurred excommunication (18 October 1460).

The origins of the virulent strife between Cardinal Cusa and Duke Sigismund need detain us but briefly.[79] In early 1450 Cusa was named Bishop of Brixen by a papal provision that violated the Concordat of Vienna and upset the chapter election of Leonard Wismair, a counselor of the Duke. The cardinal's energetic promotion of strict monastic discipline met stout resistance, particularly among the wealthy and recalcitrant nuns of the convent of Sonnenberg. More vexatious for Sigismund was the cardinal's assertion of broad territorial claims for lands that had been alienated from the bishopric for centuries. When Duke Sigismund and the clergy of the diocese repeatedly appealed against him "to a Pope better informed," Cusa imposed a general interdict over the lands of the diocese of Brixen (3 July 1458).

Pope Pius II, not greatly in sympathy with Cusa's inflexibility, searched for reconciliation. However the growing suspicions and recriminations of both parties in the dispute made rapprochement impossible. On Easter Sunday, 1460, Duke Sigismund imprisoned Cusa in the fortress of Bruneck and exacted a harsh settlement granting himself control of all the strongholds of the diocese and a large sum of cash. A few days later Cusa fled to Italy never to see his diocese again.

Pius II immediately prepared papal censures against Sigismund. Pius insisted that any investigation was unnecessary because the Duke's crimes were *notorious*, but as an act of grace he named a commission of three shrewd jurists. They quickly confirmed his judgment.[80] As a final gesture of conciliation, Pius urged Sigismund to appear at a public

---

[78] This epithet is drawn from a bull dated 31 December 1460; cited in Gebhardt, p. 43.
[79] The most accessible scholarly account of the Brixen conflict is the decidedly antipapal exposition found in Voigt, III, 305–421.
[80] Voigt, III, 364.

consistory on 4 August 1460. The Duke responded in mid-July with a
lengthy defense against Cusa and a mild appeal "to a Pope better
informed." Sigismund's envoy, Doctor Lorenz Blumenau, was imprisoned as a suspect heretic who sought to undermine obedience to
the Church, and the Duke's appeal was rejected as "foolish and frivolous."[81] Four days after the public consistory, Pius promulgated a
bull excommunicating Sigismund and laying his lands under an interdict.

On 13 August 1460 Sigismund published an appeal to a future Pope
and a future general council. Another sharper appeal followed a month
later from the pen of Heimburg. The appeals argued that the Duke was
compelled to carry his case to a higher tribunal because the Pope
persisted in arbitrarily condemning him on the basis of false information.[82] In a sense, the appeals were directed to German public opinion.
The repeated petitions and polemic that ensued passed from hand to
hand and appeared upon church doors throughout Germany as far
north as Thuringia and Lower Saxony—the large number of manuscripts extant bears witness to their wide circulation.[83] In the bull
Infructuosos palmites of 2 November 1460, Pius, on the basis of *Execrabilis*, included within the previous excommunication all those who
adhered to Sigismund's appeal to a future council.[84] But the Pope
found no effective support among German rulers and clergy. The
Tyrolean populace and most of the clergy of the diocese of Brixen
openly upheld Duke Sigismund, and many German princes condemned
the Pope's action and declared their open support for the Duke.[85]

In a stinging, powerful appeal written in January 1461[86] Heimburg

---

[81] Voigt, III, 371.
[82] Voigt, III, 376.
[83] Voigt, III, 376.
[84] Picotti, pp. 32, 50–56.
[85] Kraus, pp. 420–421.
[86] This appeal is reprinted in M. Freher and B. G. Struve, *Rerum Germanicarum scriptores varii, qui res in Germania & Imperio sub Friderico III, Maximiliano I, Impp.
memorabiliter gestas illo aevo litteris prodiderunt* (Strasbourg, 1717), II, 211–214.

accepted the gauntlet thrown down in *Infructuosos palmites*. Again he protested against being condemned without a hearing. Quoting Horace's adage that "force without counsel falls of its own weight," [87] he set out to establish that the papal condemnation of an appeal to a future council was devoid of legal foundation. In the conciliar tradition, he declared that the general councils followed in the steps of the apostles and that *Execrabilis* expressed simply the personal will of the Pope. By refusing to recognize the immortal authority of the Church, which, although dispersed, could be congregated in a general council, Pius himself was in heresy. [88] The edict of Mantua which the Pope "vomited forth rather than decreed" had been elicited by dark fears:

> Indeed the Pope hates this most holy convocation of Christians, the mother of liberty, as though it were an illegitimate claim. He hopes to destroy it with an empty decree and has condemned it before it again arose. But by this condemnation he has, on the contrary, passed judgment upon himself. The more willfully he condemns it, the more evident is his fear. What has become dull in memory because of long silence has been given new life by his odious condemnation. It is as though someone wished to smother or drown the hidden powers of quicklime by pouring cold water upon it and aroused these powers against his wish. [89]

Heimburg suggested darkly that Pius had condemned an appeal to a council in order to remove all German opposition to his schemes to exact "tribute" from the Empire under the pretext of a crusade against the Turks. Under such circumstances, the Duke and his supporters had no other recourse but to appeal to a future council. [90]

Concern in Rome was evinced in a vitriolic reply to Heimburg penned by Teodoro de Laelio, Auditor of the Rota, and shortly thereafter

---

[87] Freher and Struve, II, 211.
[88] Freher and Struve, II, 211; repeated in Laelio's *Response*, see p. 311.
[89] Freher and Struve, II, 212.
[90] Freher and Struve, II, 212.

Bishop of Feltre. Laelio's vindication of the papal censures against Sigismund was founded upon this principle: "The verdict of the Pope is valid in notorious instances without citation"; [91] an appeal from this verdict was an act of criminal rebellion. Later we shall briefly compare Laelio's defense of the papal monarchy and the Mantuan constitution with the *Defensorium* of Gabriel Biel.

In a renewal of the Duke's appeal, drafted in March in response to a bull (23 January 1461) summoning him and his adherents to appear before the Pope within sixty days, the ducal position was restated in the most emphatic terms: "It would be madness to appear before one who refuses us a hearing. So, in the last resort, there remains only the remedy of an appeal to a future council." [92] It should be noted that the Duke's persuasive appeals were being disseminated throughout Germany precisely at the time that the fortunes of Diether and the anti-papal and anti-imperial faction were attaining flood tide at the Nuremberg Reichstag. But the unity achieved at Nuremberg was to be singularly ephemeral.

The division of Wittelsbach and Hohenzollern ambitions and the selfish intrigues of the King of Bohemia, as well as other tensions, quickly stirred general mistrust and discord. Nevertheless, the threats voiced at Nuremberg did not disturb the Emperor. In April he wrote to Pius in very revealing words: "Consider, Holy Father, how boldly the factions of the Empire raise their heads and how they in deranged madness undertake to dictate laws to us, their spiritual and temporal overlords. With respect to Diether, you should now recognize the result of conferring spiritual confirmation [upon him] without consulting us; therefore, at least see that he no longer retains the archiepiscopal throne." [93] The city of Frankfurt was forbidden to hold the threatened May Reichstag within its walls. [94]

[91] See p. 305.
[92] Quoted in Voigt, III, 406.
[93] Quoted in Kraus, p. 375.
[94] Kraus, p. 375; Glaser, p. 785.

THE TWILIGHT OF THE CONCILIAR ERA

Meanwhile Pius had been quite active. The maladroit Bessarion was replaced by Rudolf von Rüdesheim, cathedral deacon of Worms, and Francis of Toledo. These skilled diplomats assured Margrave Albert of Brandenburg and other German princes that the Pope had no intent to levy a tithe without their consent and that he was not categorically opposed to a general council and certain reforms. Concessions in the matter of the tithe were enough to bring the princes to drop the questions of a general council and church reform. Even the Pfalzgraf was persuaded to withdraw his support for Diether's appeal.[95] Finally in mid-April 1461, with the utmost secrecy, Pius dispatched Johann Werner von Flassland, the cathedral deacon of Basel, to Germany to sound local support for a new archiepiscopal election.[96]

By early June Diether was almost isolated diplomatically. He was compelled to transfer the Reichstag from Frankfurt to Mainz in late May, and the sole prince present there was Landgrave Heinrich of Hesse. Only the Pope, the Pfalzgraf, the Saxon Elector, the Margrave of Brandenburg, the Duke of Tyrol, and the cathedral chapter of Brixen sent representatives.[97] Diether opened the assembly with an oration reviewing his grievances and insisting upon the strong opposition in Germany to the tithe and indulgence for the Turkish expedition. The address closed with a resounding invocation of German patriotic spirit and a repeated assertion that he had no other recourse than to appeal to a future council.[98]

The rebuttal of the papal nuncio, Rudolf von Rüdesheim, was very polished.[99] He declared to the small assembly that the Curia had

---

[95] Glaser, p. 785; Kraus, pp. 376–377; Menzel, pp. 132–135.

[96] Kraus, p. 377; Menzel, p. 138; Müller, II, 30.

[97] Kraus, p. 377; Heinrich Schrohe, *Mainz in seinen Beziehungen zu den deutschen Königen und den Erzbischöfen der Stadt bis zum Untergang der Stadtfreiheit (1462)*, vol. IV of *Beiträge zur Geschichte der Stadt Mainz* (Mainz, 1915), p. 186.

[98] Gabel, *Comm. of Pius II*, pp. 196–197; the excerpt is quoted by Georg Helwich, "Moguntia Devicta" (1626), in Serarius and Joannis, II, 141–142.

[99] Only the reconstructed Latin version of Pius II in his *Comm.* is extant; this is reprinted in Helwich, in Serarius and Joannis, II, 142–144. The address is slightly abridged in Gabel, *Comm. of Pius II*, 197–200.

expected Diether to pay only the annates traditionally exacted from Mainz and that the Pope had no intention of levying a Turkish tithe without the approval of the German princes and prelates. Diether's appeal to a council was dismissed with biting scorn:

"I have appealed to a future council," you say, Where is this future council? Where does it sit? Where will we seek its tribunal? This is a pretty invention so that crimes may go unpunished, so that the injury of others may be sanctioned without the fear of judgment! He has appealed to a judge who can never be found. A law was promulgated against this crime at the Congress of Mantua, so that anyone who appeals to a future council invites the punishment which is inflicted upon those who foment heresy and those guilty of lèse-majesté.[100]

Diether's humiliation was deep. Hoping to receive better treatment in the matter of the annates, he secretly withdrew his appeal before the papal nuncios and several witnesses. The nuncios noncommittally promised to intercede with the Pope.[101] Heimburg resigned his duties as the Chancellor of Mainz and departed.[102] Diether, however, sought clemency too late; the Pope felt strong enough to repress Diether as an example to those who would champion conciliar appeals in the future. Flassland, the secret papal nuncio, discovered a suitable candidate for the see of Mainz—Adolf von Nassau-Wiesbaden. Adolf belonged to a proud old dynasty that had included a German Emperor and two archbishops of Mainz. Under the pretext of a pilgrimage to Aachen, the hesitant Adolf met in Cologne with Flassland and an assemblage that included Archbishop Johann of Trier, Bishop George of Metz, Margrave Karl of Baden, Graf Ulric of Württemberg, Landgrave

---

[100] Helwich, in Serarius and Joannis, II, 143. Note the parallels in *Execrabilis*, p. 225.
[101] Kraus, p. 378; Menzel, pp. 147–148. Helwich's account (Serarius and Joannis, II, 144) is drawn from the *Comm.* of Pius II. See also Diether's *Defense*, p. 271.
[102] Kraus, p. 378.

Ludwig of Hesse, and several members of the Mainz cathedral chapter. Adolf was moved to accept the papal provision.[103]

After hearing Flassland's report, Pius dispatched him on 21 August 1461 to Germany again with four bulls in which he deposed Diether from his see for "manifest crimes," released all his subjects, spiritual and temporal, from their bonds of allegiance, and appointed Adolf of Nassau as Archbishop of Mainz.[104] The long bull of deposition, *In apostolicae sedis specula,* rehearsed a lengthy list of indictments against Diether: his appeal to a future council in defiance of *Execrabilis,* thus incurring the penalties of heresy and lèse-majesté; his exhortation to other prelates and cathedral chapters to join him in his rebellion; an election tainted by simony; failure to pay his annates within the allotted period; perjury of his oath to come to the Curia within a year to declare his obedience to the Pope; his sheltering and encouragement of "the publicly condemned heretic Gregor Heimburg"; the convocation of a Reichstag at Mainz without imperial consent; tyrannical violence against his subjects; and "numerous other excesses."[105] The Pope argued that there was no need for ordinary juridical process: "All agree that he must be deposed of whom such great crimes are reported and that there is no need for a formal judgment against Diether who has publicly appealed to a future council, has perjured himself, and has not been consecrated archbishop within the appointed time; notorious crimes do not require due process."[106]

On 24 September Flassland delivered the bulls to Adolf. Two days later Adolf rode into Mainz with 1,400 horsemen and, having called together the cathedral chapter, exhibited the papal bulls announcing the deposition of Diether and his own provision. Five of the seven

---

[103] Helwich, in Serarius and Joannis, II, 144–145; Kraus, p. 380; Menzel, p. 152.

[104] The four bulls are reprinted in Helwich, in Serarius and Joannis, II, 146–154.

[105] The text of *In apostolicae sedis specula* reprinted in this volume is found in Müller, II, 31–35. For these charges, see pp. 231–243.

[106] Quoted from the *Comm.* of Pius II in Müller, II, 31.

canons present were adherents of Adolf. Adolf adamantly refused the request of Diether's supporters to postpone any decision for a month until the full chapter could be assembled. On the evening of 2 October a *Te Deum* was sung in the cathedral and Adolf was seated upon the archiepiscopal throne. The new archbishop was announced and the papal bulls were read to the assembled burghers and clergy of Mainz. Because of the hostility of large numbers of the Mainz burghers, Adolf then hastily left the city.[107]

Diether withdrew to his strongholds east of the city.[108] He quickly issued an appeal "to a Pope better informed" and on 1 October published a fiery *Defense* in the vernacular "to all the princes, prelates, clergy, burghers, and people of Germany." In this exhaustive rebuttal of the papal indictment in the bull of deposition, Diether continued to affirm that he had been condemned without a summons, without an equitable hearing, and without evidence. He persisted in denouncing the Mantuan constitution as contrary to all law, divine, natural, and positive. He argued that if an appeal to a general council were no longer permissible, all were vulnerable to intolerable arbitrary papal oppression. The Pope's "daring fraud" in releasing all archiepiscopal subjects from their oaths of fealty could only introduce dissension, disruption, and bloodshed into the diocese.[109] In a letter written at this time to Duke William of Saxony, Diether stressed his willingness to submit his case to a tribunal composed of the Emperor, the Electors, the bishops of Bamberg, Würzburg, Eichstadt, Worms, and Speyer, the dukes of Austria and Bavaria, the chapter, and the representatives of twelve imperial cities of the region.[110]

Indicative of the general confusion introduced by repeated papal censures and responding appeals is Diether's contention that an excommunication or interdict was without binding force after an appeal

---

[107] Helwich, in Serarius and Joannis, II, 154–156; Schrohe, pp. 187–188.
[108] Helwich, in Serarius and Joannis, II, 156; Schrohe, p. 188.
[109] See p. 279.
[110] Reprinted in Müller, II, 48–50.

had been made.[111] This widely held assumption became very useful to the many who found it expedient or preferable to remain lukewarm supporters of both factions. For example, in March 1462 the city of Mainz appealed "to a Pope better informed" in order to suspend an interdict threatened against the city if it persisted in its adherence to Diether.[112]

Because Diether continued to occupy most of the territorial holdings of the diocese—he held all of the diocesan lands upon the right bank of the Rhine—Adolf began to search for military allies. For Adolf, the support of Margrave Karl of Baden, Archbishop Johann of Trier, Bishop George of Metz, Graf Ludwig of Veldenz, and his brother, Graf Johann of Nassau-Wiesbaden, was not significant militarily; but Diether hesitated to launch hostilities. His strongest possible ally, Pfalzgraf Frederick, was heavily involved in other struggles.[113] Accordingly, Diether entered into a tentative agreement with Adolf on 11 November. Diether voluntarily abdicated his archiepiscopal throne in return for control of the wealthy region of the Bergstrasse for life, absolution from papal censures, and resolution of his debts including the contested annates.[114] This accord suggests that neither of the protagonists relished a protracted and exhaustive struggle.

Pfalzgraf Frederick, seeing a chance to fish in troubled waters, persuaded Diether to break his accord with Adolf. Only eight days after entering into a conditional settlement with Adolf, Diether joined the Pfalzgraf and the strong noble, Graf Philip of Katzelnbogen, at Wernheim in an alliance to be binding until the end of the struggle. The allies were to divide the spoils evenly. The Pfalzgraf received the Bergstrasse, to be redeemed for 100,000 Rhenish gulden.[115] Two weeks

---

[111] See p. 267.
[112] Schrohe, p. 195.
[113] For the alignment of forces, see Kraus, p. 381; Menzel, pp. 159–160; Müller, II, 104–106.
[114] Glaser, pp. 790–791; Kraus, p. 385; Menzel, pp. 164–165.
[115] Glaser, pp. 791–792; Kraus, p. 385; Menzel, pp. 167–168.

later Diether induced the Mainz Rat to enter a defensive compact providing that the city would conclude no separate settlement with the Pope until the conclusion of the struggle. In return Diether extended a number of fiscal privileges to the burghers including the abolition of the *Pfaffenrachtung*, a particularly despised tax exemption of the Mainz clergy.[116] In early January 1462 Landgrave Heinrich of Hesse entered the alliance to advance his quarrel with his older brother, Landgrave Ludwig.[117]

During these months Adolf, too, was not idle. In addition to the adherents noted above, Adolf secured pledges of support from Margrave Albert of Brandenburg, Graf Ulric of Württemberg, Landgrave Ludwig of Hesse, Duke William of Saxony, the Bishop of Speyer, and a considerable number of small nobles and knights. Only Graf Ulric contributed significantly to the military strength of Adolf's faction. But these alliances were far more important in another respect. Each had been purchased for various sorts of concessions; the sum of these pledges of territory and treasure was enormous.[118] The doggerel of Michel Beheim's rhymed chronicle of the Stiftsfehde is graphic:

> Doch also es wolt menglich von
> sant Martins mantell ein stück han
> —das land ward in vil stuck getrandt
> und kam gar in manch fremde handt,
> das bystum ward vil flissig,
> bischoff warn mern dan drissig.[119]

By the beginning of 1462 the Pope was confronted with a whole faction in rebellion. On 8 January Pius promulgated a final bull of

---

[116] Kraus, p. 386; Schrohe, pp. 191–192.

[117] Franz Grundlach, *Hessen und die Mainzer Stiftsfehde 1461–1463* (Marburg, 1899), p. 23.

[118] These accords are discussed in detail in Helwich, in Serarius and Joannis, II, 160–162.

[119] "Michel Beheims Reimchronik," *Quellen und Erörterungen zur Bayrischen und Deutschen Geschichte*, ed. C. Hofmann (Munich, 1857), III, 92.

excommunication giving Diether and his adherents eighteen days to surrender all positions to Adolf; in the event of a refusal the faction was threatened with an interdict and the loss of all legal rights and privileges.[120] This bull was published in Strasbourg, but the Pfalzgraf forbade its publication within his lands under the pain of death. Upon his order the bull was torn down from the doors of the cathedral of Speyer, and a searing letter justifying his position and actions was dispatched to the Pope.[121] Pius's repeated reminders to the Pfalzgraf of the penalties incurred for overt rebellion against the Holy See fell upon deaf ears.[122]

German enthusiasm for Adolf's cause was not widespread. The papal censures, however, did prove a serious problem for those who lived within Diether's lands. Many inhabitants of Mainz maintained communications with the Nassau faction and with friends outside the city. In early January Diether exacted an oath from the clergy of Mainz to obey the city Rat throughout the struggle. Many members of the clergy wished to delay the oath and to await better weather before fleeing from the city. In the following days most of the clergy who favored Adolf were expelled from the city or departed willingly. A large number of monks scattered to various convents of the Rhineland.[123] It is probable that Gabriel Biel fled at this time, if not earlier, to the Rheingau, an area that firmly supported Adolf. Concern for clerical loyalty led Diether and the Pfalzgraf a few weeks later to call together all the clergy of Mainz in the chapter room of the cathedral to swear fealty to Diether upon the cathedral's holy relics. The allied princes vowed to conclude no peace until all their followers were assured of their benefices and privileges.[124]

---

[120] Kraus, p. 386; Menzel, p. 172; Voigt, III, 284.
[121] Voigt, III, 284.
[122] The Pope's letter of 23 February 1462 to the Pfalzgraf appears in translation in Karl Hegel, *Die Chroniken der deutschen Städte* (Leipzig, 1882), XVIII, 44–45.
[123] Hegel, pp. 27–28, 34–39; Schrohe, p. 194; Helwich, in Serarius and Joannis, II, 166.
[124] Hegel, pp. 39–40; Schrohe, p. 194.

The Pfalzgraf also exacted a grudging allegiance from the inhabitants of his lands. Bishop Reinhard of Worms issued a public protest against the papal censures but humbly informed the Pope that he only wished to avoid the injury to his diocese that defiance to the Pfalzgraf might incur. The University of Heidelberg published an extremely equivocal appeal "an den um Rath zu fragenden und zu unterrichtenden Papst Pius"—a very polite paraphrase of the formula, "to a Pope better informed." The university avowed its refusal to countenance the execution of papal mandates detrimental to its associates; yet it insisted emphatically that it did not waver in its obedience to the Pope and the Apostolic See. Heidelberg twice sent legations to Rome to urge the Pope to be merciful because it was impossible to comply with his commands. The envoys argued that the old doctors would be reduced to penury if the Pfalzgraf seized their incomes or the Pope removed their benefices. They also protested that Heidelberg remained "the most obedient daughter" of the Holy See and insisted that the university would have advised the Pfalzgraf, if he had consulted it, to support Adolf or to remain neutral.[125] In the *Defensorium*, Biel refers approvingly to Heidelberg's humble unwillingness in its appeal to pronounce judgment upon the wider issues at stake in the Stiftsfehde.[126] The modern historian doubtless finds the university's course of action abject and singularly unedifying.

When the bitter winter of 1461–62 was drawing to a close and serious hostilities could be opened, Diether published a *Manifesto* addressed to all the rulers and inhabitants of Germany (30 March 1462).[127] Again Diether affirmed "how [the Pope and his adherents] have presumed to undertake against all divine, natural, papal, and imperial law, ordinance, and justice, and against God, honor, and equity

---

[125] A detailed account of the university's appeal is given in Voigt, III, 286–287.
[126] See p. 155.
[127] Diether's *Manifesto* is reprinted in Müller, II, 113–117. This broadside is believed to be the oldest printed act of diplomacy and the first piece of printed political propaganda.

to depose us from our princely office." [128] He reviewed his efforts to seek the arbitration of various German rulers. Throughout the tract he emphasized the extent to which his quarrel was the concern of all Germans. But there is not much evidence that this appeal for active support had the desired effect.

Little need be said about the course of the fighting except to stress its savagery and cruelty. This warfare of raids, skirmishes, and pillaging further exhausted the adversaries. In late June the Nassau faction organized a strong attack upon Heidelberg, the Pfalzgraf's capital. The wily Pfalzgraf and Diether trapped their overconfident foe in an ambush at Seckenheim at the confluence of the Rhine and the Neckar rivers (30 June). Diether rode into battle in full armor "to defend the honor of his see." [129] The attack proved to be a rout. Margrave Karl of Baden, Bishop George of Metz, Graf Ulric of Württemberg, and a host of knights were captured and sent to await ransom in the Pfalzgraf's prisons in Heidelberg. [130] The following day the news was greeted in Mainz with the ringing of bells and the singing of a *Te Deum*. The next Sunday the clergy marched in procession through the city, bearing the sacrament. [131]

The emperor received the tidings of Seckenheim with consternation. Letters were sent to Rome pleading with the Pope to employ all possible measures against Diether and the Pfalzgraf. Pius dispatched an appeal to the powerful Duke Philip of Burgundy to assume the leadership of Adolf's forces. [132]

The adversaries spent the late summer and early autumn upon the Rhine, regrouping their forces for a decisive confrontation. Meanwhile Biel was occupied with his pastorate in the Rheingau. In early autumn he dispatched a circular letter written in the vernacular to a friend in Mainz clearly stating the duties of the faithful in a city under

---

[128] Müller, p. 116.
[129] Glaser, p. 297; Menzel, p. 183.
[130] Glaser, pp. 795–796; Menzel, pp. 180–185.
[131] Hegel, p. 50; Schrohe, p. 197.
[132] Voigt, III, 292–293.

interdict.[133] On 22 October he completed his *Defensorium obedientiae apostolicae.*

This work appeared as Adolf and his allies were contriving a plot to avenge the defeat of Seckenheim. Sympathizers in Mainz reported that Diether, the Pfalzgraf, and Graf Philip were to gather in the city for a war council on 28 October. The allies, after carefully dividing the prospective spoils, assembled their forces rapidly and stealthily at Eltville in the Rheingau.[134] During the night of 27 October a scaling party of five hundred men climbed an unguarded section of the wall of Mainz and admitted Adolf's main force into the city. The ringing of the alarm bell in St. Quintin's tower brought the burghers scrambling from their beds pell-mell to confront the city's assailants in the cattle market. Diether and Graf Philip, aroused by the tumult, fled over the city's river wall and across the Rhine in a small fishing boat to seek reinforcements; the Pfalzgraf, heeding the warning of an astrologer, had not entered the city. Cathedral canons loyal to Diether also fled. The two hundred horsemen and the small body of infantry which Diether dispatched over the Rhine to the aid of the embattled burghers proved of little avail. By early afternoon, a large portion of the city was in flames and the bodies of over four hundred burghers lay dead in the streets. To prevent a massacre and utter destruction, the burghers were compelled to surrender.[135]

---

[133] Of the three manuscripts of this letter that once existed, only two now remain: Vat palat. lat. 192, fol. 204^v–206^v, and Mainz Stadtbibliothek, HS II, 219, pp. 23–24. A manuscript copy at Frankfurt was destroyed by bombing during the Second World War. For modern editions of the letter see J. B. Ritter, *Evangelisches Denckmahl der Stadt Franckfurth am Mayn* (Frankfurt, 1726), pp. 18–23; F. W. E. Roth, "Ein Brief des Gabriel Biel, 1462," *Neues Archiv der Gesellschaft für ältere deutsche Geschichtskunde* 35 (1910), 582–585; A. Erler, "Gabriel Biel und die Mainzer Stiftsfehde," *Nassauische Annalen* 71 (1960), 222–224. An English translation of this letter is available in Heiko A. Oberman, *The Harvest of Medieval Theology* (Cambridge, Mass.: Harvard University Press, 1963), pp. 26–29.

[134] Glaser, pp. 798–799; Helwich, in Serarius and Joannis, II, 182; Hegel, p. 176.

[135] The assault and capture of Mainz is described in Glaser, pp. 798–800; Hegel, pp. 51–57; Helwich, in Serarius and Joannis, II, 182–185; Menzel, pp. 190–192; Müller, II, 159–160; Schrohe, pp. 198–202; Voigt, III, 293–294.

THE TWILIGHT OF THE CONCILIAR ERA

On the following day the victorious Adolf poured out his wrath upon eight hundred burghers gathered in the cattle market, thundering that all those "who had adhered to the deposed and excommunicated Diether against all papal bulls and imperial decrees" had broken all faith and merited the greatest punishment.[136] The city was thoroughly looted and the houses of the most prominent members of the Isenburg faction confiscated. Mainz was stripped of all charters and privileges and reduced to the status of a Landstadt, a personal fief of the Archbishop. The wretched burghers were compelled to abandon their homes and families and to seek refuge in the surrounding countryside.[137] Chroniclers report that Adolf's Swiss infantry expressed pity for the plight of the burghers, but that soldiers from the Rheingau, perhaps reflecting the preaching of Gabriel Biel, derided the citizens as oath breakers, heretics, and impious men.[138] Although most of the burghers gradually managed to return, the economy of the city suffered a nearly mortal blow.[139]

The capture of Mainz ended active fighting, although Diether remained firmly in control of the diocesan lands east of the Rhine. The adversaries had exhausted their resources. The Pfalzgraf became more inactive, preferring to assure the concessions he had won from Diether and to consolidate the victory of Seckenheim by exacting enormous ransoms from his eminent prisoners. The election of his brother Rupert to the archiepiscopal throne of Cologne in early 1463 (30 March) also cooled the Pfalzgraf's ardor to champion Diether's cause to a triumphant conclusion. To assure this gain for the Wittelsbachs, Rupert

---

[136] Helwich, in Serarius and Joannis, II, 186.

[137] Schrohe, pp. 202–206; Menzel, pp. 193–194; Helwich, in Serarius and Joannis, II, 185–188; Glaser, pp. 800–801; Voigt, III, 294–295.

[138] Hegel, p. 57; Helwich, in Serarius and Joannis, II, 186.

[139] Helwich, as Vicar of Mainz in the early seventeenth century, estimated the losses of the church of Mainz at the staggering sum of 2,000,000 Rh. gulden (Serarius and Joannis, II, 194). Hegel gives detailed evidence of economic disaster (pp. 182–184).

sought a rapprochement with the papacy and promised to urge a settlement of the Mainz Stiftsfehde. Diether, aware of altered circumstances, signed a truce with Adolf at Oppenheim on 24 April which was to last until St. Martin's Day. In early October at Zeilsheim he concluded a complete accord with Adolf.[140]

The outlines of this detailed settlement should be noted. Diether abdicated the archiepiscopal throne in exchange for extensive concessions: Adolf promised to seek release for Diether and his adherents from papal and imperial censures; Diether's commitments to the Pfalzgraf were recognized and the privileges and benefices of the clergy who had followed Diether were restored; restitution of all property lost in the conflict, with the exception of holdings in Mainz, was pledged; the new archbishop also assumed all debts Diether had contracted as archbishop, including the contested annates and Diether's personal debts to the sum of 5,000 Rhenish gulden; finally Diether was granted the important strongholds of Höchst, Steinheim, and Dieburg for life.[141] This feudal compromise thus assured Diether his personal position and Adolf an impoverished archiepiscopal throne.

On 24 October 1463, before an assembly of princes and prelates in Frankfurt, Diether formally laid down his electoral sword and surrendered the archiepiscopal see to Adolf. Bowing before the legate, Pietro Ferrici, Diether received papal absolution.[142] But the bestowal of papal forgiveness only recognized and ratified the feudal settlements of the primarily secular issues that the antagonists had concluded. The agreement achieved by arms and shrewd diplomacy bore little resemblance to the uncompromising declarations of principle which Rome had fulminated against Diether and his faction in bulls and public censures. There is no evidence that Diether's submission included

---

[140] Glaser, pp. 802–803; Helwich, in Serarius and Joannis, II, 190–191; Kraus, pp. 396–400; Menzel, pp. 213–218.

[141] Helwich gives a very detailed account of the settlement (Serarius and Joannis, II, 191–193).

[142] Kraus, p. 400; Helwich, in Serarius and Joannis, II, 191.

a formal recognition of papal supremacy as demanded in *Execra-bilis*.[143]

Repeated papal threats and censures against Duke Sigismund proved even less effective. Increasingly urgent summons to Rome and polemic of mounting violence failed to shake the Duke's strong position. At length in November 1462 the Pope reluctantly accepted the proposal of Venice to arbitrate negotiations with the Duke. The papal insistence that Sigismund submit to the Apostolic See and accept an imposed penance quickly deadlocked discussions. But Sigismund's cousin, the Emperor, spurred by dynastic territorial concerns occasioned by the death of his brother, Archduke Albert, in late 1463, offered strong new support to Sigismund, thus bringing added pressure for a settlement. Finally the deaths of Cardinal Cusa and Pope Pius II in August 1464 removed the most formidable obstacles to a reconciliation with the papacy. In early September Duke Sigismund received papal absolution from Rudolf von Rüdesheim after making an ambiguous declaration that he had never harbored evil intent against the Pope, but had only wished to maintain his position as a prince.[144] The papacy had achieved little beyond release from an exhausting and baffling conflict.

IV. THE LEGAL ISSUE

It is instructive to note Duke Sigismund's conviction that his struggle against Cardinal Cusa and Pope Pius stemmed solely from his desire to defend his princely prerogative. Both Archbishop Diether and Duke Sigismund appealed from the Pope to a future council in the defense of specific concrete personal interests; both protested against what they

---

[143] The Mainz Stiftsfehde had an ironic aftermath. Twelve years later, after brief hesitation, Pope Sixtus IV again confirmed Diether as Archbishop of Mainz. He occupied the see for the last seven years of his life (1475–1482).

[144] This summary of the conclusion of Sigismund's clash with the papacy is drawn from Gebhardt, p. 52; Kraus, pp. 422–423; Picotti, pp. 40–41; Voigt, III, 416–421. Only Gregor Heimburg was excluded from this absolution. He spent the last years of his life in comparative security as the adviser of King Georg of Bohemia and was reconciled with the Church only shortly before his death in 1472.

INTRODUCTION

felt to be intolerable papal interference within their jurisdiction. In his *Defense* Diether rebukes the Pope for contending that consideration of the common good of the German nation and Christendom was not the concern of the Archbishop of Mainz; he insists that in such extreme necessity he only fulfills his duty as an Elector and as the deacon of the electoral college in convoking the German princes to consider redress for his grievances.[145] His *Manifesto* to the German princes closes with a lengthy catalogue of feudal obligations violated by Adolf and his adherents in taking up arms against him with the blessing of the Pope. He concludes that if the Pope can absolve those bound to the Archbishop by feudal ties, no written charter of privileges and prerogatives thereafter will be safe from papal tampering.[146] In August 1461, writing to Cusa in the Duke's defense, Heimburg sharply asserted that the Austrian princes enjoyed a "plenitudo potestatis" in their lands as did the Roman Emperor. Cusa was reminded that his predecessors in the see of Brixen had recognized the Duke of Tyrol as lord; the cardinal had unfortunately chosen to follow the example of the builders of the Tower of Babel and Lucifer in revolt against God.[147] The intent of his violent imagery is clear.

The legal sanction in the conciliar tradition that Diether and Sigismund invoked in their appeals to a future general council was broad and almost unparticularized. Diether's first appeal, launched at the Diet of Nuremberg (1461), noted "the decrees of Constance and Basel," but alluded only to *Frequens* by name. The Pfalzgraf at Nuremberg protested in Diether's behalf that papal measures "opposed to the decrees of the holy Council of Basel" forced him to appeal. Heimburg repeatedly founded the right of appeal upon *Frequens*.[148] The clearest

---

[145] See p. 269.
[146] Müller, I, 114–116.
[147] Freher and Struve, II, 265.
[148] Freher and Struve, II, 194, 236; Ferdinand de Gudenus, *Codex diplomaticus anecdotorum, res Moguntinas, Francicas, Trevirenses, Hassiacas, finitimorumque regionum, necnon ius Germanicum et S.R.I. historiam vel maxime illustrantium* (Frankfurt and Leipzig, 1758), IV, 344–345.

42

direct citation of the conciliar heritage occurs in Sigismund's appeal of March 1461, which denies the validity of *Execrabilis*: "But we have been instructed that the great council of Constance decreed that a universal council possesses authority over the Pope from Christ directly in those matters which involve faith, reform, and peace. The holy Council of Basel renewed [this decree] and the Roman pontiffs Eugenius and Nicholas recognized it."[149]

The focus of these appeals to the tribunal of a council lay, however, in the contention that the Pope had condemned their cases without judicial citation or investigation—"non vocatum et indefensum," to quote Biel's restatement of Diether's case in the *Defensorium*.[150] It will be recalled that Diether in his *Defense* and *Manifesto* angrily avowed that the papal condemnation of his appeal was opposed to all divine, natural, and positive law. Sigismund in his appeal of March 1461 stated his objection to *Execrabilis* in similar terms: "A hearing has been denied us and a defense has been withdrawn; we deny this censure which the Pope willfully has breathed out against us as contrary to the Law of Nature."[151]

The papacy adamantly disavowed the legality of such appeals as endangering the unity of the Church. In the Mantuan decretal Pope Pius declared that the practice of appealing from the Pope to a future council had been aroused by "a spirit of rebellion" and a desire to evade judgment. If such appeals went unchallenged, he said, all church discipline and the hierarchy itself would be overthrown. Consequently such appeals incurred the penalties for heretical rebellion and lèse-majesté.[152] In a letter written to the city of Nuremberg, Pius argued that the very life of the Church was threatened if those who scorned Christ's Vicar were not punished: "Under the pretence of an appeal, they are earnestly striving to destroy the unity of the Church...These malevolent

---

[149] Freher and Struve, II, 194.
[150] See p. 128.
[151] Freher and Struve, II, 193.
[152] See p. 225.

tricksters and perverse men presume to evade justice through the
mockery of frivolous appeals to a future council—to something which
does not exist, cannot be found, and cannot be above the Vicar of
Christ. Thus they rashly and wrongly turn aside from the obedience
which concerns itself with the needs of the Church and the salvation of
all." [153] To seek redress from a tribunal other than the Roman See was
a manifestation of "the spirit of rebellion." [154]

The Pope repeatedly insisted that the censures imposed upon such
notorious offenders as Diether, Sigismund, and their adherents admitted
no citation or investigation. In preparing censures against Sigismund,
the Pope granted a perfunctory investigation while maintaining that
the notoriety of his offense made it unnecessary.[155] Later, in threaten-
ing the Pfalzgraf with the full displeasure of the Roman see for his reported adherence to Diether's cause (23 February 1462), Pius warned
him that his offense was notorious and his rebellion manifest.[156] We
have already noted the conclusion drawn by Pius in his *Commentaries*
on the deposition of Diether: "Notorious crimes do not require due
process." [157]

Teodoro Laelio insisted that the proposition "notorious and manifest
matters do not require an investigation" [158] was a rudimentary principle
of canon law. The Holy Scriptures, he argues, are filled with instances
in which formal judgment was omitted because guilt was apparent;
he cites, among others, the examples of Elijah and the priests of Baal,
King Ahaziah, Ananias and Sapphira, and the Corinthian fornicator
excommunicated by St. Paul.[159] He further alludes to decisions of
popes Gelasius, Innocent III, Innocent IV, and Clement IV to establish

---

[153] Freher and Struve, II, 209.
[154] Freher and Struve, II, 209; cf. *Execrabilis*, p. 225.
[155] Voigt, III, 276, 288, 364.
[156] Helwich, in Serarius and Joannis, II, 165.
[157] Müller, I, 31.
[158] See p. 301.
[159] See pp. 299–301.

a papal tradition of valid condemnation in notorious instances without formal citation.[160]

Biel accuses Diether of deception in claiming that he was condemned "unsummoned and undefended" contrary to divine, natural, and positive law. It is notorious, he says, that Diether never was properly ordained and sought no dispensation to remove this impediment.[161] A frivolous appeal cannot absolve one from such manifest irregularity. Biel presents a far longer list of scriptural malefactors who received summary chastisement although "non vocatum et indefensum."[162] He adduces many examples of swift justice rendered by God or his servants to prove that such condemnation of manifest evildoers cannot be contrary to divine law. He argues that, because a judge already knows the truth of the matter when dealing with a notorious criminal, a formal judgment would be a futile action and therefore contrary to nature, which does nothing in vain.[163] Although he notes that the Pope is not bound by positive law, he goes on to demonstrate that not even positive law can offer Diether a refuge. He lists nine canon law references as only representative condemnations and depositions of kings and prelates by the decrees of the Pope and universal councils without judicial citation. He closes with specific examples of flagrant breaches of church discipline and the feudal bond which incur condemnation by their intrinsic nature.[164]

Heimburg's response to the line of argument followed by Laelio and

----

[160] See p. 305.
[161] See p. 129.
[162] See pp. 131–139.
[163] See p. 141.
[164] See p. 142; the pronouncements of Pius II, Laelio, and Biel rested in canon law, ultimately in Gratian's dictum that no condemnation is needed for those who follow a heresy already condemned (e.g. c. 1, C. XXIV, qu. 1 [RF I, 966]). This canon was part of the important strand of canonist thought that argued that a pope guilty of notorious heresy incurred "ipso facto" deposition. Important representatives of this view were Huguccio, Joannes Teutonicus, and Occam. See Brian Tierney, *The Foundations of Conciliar Theory: The Contribution of the Medieval Canonists from Gratian to the Great Schism* (Cambridge, Eng., 1955), pp. 62–67.

Biel is noteworthy. The examples of Scripture are dismissed because, while "the Spirit of God" is evident in these instances, it is presumptuous to invoke the "Spirit" for the arbitrary papal censures of the present.[165] Even the ruler who is unrestrained by any law is obligated to investigate before passing judgment, except in rare instances of extraordinary crisis. He emphatically concludes that only God from whom no secrets are hidden can condemn one "non vocatum vel inauditum."[166] The modern historian can only concur with Heimburg; he does not share the confidence of Pius II, Laelio, and Biel in "revealed justice" which renders the evaluation of all available evidence unnecessary.

V. THE ISSUE OF CHURCH AUTHORITY: TEODORO LAELIO, GREGOR HEIMBURG, AND GABRIEL BIEL

An important consideration in the inclusion of Laelio's work in this volume is its heightened repetition of much of Heimburg's position. Laelio's work is, as Heimburg's, swollen and rhetorical in character. His stated intent is to defend the justice of the papal position against Heimburg's blasphemous polemic which has been scattered throughout Italy and Germany. With horror he compares Heimburg to the great heretics of the ancient world; he even suggests that Heimburg repeats the antitrinitarian errors of the Greeks in impugning the primacy of the Vicar of Christ. Heimburg has chosen also to walk in the path of modern heretics such as Marsilius of Padua, John of Jandun, John Wyclif, and John Huss. Those who slander Christ's Vicar are guilty of a form of homicide.[167] (This statement finds echo in Biel's sixth proposition: "Those who revile the Supreme Pontiff and the obedient faithful slander their own good names and sin damnably and without hope of mercy unless they make good their slander as far as possible."[168])

---

[165] Freher and Struve, II, 241–242.
[166] Freher and Struve, II, 243–244.
[167] See pp. 289, 293, 345.
[168] See p. 183.

THE TWILIGHT OF THE CONCILIAR ERA

Laelio dismisses an appeal from the Pope to a future council as criminal and as a device to evade the merited penalty for notorious crimes. Heimburg, he claims, bases his case upon three ludicrous principles: "He contends that councils are the foundations of the Christian faith that have informed the actions of popes and have corrected their errors; that councils rule in Christ's stead and have received their authority from him; and that, therefore, councils are superior to Peter and his successors."[169] But the power of the keys has been given by Christ solely to the apostle Peter and his successors in order to avoid schism in the Church.[170]

Laelio's defense of the papal monarchy repeats in simplified form arguments of medieval canonists and philosophical commonplaces. In the defense of papal primacy he cites, with Biel, the canons *Sacrosancta romana ecclesia* and *Ita dominus noster*, as well as St. Bernard of Clairvaux's *De consideratione libri quinque ad Eugenium Tertium*[171]—a work which balances a lofty conception of papal prerogatives with an equally weighty view of the Pope's responsibilities. He posits the natural order and numerical perfection of monarchial rule—"Where there is unity, there is perfection."[172] However, he places even more emphasis upon his second argument that a harmonious body subjected to one head assures peace and concord.[173] To his contemporaries, deeply swayed by the ideal of unity and still in the shadow of the Great Schism, Laelio's conclusion must have had great impact: "If there were various heads in the Church, the bonds of unity would be broken."[174] It is of interest to mark the parallels to Laelio's arguments that occur in Pius II's long panegyric on ecclesiastical monarchy and Roman primacy in the decretal *In minoribus agentes* (26 April 1463).[175]

---

[169] See p. 313.
[170] See p. 313.
[171] See pp. 294, 320, 326.
[172] See p. 315.
[173] See p. 317.
[174] Laelio quotes from the *Glosa Ordinaria*; see p. 337.
[175] See pp. 359–363.

47

Gregor Heimburg, in his rigorous restatements of conciliar doctrines, was an anachronism by the period of the Mainz Stiftsfehde; his polemical power lay in his vigorous German patriotism and fiery resistance to ecclesiastical injustices experienced, if not articulated, by the majority of Germans. With evident conviction, he rebuffed Laelio's vitriolic accusations of heterodoxy. He professed the utmost abhorrence for the heresies of the Arians, Macedonians, Donatists, Pelagians, and Patarines, and proudly reminded Laelio that the heresies of Wyclif, Huss, and Jerome of Prague had been condemned by the Council of Constance.[176]

With the Nicene Creed, Heimburg professes "one holy Catholic and Apostolic Church."[177] He pungently observes that the unity of the Church lies in Christ and not in St. Peter or Pius.[178] In the conciliar tradition, he contends that the authority of the Church, the "congregatio fidelium," is immortal, and although the Church is dispersed throughout the world, it can be assembled in an ecumenical council.[179] Irately he asserts that the only unity that Laelio can comprehend is the literal unity of the number one. While he is prepared to recognize a corporal unity in the Church in which many members are subjected to one head, Heimburg finds it as inadmissible to permit the head to usurp the office of the hand or foot as to imagine the sun disturbing the course of the stars.[180] He depicts the current state of the Church with malevolent bitterness: "The Pope alone disturbs the bonds of the Church, impedes the functions of the members by choking them, and stifles them by oppression. Lest any bishop may be able to fulfill his function in peace he looses the bonds [of unity], upsets the harmony of the whole, and arrogates the functions of all to himself alone."[181]

The fact that the Duke's antagonist, Cardinal Cusa, based the validity

---

[176] Freher and Struve, II, 252–254.
[177] Freher and Struve, II, 195.
[178] Freher and Struve, II, 246.
[179] Freher and Struve, II, 213.
[180] Freher and Struve, II, 244–245, 251.
[181] Freher and Struve, II, 244.

of the papal censures against the Duke upon the Mantuan decretal enraged Heimburg; he considered this a profound betrayal of the conciliar tradition. The irony of defending a position abandoned by the author of *De concordantia catholica* two decades before did not escape him. In a passionate *Invectiva* directed to Cusa, he charged the former conciliarist with an appeal to the Pope to destroy the faithful; the cardinal's invocation of "the sacrilegious constitution which forbids an appeal to a council" [182] overlooked the practical consideration that papal constitutions in experience are frequently altered, revoked, or repudiated. To argue that appeals to councils would postpone the execution of justice seemed to Heimburg frivolous and evasive; but to contend that the Pope could condemn the Duke unsummoned and undefended could only be regarded as malevolent folly.[183]

Heimburg's critique of papal primacy rested firmly upon the conciliar heritage. He grants that the Bishop of Rome, as the Vicar of Christ and the successor of St. Peter, who has received immediately from Christ the power to bind and loose, is the "caput ministeriale" of the Church. Yet, because it is Christ who binds and looses, and because the Pope, as Christ's servant, only in fact judges whether one is bound or loosed, the Pope's judgment is subject to error.[184] With the conciliarists, he maintains that the authority of the keys was bestowed by Christ directly upon all the apostles; as the successors of the apostles, therefore, general councils remain the seat of ultimate authority within the Church. Following Augustine, Heimburg insists that the Rock upon which the Church is founded is Christ. Heimburg emphasizes that Christ offered assurance to the universal church that he would remain its eternal head in Matthew 28:20: "Lo, I am with you always, even unto the end of the world"; this promise, he declares, could not have been reliably made to the Roman see which suffers vacancy and

---

[182] Freher and Struve, II, 259.
[183] Freher and Struve, II, 260.
[184] Freher and Struve, II, 263

vicissitude.[185] Consequently, the authority of the Church Universal must be considered above that of the Roman church. To support this affirmation he invokes the authority of the Fathers, including the cherished quotation of the conciliarists drawn from Jerome: "siquidem orbis major est urbe."[186] The volatile jurist vigorously declares that a general council must assume active responsibility when the Church is confronted with mortal crisis such as schism, rampant heresy, or a pope guilty of simony or notorious heresy.[187]

Gabriel Biel is a figure of more complexity than Teodoro Laelio or Gregor Heimburg.[188] It is perhaps not irrelevant to note that Biel, unlike Laelio or Heimburg, was a trained theologian. Yet, in contrast to the great theologians of the Conciliar Era such as d'Ailly and Gerson, he manifests an absence of hostility to the canonists as the champions of papal prerogatives.[189] Indeed, in the *Defensorium* Biel shows considerable skill in the marshaling of evidence from canon law and firmly insists that papal mandates bind all the faithful.

For Biel, the Church's authority is a matter of central significance. His vast respect for the authority of the definitions of the Church is manifested throughout all his writings. "What the holy Church, our Mother, defines and accepts as catholic truth," he maintains, "must be believed with the same reverence as though it were stated in Holy Scripture."[190] Indeed he misquotes Augustine: "I would not believe unless the authority of the Church *compelled* me."[191] In locating authority within the Church, Biel appears to stand with d'Ailly and Gerson in affirming the supremacy of a general council over the Pope in the event of conflict; however, he apparently views such conflict as a highly

---

[185] Freher and Struve, II, 211, 213, 252–253.
[186] Freher and Struve, II, 211.
[187] Freher and Struve, II, 261.
[188] For a biographical sketch of Biel, see Oberman, *Harvest of Medieval Theology*, pp. 1–21.
[189] See Oberman's discussion, pp. 401–403.
[190] See p. 75.
[191] See pp. 75–77.

abnormal situation, such as the extraordinary crisis that provoked the Council of Constance. The authority of the Church in normal circumstances resides with the Pope who periodically convenes a council to aid him in the exercise of that authority.[192]

Biel finds the bulwark of the Church's authority in unity; and again this unity is indissolubly connected with the See of Rome. Biel's principal concern in the *Defensorium* is "to preserve the unity of our Lord's sheepfold."[193] With Augustine he professes that the church in which schism dwells is not the true Church. He argues with St. Bernard that Christ, in his charge to St. Peter, "Feed my sheep," commended all flocks (that is, churches) to his pastorate in order to confirm the unity of the whole flock (that is, the Church).[194]

This commission becomes the cornerstone of Biel's exposition of the prerogatives of the Apostolic See. He pointedly stresses the exalted pastoral charge given to St. Peter alone; St. Peter was set over all the apostles and all the faithful, and the Roman Church exercises primacy over all churches.[195] St. Peter and his successors are bound together with the Church in bonds of mutual obligation—St. Peter and his successors are obligated to rule the Church committed to St. Peter by Christ, and all the Church is bound to obey St. Peter and his successors.[196] Biel shares Heimburg's confidence in the immortal nature of the Church's authority, but joins it firmly to the Apostolic See. "How," he asks, "could Christ have provided sufficiently for his Church if he had not perpetuated in the Church the authority granted to Peter to rule it?"[197]

The character of the primacy exercised by the Pope is only implicitly

---

[192] See Oberman, *Harvest of Medieval Theology*, pp. 418–419; Cf. *Canonis misse expositio Gabrielis Biel*, ed. H. A. Oberman and W. J. Courtenay G–O (Wiesbaden, 1963–1967), vol. I, Lect. XXII D, Lect. XXIII G–O.
[193] See p. 71.
[194] See pp. 81, 83.
[195] See pp. 85–87.
[196] See p. 87.
[197] See p. 91.

defined in this work. Biel himself states that "every Roman pontiff possesses all the ruling power and pastoral authority that St. Peter received from the Lord to rule the Church Universal,"[198] and he cites Bernard of Clairvaux's ascription of "plenitudo potestatis" to the Pope with evident approbation. The Roman Church must be revered as the mother and head of all churches.[199] All religious matters must be referred to the Roman see from which spiritual authority descends into the entire hierarchy of the Church. Lower authority must be subject to higher authority. Thus follows the precept that no lesser prelate can reject a papal precept or excuse anyone from any duty enjoined by the Pope.[200]

Biel admits that the Pope can conceivably abuse his authority. He insists that this authority may properly be exercised only for the Church's edification, thus echoing a fundamental tenet of the conciliarists.[201] Papal mandates and pronouncements bind none to observance when they are opposed to Scripture and divine and natural law—yet unless such opposition is established with utter certainty, all the faithful must give assent to all papal mandates and obey as far as they are able.[202] Such opposition would appear to be almost hypothetical, because Biel holds that the Church enjoys the authority to interpret Scripture, the vehicle of divine law which the voice of conscience cannot contradict, and that the Pope under all normal circumstances exercises this authority.[203] Moreover, Biel relentlessly demonstrates the self-evident guilt of Diether von Isenburg on the grounds that he has refused to observe papal mandates sufficiently publicized.[204]

Biel's passing reference to *Execrabilis* in the second part of the *Defensorium* should not be interpreted as an allusion to the question of

---

[198] See p. 91.
[199] See p. 95.
[200] See p. 111.
[201] See p. 91.
[202] See pp. 115–121.
[203] See Oberman, *Harvest of Medieval Theology*, p. 414.
[204] See p. 129.

conciliar supremacy. His concern is unwarranted disobedience to the mandates of the Apostolic See.[205] Indeed, it is suggestive that Biel does not concern himself with the conflicting claims of curialists and conciliarists that opposed Pope and Council to one another. It is upon legal grounds that he contends that a frivolous appeal from the juris- diction of the papal courts—particularly when guilt is self-evident— would call the final nature of verdicts into question and delay the exe- cution of justice.[206]

Biel's focus shifts significantly from the question of the location of ultimate authority within the Church to an emphasis upon the preser- vation of that authority as vested in the Apostolic See; it may be pro- visionally concluded that his writings express a *via media* between papalism and anticurialism that reflects widespread feeling in contem- porary theological circles. The memory of schism and conciliar failure at Basel had radically reduced the effective attraction of a general council. But it is evident that the unity championed by Biel and others was fragile and gravely threatened in reality. Although Diether von Isenburg, Duke Sigismund, and their impassioned spokesman, Gregor Heimburg, won little serious support for reopening the explosive question of ultimate authority in the Church, their physical resources and burning sense of material injustice posed a formidable threat to ecclesiastical unity. Other aggressive territorial princes and worldly prelates, while rendering formal obeisance to the Apostolic See, were nonetheless ruthlessly pursuing ambitions that threatened the fabric of Christendom. Yet even more ominous were the consequences in the moral and intellectual sphere of rigid appeals for submission and unity such as the *Defensorium*. A modern historian readily suspects that rigorous theological objection, particularly when painful to vested interests, was too easily dismissed as rebellious and deleterious to church harmony. The following turbulent century was to demonstrate that the

---

[205] See p. 129.
[206] See p. 149.

demands of individual religious conviction could not be permanently subordinated to a unity precariously based on rivalry among the secular powers.

German resentment against the Curia continued to seethe in the decades following the Mainz Stiftsfehde; but the cry for a general council in Germany grew faint. It was Martin Luther who ignited the tinder. The frustrated wrath and indignation of generations of Germans against "the devilish rule of Rome" found a tumultuous outlet in Luther's *Open Letter to the Christian Nobility of the German Nation* (1520). As his assault upon "Roman tyranny" waxed in scope and vehemence, the issue of ecclesiology attained critical urgency. The papacy found eager champions in men such as Sylvester Prierias, Johann Eck, Ambrosius Catharinus, and Cajetan; it is significant that their arguments echo the polemic of Biel, Laelio, and Pius II.[207]

The Mainz Stiftsfehde anticipated the following century in physical violence as well as polemic. Virtually every armed conflict in the fourteenth and fifteenth centuries involved ecclesiastical questions because the spheres of church and state were so intricately interwoven. Prelates in Germany were deeply involved in the endemic warfare that raged throughout this period. As in the Mainz Stiftsfehde, disputed elections often became the centers of armed political struggle; the sees of Constance (1472–1479) and Utrecht (1423–1449) suffered

---

[207] For Luther's relation to conciliarism on the eve of the Reformation, see Christa Tecklenburg Johns, *Luthers Konzilsidee in ihrer historischen Bedingtheit und ihrem reformatorischen Neuansatz* (Berlin Töpelmann, 1966), particularly pp. 97 ff. The most important defenses of the doctrine of papal primacy written against Luther are: Sylvester Prierias, *In praesumptuosas Martini Lutheri conclusiones de potestate Papae dialogus* (1517), ed. H. Schmidt, in *D. Martini Lutheri opera Latina varii argumenti ad reformationis historiam imprimis pertinentia* (Erlangen, 1865), I, 344–377; Ambrosius Catharinus, *Apologia pro veritate catholicae et apostolicae fidei ac doctrinae adversus impia ac valde pestifera Martini Lutheri dogmata* (1520) ed. A. Franzen, in *Corpus catholicorum* (Munster, 1956), XXVII; Cajetan, *De divina institutione pontificatus Romani pontificas* (1521), ed. F. Lauchert, in *Corpus catholicorum* (Munster, 1925), X; Johann Cochlaeus, *De authoritate ecclesiae et scripturae, adversus Lutheranos* (Strasbourg, 1524).

particularly acute schisms.[208] German rulers sought to extend their power by attaining high office in the Church for their relatives or followers; in turn, ambitious prelates attempted to amass church offices and to wrest temporal prerogatives from neighboring rulers. The Mainz Stiftsfehde suggests the price of such ambition. When scholarship has more fully explored the records of the late medieval German Church, much light will undoubtedly be shed on the forces unleashed by the Lutheran reformation.

VI. THE *DEFENSORIUM* TEXT

The text presented here is based on an examination of all the manuscripts and editions of the *Defensorium* known to date; the collation itself was prepared from the manuscripts and the first two printed editions. Hitherto no manuscripts of the *Defensorium* were believed to exist. The earliest known copy was the first printed edition of John Otmar at Tübingen in 1500. In 1965, however, two manuscripts, previously hidden by miscataloguing, were uncovered, and these can be dated within the decade immediately following the writing of the *Defensorium* in 1462. The two manuscripts enable us to determine the amount of editing done by Biel's disciple, Wendelin Steinbach, who prepared the text for its first publication, and they give us a clearer picture of the work as it was known in the sixties and seventies of the fifteenth century. The manuscripts and editions are as follows:

Mainz Stadtbibliothek, HS II, 219, pp. 25–41. Paper, 112 pages, double columns; a firm, clear hand with few corrections.
Vatican Library, Codex palat. lat. 192, fol. 186^r–200^v. Paper. 218 fol.; a clear hand, but with many corrections and errors.
Tübingen: John Otmar for Frederick Meynberger, 1500
Hagenau: Henry Gran for John Rynmann, 1510

---

[208] An interesting sketch of the Utrecht controversy can be found in R. R. Post, *Kerkgeschiedenis van Nederland in de Middeleeuwen* (Utrecht, 1957), II, 1–21.

Hagenau: Henry Gran for John Rynmann, 1515
Hagenau: Henry Gran for John Rynmann, 1519
Basel: Adam Petri, 1519
Hagenau: Henry Gran for John Rynmann, 1520

All the printed editions are based on that of Tübingen, 1500, although the later ones use the revised or classicized orthography of the Hagenau, 1510, and repeat several changes that were made by that edition. For the collation therefore it was necessary to use only the two manuscripts and the first two printed editions. Among these it was found that there were two manuscript traditions, one to which the Mainz and Vatican manuscripts belonged, and another to which the Tübingen edition belonged. The Tübingen text contains passages that do not appear in the Mainz and Vatican manuscripts and that do not seem to be the result of editorial revision. Each passage in question contains no new concepts and fits nicely into the general argument. Since each begins with the same word or phrase as the passage following it, they could most easily be explained as scribal errors made in the copy that formed the basis for the Mainz and Vatican manuscripts. In such cases the Tübingen edition bears witness to a more accurate manuscript tradition than the Mainz and Vatican manuscripts. In other cases, however, the Tübingen edition shows an editorial refinement both in orthography and phrasing. Some passages are clarifications and extensions of the argument that cannot be explained as errors on the part of the Mainz and Vatican manuscript tradition but seem rather to be the work of editing. Since the Mainz manuscript proved to be much more accurate than the Vatican copy, we have relied mainly on the Mainz manuscript and the Tübingen edition.

The variant readings given in the critical apparatus do not represent every variant that was found in the texts. Meaningless scribal and typographical errors have not been given. Some variations, such as those centering around the difference between a *t* and a *c* or between a *u* and an *n*, are extremely difficult to ascertain in manuscripts; those we have included, such as *nobis—vobis*, represent but a small proportion

of the possible variants of this type, and it was only after hesitation that we included the small group that could be depended on. Variants in orthography, while useful in helping to determine text tradition, add nothing to the meaning of the text and therefore have not been placed in the apparatus. The orthography of the present edition is in conformity with classical usage, thus completing a trend already in evidence in the Hagenau editions.

Besides the variant readings another important difference between the manuscripts and the printed editions is the location of the reference notes for the passages quoted in the text. In the printed editions these references are included in the body of the text itself, but in the manuscripts they occur in the margin, having been added by the same hand that copied the text. This medieval system of marginal references (the ancestor of the modern footnote) has the advantage of keeping the text uncluttered so that the author's argument moves more quickly. The sixteenth-century editors of the printed editions placed these references in the main body of the text, thus freeing the margins for the marks and comments of the purchaser of the volume. From one point of view it would have been preferable for us to have placed these references as footnotes so that the text would flow as easily as does that of the Mainz and Vatican scribes. This, however, would have given the false picture that the elaborate and precise references are a modern addition and not the work of Biel himself. We have therefore left the references in the text and have corrected or extended them where necessary by our footnotes so that the reader can distinguish between the contributions of the fifteenth century and the comments of the twentieth.

Biel completed the *Defensorium* on 22 October 1462 while in exile in the Rheingau, probably at Eltville.[209] Like the letter he had written in the previous month, this work was intended for circulation in Mainz and was a defense of the position he had taken in the struggle between

---

[209] For a more complete discussion, see W. J. Courtenay, "Zur Chronologie der Schriften Gabriel Biels von 1462 und zu seiner Rolle in der Mainzer Stiftsfehde," *Trierer Theologische Zeitschrift* 74 (1965), 374–376.

INTRODUCTION

Diether von Isenburg and Adolf von Nassau for the archiepiscopacy of
Mainz. Originally the work was without title, beginning simply with the
words *Olim surrecturos*, but towards the end of the fifteenth century it
was by common usage referred to as the *Defensorium obedientiae
apostolicae.*[210] According to Steinbach the work was sent to Pope
Pius II and was approved by him.[211] We no longer possess either the
original autograph of Biel or any of the early copies that must have been
made at the time of its circulation. The earliest copies, the two manuscripts of which we have already spoken, exist in collections of documents relating to the Mainz controversy and were compiled shortly
after the victory of Adolf.

The Mainz manuscript contains documents covering the twelve year
period 1452–1464 and falls roughly into three sections. The first section
(pp. 1–22) contains trial briefs of the Mainz vicar general Hermann
Rosenberg, almost all referring to events in 1452. The second section
(pp. 23–49) concerns the archiepiscopal controversy itself and contains
papal and imperial letters, university judgments, letters of Diether and
Adolf, and Biel's two works, his letter of 1462 and his *Defensorium.*
Most of these documents are from the two year period 1461–1462. The
third section (pp. 50–112) is a more general collection of various documents, covering the period 1459–1464, which directly or indirectly
concern the controversy. The second and third sections, both of which
deal with the archiepiscopal controversy, have no connection with the
first section and seem to have been accidently bound in with it. These
last two sections support, in their choice of documents, the case of
Adolf von Nassau and may therefore have been compiled during the
time when the legality of Adolf's claim was still disputed and such
documents could arouse interest, that is in 1464, the date of the last
document in the collection, or shortly thereafter. That the *Defensorium*

---

[210] "Annals of the Wolf Brethren House," Staatsarchiv, Koblenz, Abt. 701, nr. 92,
fol. 20ᵛ; *Sermones* (Tübingen, 1500) [fol. 153ʳ].
[211] *Sermones* (Tübingen, 1500) [fol. 17ᵛ, 153ʳ].

58

in the Mainz manuscript lacks what, according to Steinbach, was its common title, also argues for an early date.

The Vatican manuscript is very similar to that of Mainz in that it is a collection of documents relating to the archiepiscopal controversy. It is much shorter, however, consisting of only two quires of six sheets each. Only half of the documents of the middle section of the Mainz manuscript are here, and they occur in the same order except for the letter of Biel, which is placed at the end instead of at the beginning. None of the documents supporting Diether are given in the Vatican manuscript. There is no indication in this collection as to the purpose of its compilation or the person or persons for whom it was copied. We know only that the manuscript was seized during the Thirty Years War and sent to Rome, and thus it became part of the Vatican holdings.

A gap of about thirty years exists between these manuscripts and the first printed edition which appeared in 1500. During this period Biel rose to the peak of his career both as a leader of the *Devotio moderna* in Germany and as a professor of theology at the newly founded University of Tübingen. Toward the end of this period Wendelin Steinbach, disciple and successor of Biel at Tübingen, began to edit and publish Biel's works, beginning with the *Canonis misse expositio* in 1488. As the last stage of this project Steinbach edited the *Sermones* of Biel and into this collection he placed several small treatises, including the *Defensorium.*

After the Hagenau edition of 1520 the *Defensorium*, along with the *Sermones* with which it was usually bound, ceased to be printed. Because of the rarity of those early editions and the immediately related documents, the discovery of the two manuscripts, and the importance of the archiepiscopal controversy in which Biel played a part, we have prepared the present critical edition.

59

Note to the Reader

In this volume the editors have followed classical Latin orthography. Thus *ae* appears for *e*, *m* for *n*, and so forth. The vowel *i* is distinguished from the consonant *j*; likewise, the distinction between *u* and *v* is retained. Such changes slightly impair the flavor of the original late-medieval Latin, but the meaning is not affected. Inconsistencies of spelling in the German document have been retained, since any alterations would have been artificial and arbitrary.

The editors have introduced punctuation and paragraphing throughout. Abbreviations have occasionally been expanded in the interest of clarity; their English equivalents are given in full in the translation. The names of authorities cited in the texts have been printed in capital letters to approximate late-medieval practice and to assist the reader. All direct quotations have been printed in italic; when such quotations depart from the original, one or two asterisks have been added to the footnote.

The footnotes complete the information in the texts; when the reference is erroneous, the correct source is given. In the texts the footnote number immediately follows the author's name and the title of the work, when both appear; when no title is given, the number immediately follows the author's name. When neither author nor title is given, the footnote number directly follows the citation. The footnote number immediately precedes all direct quotations.

All scriptural citations in the footnotes refer to the Vulgate Bible; the translation of New Testament citations follows the New English Bible where the Latin permits.

Symbols and Abbreviations

*	citation not exact
**	citation quite free
M	Mainz manuscript of the *Defensorium obedientiae apostolicae*
V	Vatican manuscript
T	Tübingen edition
H	Hagenau edition. The four variants are indicated by H^1, H^2, H^3, and H^4.

a, b,   variants in the text of the *Defensorium*. For example, ^{c}concernens *T* (the Tübingen edition gives the word "concernens" for the reading of the other sources, "concernentes"); $^{a-a}$ex verbis *V* (the Vatican manuscript gives the phrase "ex verbis" for the reading of the other sources, "et verbo").

add.   *addit*. For example, ^{a}*add*. et *M* (the Mainz manuscript adds "et"); $^{a-a}$*add*. quae talis est *M V* (the Mainz and Vatican manuscripts add "quae talis est").

om.   *omittit*. For example, ^{c}*om*. *T H* (the Tübingen and Hagenau editions omit "pater"); $^{f-f}$*om*. *M V* (the Mainz and Vatican manuscripts omit "et caetera").

CCh	*Corpus Christianorum*, Latin series (Turnhout, Belgium, 1953–).
CSEL	*Corpus scriptorum ecclesiasticorum Latinorum* (Vienna, 1866–).

Magnum Bullarium Romanum   *Bullarium diplomatum et privilegiorum sanctorum Romanorum pontificum*, ed. S. Franco and A. Dalmazzo, vol. V (Turin, 1860).

Moos	Thomas Aquinas, *In scripto sententiarum*, ed. A. Moos, 4 vols (Rome, 1947).
Parma	Thomas Aquinas, *Opera omnia*, 25 vols. (Parma, 1852–1873).
PG	*Patrologia Graeca*, ed. J. P. Migne (Paris, 1857–1912).
PL	*Patrologia Latina*, ed. J. P. Migne (Paris, 1844–1890).
RF	*Corpus iuris canonici*, ed. E. Friedberg and L. Richter, 2 ed., 2 vols. (Leipzig, 1922).
Wadding	Duns Scotus, Joh., *Opera omnia*, ed. L. Wadding, 26 vols. (Paris, 1891–1895).

Sources

Acta sanctorum septembris, vol. VI (Antwerp, 1757).

Aristotle, *Opera*, ed. Academia Regia Borussica (Berlin, 1831–1870).

Biblie iampridem renovate pars prima (-sexta) cum glosa ordinaria (et interlineari) et expositione lyre litterali et morali: necnon additionibus ac replicis, 6 vols. (Basel, 1502).

Biel, Gabriel, *Canonis misse expositio*, ed. H. A. Oberman and W. J. Courtenay, 4 vols. (Wiesbaden, 1963–1967).

———, *Collectorium in quattuor libros sententiarum*, 2 vols. (Basel, 1512).

———, *Epistola* 1 (18 Sept. 1462) Incip.: "Gnade und erluchtunge des heyligen geystes . . ." Explic.: ". . . fronefasten anno etc. LXII. Gabriel Byel." Stadtbibliothek Mainz, HS II, fol. 23ʳ–23ᵛ. Ed. F. W. E. Roth, "Ein brief des Gabriel Biel, 1462," *Neues Archiv der Gesellschaft für ältere deutsche Geschichtskunde* 35 (1910), 582–585; trans. as "Biel's Letter to the Church at Mainz under Interdict" in H. A. Oberman, *The Harvest of Medieval Theology* (Cambridge, Mass.: Harvard University Press, 1963), pp. 26–29.

Bullarium diplomatum et privilegiorum sanctorum Romanorum pontificum, ed. S. Franco and A. Dalmazzo, vol. V (Turin, 1860).

Corpus Christianorum, Latin series (Turnhout, Belgium, 1953–).

Corpus iuris canonici, ed. E. Friedberg and L. Richter, 2 ed., 2 vols. (Leipzig, 1922).

Corpus scriptorum ecclesiasticorum Latinorum (Vienna, 1866–).

Decretales Gregorii noni Pont. Max. cum epitomis, divisionibus, et glossis ordinariis (Venice, 1567).

Denzinger, H., and A. Schönmetzer, *Enchiridion symbolorum definitionum et declarationum de rebus fidei et morum*, 33 ed. (Freiburg i. Br., 1965).

Duns Scotus, Joh., *Opera omnia*, ed. L. Wadding, 26 vols. (Paris, 1891–1895).

Freher, M., and B. G. Struve, *Rerum Germanicarum scriptores varii, qui res in Germania & imperio sub Friderico III, Maximiliano I. Impp. memorabiliter gestas illo aevo litteris prodiderunt*, vol. II (Strasbourg, 1717).

Goldast, M., ed., *Monarchia seu Romani imperii*, vol. II (Frankfurt, 1668).

Gratiani decreta cum glossis (Paris, 1542).

Gudenus, F. de, *Codex diplomaticus anecdotorum, res Moguntinas, Francicas, Trevirenses, Hassiacas, finitimorumque regionum, necnon ius Germanicum et S.R.I. historiam vel maxime illustrantium*, vol. IV (Frankfurt and Leipzig, 1758).

Horace, *Ars poetica*, Loeb Classical Library, vol. 194 (Cambridge, Mass.: Harvard University Press, 1955).

John Runsic of Freiburg, *Summa confessorum* (Lyons, 1518).

SOURCES

Liber sextus decretalium d. Bonifacii Papae VIII suae integritati una cum Clementinis et extravagantes earumque glossis cum glossa J. Andreae (Paris, 1585).

Marsilius of Padua, *Defensor pacis*, ed. C. W. Previté-Orton (Cambridge, England, 1928).

Missale Aquileia (Venice, 1519).

Müller, J. J., *Des Heiligen Römischen Reichs Teutscher Nation Reichstag Theatrum, wie selbiges unter Keyser Friedrichs V allerhöchsten Regierung von Anno MCCCCXL bis MCCCCXCIII gestanden* . . . , 2 vols. (Jena, 1713).

Patrologia Graeca, ed. J. P. Migne (Paris, 1857–1912).

Patrologia Latina, ed. J. P. Migne (Paris, 1844–1890).

Pliny, *Natural History*, Loeb Classical Library, vol. 353 (Cambridge, Mass.: Harvard University Press, 1956).

Schatzgeyer, Caspar, *Apologia status fratrum ordinis minorum de observantia* (Nuremberg, 1516).

Thomas Aquinas, *Opera omnia*, 25 vols. (Parma, 1852–1873).

——— *In Scripto sententiarum*, ed. A. Moos, 4 vols. (Rome, 1947).

THE DOCUMENTS

DEFENSORIUM OBEDIENTIAE
APOSTOLICAE

Sequitur tractatulus DEFENSORIUM OBEDIENTIAE APOSTO-
LICAE intitulatus, a venerabili viro Gabriele Biel de Spira in Ringkavia
editus, Pio papae secundo dedicatus, et ab eodem approbatus. Accer-
situmque auctorem, Pius papa condigne omni, qua voluit, munificentia
5 decorare statuit; sed mercedem ab altissimo spectans temporalia
sprevit, perennis gloriae laurea coronandus.

Is in duas scinditur partes. In prima parte habentur novem veritates,
quae apostolicae sedis obedientiam debitam extollunt et ostendunt. In
secunda parte propositiones duodecim ex praemissis novem veritatibus
10 eliciuntur, factum domini Dietheri de Isenberg, quondam electi
ecclesiae[a] Moguntinensis, et provisionis reverendissimi in Christo
Patris et Domini domini Adolphi de Nassau electi et[b] confirmati: jam
dictae ecclesiae metropoliticae Moguntinensis et cetera concernentes[c].
DEFENSORIUM OBEDIENTIAE APOSTOLICAE AD PIUM

---

[a] *om.* $H^2 H^3$ [b] *om.* $H^2 H^3$ [c] concernens T

A DEFENSE OF APOSTOLIC
OBEDIENCE

[The Hagenau edition of 1510 begins here.]

Here follows a short treatise entitled DEFENSORIUM OBEDIEN-
TIAE APOSTOLICAE. This work was published by the venerable
Gabriel Biel of Speyer in the Rheingau, dedicated to Pope Pius II, and
approved by the Pope. Pope Pius summoned the author and promised to
bestow upon him any reward he desired; but he spurned temporal goods
expecting the recognition of heaven—the laurel crown of everlasting
glory.

This work is divided into two parts. Part One asserts nine truths which
declare and extol the obedience due to the Apostolic See. In Part Two
twelve propositions are deduced from these nine truths. These propositions deal with the deeds of Graf Diether von Isenburg, formerly elected
to the church of Mainz, and with the provision of the Very Reverend,
Father and Lord in Christ, Graf Adolf von Nassau, elected and confirmed,
and with other matters that concern the metropolitan church of Mainz.
[The Tübingen edition of 1500 begins here.]
THE *DEFENSORIUM OBEDIENTIAE APOSTOLICAE* WAS

DEFENSORIUM OBEDIENTIAE APOSTOLICAE

PAPAM SECUNDUM DESTINATUM AC AB EODEM APPROBATUM.

PARS PRIMA

Olim surrecturos pseudoprophetas, seductores multorum, evangelica tuba[a] prodidit MATTHEI xxiiii.[1] Sed et magistri sententiam fidelis
5 discipulus publicavit; ait etenim ad Timotheum scribens I AD TIMOTHEUM iiii:[2] *Spiritus manifeste dicit, quia in novissimis temporibus discedent demoniorum quidam a fide, attendentes spiritibus erroris et doctrinis demoniorum, in hypocrisi loquentium mendacium.* Causam[b] quoque[b] veritas aperit, dum prioribus continuo subjungit:[3] *quia*
10 *abundabit iniquitas, multorum charitas refrigescet.* Quam praeco veritatis Paulus, extendens II TIMO. iii:[4] *Hoc,* inquit, *scito, quod in novissimis diebus instabunt tempora periculosa, et erunt homines seipsos amantes, cupidi, elati, superbi, blasphemi, parentibus, haud dubium quin et spiritualibus, non obedientes, ingrati, scelesti, sine affectione, sine pace, crimina-*
15 *tores, incontinentes, immites sine benignitate, proditores, protervi, tumidi, voluptatum amatores magis quam Dei, habentes speciem[c] quidem pietatis, virtutem autem eius abnegantes, et hos devita. Tunc erit tempus, cum sanam doctrinam non sustinebunt,* II TIM. iiii,[5] *sed ad sua desideria coacervabunt sibi magistros prurientes auribus, et a veritate quidem[d]*
20 *auditum avertent, ad fabulas autem convertentur.* Hos dies nos apprehendisse dolenda probat experientia, qua homines pestiferos, *qui dissensiones et offendicula, praeter doctrinam Christi, faciunt,* AD ROM.

---

[a] turba *H*   [b–b] Hujus causam *T H*   [c] spem *T*   [d] quit *T*

[1] *Matth.* 24, 11.**
[2] *I Tim.* 4, 1–2.
[3] *Matth.* 24, 12.*
[4] *II Tim.* 3, 1–5.
[5] *II Tim.* 4, 3–4.

68

A DEFENSE OF APOSTOLIC OBEDIENCE

DISPATCHED TO POPE PIUS II AND RECEIVED PAPAL APPROVAL.

[The Mainz and Vatican manuscripts begin here.]

PART ONE

Christ, the Evangelical Trumpet, proclaimed in MATTHEW 24 that *many false prophets will arise, and will mislead many*; and Paul, his faithful disciple, made known abroad the Master's teaching when he wrote to Timothy in I TIMOTHY 4: *The Spirit says expressly that in aftertimes some will desert from the faith and give their minds to subversive doctrines inspired by devils, through the specious falsehoods of men.* When Truth adds immediately to his previous words that *the love of many will grow cold, because lawlessness will abound,* he discerns the cause. Paul, Truth's herald, said later in II TIMOTHY 3: *You must face the fact: the final age of this world is to be a time of troubles. Men will love nothing but money and self; they will be arrogant, boastful, and abusive, with no respect for their parents, much less their spiritual parents, no gratitude, no piety, no natural affection; they will be implacable in their hatreds, scandalmongers, intemperate and fierce, traitors, adventurers, swollen with self-importance. They will be men who put pleasure in the place of God, men who preserve the outward form of religion, but are a standing denial of its reality. Keep clear of men like these. For the time will come when they will not stand wholesome teaching* (II TIMOTHY 4) *but will follow their own fancy and gather a crowd of teachers to tickle their ears. They will stop their ears to the truth and turn to mythology.* Painful experience proves that we have fallen upon those days in which there are pernicious men *who stir up quarrels and offend against the teaching of Christ* (ROMANS 16). *Such people are servants*

69

DEFENSORIUM OBEDIENTIAE APOSTOLICAE

xvi,[1] *qui non Christo domino sed suo ventri serviunt, per dulces sermones et per benedictiones, lugemus*[a] *corda seducere innocentum.*

Domini itaque vicem dolens, ego, Gabriel Biel de Spira, ecclesiae Moguntinensis vicarius, inter orthodoxos praedicatores minimus, oves
5 dominicas contra hujuscemodi rapacium luporum insidias veritatis aeternae clipeis munire satagens, quemadmodum injuncti officii exigit sollicitudo, ad fidei catholicae normam, sanctae sedis apostolicae obedientiam et dominici ovilis matris ecclesiae unitatem servandam, secundum datam mihi gratiam non desino erudire. Eapropter praefa-
10 torum pseudoprophetarum quasi sator errorum fama referente lacescor.

Cupiens perinde[b] ejus, quae in me est[c], fidei rationem reddere, simul et omnibus doctrinam meam[d], verius Christi et sanctae matris ecclesiae, patefieri. Sciens illud evangelii:[2] *Qui facit veritatem, venit ad lucem, ut manifestentur opera ejus, quia in Deo facta sunt,* orthodoxorum non
15 refugio judicium. Quin immo corde avido ad lucem districti examinis una cum impugnatoribus meis venire desiderans, universa per[e] me in districto, Ringkau vulgariter nuncupato, praedicata, sub catholicarum, quae sequuntur, veritatum propositionumque coartavi compendio in publicum omnibus offerendo.

PRIMA[f] VERITAS[f]

20   In primis secundum Niceni tenorem symboli corde credo et ore confiteor: *Unam sanctam catholicam et apostolicam ecclesiam.*

Hujus sanctae ecclesiae unitatem unitatisque rationem apostolus manifestat, cum EPHESIIS ait capitulo iiii:[3] *Solliciti servare unitatem*

---

[a] longenius *M V*   [b] proinde *T H*   [c] *om. V*   [d] *om. T H*   [e] pro *M T H*   [f-f] *om. M V*

[1] *Rom.* 16, 17–18.*
[2] *Joan,* 3, 21.
[3] *Ephes.* 4, 3–6.

not of Christ our Lord but of their own appetites, and they seduce the minds of innocent people with smooth and specious words.

Therefore, suffering for the sake of our Lord, I, Gabriel Biel of Speyer, vicar of the church of Mainz, the least among orthodox preachers, devote my energies to guarding the Lord's flock with the shields of eternal truth against the stratagems of ravenous wolves. As the duties of my charge require, and according to the measure of grace given to me, I do not cease to instruct in accordance with the rule of the Catholic faith and the obedience due to the holy Apostolic See. This I do to preserve the unity of our Lord's sheepfold, our mother, the Church. I am aroused to write, therefore, on account of these false prophets and the reported rumor that I am a sower of error.

Likewise I wish to render an account of that faith which is in me, and at the same time to make known to all that my teaching is truly that of Christ and of our holy mother, the Church. I do not flee the judgment of the orthodox since I am aware of those words of the Gospel: *The honest man comes to the light so that it may be clearly seen that God is in all he does.* Indeed because I desire with an eager heart to come to the light of a strict examination by my assailants, I have gathered together all my preachings in the district, commonly called the Rheingau, into a compendium of catholic truths and propositions in order to present them to the general public.

FIRST TRUTH

First, in accordance with the contents of the Nicene Creed I believe with my heart and I confess with my mouth *one holy Catholic and Apostolic Church.*

The Apostle proclaims the unity of this holy Church and the nature of her unity when he writes to the EPHESIANS in chapter 4: *Spare no*

71

DEFENSORIUM OBEDIENTIAE APOSTOLICAE

Spiritus in vinculo pacis, unum corpus et unus Spiritus sicut vocati estis in una spe vocationis vestrae, unus Dominus, una fides, unum baptisma, unus Deus et Pater omnium. Corpus Christi ecclesiam, jam dixerat, dum eisdem de Christo loquens EPH. i[1] praetulit, *ipsum dedit* 5 *caput super omnem ecclesiam, quae est corpus ipsius.* Ecce ea ratione unum dicit corpus, quod est ecclesia, quia unus est spiritus, eam inhabitans; unus dominus Christus[a], eam sibi tamquam capiti corpus connectens; unus Deus, pater[b] omnium, eam paterna sollicitudine defendens; una denique fides, spirituale aedificium tamquam funda-10 mentum solidissimum sustentans; una spes vocationis, aeternam beatitudinem promittens; unum baptisma, cunctos regenerans, cetero-rumque sacramentorum identitate[c] regeneratos fovens et enutriens ad perfectum. Et quia una est sancta mater ecclesia, cujus[d] unitatem perversorum nemo scissuris dirumpere praevalet, licet ab ea seipsum 15 damnabiliter poterit separare.

Hinc beatus martyr CYPRIANUS, in EPISTOLA ad Normacium, dicit, et habetur xxiiii, quaest. i, *Loquitur:*[2] *Nemo veritatem fidei perfida praevaricatione[e] corrumpat. Ecclesia una est, quae in multitudine latius, incremento fecundius ostenditur, quomodo solis multi radii[f] sunt[f], sed* 20 *lumen unum, et[g] rami arboris multi sunt[h], sed robur unum tenaci radice fundatum. Et quomodo de fonte uno rivi plurimi defluunt, et numerositas licet diffusa videatur exundantis copiae largitate, unitas[i] tamen servatur integra origine. Avelle radium solis a corpore, divisionem unitas lucis non capit. Ab arbore frange ramum, germinare non poterit. A fonte praescide[j]* 25 *rivum praecisus arescit. Sic et ecclesia Dei luce perfusa per totum orbem radios suos porrigit; unum tamen est, quod ubique diffunditur nec unitas corporis separatur; ramos suos per universam terram, copia[k] suae ubertatis extendit, profluentes[m] largiter rivos latius pandit; unum tamen caput*

---

[a] Christo *T H*   [b] *om. T H*   [c] identitas *M V T H*   [d] ejus *T H*   [e] praedictione *H*
[f-f] sunt radii *V*   [g] *om. M V*   [h] *om. M V*   [i] uni *V*   [j] praescinde *T H*
[k] copias *M V*   [m] *om. M V*

---

[1] *Ephes.* 1, 22–23.
[2] c. 18, C. XXIV, qu. 1 (RF I, 972)*; *De unitate ecclesiae*, c. 5 (*PL* 4, 501A–502B).

A DEFENSE OF APOSTOLIC OBEDIENCE

effort to make fast with bonds of peace the unity which the Spirit gives. There is one body and one Spirit, as there is also one hope held out in God's call to you; one Lord, one faith, one God and Father of all. Previously Paul had said that the Church was the body of Christ, when speaking to the EPHESIANS about Christ. Paul affirmed that *he* [God the Father] *appointed him as supreme head to the Church which is his body.* He says that the body which is the Church is one for the following reasons: there is one Spirit which dwells within her; one Lord, who joins her to himself as the body is joined to its head; one God, who is the Father of all, and who defends her with fatherly concern; one faith which supports the spiritual edifice as the firmest foundation; one hope of vocation which promises eternal beatitude; one baptism which regenerates all and together with the other sacraments sustains the regenerate and nourishes them toward perfection. Because our holy mother the Church is one, none of the wicked will prevail in destroying her unity with schisms. Although the wicked man be able to separate himself from the Church, he will only achieve his own damnation.

The blessed martyr CYPRIAN writes in his EPISTLE to Normacius (Cause xxiv, question 1, *Loquitur*): *Let no one corrupt the truth of the faith with perfidious falsehood. There is only one Church, which has spread abroad far and wide into a multitude by its increase of fruitfulness. She resembles the sun which has many rays but remains one light, and a tree which has many branches but bases its one strength in its sturdy root; she resembles a spring from which many streams flow: although there is an apparent multiplicity in its overflowing abundance, its unity is preserved in its untarnished source. Separate a ray of the sun from its body of light; the unity of light does not undergo division. Break a branch from a tree; it will not be able to sprout. Cut off a stream from its spring; it will dry up. Thus also the Church of God, filled with light, sheds her rays throughout the world; yet she is one light which is everywhere diffused and the unity of her body is not jeopardized. In fruitful abundance, she extends her branches over the whole world. She broadly expands her rivers, profusely flowing; yet she has*

73

est et una origo, et una mater fecunditatis copiosa adulterari non potest. Christi sponsa incorrupta est et pudica, unam domum novit, unius cubilis sanctitatem casto pudore custodit.

Haec autem ecclesia, quia sancta, ideo sicut semper recta fide, ita
5 ornata creditur justitia et charitate. Propter quod apostolus AD EPH. v:[1] *Christus*, inquit, *dilexit ecclesiam et seipsum tradidit pro ea, ut illam sanctificaret, mundans illam lavacro aquae*[a] *in verbo vitae, ut exhiberet ipse sibi gloriosam ecclesiam non habenten maculam neque rugam vel aliquid hujusmodi, sed ut sit sancta et immaculata.* Siquidem fidei
10 indeficientiam Christus suae ecclesiae promisit, dum beato Petro, futuro ejus pastori, ait, LUCE xxii:[2] *Ego rogavi pro te, ut non deficiat fides tua.* Dum rectorem Spiritum Sanctum, ab ea nunquam separandum, pollicetur: *Rogabo*[b], inquit, JOANNIS xiiii,[3] *patrem meum et alium paracletum dabit vobis, ut maneat vobiscum in aeternum.* Dum eam patri
15 in suo nomine semper conservandam[c] commisit, cui dixit JOAN. xvii;[4] *Pater sancte, serva eos in nomine tuo, quos dedisti mihi.* Et sequi-tur:[5] *Non autem pro his tantum rogo*, videlicet apostolis, *sed et*[d] *pro eis, qui credituri sunt per verba eorum in me. Dum*[e] *denique suiipsius* praesen-tiam gratiosam ab ecclesia numquam subtrahendam pacto firmissimo
20 approbavit, dicens MATTH. xxviii:[6] *Ego vobiscum sum omnibus diebus usque ad consummationem saeculi.* Ex quibus emergunt duae assertiones[f] corollariae, his accomode quae sequuntur.

Prima veritas, quam sancta mater ecclesia tamquam catholicam diffinit vel acceptat, eadem veneratione credenda est, quasi in divinis
25 litteris sit expressa. Huic simile est, quod beatus[g] AUGUSTINUS

---

[a] *om. M V*   [b] Rogo *M V*   [c] servandam *T H*   [d] *om. M T H*   [e] Cum *H*
[f] fundamentales veritates *T H*   [g] *om. T H*

[1] *Ephes.* 5, 25–27.
[2] *Luc.* 22, 32.
[3] *Joan.* 14, 16.
[4] *Joan.* 17, 11.
[5] *Joan.* 17, 20.
[6] *Matth.* 28, 20.

A DEFENSE OF APOSTOLIC OBEDIENCE

but one head and one source. *As the one mother who is boundless in fecundity, she cannot be defiled. The Bride of Christ is pure and chaste; she knows one home and preserves with chaste modesty the sanctity of one marital bed.*

Moreover, the Church, because she is holy, is believed always to be distinguished by correct faith, by justice, and by love. For this reason, the Apostle wrote in EPHESIANS 5: *Christ loved the Church and gave himself up for her, to consecrate her, cleansing her by washing in the word of life, so that he might present the Church to himself all glorious, with no stain or wrinkle or anything of the sort, but holy and without blemish.* Indeed Christ promised his Church that she would not lapse from the faith, when he said to St. Peter, her future pastor (LUKE 22): *For you I have prayed, that your faith may not fail.* When he promised that her guide, the Holy Spirit, would never be taken away from her, he said (JOHN 14): *I will ask the Father and he will give you another to be your advocate, who will be with you forever.* When he committed her to the Father to preserve her always for his sake, he said (JOHN 17): *Holy Father, for thy sake keep those whom thou hast given me.* Subsequently he continued, *It is not for these alone that I pray*, namely, the apostles, *but for those also who through their words put their faith in me.* Finally (MATTHEW 28) he affirmed in a steadfast covenant that he would never withdraw his gracious presence from his Church: *I am with you always, to the close of the age.* From these statements of our Lord arise two corollary assertions which clearly follow these.

The first: What the holy Church, our Mother, defines and accepts as catholic truth must be believed with the same reverence as though it were stated in Holy Scripture. In his reply to the Manichaeans, ST. AUGUSTINE writes to similar effect: *I would not believe unless the*

contra EPISTOLAM fundamenti scribens ait:[1] *Evangelio non crederem
nisi ecclesiae auctoritas me* compelleret. Cui beatus BERNARDUS, in
sermone DE VIGILIA NATIVITATIS DOMINI,[2] qui incipit *Hodie
scietis,* consonare videtur in haec verba: *Ecclesia secum habet consilium*
5 *et spiritum sponsi et Dei sui,* "*cui dilectus inter ubera commoratur,*"[3]
*ipsam cordis sedem principaliter possidens et conservans. Nimirum ipsa
est, quae vulneravit cor ejus, et in ipsam abyssum*[a] *secretorum Dei oculum
contemplationis immersit, ut et illi in suo et sibi in ejus corde perennem
faciat*[b] *mansionem. Cum ergo ipsa in scripturis divinis verba vel alterat*
10 *vel alternat, fortior est illa compositio quam positio prima verborum; et
fortasse tanto fortior, quantum distat inter figuram et veritatem, inter
lucem et umbram, inter dominam et ancillam.*

Secunda[c]: Praeceptis universalis ecclesiae, cujus perpetua est sanctitas
et justitia, necesse est fideles quoslibet obedire. Pro qua sufficiat illud
15 sponsi ejus testimonium, MATTHEI xviii:[4] *Si ecclesiam non audierit, sit
tibi sicut ethnicus et publicanus.* Facit ad idem canon beati GREGORII,
xv dist. *Sicut sancti,* de quattuor consiliis evangelicis ita loquentis:[5] *Quia
dum universali sunt consensu constituta, se et non illa destituit, quisquis
praesumit absolvere, quod ligant*[d], *aut religare quod absolvunt*, ubi consi-
20 liorum[e] auctoritatem, quam tamquam evangelii suscipiendam testatur,
in universalis ecclesiae consensu fundat.

Quia etiam ecclesia haec catholica est, id est, universalis. ISIDORUS,
lib. I, DE SUMMO BONO, cap. xvi:[6] *Praeter hoc, quod per universum
orbem diffunditur, non in aliquo angulo coartatur, omnes regni aeterni
25 filios comprehendit.* Propter quod extra illam quisquis manserit, salutem

---

[a] *add.* secretum *M V*   [b] faciant *M*   [c] *add.* veritas *M V*   [d] religant *M V*
[e] conciliorum *M V*

[1] *Contra epist. manichei,* L. I. (*PL* 42, 176)**; Aug. habet *commoveret.*
[2] *Serm.* 3 (*PL* 18, 94D–95A).
[3] *Cant.* 1, 12.**
[4] *Matth.* 18, 17.
[5] c. 2, D. XV (RF I, 36).*
[6] *Sent.,* L. I, c. 16 (*PL* 83, 572B).

A DEFENSE OF APOSTOLIC OBEDIENCE

authority of the Church compelled me. ST. BERNARD also seems to be in accord with this position in his sermon, DE VIGILIA NATIVITATIS DOMINI, which begins *Today you will know.*: *The Church has the counsel and spirit of her bridegroom and God. She has the Beloved "abiding between her breasts," preserving her heart, and occupying it like a king upon his throne. Indeed, she is the spouse who has pierced his heart, and who with the eye of contemplation penetrates the abyss of God's hidden designs, and so makes an everlasting dwelling place for herself in his heart and for him in her own. Whenever, therefore, she changes or shifts the arrangement of a text in Holy Scripture, the new construction possesses greater weight than the original word order. Perhaps this construction surpasses the original to the degree that the reality exceeds the image; the light, the shadow; the mistress, the maidservant.*

The second: All the faithful must obey the precepts of the Church Universal whose sanctity and justice is everlasting. For this, the testimony of her Bridegroom suffices (MATTHEW 18): *If he will not listen even to the Church, you must then treat him as you would a pagan or a tax-gatherer.* The canon of ST. GREGORY (distinction xv, *Sicut sancti*) supports the same conclusion in discussing the four evangelical counsels: *Because these counsels are constituted by universal consent, whoever presumes to absolve what they enjoin or to enjoin what they absolve forsakes himself, and not them.* Thus he founds the authority of these counsels in the consensus of the Church Universal and asserts that they must be regarded with the authority of Scripture.

Furthermore, the Church is [not only holy, but] also catholic, that is, universal. ISIDORE (DE SUMMO BONO, Book 1, chapter 16) asserts that since the Church is diffused through the whole world and is not confined in any corner, she includes all children of the eternal kingdom. Thus whoever remains outside her will be unable to attain salvation.

consequi non valebit, quod beatus AUGUSTINUS in DE FIDE ad Petrum capitulo xxxv approbat dicens:[1] *Firmissime tene et nullatenus dubites, non solum omnes paganos sed et omnes judaeos et haereticos atque schismaticos, qui*[a] *extra ecclesiam sanctam praesentem finiunt vitam, "in*
5 *ignem aeternum ituros, qui praeparatus est diabolo et angelis ejus."*[2] Item ibidem capitulo xxxvi:[3] *Omni homini, qui ecclesiae non*[b] *tenet unitatem, neque baptismus nec eleemosyna quaelibet*[c] *copiosa, neque mors pro nomine Christi suscepta, proficere poterit*[d] *ad salutem.* Et in EPISTOLA CONTRA DONATISTAS xxii, quaest. iiii, *Si quis:*[4] *Si quis, ait, a catholica ecclesia*
10 *fuerit separatus, quantumlibet laudabiliter se vivere existimet, hoc solo scelere, quod a christianitate*[e] *disjunctus est, non habebit vitam, et ira Dei manet super eum.* Beatus quoque CYPRIANUS xxiiii, quaest. i, *Alienus,* idipsum testatur dicens:[5] *Alienus est, profanus est, hostis est; habere non potest Deum patrem, qui universalis ecclesiae non tenet unitatem.* Sed et
15 Dominus ipse in evangelio idem designat, cum JOANNIS iii[f],[6] neminem ad caelum ascendere posse, nisi filium hominis, asserit[g]. Necesse ergo est membrum Christi fore, quisquis voluerit in caelum recipi. Sed quomodo membrum[h] esse poterit, qui a corpore Christi, quod est ecclesia, separatur?
20 Quia demum ecclesia est apostolica, in apostolorum videlicet fide fundata, apostolorum praedicatione collecta, apostolorum doctrinis, ordinationibus et praeceptis fulcita, apostolorumque successione legitima per summos, scilicet, pontifices, episcopos et praelatos continuata, quicumque huic ordinationi resistit, in sanctam ecclesiam vehementer
25 impingit, quam usque in saeculi finem, donec ad judicium Dominus

---

[a] quo *M*   [b] *om. T H*   [c] quamlibet *T*, quantumlibet *H*   [d] potest *M V*
[e] catholica ecclesia *M V*   [f] *add.* dicit *M V*   [g] *om. M V*   [h] *add.* Christi *T H*

[1] Pseudo-Aug., c. 38 (*PL* 40, 776).
[2] *Matth.* 25, 41.*
[3] Pseudo-Aug., c. 39 (*PL* 40, 776).
[4] c. 7, C. XXIII, qu. 4 (RF I, 900–901).
[5] c. 19, C. XXIV, qu. 1 (RF I, 972).
[6] Cf. *Joan.* 3, 13.

A DEFENSE OF APOSTOLIC OBEDIENCE

ST. AUGUSTINE agrees when he says (DE FIDE AD PETRUM, chapter 35): *Hold steadfast and entertain not the slightest doubt that not only all those pagans but also all those Jews, heretics, and schismatics who die outside the holy Church "will depart to eternal fire that is ready for the devil and his angels."* He writes likewise later in the same treatise (chapter 36): *For any man who does not abide in the unity of the Church, neither baptism nor alms, no matter how generous, nor even death suffered for the name of Christ will avail to salvation.* And in his EPISTLE AGAINST THE DONATISTS (Cause xxiii, question 4, *Si quis*), he says: *If any man separates himself from the Catholic church, no matter how praiseworthy he deems his manner of life, for this sin alone—that he has isolated himself from the body of Christians—he will not have eternal life and the wrath of God will remain upon him.* ST. CYPRIAN also asserts the same (Cause xxiv, question 1) when he says: *He is an alien; he is impious; he is an enemy. He cannot have God as his father who does not preserve the unity of the Church Universal.* The Lord himself suggests the same in the Gospel, when he asserts (JOHN 3) that no one can go up into heaven except the Son of Man. Therefore whoever wishes to be received into heaven must be a member of Christ. But how can anyone be a member of Christ who is separated from the body of Christ, which is the Church?

Finally, the Church is apostolic, that is, founded in the faith of the apostles, gathered through the preaching of the apostles, enlightened by the teachings, ordinances, and precepts of the apostles, and continued manifestly in legitimate succession from the apostles through popes, bishops, and prelates. Therefore whoever resists this order of the Church

DEFENSORIUM OBEDIENTIAE APOSTOLICAE

veniet, duraturam testatur apostolus, EPH. iiii[1] dicens: *Ipse qui ascendit super omnes caelos, dedit quosdam quidem apostolos, quosdam autem prophetas, alios vero evangelistas, alios pastores et doctores, ad consummationem sanctorum, in opus ministerii, in aedificationem corporis Christi,*
5 *donec occurramus omnes in unitatem fidei et agnitionis filii Dei, in virum perfectum, in mensuram aetatis plenitudinis Christi;* qui occursus[a] in extremo judicio fiet, secundum omnium doctorum expositionem[2].

De hac etiam successione loquitur sanctus AUGUSTINUS libro CONTRA MANICHAEOS, xi dist., *Palam:*[3] *Palam est,* inquit, *quod in re*
10 *dubia ad fidem et certitudinem valeat[b] ecclesiae catholicae auctoritas, quae ab ipsis fundatissimis apostolorum sedibus usque ad hodiernam diem succedentium, sibimet et episcoporum serie, et tot consensione populorum firmatur.* Et rursus idem ait, xxiii, quaest. 1, *Pudenda,* juxta finem:[4] *Quod si nullomodo recte[c] potest dici ecclesia, in qua schisma est, restat, ut, quoniam*
15 *ecclesia nulla esse non potest ea sola sit, quam in sedis apostolicae per successiones episcoporum radice constitutam, hominum nullorum malitia ullo[d] modo valeat extinguere.* In hac catholica professione multa sequentium fundabuntur.

SECUNDA VERITAS[e]

Christus Dominus ad caelum ascensurus beatum Petrum, apostolum,
20 ecclesiae suae praefecit generalem pastorem, caput, principem, et praelatum.

---

[a] occursurus *V*   [b] variae et *M V*   [c] id est certe *M V*   [d] nullo *M V*
[e] *add.* est haec *M V*

---

[1] *Ephes.* 4, 10–13.
[2] *Biblie iampridem renovate pars prima (-sexta) cum glosa ordinaria (et interlineari) et expositione lyre litterali et morali: necnon additionibus ac replicis* (Basel, 1502), VI, f. 94ʳ.
[3] c. 9, D. XI (RF I, 25).
[4] c. 33, C. XXIV, qu. 1 (RF I, 979).

assails the holy Church herself which the Apostle states (EPHESIANS 4) will endure until the end of time when the Lord will come in judgment: *He who ascended far above all the heavens ordained some to be apostles, some prophets, some evangelists, some pastors and teachers, to the perfecting of the saints, to the work of his service, to the building up of the body of Christ: so shall we all at last attain to the unity inherent in our faith and our knowledge of the Son of God—to mature manhood, measured by nothing less than the full stature of Christ.* This attainment will take place in the Last Judgment, according to the exposition of all the doctors.

ST. AUGUSTINE also speaks of this succession in his book, CONTRA MANICHEOS (cited in distinction xi, *Palam*) when he writes: *It is plain that in a dubious matter the authority of the Catholic Church can establish faith and certitude. This authority is rooted in a succession of bishops succeeding one another up to the present time from those sees founded by the apostles themselves, and in the acceptance of so many people.* He reiterates this assertion (Cause xxiv, question 1, *Pudenda* near the end):[1] *Now therefore in no manner can a church in which schism dwells be rightly termed the Church.*

It remains that because such a body cannot be the Church, that only is the true Church which was constituted in the foundation of the Apostolic See through the succession of bishops. This Church alone cannot be extinguished by the malice of men. Much of what follows will be founded in this Catholic profession.

SECOND TRUTH

Christ, the Lord, before he ascended into heaven, appointed St. Peter, the Apostle, the general pastor, head, ruler, and prelate of his Church.

---

[1] E. Friedberg attributes this to Pope Pelagius.

DEFENSORIUM OBEDIENTIAE APOSTOLICAE

Hanc veritatem evangelica pandit historia. Interrogato siquidem Petro, JOANNIS ultimo:[1] *Petre, amas me plus his?* vice trina. Ipso quoque totiens respondente: *Tu scis, Domine, quia amo te.* Subjunxit Dominus ad quamlibet Petri responsionem: *Pasce oves meas.* In quibus verbis *Oves*
5 *suas* indistincte Petro singulariter tamquam pastori universali Dominus commendavit. *Nam non designasse aliquas est assignasse omnes*[a], ait BERNARDUS libro II[b] DE CONSIDERATIONE ad Eugenium papam.[2] Quod autem[c] singulariter Petro haec verba Dominus locutus fuerit, et[d] eum in persona propria dixerit[e] non[f] aliorum condiscipulorum[f]
10 convincitur manifeste per regulam beati AUGUSTINI in libro OCTO-GINTATRIUM QUAESTIONUM,[3] quaestione lxix, dicentis: *Solet*[g] *circumstantia scripturae illuminare sententiam, cum ea, quae circa scripturam sunt praesentem quaestionem contingentia, diligenti discussione tractantur.* Sic in proposito, ad quem verba sua Christus direxerit, ex praecedentibus
15 et sequentibus colligi clare potest. Quaerens namque a Petro Dominus, *an se diligeret*, addidit, *plus his. Petre*, inquit,[4] *diligis me plus his?* Discernens ergo Petrum ab *his*, id est, aliis praesentibus apostolis et discipulis, ad ipsum in persona sua singulariter, non aliorum, a quibus aperte discernitur, amoris dirigit[h] quaestionem. Quo respondente[5]: *Tu scis, Domine,*
20 *quia amo te*, continuo ovium suarum pasturam injungit, dicens:[6] *Pasce agnos*[i] *meos*[i]. Quis dubitat, quin illi, quem de[j] suo amore quaesivit, siquidem—ut omnibus patenter[k] causam[m] Dominus[m] insinuaret, cur specialiter Petro plus ceteris ovium suarum, quas ipse dilexerat curam committeret—de amore quaestionem ad Petrum, si se plus ceteris
25 diligeret[n], praemittebat.

---

[a] *add.* ut *T H*   [b] III *T H*   [c] vero *T H*   [d] *add.* ad *V*   [e] direxit *M*, direxerit *T H*
[f-f] *om. T H*   [g] Solent *T*   [h] *om. V*, dixit *H*   [i-i] oves meas *V*   [j] a *V*   [k] patentur *T H*
[m-m] Dominus causam *T H*   [n] *add.* in persona propria *T H*

[1] *Joan.* 21, 15–17.
[2] L. II, c. 8 (*PL* 182, 751D).*
[3] *PL* 40, 75.
[4] *Joan.* 21, 15.
[5] *Joan.* 21, 16.
[6] *Joan.* 21, 17.

A DEFENSE OF APOSTOLIC OBEDIENCE

The gospel account reveals this truth: Peter was asked three times (JOHN 21): *Peter, do you love me more than these?* And each time, he responded: *You know, Lord, that I love you.* To each response of Peter, the Lord replied: *Feed my sheep.* In these words, *my sheep,* the Lord commended his flock undivided to Peter alone as a universal pastor. *Instead of designating some portion of the flock, he rather assigns the whole,* declares ST. BERNARD to Pope Eugenius (DE CONSIDERATIONE, Book II). It is clearly manifest that the Lord addressed these words to Peter only and addressed him personally and not the other disciples, if one follows the rule of ST. AUGUSTINE (OCTOGINTATRIUM QUAESTIONUM, question 69): *Usually the context of a passage illuminates its meaning. Those matters which are related to the present question are treated in a careful discussion in the context of the passage.* Thus in the instance above, it can clearly be gathered from the preceding and following words to whom Christ directed his words, since the Lord in asking Peter *whether he loved him* added, *more than these? Peter,* he asked, *do you love me more than these?* Therefore he distinguished Peter from the others, that is, from the other apostles and disciples present, and directed his question of love to Peter personally, and not to the others from whom Peter is clearly distinguished. When Peter responded, *You know, Lord, that I love you,* the Lord immediately assigned him the pastoral care of his sheep: *Feed my sheep.* Who may doubt but that the Lord when he questioned Peter about his love—since he posed the question of love to Peter personally, that is, whether he loved him more than the others— did so to make known publicly to all the reason he committed the care of his sheep, whom he loved, more specifically to Peter than to the other apostles?

DEFENSORIUM OBEDIENTIAE APOSTOLICAE

Sic cum tertia[a] repetita quaestione Petrique responsione addidisset: *Pasce oves meas*, statim subdit:[1] *Amen, amen, dico tibi, cum esses junior, cingebas te, et ambulabas, quo volebas* et cetera. Quae ad Petrum in persona propria fuisse dicta, etiam evangelista testatur, cum dicit:[2] *Hoc autem*
5 *dixit significans qua morte esset clarificaturus Deum.* Cum itaque in principio hujus sententiae et in fine similiter ad personam Petri, ut suam[b] Dominus sermonem direxerit, frivolum est omnino, protervum, et omni ratione vacuum, dicere in medio illius sententiae, maxime quia ex principio dependet, nullo modo loquendi mutato, servata eadem verborum
10 forma, ad alium vel etiam ad eundem in persona aliorum verborum sententiam direxisse.

Huic catholico intellectui favent alia sancti evangelii verba, quibus secundum sanctorum expositiones beatus Petrus futurus pastor et caput universalis ecclesiae designatur. Sicut illa: *Tu vocaberis Cephas*, JOAN.
15 i;[3] *Tu es Petrus et super hanc petram aedificabo ecclesiam meam*, MATTH. xvi[4]; *Ego pro te rogavi Petre, ut non deficiat fides tua, et tu aliquando conversus confirma fratres tuos*, LUCE xxii.[5]

Hanc denique veritatem tenuerunt et firmiter credendam tradiderunt sancti patres, summi pontifices, et ecclesiae doctores, a temporibus apo-
20 stolorum usque ad tempora nostra, continua sibi serie succedentes. Hoc Anacletus, hoc Clemens, apostolorum discipuli, a beato Petro in divinis scripturis instructi, sancti martyres et pontifices summi. Hoc beati martyres Marcellus, Cyprianus, sanctique doctores Eusebius Caesariensis, Hieronymus, Ambrosius, Augustinus, Chrysostomus, Gregorius
25 maximus, Leo et Bernardus, alii quoque innumeri senserunt, docuerunt et in scripturis reliquerunt, unanimiter contestati: beatum Petrum caput et praelatum apostolorum omniumque fidelium, ecclesiam quoque

---

[a] tertio *T H* [b] suum *M*

[1] *Joan.* 21, 18.
[2] *Joan.* 21, 19.
[3] *Joan.* 1, 42.
[4] *Matth.* 16, 18.
[5] *Luc.* 22, 32.

A DEFENSE OF APOSTOLIC OBEDIENCE

Thus when he had repeated the question three times and had answered Peter's response three times, *Feed my sheep*, he immediately added, *And further, I tell you this in very truth: when you were young you fastened your belt about you and walked where you chose*, and so forth. The evangelist bears witness that these words were addressed to Peter personally when he writes: *He said this to indicate the manner of death by which Peter was to glorify God*. Therefore since at the beginning and at the end of this passage the Lord directed his words in the same manner to the person of Peter, it is utterly frivolous, impudent, and devoid of all reason to say that in the middle of that passage he directed his words to another or to Peter in a different fashion, particularly because this passage is dependent upon the beginning, the manner of speaking is in nowise changed, and the same form of the verb is maintained.

Other texts of Holy Scripture in which St. Peter is designated future pastor and head of the Church Universal, according to the expositions of the saints, support this catholic interpretation: *You shall be called Cephas* (JOHN 1); *You are Peter, and on this rock I will build my church* (MATTHEW 16); *For you I have prayed, Peter, that your faith may not fail* (LUKE 22).

Finally, the holy Fathers, popes, and doctors of the Church succeeding one another in an unbroken line from the time of the apostles until our time have maintained this truth and taught that it must be firmly believed. To this truth Anacletus and Clement, holy martyrs and popes, and disciples of the apostles who were instructed by St. Peter in the divine Scriptures, gave their assent. This truth the blessed martyrs, Marcellus and Cyprian, and the holy doctors, Eusebius of Caesarea, Jerome, Ambrose, Augustine, Chrysostom, Gregory the Great, Leo, Bernard, and innumerable others, held, taught, and bequeathed in their writings and unanimously attested: that St. Peter is the head and prelate of the apostles and all the faithful and that the Roman church, the see which

---

romanam, quam sibi et successoribus jubente Domino sedem constituerat,
super omnes ecclesias primatum habere. Quorum aliquae[a] in DECRETO
collegit GRATIANUS, ut dist. xxii, *Sacrosancta*, et cap. *Omnes*,[1] dist.
lxxx, *In illis*,[2] xxiiii, quaest. 1, *Rogamus*,[3] et cap, *Cum beatissimus*,[4] et
5 cap. *Loquitur*[5] eadem quaestione et causa[b], 1 dist., *Hi qui*, sect. *sed
exemplo*[6] et duobus capitulis sequentibus, dist. xix, *Ita dominus*,[7] xxi
dist., sect. 1 *in verbo Petrum vero*[8] et cap. *In novo*[9] et cap. *Quamvis* eadem
distinctione,[10] dist.[c] xi, *Nolite*,[11] DE ELECTIONE, *Significasti*,[12] DE
MAJORITATE ET OBEDIENTIA, *Solitae*[13] et in aliis pluribus locis[d].

TERTIA VERITAS[e]

10 Omnes oves Christi universi, scilicet, fideles, regimini beati Petri
tenebantur subesse, ac de necessitate salutis vocem ejus tamquam veri
pastoris sequi, praeceptis ejus et jussionibus obedire.

Patet haec veritas, quia non minus tenetur regendus subesse, quam
rector regere. Quippe frustra est obligatio alicujus ad regendum, ubi
15 nulli obligati sunt ad parendum[f]. Fuit autem beatus Petrus obligatus
post commissionem ecclesiae sibi a Domino factam ad regendum eam,
quare omnes de ecclesia regimini suo subici tenebantur.

Si auctoritas quaeritur, Dominum audiamus, JOAN. x, de pastore et

---

[a] aliqua *T H* [b] *om. T H* [c] *om. T H* [d] *add.* sequitur *M V*
[e] *add.* quae talis est *M V* [f] *add.* et *M*

---

[1] c. 2, D. XXII (RF I, 73–75); c. 1, D. XXII (RF I, 73).
[2] c. 2, D. LXXX (RF I, 280).
[3] c. 15, C. XXIV, qu. 1 (RF I, 970).
[4] c. 16, C. XXIV, qu. 1 (RF I, 971).
[5] c. 18, C. XXIV, qu. 1 (RF I, 971).
[6] Cf. c. 9, C. III, qu. 4 (RF I, 513).
[7] c. 7, D. XIX (RF I, 62).
[8] D. XXI (RF I, 67); *Gratiani decreta cum glossis* (Paris, 1542).
[9] c. 2, D. XXI (RF I, 69–70).
[10] c. 3, D. XXI (RF I, 70).
[11] c. 3, D. XI (RF I, 23).
[12] c. 4, X (1,6) (RF II, 49–50).
[13] c. 6, X (1,33) (RF II, 196–198).

A DEFENSE OF APOSTOLIC OBEDIENCE

Peter established for himself and his successors by the Lord's command, enjoys primacy over all churches. GRATIAN presents some of these affirmations in the DECRETUM (distinction xxii, *Sacrosancta* and *Omnes*; distinction lxxx, *In illis*; Cause xxiv, question 1, *Rogamus*; the canons *Cum beatissimus* and *Loquitur* in the same cause and question; the distinction 1, *Hi qui,* under the section *sed exemplo* and the following two canons; distinction xix, *Ita dominus*; distinction xxi under the section *in verbo Petro vero*; the canon *In novo*; the canon *Quamvis* in the same distinction; distinction xi, *Nolite*; in DE ELECTIONE under *Significasti*; in DE MAJORITATE ET OBEDIENTIA under *Solite*; and in many other places).

THIRD TRUTH

All the sheep of Christ, namely, the faithful, are subject to the rule of St. Peter and bound for their salvation to follow his voice as that of the true shepherd and to obey his precepts and commands.

This truth is quite evident since the one ruled is no less bound to be subordinate than the ruler is bound to rule. Indeed, any obligation to rule is void where none are bound to obey; but St. Peter was bound to rule the Church after it was committed to him by the Lord; therefore all the members of the Church are bound to be subject to his rule.

If authority is sought, let us hear the Lord who speaks thus concerning the shepherd and his sheep (JOHN 10): *The sheep hear his voice.* He adds,

ovibus sic loquentem:[1] *Oves vocem ejus audiunt.* Et infra:[2] *Cum proprias oves emiserit ante eas vadit, et oves illum sequuntur.* Non ergo est ovis propria, quae pastorem suum non audit, docentem auscultando, nec sequitur mandatis obsequendo[a]. Facit ad idem verbum Christi ad omnes
5 discipulos dictum LUCAE x:[3] *Qui vos spernit me spernit, et qui spernit me, spernit eum, qui misit me.* Et apostolus AD ROM. xiii:[4] *Qui potestati, inquit, resistit, Dei ordinationi resistit; qui autem resistunt, ipsi sibi damnationem adquirunt.*

QUARTA VERITAS

Romanus pontifex, canonice intrans, super cathedram Petri sedet,
10 ejusque verus et legitimus est sucessor.

Huic veritati consonat beatus HIERONYMUS, qui romanum allo-quens pontificem ait[b] ita[b] xxiiii, quaest. i, *Quoniam vetus:*[5] *Cum suc-cessore[c] piscatoris discipulo Christi loquor. Ego nullum premium nisi Christum sequens beatitudini tuae, id[d] est[d], cathedrae Petri[e] consortio super
15 illam petram ecclesiam fundatam scio.* Iterum ad Damasum papam scri-bens ait, xxiiii, quaest. i, *Haec est:*[6] *Emendari cupimus a te, qui Petri et sedem tenes et fidem.* SIXTUS quoque papa ait, xxiiii, quaest. i, *Memor:*[7] *Memor sum me sub illius nomine praesidere ecclesiae, cujus confessio a Domino glorificata est.* Cui concordat illud INNOCENTII III in cap.
20 *Solite,* DE MAJORITATE ET OBEDIENTIA:[8] *Nobis autem in beato Petro sunt oves Christi[f] commissae a Domino, dicente,*[9] *"Pasce oves meas,"* non

---

[a] *add.* et *M*   [b-b] ita ait *T H*   [c] successori *M V*   [d-d] idem *M T H*   [e] petrae *M T H*
[f] *om. M V*

[1] *Joan.* 10, 3.
[2] *Joan,* 10, 4.
[3] *Luc.* 10, 16.
[4] *Rom.* 13, 2.
[5] c. 25, C. XXIV (RF I, 976).
[6] c. 14, C. XXIV (RF I, 970).
[7] c. 10, C. XXIV (RF I, 969).
[8] c. 6, X (1,33) (RF II, 198).
[9] *Joan.* 21, 17.

A DEFENSE OF APOSTOLIC OBEDIENCE

When he has brought his own sheep out, he goes ahead and the sheep follow him. Therefore the sheep which does not hear his shepherd is not the shepherd's; such sheep hear the teacher but do not follow him by heeding his commands. These words of Christ to all the disciples are to the same effect (LUKE 10): *Whoever rejects you rejects me. And whoever rejects me rejects the One who sent me.* The apostle Paul also says (ROMANS 13): *Anyone who rebels against authority is resisting a divine institution, and those who so resist have themselves to thank for their own damnation.*

FOURTH TRUTH

The Roman pontiff, canonically elected, who sits upon the chair of St. Peter is his true and legitimate successor.

ST. JEROME affirms this truth in addressing the Roman pontiff thus (Cause xxiv, question 1, *Quoniam vetus*): *I address myself to the successor of the fisherman, to the disciple of Christ. As I seek no reward but Christ, so I join in supporting your blessedness, that is, the chair of Peter. I know that the Church is built upon this rock.* Again JEROME wrote to Pope Damasus (Cause xxiv, question 1, *Haec est*): *We desire to be corrected by you, who defend the see and faith of Peter.* POPE SIXTUS also says (Cause xxiv, question 1, *Memor*): *I am aware that I have the care of the Church in the name of him whose confession was glorified by the Lord.* POPE INNOCENT III agrees with this (chapter *Solite*, DE MAJORITATE ET OBEDIENTIA): *To us were the sheep of Christ committed in St. Peter by the Lord. When he said "Feed my sheep," he did not distinguish between "these" sheep and*

DEFENSORIUM OBEDIENTIAE APOSTOLICAE

distinguens inter oves et alias, ut alienum a[a] *suo demonstraret*[a] *ovili, qui Petrum et successores illius magistros non recognosceret et pastores.* Et DE TRANSLATIONE, cap. *Licet,* idem de romano pontifice dicit:[1] *Successor est Petri et vicarius Jesu Christi.*

QUINTA VERITAS

5 Omnem regitivam potestatem atque pastoralem auctoritatem habet[b] pontifex quilibet romanus, quam ad regendum universalem ecclesiam a Domino acceperat sanctus Petrus.

Nisi etenim eadem apud romanum pontificem resideret regendi auctoritas, quae apud Petrum, quomodo successor Petri vere diceretur
10 et esset, cum successor sicut antecessor, pari[c] immo eadem fungitur auctoritate, ut innuit INNOCENTIUS tertius in cap. *Innotuit,* DE ELECTIONE.[2] Quomodo etiam sufficienter ecclesiae suae providisset Christus, si potestatem Petro ad regendum ecclesiam concessam in ecclesia non perpetuasset? Neque enim propter utilitatem propriam
15 universalis ecclesia Petro, nec aliqua particularis ecclesia praelato cuilibet est commissa, dicente apostolo, II COR. ultimo:[3] *Potestatem*[d] *mihi dedit in aedificationem*—haud dubium quin ecclesiae—*non in destructionem.* Et iterum AD EPH. iiii:[4] *Eis quos ordinavit apostolos, pastores, doctores, et*[e] *cetera*[e] *potestatem dedit ad consummationem sanc-*
20 *torum, in opus ministerii, in aedificationem corporis Christi,* quod est ecclesia, ut supra allegatum est. Indiget sane semper ecclesia regitiva potestate Petro concessa. Nunquam ergo privabitur illa, quam in necessariis ad salutem sponsus suus deficere non permittit. Hanc autem, si romanus pontifex, successor Petri, non habet, sine dubio alius nemo
25 habet.

[a–a] demonstraret a suo *M V*   [b] *add.* summus *V*   [c] patri *M*   [d] *om. M V*   [e–e] *om. T H*

[1] c. 4, X (1,7) (RF II, 100).
[2] c. 20, X (1,6) (RF II, 61–63).
[3] *II Cor.* 13, 10.
[4] *Ephes.* 4, 11–12.**

"other" *sheep so that he might clearly indicate that anyone who does not* *recognize Peter and his successores as masters and pastors is a stranger in* *his sheepfold.* INNOCENT also writes concerning the Roman pontiff (canon *Licet,* DE TRANSLATIONE): *He is the successor of Peter and* *the vicar of Jesus Christ.*

FIFTH TRUTH

Every Roman pontiff possesses all the ruling power and pastoral authority that St. Peter received from the Lord to rule the Church Universal.

For unless the same authority to rule resides in the Roman pontiff as resided in St. Peter, how can he truly be said to be the successor of St. Peter? A successor is as his predecessor; he commands equal authority, as INNOCENT III declares in DE ELECTIONE in the canon which begins *Innotuit.* How could Christ have provided sufficiently for his Church if he had not perpetuated in the Church the authority granted to Peter to rule it? The Church Universal was not committed to Peter for his own advantage; nor is a particular church committed to any prelate for his own advantage, as the Apostle says in the last chapter of II CORINTHI-ANS: *The Lord gave me authority for building up*—there is no doubt that Paul refers to the Church—*and not for pulling down.* Again Paul writes in EPHESIANS 4: *He ordained some to be apostles, some pastors and teachers,* *giving them power for the perfecting of the saints in the work of his service in* *the building up of the body of Christ.* This is the Church, as stated previously. Indeed the Church always requires the ruling power granted to St. Peter. Therefore she will never be destitute, rather her spouse will not permit her to be wanting in those matters necessary to salvation. If the Roman pontiff who is the successor of St. Peter does not have this power, without a doubt none other possesses it.

DEFENSORIUM OBEDIENTIAE APOSTOLICAE

Huic denique veritati praeclarum testimonium perhibet egregius doctor ecclesiae beatus BERNARDUS, lib. ii, DE CONSIDERATIONE ad Eugenium papam ita scribens:[1] *Tu quis es? Sacerdos magnus, pontifex summus, tu princeps episcoporum, tu haeres apostolorum, tu primatu*
5 *Abel, gubernatu Noe, patriarchatu Abraam, ordine Melchisedech, dignitate Aaron, auctoritate Moyses, judicatu Samuel, potestate Petrus, unctione Christus. Tu es, cui claves traditae, cui oves creditae sunt. Sunt quidem et alii caeli janitores et gregum pastores, sed tu "tanto gloriosius quanto et differentius, utrumque prae ceteris nomen haereditasti."*[2] *Habent illi*
10 *assignatos sibi greges singulos, tibi universi crediti uni sumus. Nec modo ovium, sed et pastorum tu unus omnium pastor. Unde id probem quaeris? Et*[a] *verbo*[a] *Domini: Cui enim, non dico episcoporum sed etiam apostolorum, sic absolute et indiscrete totae commissae sunt oves? "Si me amas, Petre, pasce oves meas."*[3] *Quas? Illius vel illius civitatis populos, aut*[b]
15 *regionis, aut certae regni? "Oves meas," inquit. Cui*[c] *non planum, non designasse aliquas, est assignasse omnes? Nihil excipitur, ubi distinguitur nihil. Et forte praesentes ceteri condiscipuli erant, cum committens uni omnes, unitatem commendaret in uno grege et*[d] *uno pastore secundum illud:*[4] *"Una est columba mea, formosa mea, perfecta mea."*
20 Et paulo post:[5] *Ergo juxta canones tuos alii in partem sollicitudinis, tu in plenitudinem potestatis vocatus es. Aliorum potestas certis artatur limitibus, tua extenditur et in ipsos, qui potestatem super alios acceperunt. Nonne si causa extiterit, tu episcopo caelum claudere, tu ipsum ab episcopatu deponere, etiam et tradere Satanae potes? Stat ergo*[e] *inconcussum*[f] *tuum*
25 *privilegium tibi, tam in datis clavibus, quam in ovibus commendatis.* Et post pauca:[6] *Ita cum quisque ceterorum habeat suam, tibi una commissa est*

[a-a] ex verbis *V*   [b] non *M V*   [c] Cum *M V*   [d] add. in *M V*   [e] enim *M V*
[f] concussum *T H*

---

[1] L. II, c. 8 (*PL* 182, 751C–752A)
[2] *Hebr.* 1, 4.
[3] *Joan.* 21, 15.**
[4] *Cant.* 6, 8.*
[5] *De consideratione*, L. II, c. 8 (*PL* 182, 752B)
[6] *Ibid.*

92

A DEFENSE OF APOSTOLIC OBEDIENCE

Finally, the eminent Doctor of the Church, ST. BERNARD, bore a remarkable witness to this truth when he wrote to Pope Eugenius (DE CONSIDERATIONE, Book II): *Who are you? You are the high priest and the supreme pontiff. You are the prince of bishops and the heir of the apostles. By your primacy, you are Abel; by your office as helmsman, Noah; by your patriarchate, Abraham; by your orders, Melchizedech; by your dignity, Aaron; by your authority, Moses; by your judicial power, Samuel; by your jurisdiction, Peter; and by your anointment, Christ. You are the one to whom the keys have been given and the sheep entrusted. There are indeed other gatekeepers of heaven, and there are other shepherds of the flock; but you are in both respects more glorious and exceptional than they "in as much as you have inherited a title superior to theirs." They have assigned to them particular portions of the flock, but you have been given charge of all the sheep. You are the one shepherd not only of the sheep but of all the shepherds. Do you wish to know how I prove this? I prove it from the words of the Lord. To which apostle—I do not speak of bishops, but apostles— were all the sheep committed so absolutely and so indiscriminately? "If you love me, Peter, feed my sheep." To what sheep did Christ refer? Was it to the people of this or that city, of this or that region or kingdom? "My sheep," the Lord said. Who does not see clearly that Christ instead of designating some sheep of the flock rather assigned the whole flock? There can be no exception where there is no distinction. And probably the other disciples were present when the Lord committed all the sheep to the care of one alone, and thus commended unity to all in one flock and one shepherd, according to the text: "There is but one who is my dove, my beautiful one, my perfect one."*

BERNARD shortly continues: *Therefore, according to your own canons, while the other bishops are called to a share in the burdens of government, you are invested with the plenitude of power. Their authority is confined within certain limits, but yours extends itself even to them that have received power over others. Do you not have the power, if the need arises, to close heaven even to a bishop, to deprive him of his see, even to consign him to Satan? Your prerogative therefore is firmly established, both because the keys have been entrusted to you and because the sheep have been committed to your care.*

grandissima navis facta ex omnibus, ipsa universalis ecclesia, toto orbe diffusa. Haec BERNARDUS, in quibus plane omnia attribuit papae Eugenio, quae ad regendum ecclesiam concesserat Dominus Petro.

Propter hanc autem potestatem romano pontifici in beato Petro
5 collatam, qua dicitur pastor, rector, universalis ecclesiae caput, ac pater patrum, ecclesia[a] romana[a] similiter mater[b] et caput omnium ecclesiarum esse, ac tenere in omnibus principatum sancti patres contestantur; et hoc non humana, sed Christi salvatoris nostri ordinatione, pro eo, quod beatus Petrus a Christo immediate hanc potestatem pro se et suis
10 successoribus accepit, pro quibus jubente Domino in romana urbe sedem constituit et elegit.

De quo beatus ANACLETUS papa ita dicit xxii dist. *Sacrosancta:*[1] *Sacrosancta romana ecclesia non ab apostolis, sed ab ipso Domino, salvatore nostro, primatum obtinuit, sicut beato Petro apostolo dixit*[2] *"Tu es petrus et*
15 *super hanc petram"* et cetera. Et sequitur:[3] *Inter beatos apostolos quaedam potestatis discretio fuit, et post, licet omnes[c] essent apostoli[c], Petro tamen concessum est a Domino. Et ipsi inter se idipsum voluerunt, ut reliquis omnibus praeesset apostolis, et Cephas, id est, caput et principium teneret apostolatus. Qui eandem formam suis successoribus et reliquis episcopis*
20 *tenendam tradiderunt.* Et post pauca:[4] *Haec vero apostolica sedes, caput et cardo a Domino, ut praefatum est, et non ab alio, constituta est. Et sicut cardine ostium regitur, sic; hujus apostolicae sedis auctoritate omnes ecclesiae Domino disponente reguntur.*

Hanc quoque veritatem omni firmitate oportet suscipere[d], qui crimen
25 haeresis maluerit evitare. Sicut[e] NICOLAUS papa Mediolanensibus

---

a–a ecclesiam romanam *T H*   b matrem *T H*   c–c essent apostoli omnes *M*
d suscipe *V*   e Sic *V*

[1] c. 2, D. XXII (RF I, 73–74).
[2] *Matth.* 16, 18.
[3] c. 2, D. XXII (RF I, 74).
[4] *Ibid.*

A DEFENSE OF APOSTOLIC OBEDIENCE

BERNARD goes on: *Thus although each of the other bishops has his own ship, the largest ship of all is entrusted to you. Your ship is the Church Universal, made up of all the particular churches and extending throughout the world.* Thus Bernard clearly attributes to Pope Eugenius all the authority which the Lord granted to St. Peter to rule the Church.

Moreover, because the authority is conferred through St. Peter to the Roman pontiff, upon which grounds he is termed pastor, ruler, head of the Church Universal, and father of fathers, the holy Fathers bear witness that the Roman church likewise is mother and head of all churches and exercises primacy over all other churches. This is not founded in human sanction, but in that of Christ, our Savior; in view of the fact that St. Peter received this authority directly from Christ for himself and for his successors,[1] he chose and established his see in the city of Rome in accord with the Lord's command.

On this matter POPE ANACLETUS declares (distinction xxii, *Sacrosancta*): *The most holy Roman Church obtained its primacy not from the apostles, but from the Lord, our Savior, when he said to the apostle Peter: "You are Peter and upon this rock* and so forth. He continues: *There was a certain inequality in authority among the holy apostles—though all were apostles. Nevertheless, the apostles concurred in the Lord's grant to Peter to rank above them all and to hold primacy among them—indeed, Cephas signifies "head"; they have handed down to their successors and the other bishops that this be strictly observed.* The canon adds shortly: *The Apostolic See, the head and hinge of all the churches, was constituted by the Lord, and not by another, as has been said before. As the door is guided by the hinge, so are all churches, the Lord providing, guided by the authority of the Apostolic See.*

All who wish to avoid the crime of heresy must defend this truth with the utmost vigor. To this, POPE NICHOLAS, writing to the people of

---

[1] The traditional canonist defense of the "plenitudo potestatis" of the Pope argued that Peter alone received this ordination immediately from Christ; the conciliarist position insisted that all the apostles shared immediately in this ordination.

95

scribens, testatur xxii dist. *Omnes:*[1] *Omnes, inquit, sive patriarchae, sive metropoleon, in cujuslibet apicem primatus aut episcoporum cathedras, vel ecclesiarum cujuslibet ordinis dignitatem, instituit romana ecclesia. Illam vero solus ipse fundavit et supra petram fidei mox nascentis ecclesiae erexit,*
5 *qui beato Petro, vitae aeternae clavigero, terreni simul et caelestis imperii jura commisit. Non ergo quaelibet*[a] *terrena sententia, sed*[b] *illud verbum, quo constructum est caelum et terra, per quod denique omnia condita sunt elementa, romanam fundavit ecclesiam, illius certe privilegio fungitur, illius auctoritate fulcitur. Unde non dubium est, quia quisquis cuilibet*[c] *ecclesiae*
10 *jus suum detrahit, injustitiam facit. Qui autem romanae ecclesiae privilegium ab ipso omnium summo ecclesiarum capite traditum auferre conatur, hic proculdubio in haeresim labitur. Et cum ille vocetur injustus, hic est dicendus haereticus. Fidem quippe violat qui adversus illam agit, quae est mater fidei; et illi contumax invenitur, qui eam cunctis ecclesiis praetulisse*
15 *cognoscitur. Et infra. Unde tanctus Ambrosius se in omnibus magistram*[d] *sanctam romanam ecclesiam profitetur.*

SEXTA VERITAS

Reverentiam, honorem, et obedientiam tenentur universi fideles diffinitionibus et praeceptis summi pontificis pro tempore ecclesiam Dei regentis, quam debent beati Petri sanctionibus ore proprio publicatis.
20   Siquidem simili, immo verius eidem auctoritati, dissimilis obedientia non debetur. Hinc AGATHON papa dicit xix dist., *Sic omnes:*[2] *Sic omnes apostolicae sedis sanctiones accipiendae sunt tamquam ipsius divina voce Petri firmatae.* Beatus quoque BERNARDUS, attendens, quod secundum apostolicum dictum[3] *omnis potestas a Deo est,* etiam de inferiorum

---

[a] quilibet *T H*   [b] secundum *T H*   [c] cujuslibet *M V*   [d] in gratiam *V*

[1] c. 1, D. XXII (RF I, 73).
[2] c. 2, D. XIX (RF I, 60).
[3] *Rom.* 13, 1.*

A DEFENSE OF APOSTOLIC OBEDIENCE

Milan, bears witness (distinction xxii, *Omnes*): *The Roman Church in-stituted the dignity of every ecclesiastical order, whether the superior rank of patriarchs, the primacy of metropolitans, or the jurisdictions of bishops. He alone who granted to St. Peter the possession of the keys of eternal life and dominion over the earthly and heavenly realms founded the Roman church and erected it upon the rock of the faith of the Church that straightway arose. Therefore no earthly oracle, but the Word which made heaven and earth and established all the elements founded the Roman church. In truth, it is ad-ministered upon the basis of this prerogative and is supported by its authority. Henceforth, there should be no doubt that anyone who disparages its claim over every church does so most unjustly, but he who attempts to remove force-fully the prerogative bestowed upon the Roman church by the supreme head of all the churches without doubt falls into heresy. The one* [who disparages its claim] *must be termed unjust but he* [who assails it] *heretical. Indeed, he assails the faith who attacks that church which is the mother of the faith; and he shows contempt for that church which is recognized as placed over all churches. Hence, St. Ambrose avows that in all matters he follows as his in-structor the holy Roman Church.*

SIXTH TRUTH

All the faithful owe as much reverence, honor, and obedience to the definitions and precepts of the supreme pontiff ruling the Church of God in their time as they owe to decrees declared by the mouth of St. Peter himself.

Equal authority certainly does not command unequal obedience. Pope AGATHON writes (distinction xix, *Sic omnes*): *Thus all the rulings of the Apostolic See must be accepted as if they were asserted by the holy voice of Peter himself.* And ST. BERNARD, heeding the apostolic text, *all authority is from God,* writes concerning the precepts of lower prelates

97

DEFENSORIUM OBEDIENTIAE APOSTOLICAE

praelatorum praeceptis in libro DE DISPENSATIONE ET PRAECEP-
TO ait:[1] *Sive Deus, sive homo vicarius Dei mandatum quodcumque tradiderit, pari profecto prosequendum est cura, pari reverentia deferendum.* Et
infra:[2] *Quicquid vice Dei praecipit homo, quod tamen*[a] *non*[a] *sit certum*
5 *displicere Deo, haud secus omnino accipiendum est, quam si praecipiat
Deus. Quid enim interest, utrum per se vel suos ministros, homines vel
angelos, hominibus innotescat suum beneplacitum Deus?*
Verum ut luculentius clareat, quanta obedientiae reverentia sedi
apostolicae subdi oportet, quamque sit detestabile—licet dura sint,
10 quae praecipit—illi temere obniti, patrum sententiis paulo plus censeo
demonstrandum. De hoc itaque ait beatus martyr CYPRIANUS, xciii
dist., *Qui cathedram:*[3] *Qui cathedram Petri, super*[b] *quam fundata est
ecclesia, deserit, in ecclesia se esse non confidat.* Beatus quoque AM-
BROSIUS hunc solum reputat catholicum, qui cum romana convenit
15 ecclesia; xxiiii, quaest. i, *Advocavit.*[4] Cum illa vero[c] convenire, quid aliud
est quam fide et obedientia illi subesse? Beatus HIERONYMUS similiter,
xxiiii, quaest. i, *Quoniam vetus,* ad apostolicum de eremo adjacenti Syrie
scribens ait:[5] *Mihi cathedram Petri et fidem apostolico ore laudatam censui
consulendam*[d]*, inde nunc*[e] *animae meae*[e] *postulans cibum, unde olim*
20 *Christi vestimenta suscepi.* Sequitur:[6] *Profligato a sobole mala patrimonio*[f]*,
apud vos solos incorrupta patrum servatur auctoritas. Ibi caespite terra
fecundo seminis puritatem, centeno fructu refert.* Et sequitur:[7] *Cum
successore*[g] *piscatoris*[h] *et discipulo christi loquor. Ego nullum praemium
nisi Christum sequens, beatitudini tuae, id est, cathedrae Petri communione*

---

a–a non tamen *T*   b per *V*   c verbo *M T H*   d consulendum *T H*
e–e unicam meae animae *M V*   f patrimonia *M*   g successori *M*   h piscatorum *M V*

[1] c. 9 (*PL* 182, 871).
[2] c. 9 (*PL* 182, 873).
[3] c. 3, D. XCIII (RF I, 321).
[4] c. 23, C. XXIV, qu. 1 (RF I, 974).
[5] c. 25, C. XXIV, qu. 1 (RF I, 975).
[6] *Ibid.*
[7] c. 25, C. XXIV, qu. 1 (RF I, 976).

A DEFENSE OF APOSTOLIC OBEDIENCE

in his book, DE DISPENSATIONI ET PRAECEPTO: *Whether God himself or a man who is God's vicar promulgates a law, it must certainly be executed with equal care and received with equal respect.* BERNARD adds somewhat later: *Whatever God's vicar decrees that is not clearly displeasing to God must be accepted as though it were God's order. In effect, does it matter whether God makes known his good pleasure to man through himself or through his servants, whether angels or men?*

But so that it may be made even clearer with what reverent obedience one must subject oneself to the Apostolic See, and how detestable it may be to oppose it rashly—although what it enjoins may be harsh—I think it should be clarified somewhat more with citations from the Fathers. ST. CYPRIAN declares on this subject (distinction xciii, *Qui cathedram*): *He who abandons the see of Peter upon which the Church was founded should not believe that he is in the Church.* And ST. AMBROSE (Cause xxiv, question 1, *Advocavit*) regards him only as Catholic who is in agreement with the Roman church. What can it mean to be in agreement with the Roman church but to submit to its obedience and teaching? ST. JEROME speaks likewise writing to the Pope from the desert which borders Syria (Cause xxiv, question 1, *Quoniam vetus*): *I think it my duty to consult the chair of Peter, and to turn to a church whose faith has been praised by Paul. I appeal for food for my soul to the church, whence once I received the garb of Christ.* He continues: *Wicked children have squandered their inheritance; you alone preserve the authority of the Fathers intact. There* [in Rome] *the fertile soil, when it receives the pure seed, yields fruit an hundredfold.* Again he goes on: *I speak to the successor of the fisherman, to the disciple of Christ. As I seek no reward but Christ, so I join in supporting your blessedness, that is, the chair of Peter. I know that the Church*

consortior, super illam petram fundatam ecclesiam[a] *scio*[a]. *Quicumque extra hanc domum agnum comederit, profanus est. Si quis in Noe arca non fuerit, peribit, regnante diluvio. Et quia pro facinoribus meis ad eam solitudinem commigravi, quae Syriam*[b] *juncto barbariae fine determinat, non*
5 *possum sanctum Domini*[c] *a tua sanctimonia tot interjacentibus spaciis semper expetere. Ideoque collegas tuos, Egyptios confessores, sequor, et sub onerariis parva navicula delitesco. Non novi Vitalem, Miletum respuo, ignoro Paulinum. Quicumque tecum non colligit, spargit, hoc est, qui non est Christi, antichristi est.* Ex quibus verbis expresse innuit beatus
10 HIERONYMUS, quod schismatici romanae, scilicet, ecclesiae inobedientes, quales fuere quos nominavit, profani sunt et a statu salutis penitus alieni. Sunt autem schismatici secundum beatum THOMAM ii, ii, quaest. xxxix,[1] *qui subesse renuunt summo pontifici, qui membris ecclesiae ei subjectis communicare recusant*[d].

15 AUGUSTINUS etiam, in ii libro DE DOCTRINA CHRISTIANA, decretales papae epistolas inter canonicas scripturas numerandas esse testatur, dist. xix in canoni dicens:[2] *In canonicis scripturis ecclesiarum catholicarum*[e] *quamplurimum divinarum scripturarum sollertissimus indagator auctoritatem sequatur. Inter quas sane et illae sunt, quas et aposto-*
20 *lica sedes habere, et ab ea*[f] *meruerunt accipere*[g] *epistolas.* Canonicis[h] scripturis certa debetur fides et obedientia, alioquin canonicae non essent. Ideo epistolis papalibus, diffinitivis et praeceptivis[i], fidem praestare et obedientiam est necesse. Cui consonat constitutio NICOLAI papae, dist. xix, *Si romanorum* qua dicitur:[3] *Si romanorum pontificum*
25 *decreto cunctorum opuscula tractatorum approbantur vel reprobantur; ita ut, quod vere sedes*[j] *apostolica approbavit, hodie teneatur acceptum, et quod illa repulit, hactenus inefficax habeatur. Quanto ergo potius, quae ipsa pro*

---

a–a scio ecclesiam *M V*   b Syriae *V*   c Dominum *V*   d praesumunt *M V*   e *om. M V*
f *add.* alii *T H*   g *om. M V*   h *add.* enim *T H*   i praeceptis *V*   j fides *M V*

1 *Summa theol.*, P. II, II, qu. 39, a. 1 (Moos 1629a; Parma III, 154).
2 c. 6, D. XIX (RF I, 61–62); c. 8 (*PL* 34, 40).
3 c. 1, D. XIX (RF I, 58–59).

A DEFENSE OF APOSTOLIC OBEDIENCE

is built upon this rock. Whoever will eat the lamb outside this house is an outcast. Anyone who is not in Noah's ark will perish when the flood comes. But since, driven by my sins, I have traveled to this desolate place which lies between Syria and the uncivilized regions, I cannot, because of the great distance which separates us, always ask of your holiness the holy thing of the Lord. Consequently, I follow the Egyptian confessors who share your faith and conceal my frail craft under the shadow of such great ships. I know nothing of Vitalis;[1] I reject Meletius;[2] I do not know Paulinus.[3] He that does not gather with you scatters; that is, he that is not of Christ is of the Antichrist. In these words, St. Jerome expressly declares that schismatics, namely, those disobedient to the Roman church (as were those whom he named), are outcasts and are utterly removed from the state of salvation. *Those are schismatics,* according to ST. THOMAS (II, II, question 39), *who refuse to obey the supreme pontiff and who disdain to have communion with those members who are subject to him.*

AUGUSTINE also affirms in DE DOCTRINA CHRISTIANA, Book II, that papal letters and decretals must be reckoned as canonical Scripture (distinction xix in canon law): *In regard to canonical Scriptures, the assiduous investigator of Holy Writ must follow the authority of the greater number of Catholic churches; and among these, of course, he must follow the authority of those worthy to be the see of an apostle or to receive epistles.* For firm faith and obedience are owed to canonical writings; otherwise they are not canonical. Therefore it is necessary to lend faith and obedience to letters of the Pope which define and instruct. The constitution of POPE NICHOLAS (distinction xix, *Si romanorum*) is in agreement: *If literary works upon any subject have been approved or condemned by the decree of the Roman pontiffs, so that what the Apostolic See officially approved is still today considered accepted, and what it rejected is still regarded null and void, how much more, therefore, should those*

---

[1] Schismatic Arian Bishop of Antioch, appointed in 371 (?) by the community established by Appollinarius of Laodicea.
[2] Arian Bishop of Antioch, 360 (d. 381).
[3] Schismatic Arian Bishop of Antioch, appointed in 362.

catholica fide, pro sanis dogmatibus, pro variis et multifariis ecclesiae
necessitatibus, et fidelium moribus diverso tempore praescripsit, omni
debent[a] *honore praeferri, et ab omnibus prorsus, in quibuslibet*[b] *opportuni-*
tatibus, dispensatione vel discretione, magistra reverenter assumi[c].

5   Rursus de obedientia, quae apostolicae sedi debetur, pulchre loquitur
beatus[d] GREGORIUS, divino miraculo ad papatum electus, ita dicens
xii dist., *Praeceptis:*[1] *Praeceptis apostolicis non dura superbia resistatur,*
sed per obedientiam, quae a sancta romana ecclesia[e] *et apostolica auctoritate*
jussa sunt, salutifere impleantur, si ejusdem sanctae Dei ecclesiae, quae est
10 *caput vestrum, communionem habere desideratis. Non novum aliquod*
praesenti jussione praecipimus, sed illa, quae olim videntur indulta,
firmamus, cum nulli dubium sit, quod non solum pontificalis accusatio,
sed omnis sanctae religionis relatio ad sedem apostolicam, quasi ad caput
ecclesiarum debet referri, et inde normam sumere unde sumpsit exordium,
15 *ne caput institutionis videatur omitti. Cujus auctoritatis sanctionem omnes*
teneant sacerdotes, qui nolunt[f] *ab*[g] *apostolicae petrae, super quam Christus*
fundavit universalem ecclesiam, soliditate divelli.

    Et iterum idem ait, xix dist. *Nulli:*[2] *Nulli fas est vel velle vel posse trans-*
gredi apostolicae sedis praecepta, nec nostrae dispositionis ministerium,
20 *quod vestrum sequi oportet caritatem. Sit ergo ruinae suae dolore prostra-*
tus[h], *quisquis apostolicis voluerit contraire praeceptis vel decretis, nec locum*
inter sacerdotes deinceps habeat, sed extorris a sancto fiat ministerio, non de
ejus judicio quisquam[i] *postea curam habeat, quoniam*[j] *jam damnatus a*
sancto[k] *synodo et ab*[k] *apostolica ecclesia, sua inobedientia atque praesump-*
25 *tione a quoquam esse non dubitatur, quia*[m] *majoris excommunicationis*
dejectione est abiciendus[n], *cui sanctae ecclesiae commissa fuerit disciplina,*
qui[o] *non solum praelatae*[p] *sanctae ecclesiae jussionibus parere debuit, sed*

---

[a] dicuntur *M V* [b] necessitatibus vel *T H* [c] *add.* et cetera *T H* [d] *om. V*
[e] *om. M V* [f] noluerint *T H* [g] a *V* [h] stratis *T H* [i] *om. M V* [j] quin *M V*
[k-k] sancta et *T H* [m] quare *M V* [n] eiciendus *V* [o] quia *T H* [p] praefatae *T H*

---

[1] c. 2, D. XII (RF I, 27).
[2] c. 5, D. XIX (RF I, 61).

A DEFENSE OF APOSTOLIC OBEDIENCE

things it enjoined at various times for the Catholic faith, for sound doctrine, for the various manifold needs of the Church, and for the conduct of the faithful be preferred with all honor, and its distinctions and dispositions received by all with the utmost reverence in every contingency.

Again ST. GREGORY, who was elected pope by divine intervention, writes eloquently concerning the obedience owed to the Apostolic See (distinction xii, *Praeceptis*): *Apostolic precepts must not be resisted with obstinate pride, but those things which are imposed by the holy Roman Church and apostolic authority must be fulfilled obediently in a salutary manner if you wish to remain in communion with that holy Church of God which is your head. We do not enjoin anything new in this ordinance, but we affirm what in time past was granted. There can be no doubt that not only every episcopal complaint, but everything related to the Church ought to be referred to the Apostolic See, as the head of the other churches. Thence it should take its rule where it took its beginning, lest the head of this foundation seem to be lacking. All priests should sustain the establishment of this authority who do not wish to be torn from the firm apostolic rock upon which Christ founded the Church Universal.*

And again GREGORY[1] writes (distinction xix, *Nulli*): *It is lawful for no man to intend to transgress or to transgress in deed the precepts of the Apostolic See or to obstruct the implementation of our decisions, to which your love compels you. Therefore may he who wishes to oppose apostolic precepts or decrees be overwhelmed by the sorrow of his own ruin. Let no one doubt that such a man should not be regarded henceforth as a priest, but as ousted from the sacred ministry. Let none hereafter grant any weight to his judgment; he is already condemned by the holy and apostolic church for his disobedience and presumption. He must be brought to his knees by the total excommunication[2] of the Pope to whom the discipline of the holy Church was assigned, for he has not only disobeyed the mandates of the aforesaid church,*

---

[1] Gregory IV (827–844).
[2] Total ban from all sacraments and association in Christian society.

---

etiam aliis, ne praeterirent insinuare. Sitque alienus a divinis et pontifi-
calibus officiis, qui noluerit praeceptis obtemperare apostolicis.

Aliud[a] item GREGORIUS papa, lxxxi dist., *Si qui sunt presbyteri:*[1]
Peccatum, inquit, *paganitatis incurrit quisquis, dum christianum se esse*[b]
5 *asserit, sedi apostolicae obedire contemnit.* Cui consonat illud ADRIANI
papae, xxv, quaest. i, *Generali:*[2] *Generali decreto*[c] *constituimus, ut*
execrandum anathema fiat, et velut praevaricator fidei catholicae semper apud
Deum reus existat, quicumque regum, seu episcoporum, vel potentum,
deinceps romanorum pontificum decretorum censuram in quoquam credi-
10 *derit vel permiserit violandam.*

Plane[d] ad idem loquitur beatus LEO dicens dist. xix, *Ita dominus:*[3]
Ita, inquit[e], *dominus Jesus Christus, humani generis salvator, instituit,*
ut veritas, quae antea legis et prophetarum praeconio continebatur, per
apostolicam tubam in salutem universitatis exiret, sicut scriptum est:[4] "*In*
15 *omnem terram exivit sonus eorum et in fines orbis terrae verba eorum.*" *Sed*
hujus muneris sacramentum ita Dominus ad omnium apostolorum officium
pertinere voluit, ut in beatissimo Petro, summo apostolorum omnium,
principaliter collocaret[f], *et ab ipso quasi a quodam capite dona sua velut in*
corpus omne diffunderet, ut exsortem ministerii se intelligeret esse divini,
20 *qui ausus fuisset a Petri soliditate recedere. Hunc enim in consortium in-*
dividuae unitatis assumptum, id, quod ipse erat, Dominus voluit nominari,
dicendo[5]: "*Tu es Petrus, et super hanc petram aedificabo ecclesiam meam,*"
ut[g] *aeterni templi aedificatio*[h] *mirabili munere gratiae Dei in soliditate*
Petri consisteret. Hanc etiam ecclesiam suam firmitate corroborans, ut
25 *illam nec humana temeritas posset appetere, nec portae inferi contra eam*
praevalere.

---

[a] Alius *V, om. T H*   [b] *om. M V*   [c] *add.* censemus et *T H*   [d] *om. V*   [e] *om. T H*
[f] collocavit *M V*   [g] et *M V*   [h] aedificio *M V*

[1] c. 15, D. LXXXI (RF I, 285).
[2] c. 11, C. XXV, qu. 1 (RF I, 1009–1010).
[3] c. 7, D. XIX (RF I, 62).
[4] *Psal.* 18, 5.
[5] *Matth.* 16, 18.

A DEFENSE OF APOSTOLIC OBEDIENCE

but he has urged others to disregard them. *Let him be removed from divine and episcopal office who does not wish to heed apostolic precepts.*

Pope GREGORY[1] writes elsewhere (distinction lxxxi, *Si qui sunt presbyteri*): *He betrays himself a heathen who, while he declares himself a Christian, disdains to obey the Apostolic See.* Pope HADRIAN agrees with him (Cause xxv, question 1, *Generali*): *We have settled by a general decree that any king, bishop, or ruler who henceforth supports or permits the violation of a censure decreed by the Roman pontiffs is cursed with anathema and stands indicted forever before God as an apostate against the Catholic faith.*

ST. LEO clearly says the same thing (distinction xix, *Ita dominus*): *Thus our Lord Jesus Christ, the Savior of mankind, instituted that the truth, which previously was confined to the proclamation of the law and the prophets, might go forth through the apostles' trumpet blast for the salvation of all men, as it is written: "Their voice goes out through all the earth and their words to the end of the world."* The Lord wished this sacramental office to be the concern of all the apostles, but he has placed the principal burden upon the most blessed Peter, chief of all the apostles. From Peter, as from the head, he wishes his gifts to flow into all the body. Therefore anyone who dares to withdraw from the solid rock of Peter may understand that he has no part in the divine ministry. The Lord wished Peter's true function to be expressed, namely, his assumption into this bond of profound unity, when he said: *"You are Peter, and on this rock I will build my church,"* so that the eternal temple might be built by the wonderful gift of God's grace upon the solid rock of Peter. He strengthened his Church to such a degree that neither human rashness could assail it nor the gates of Hell prevail against it.

---

[1] Gregory VII (1073–1085).

DEFENSORIUM OBEDIENTIAE APOSTOLICAE

Verumtamen hanc Petri istius sacratissimam firmitatem, Deo, ut diximus, aedificante, constructam, nimis impia vult praesumptione violare, quisquis ejus potestatem temptat infringere, favendo[a] *cupiditatibus suis, et id quod accepit a veteribus, non sequendo.*

5 Venerabilis quoque BEDA SUPER MATTHEUM ait:[1] *Quicumque ab unitate fidei vel societatis Petri apostoli se quolibet*[b] *modo*[b] *segregaverint, nec vinculis peccatorum absolvi, nec januam possunt ingredi regni caelestis.* Rursus NICOLAUS papa, universali synoda praesidens, statuit xxv, quaest. ii *Si quis:*[2] *Si quis dogmata, mandata, interdicta, sanctiones vel* 10 *decreta pro catholica fide vel ecclesiastica disciplina, pro correptione imminentium vel futurorum malorum, a sedis apostolicae praesule salubriter promulgata contempserit, anathema sit.*

Neque in his, quae placent, solum, sed in eis etiam[c], quae dura sunt, obtemperare oportet romanae sedi. Sicut ad Joannem Ravennati 15 episcopum scribens, beatus GREGORIUS tradidit[d], c dist., *Contra morem:*[3] *Contra morem,* inquit, *ecclesiasticum est, si non patientissime toleratur, quod a nobis absit*[e]*, etiam*[e] *injusta correctio.* Cui concordat illud ex capitulis CAROLI imperatoris, xix dist., *In memoriam:*[4] *Licet vix ferendum ab illa*[f] *sancta sede imponatur jugum, tamen feramus et pia* 20 *devotione toleremus.*

Longum nimis pariter et taediosum foret omnes sanctorum patrum constitutiones, veritatem istam approbantes, adducere. Manifestum satis est et nemo dubitat, nisi desipiat, quam detestabile sit tot canonum decreta, ab universali ecclesia accepta ac corpori juris inserta, per 25 inobedientiam violare; quisquis talis est, rebellis plane convincitur et blasphemus, teste DAMASO papa, qui ait xxv, quaest. i *Violatores:*[5]

---

[a] favere *M V* [b–b] quomodolibet *T H* [c] om. *M V* [d] tradit *T H*
[e–e] etiam absit *M*, etiam quod absit *V* [f] ipsa *M V*

[1] c. 27, C. XXIV, qu. 1 (RF I, 977).
[2] c. 18, C. XXV, qu. 2 (RF I, 1016).
[3] c. 8, D. C (RF I, 354).
[4] c. 3, D. XIX (RF I, 60–61).
[5] c. 5, C. XXV, qu. 1 (RF I, 1008).

A DEFENSE OF APOSTOLIC OBEDIENCE

But a man seeks in wicked arrogance to attack the most holy authority of the rock, erected, as we have said, by God, when he attempts to infringe its power by fostering his own desires and not following ancient tradition.

The VENERABLE BEDE says the same in his *Commentary upon Matthew: Any who will separate themselves in any manner whatsoever from the unity of the faith of the fellowship of the apostle Peter cannot be released from the bonds of their sins or enter the gate of the celestial kingdom.* Again Pope NICHOLAS, presiding over a universal council,[1] declared (Cause xxv, question 2, *Si quis*): *If any will disdain the teachings, mandates, sanctions, or decrees promulgated by the occupant of the Apostolic See for the Catholic faith, for church discipline, and for the correction of immediate or future ills, let him be anathema.*

It is necessary to obey the Roman see not only in those matters which are pleasant to fulfill, but also in those which are difficult. Thus ST. GREGORY proposed in writing to John, the Bishop of Ravenna (distinction c, *Contra morem*): *It is contrary to church morals not to bear most patiently what displeases us, namely, unjust correction.* In his capitulary CHARLEMAGNE concurs (distinction xix, *In memoriam*): *Granted that the yoke imposed by that see may scarcely be borne, nevertheless let us bear it and let us tolerate it with devout devotion.*

It would be far too long and too tedious to adduce all the definitions of the holy Fathers which support this truth. It is plain enough (and none may doubt it unless he is void of all understanding) how abominable it is to transgress defiantly so many canons accepted by the Church Universal and introduced into the body of law. Such a transgressor is a rebel and, no matter who he may be, he is incontestably exposed as a blasphemer, as Pope DAMASUS attests (Cause xxv, question 1, *Violatores*): *Intentional*

---

[1] Biel is in error; Nicholas I (858–867) did not preside over a general council, but a local Italian synod.

DEFENSORIUM OBEDIENTIAE APOSTOLICAE

Violatores canonum voluntariae graviter a sanctis patribus judicantur, et a
Sancto Spiritu, instinctu cujus ac dono dictati sunt damnantur, quoniam
blasphemare Spiritum Sanctum non incongrue videntur, qui[a] *contra*
eosdem sacros canones, non necessitate compulsi sed libenter, ut praemissum
5 *est, aliquid aut proterve agunt, aut loqui praesumunt, aut facere volenti-*
bus sponte consentiunt. Talis enim praesumptio manifeste unum genus est
blasphemantium Spiritum Sanctum, quoniam ut, jam praelibatum est,
contra eum agit, cujus nisu et gratia canones editi sunt. Nec mirum, quod
talia in novo testamento, cujus non immerito perfectior debet[b] esse[b]
10 obedientia, sicut et gratia, statuit Dominus, qui in veteri lege, DEUT.
xvii,[1] sub ultimi supplicii poenis, summi sacerdotis judicio obedire
praecepit. Dathan quoque et Abyron, contemptores Moysi, quem populi
sui ducem constituit, poena prius invisa et horribili condemnavit, NUM.
xvi.[2]

15   Verumtamen non in omni casu mandatum a sede apostolica primo
emissum, statim ad sui executionem obligare intelligitur. Fert enim
patienter in certis casibus sedes apostolica, si secunda jussio expectatur,
dum tamen causam rationabilem, cur hujusmodi mandatum adimpleri
non convenit,—puta, si id praecipitur, quod sedi apostolicae prava
20 insinuatione suggestum est, aut quod sine scandalo non quidem accepto,
sed dato impleri non valet, aut aliud hujusmodi—is, cui mittitur, apostolicae sedi per litteras suas intimare curaverit. De quo in cap. *Si quando,*
DE RESCRIPTIS,[3] et cap. *Cum teneamur,* DE PRAEBENDIS.[4] In quibus
casibus non censetur parvipendere apostolicae sedis auctoritatem, nec
25 mente[c] papae mandatis[d] per inobedientiam obsistere, qui secundum
juris formam mandati executionem differt, secundam expectans jus-
sionem. Si tamen purum habeat intentionis oculum, ut non in fraudem

---

[a] quo *V*   [b–b] esse debet *T H*   [c] menti *M V*   [d] mandantis *M V*

[1] Cf. *Deut.* 17, 12.
[2] Cf. *Num.* 16, 31–35.
[3] c. 5, X (1,3) (RF II, 18).
[4] c. 6, X (3,5) (RF II, 465–466).

A DEFENSE OF APOSTOLIC OBEDIENCE

transgressors of the canons are harshly judged by the holy Fathers and are condemned by the Holy Spirit by whose inspiration and gift the canons were dictated.[1] *Quite consistently are those men said to rebel shamelessly who willfully, and not driven by necessity, as said previously, presume to speak against the sacred canons and freely lend approval to those who wish to do likewise; for they blaspheme against the Holy Spirit, since, as has just been declared, the transgressor acts against the Spirit by whose exertion and grace the canons were promulgated.* No wonder the Lord, who in the old law (DEUTERONOMY 17) ordered obedience to the judgments of the high priest[2] under the pain of death, commanded such in the new covenant, in which obedience as well as grace ought not unjustly to be more perfect. He also condemned Dathan and Abyron, who did not respect the authority of Moses, whom God had appointed leader of his people, to an unprecedented, horrible sentence (NUMBERS 16).

However, a mandate issued by the Apostolic See need not in every case bind the recipient immediately. The Apostolic See, in certain instances, endures patiently if the recipient awaits a second order, provided nevertheless, that reasonable cause does exist why the first mandate may not be fulfilled—for example, if what is ordered has been suggested to the Apostolic See by wicked counsel;[3] if what is ordered has given cause for scandal in acceptance, and furthermore cannot be fulfilled; and other causes of this nature. In cases such as these, the Apostolic See will forbear if the recipient will take the trouble to make these objections known by letter to the Apostolic See. This is discussed in the chapter *Si quando*, DE RESCRIPTIS and in the chapter *Cum teneamur*, DE PRAEBENDIS. In these cases, it is not suggested that papal authority is diminished, nor that the intent of the pope who enjoins is resisted by one who postpones execution of a mandate in accord with legal form, awaiting a second order. But if his intentions are pure, so that he does not seek delay to the detriment of

---

[1] The concept of the literal inspiration of Holy Scripture is here extended to canon law as well.

[2] The Vulgate text reads "priest," not "high priest."

[3] Biel here refers to an appeal "to a pope better informed."

obedientiae dilationem quaerat, sed ut apostolicae sedis certius mentem discat, paratus animo semper ea intellecta, sine dolo, qualibet[a] postposita obedire.

SEPTIMA VERITAS

Ab obedientia summi pontificis nullius inferioris praeceptum aliquem
5 poterit absolvere aut quomodolibet excusare.

Patet haec veritas, quoniam, sicut ACT. v dicitur,[1] *Deo magis obedire oportet quam hominibus*, eo quod *ab ipso est omnis potestas*, secundum Pauli AD ROM. xiii[2] sententiam. Ita et summo pontifici, Dei in terris vicario, a quo tamquam a capite omnis ecclesiastica fluit potestas in
10 reliquos[b] ecclesiae ministros, ut ex supra allegatis manifestum est, plus ceteris est parendum. De quo beatus BERNARDUS in libro DE DIS-PENSATIONE ET PRAECEPTO ait:[3] *Cujus inter praeceptores reverentior in nobis imminet auctoritas[c], ejus gravior formidetur offensio. Melius siquidem est obedire Deo quam hominibus, et in ipsis melius magistris quam*
15 *condiscipulis. Quibus autem melius constat obedire, ipsis procul dubio et non obedire detestabilius est.* Unde numquam praecepto inferioris contra mandatum summi pontificis obtemperandum est. Sed si quis aliquid mandato apostolico contrarium, praeceperit, contempto inferiorum[d] mandato, praecepto summi pontificis obedire oportet, quoniam in
20 potestatibus ordinatis, potestas inferior non obligat contra superiorem. AUGUSTINO teste, qui libro ii suarum CONFESSIONUM ait:[4] *In potestatibus societatis humanae major potestas minori ad obediendum praeponitur;* dist. viii. *Quae contra.*[5] Quod etiam clare GLOSSA[6] super illud AD ROM. capitulo xiii[7] *Qui potestati resistit, ipse sibi damnationem*

---

[a] *add.* dilatione *T H*   [b] reliquas *V*   [c] *om. M V*   [d] inferioris *T H*

---

[1] *Act.* 5, 29.
[2] Cf. *Rom.* 13, 1.
[3] c. 7 (*PL* 182, 869B).
[4] L. III, c. 8 (*CSEL* 33, 57; *PL* 32, 690).
[5] c. 2, D. VIII (RF I, 14).
[6] *Biblie iampridem renovate* . . . , VI, f. 28[r].
[7] *Rom.* 13, 2.*

obedience but so that he may ascertain more clearly the intent of the Apostolic See, he is always prepared to obey that intent without deceit and without delay.

SEVENTH TRUTH

The precept of an inferior cannot absolve or excuse in any way disobedience to the Supreme Pontiff.

This truth is evident since, as it is written in ACTS 5, *One must obey God rather than men,* since *all authority is from God,* according to Paul's statement in ROMANS 13. To the extent that all authority in the Church flows from the Supreme Pontiff, God's vicar on earth, as from the head, as we have asserted previously, it is evident that he must be obeyed more than others. ST. BERNARD writes upon this matter in his book, DE DISPENSATIONE ET PRAECEPTO: *That authority commands more respect with us whose infraction threatens the graver consequences. It is certainly better to obey God than men; it is better to obey our teachers than our fellow students. Moreover, it is clearly better to obey those whom, without a doubt, it is execrable to disobey.* Thus the precept of an inferior which is opposed to a command of the Supreme Pontiff must never be obeyed. Therefore one must obey the precept of the Supreme Pontiff rather than the scornful order of an inferior if anyone orders something contrary to the apostolic mandate, because in a hierarchy of authorities the inferior authority is not binding when contrary to the superior. AUGUSTINE can be cited, who writes in the second book of his CONFESSIONS (distinction viii, *Quae contra*): *Among the authorities of human society, the greater authority is obeyed before the lesser.* The gloss upon the passage (ROMANS 13), *He who resists authority acquires only punishment for*

111

acquirit, innuit, et est beati AUGUSTINI in libro DE NATURA BONI, xi, quaest. lii, *Qui resistit:*[1] *Si illud,* inquit, *jubeat potestas, quod non debes facere, hic sane contemne potestatem timendo potestatem majorem*[a]*, ipsos humanarum legum gradus adverte. Si quid*[b] *jubeat curator numquam*[c]
5 *faciendum est, si contra praesulem*[d] *jubeat? Rursus si ipse proconsul*[e] *aliquid jubeat, et aliud*[f] *jubeat imperator, numquam*[g] *dubitatur illo contempto, illi serviendum esse? Nec contemnis*[h] *potestatem, sed eligis majori servire. Nec hinc debet minor irasci, si major praelatus est.*

Ex quibus manifestum est, quod jussionibus et sententiis summi
10 pontificis, non obstante cujuscumque alterius hominis contrario mandato, sine cunctatione obediendum est. Quod etiam sacri canones aperte statuerunt. Unde NICOLAUS papa ait, ix, quaest. iii. *Patet:*[2] *Patet profecto sedis apostolicae cujus auctoritate majus non est, judicium a nemine fore retractandum. Neque cuiquam de ejus liceat judicare judicio.*
15 Et GELASIUS papa, ix, quaest. iii, *Ipsi sunt:*[3] *Ipsi sunt canones,* inquit, *qui appellationes totius ecclesiae ad hujus sanctae sedis examen voluerunt deferri. Ab ipsa vero numquam*[i] *prorsus appellare debere sanxerunt, ac per hoc illam de tota ecclesia judicare. Ipsam vero ad nullius commeare judicium, nec de ejus umquam praeceperunt judicio judicari. Sententiamque*
20 *ejus constituerunt non oportere dissolvi, cujus potius sequenda decreta mandaverunt.* Concordat[j] canon: *Cuncta per orbem.*[4]

---

[a] minorem *T H* [b] quod *M* [c] numquid *T H* [d] praeconsulem *V* [e] praeconsul *T H*
[f] aliquid *T H* [g] numquid *T H* [h] contemptus *M* [i] nusquam *T H*
[j] *add.* ibidem *T H*

---

[1] c. 97, C. XI, qu. 3 (RF I, 670)*; *Serm.* 62, c. 8 (*PL* 38, 420–421).*
[2] c. 10, C. IX, qu. 3 (RF I, 609).
[3] c. 16, C. IX, qu. 3 (RF I, 611).
[4] c. 17, C. IX, qu. 3 (RF I, 611).

A DEFENSE OF APOSTOLIC OBEDIENCE

himself, suggests this, as does ST. AUGUSTINE in his book DE NATURA BONI (Cause xi, question 3, *Qui resistit*): *If that authority enjoins something you ought not to do, then by all means ignore that authority for fear of a greater authority. Consider the several levels of human laws. If the magistrate orders something, must it be carried out, if the proconsul orders the contrary? Again if the proconsul orders something and the emperor orders something else, is there any doubt that disregarding the former, you should obey the latter?* Do not disdain authority, but rather choose to obey the greater authority. Therefore the lesser authority should not be irate if a greater authority is accorded greater respect.

On these grounds, it is quite clear that the commands and judgments of the Supreme Pontiff, notwithstanding a contrary order of any other man, must be obeyed without delay. The sacred canons explicitly support the same opinion. Thus Pope NICHOLAS declared (Cause ix, question 3, *Patet*): *Indeed it is evident that the judgment of the Apostolic See must be disputed by none whose authority is not greater, nor may any pass judgment upon its judgment.* And Pope GELASIUS[1] (Cause ix, question 3, *Ipsi sunt*): *There are strict canons which ordain that appeals of the whole Church be transferred to the investigation of this holy see. Indeed, in absolutely no circumstance do they sanction appeals from the holy see and thus judgment passed upon it for the whole Church. Certainly they never enjoined the holy see to consult the judgment of anyone or prescribed that its judgments be reviewed.[2] They determined that its decision ought not to be annulled, but commanded rather that its decrees be fulfilled.* For the same point, consult the canon *Cuncta per orbem.*

---

[1] Pseudo-Gelasius.
[2] Cf. *Execrabilis;* see p. 225.

DEFENSORIUM OBEDIENTIAE APOSTOLICAE

OCTAVA VERITAS

Summi pontificis diffinitiones et praecepta, si contra scripturam canonicam, legem divinam, aut naturalem emanarent, neminem ad sui observantiam obligarent.

Sequitur haec veritas ex praecedenti. Cum enim nec contra Dominum
5 suum vicarius, nec inferior contra superiorem potestatem sibi concedentem sit audiendus, sequitur, quod nec summus pontifex, vicarius Christi, audiendus est, immo nec creatura aliqua contra Deum, teste apostolo, II COR. xiii,[1] dicente[a]: *Non possumus aliquid adversus veritatem, sed pro veritate.* Et beato Petro, ACT. v:[2] *Oportet Deo plus obedire quam homini-*
10 *bus.* Scriptura autem canonica, utrumque videlicet testamentum, Spiritu Sancto dictante et inspirante scripta creditur, secundum illud II PETRI i:[3] *Spiritu Sancto inspirati locuti sunt sancti Dei homines.* Lex quoque naturalis divinae legi innititur, quia a Deo cordibus hominum est impressa, dicente propheta PSAL. iiii:[4] *Signatum est super nos lumen*
15 *vultus tui, Domine.* Et apostolus ait, ROM. ii:[5] *Ostendunt[b] opus legis scriptum in cordibus suis.* Ad idem valet illud beati HIERONYMI super epistolam AD EPH. xi, quaest. iii, *Si dominus:*[6] *Si dominus jubet ea, quae non sunt contraria fidei vel adversa sacris scripturis, subiciatur domino servus. Sin vero contraria praecipit, magis obediatur[c] Christo quam*
20 *corporis domino. Et infra: Si bonum est, quod praecipit imperator, jubentis exsequere voluntatem. Si malum, responde: "Oportet magis obedire Deo quam hominibus."*[7] Et beatus AUGUSTINUS in DE NATURA BONI, xi, quaest. iii, *Qui resistit:*[8] *Si aliud jubeat imperator, aliud Deus, major*

---

[a] *om. T H*   [b] Ostendit *T H*   [c] obediatis *T H*

[1] *II Cor.* 13, 8.
[2] *Act.* 5, 29.
[3] *II Petr.* 1, 21.
[4] *Psal.* 4, 7.
[5] *Rom.* 2, 15.*
[6] c. 93, C. XI, qu. 3 (RF I, 669)*; *Comm. in epist. ad Titum,* c. 2 (*PL* 26, 619C et 626C).
[7] *Act.* 5, 29.
[8] c. 97, C. XI, qu. 3 (RF I, 670); *Serm.* 62, c. 8 (*PL* 38, 421).

A DEFENSE OF APOSTOLIC OBEDIENCE

EIGHTH TRUTH

The definitions and precepts of the Supreme Pontiff bind no one, if they are issued against canonical Scripture, divine law, or natural law.

This truth follows from the previous one. Since no vicar must be obeyed against the command of his master and since no inferior must be obeyed against the command of his superior who has given him his authority, it follows that not even the Supreme Pontiff, the Vicar of Christ—indeed, no creature—must be obeyed against the command of God. The apostle Paul supports this (II CORINTHIANS 13): *We have no power to act against the truth, but only for it.* St. Peter does so also (ACTS 5): *God must be obeyed rather than men.* Canonical Scripture, namely, both Testaments, is believed to be written by the dictation and impulse of the Holy Spirit, as is asserted in II PETER 1: *Inspired by the Holy Spirit, the holy men of God spoke.* Natural law also rests upon divine law,[1] because it has been impressed by God in the hearts of men, as the prophet says (PSALM 4): *The light of thy countenance, O Lord, is impressed upon us.* The apostle Paul says (ROMANS 2): *They display the effect of the law inscribed on their hearts.* ST. JEROME writes to the same effect in his *Commentary upon the Epistle to the Ephesians* (Cause xi, question 3, *Si dominus*): *If a master orders things that are not contrary to the faith or against Holy Scripture, the servant ought to be subject to his master. If, however, he orders what is opposed to faith and Scripture, Christ should be obeyed rather than the master of the body. Moreover, if the emperor orders what is good, fulfill his will; if evil, respond: "God must be obeyed rather than men."* ST. AUGUSTINE declares in DE NATURA BONI (Cause xi, question 3, *Qui resistit*): *If the emperor enjoins one thing and God*

---

[1] Cf. Heiko A. Oberman, *The Harvest of Medieval Theology* (Cambridge, Mass.: Harvard University Press, 1963), pp. 103–111.

DEFENSORIUM OBEDIENTIAE APOSTOLICAE

est potestas Dei. O, imperator, da veniam, tu carcerem, ille minatur gehennam. Et par ratio est de quolibet mortali contra Deum praecipiente. Hinc ISIDORUS, generaliter loquens, ait, xi, quaest. iii, *Si is qui:*[1] *Si is, qui praeest, fecit*[a] *aut cuiquam, quod a Deo prohibitum est,*[a] *fecerit, aut*
5 *cuiquam, quod a Deo prohibitum est, facere jusserit, vel quod praeceptum est praeterierit, aut praeterire mandaverit, sancti Pauli apostoli AD GAL. i sententia ingerenda est:*[2] *"Et si angelus de caelo evangelizaverit vobis*[b] *praeter quod*[c] *evangelizavimus, anathema sit."* Beatus quoque BERNARDUS in DE DISPENSATIONE ET PRAECEPTO ad idem ait[d]:[3]
10 *"Labia sacerdotis custodiunt scientiam," MALACH. ii,*[4] *"et legem ex ore ejus requirant." Requirant, dixerim, legem non quam vel authentica ulla*[e] *scriptura tradiderit, vel ratio manifesta probaverit, de hujusmodi quippe nec praeceptor expectandus, nec prohibitor auscultandus est.*

Cui consentire videtur GRATIANUS dist. xix, *Ita Dominus,*[5] sect.
15 hoc[f] autem[f], ubi loquens de suscipiendis decretalibus epistolis papae addit: *Hoc autem intelligendum est de illis sanctionibus et decretalibus epistolis, in quibus nec praecedentium patrum decretis, in*[g] *lege divina vel naturali fundatis*[g]*, nec evangelicis praeceptis aliquod contrarium invenitur.*

20 Et iterum dist. x, sect. 1:[6] *Constitutiones ecclesiasticae vel saeculares, si naturali juri*[h] *contrariae*[i] *probantur, penitus sunt excludendae.* Alioquin qui mandato hominis contra Deum obtemperat, recte cum phariseis a Domino exprobari[j] meretur, dicente MATT. xv:[7] *Quare transgredimini mandata Dei propter traditiones vestras?*

[a-a] *om. T H* [b] *nobis M V* [c] *quae M V* [d] *dicit T H* [e] *illa M V* [f-f] *om. M*
[g-g] *om. T H* [h] *jure T H* [i] *contraire M* [j] *exprobrari M*

[1] c. 101, C. XI, qu. 3 (RF I, 671); cf. Basilii, *Regulae brevius tractatae*, c. 114 et c. 303 (*PG* 31, 1159A–D et 1297D–1298D).
[2] *Gal.* 1, 8.*
[3] c. 9 (*PL* 182, 873C).
[4] *Malach.* 2, 7.
[5] c. 7, D. XIX (RF I, 62); Gratiani.
[6] c. 11, D. IX (RF I, 18); Gratiani.
[7] *Matth.* 15, 3.

another, the authority of God is greater. O emperor, with your indulgence, you threaten prison, but he threatens Hell! The same conclusion applies to any mortal who orders something against the command of God. Upon this basis, ISIDORE, speaking in general terms, says (Cause xi, question 3, *Si is qui*): *If he who rules has done or will do to someone what is forbidden by God, if he will order someone to do what is prohibited by God, or if he will disregard or command others to disregard what has been enjoined, the words of St. Paul the apostle must be brought forward (GALATIANS 1):* "*If an angel from heaven should preach a gospel at variance with the gospel we preached to you, let him be anathema.*" ST. BERNARD writes to the same effect in DE DISPENSATIONE ET PRAECEPTO: "*The lips of a priest guard*[1] *knowledge, and men should seek the law from his mouth*" (*MALACHI 2*). *They should seek, I should say, not the law which any authentic scriptural text will present or evident reason will approve; indeed, in matters of this nature, no instructor must be expected nor any censor be heeded.*

GRATIAN seems to agree, because when he is speaking about the receipt of the decretals of the Pope (distinction xix, *Ita dominus*, section *hoc autem*), he adds: *This must be understood of those sanctions and decretals in which nothing is found that is contrary to the decrees of the preceding Fathers* founded[2] *in divine or natural law*[2] *or contrary to evangelical precepts.*

Or again, distinction x, section 1, may be cited: *Ecclesiastical or secular statutes, if proven opposed to natural law, must be completely rejected.* But he who heeds a human statute against the command of God justly deserves to be included in the Lord's reproach to the Pharisees (MATTHEW 15): *Why do you break God's commandments in the interest of your traditions?*

---

[1] The Revised Standard Version reads "should guard."
[2-2] Biel's addition.

DEFENSORIUM OBEDIENTIAE APOSTOLICAE

NONA VERITAS

Sanctionibus ac decretis apostolicis, quas scripturae sacrae, legi divinae, et naturali obviare certum non est, etiam si dubium fuerit, assensus et obedientia est praestanda.

Patet haec veritas praesertim, quantum ad illa dubia, quae quis scire
5 non tenetur, per beatum AUGUSTINUM, qui CONTRA MANICHAEOS scribens ait:[1] *Vir justus, si forte sub rege sacrilego militet, recte potest illo jubente bellare, vice pacis ordinem servans, si quod jubetur aut non esse contra Dei praeceptum certum est, vel, utrum sit, certum non est; ita ut fortasse reum faciat regem iniquitas imperandi, innocentem tamen militem*
10 *ostendat ordo serviendi*[a]. Ecce si regi sacrilego in dubiis miles obedire tenetur, etiam in fundendo humanum sanguinem, quia in bello, quanto magis in dubiis papae est obediendum.

Hinc etiam beatus BERNARDUS in DE DISPENSATIONE ET PRAECEPTO ait:[2] *Quod ita latere aut in dubium venire possit, utrum nam*
15 *Deus sic an*[b] *aliter forte velit in hujuscemodi, lex ex ore sacerdotis requirenda est. A quo denique divina potius consilia requirentur quam ab illo, cui credita est dispensatio mysteriorum Dei? Ipsum proinde, quem pro Deo habemus, tamquam Deum in his, quae aperte non sunt, contra Deum audire debemus;* et cetera, quae ibi sequuntur. Demum nisi[c] in dubiis
20 papae esset assentiendum et obsequendum, frustra ad ejus sedem causae dubiae per ipsum ultimatae et improvocabiliter terminandae referrentur; quippe frustra fit diffinitio, cui standum non erit. Ad apostolicum autem causae dubiae referendae sunt, et maxime in fide, sicut GELASIUS papa constituit ita, dist. ix quaest. iii, *Cuncta*,[3] dicens[d]: *Cuncta per mundum*
25 *novit ecclesia quod sacrosancta romana ecclesia fas habet de omnibus judicandi, neque*[e] *cuiquam de ejus liceat judicare judicio. Siquidem ad illam de*

---

[a] militandi *V*   [b] vel *M V*   [c] ubi *M V*   [d] om. *T H*   [e] nec *T H*

[1] *Contra faustum*, L. XXII, c. 75 (*PL* 42, 448).*
[2] c. 9 (*PL* 182, 873C–D).
[3] c. 17, C. IX, qu. 3 (RF I, 611).

A DEFENSE OF APOSTOLIC OBEDIENCE

NINTH TRUTH

Assent and obedience must be given, even if doubt exists, to papal sanctions and decrees which Holy Scripture, divine law, and natural law do not categorically reject.

This truth is particularly evident respecting those matters which one is not expected to understand, as ST. AUGUSTINE wrote against the Manichaeans: *A just man who perhaps serves under an ungodly king can rightly fight upon his command or in turn preserve the posture of peace, if it is clear that his orders are not opposed to God's precept, or if, when they are opposed, this is not clear. In the latter event, the king may be guilty of an unjust command, but the soldier innocent, as the order of responsibility demonstrates.* Therefore, if a soldier is expected to obey an ungodly king in case of doubt, even in shedding human blood, because he is at war, how much more must a pope be obeyed in case of doubt.

Thus ST. BERNARD declares in DE DISPENSATIONE ET PRAECEPTO: *When it is hidden or subject to doubt whether God wills in one manner or perhaps in another, the law must be sought from the mouth of the priest. In the end, where may divine counsels be sought if not from him who has received the authority to dispense the mysteries of God? Therefore, we ought to hear him whom we regard as God's lieutenant as if he were God, in those things not openly opposed to God;* and he continues in the same vein. After all, unless one is bound to obey and give assent to the Pope in doubtful instances, it would be an empty gesture to refer such cases to his tribunal for final settlement. Indeed, a final decision would become empty and lose its binding force. Doubtful instances must be referred to papal judgment, particularly in matters of faith, as Pope GELASIUS defined, saying (distinction ix, question 3, *Cuncta*): *Every church in the world acknowledges that the most holy Roman Church enjoys the right to judge all things and none is permitted to pass judgment upon its judgment.*

---

qualibet mundi parte appellandum est, ab illa autem nemo est appellare permissus; et hoc quantum ad omnes causas generaliter.

Quantum vero ad causas fidei, ait INNOCENTIUS papa, xxiiii, quaest. i, *Quotiens:*[1] *Quotiens fidei ratio ventilatur, arbitror omnes fratres*
5 *et coepiscopos nostros nonnisi ad Petri, id est sui nominis et honoris auctoritatem referre debere.* Et in cap. *Majores,* DE BAPTISMO ET EJUS EFFECTU idem ait:[2] *Majores ecclesiae causas, praesertim articulos fidei contingentes, ad Petri sedem referendas intelligit*ᵃ, *qui eum*ᵇ *quaerenti Domino, quem discipuli ipsum esse dicerent, respondisse notabit:*[3] *"Tu es*
10 *Christus filius Dei vivi"; et pro eo Dominum exorasse, ne deficiat fides ejus.* Hincᶜ haereticorumᵈ malleus beatissimus HIERONYMUS, dum fidei suae confessionem summi pontificis judicio obtulisset, ait, xxiiii, quaest. i, *Haec est:*[4] *Si autem haec nostra confessio apostolatus tui judicio comprobatur, quicumque me culpare voluerit, se imperitum aut malivolum vel etiam*
15 *non catholicum, sed haereticum comprobabit.*

SECUNDA PARSᵉ

His itaque veritatibus a sancta matre ecclesia, quam sentire posse errare haereticum est, acceptatis et approbatis, aut ex eisdem sanctorumque patrum irrefragabilibus testimoniis evidenter deductis innixusᶠ, ad nostrum propositumᵍ particularius descendendo, alias subicio pro-

---

ᵃ intellexit *M V*   ᵇ cum *T H*   ᶜ Hic *T*   ᵈ *add.* ille *T H*
ᵉ *add.* HUJUS DEFENSORII OBEDIENTIAE APOSTOLICAE *T H*   ᶠ innixius *M V*
ᵍ praepositum *M*

---

[1] c. 12, C. XXIV, qu. 1 (RF I, 970).
[2] c. 3, X (3,42) (RF II, 644).
[3] *Matth.* 16, 16.
[4] c. 14, C. XXIV, qu. 1 (RF I, 970); ibi Hieronymo ascribitur.

A DEFENSE OF APOSTOLIC OBEDIENCE

Indeed, every part of the world must appeal to Rome; none, however, is permitted to appeal from Rome. This applies to the same extent in general to all cases.

Pope INNOCENT[1] applies this rule to cases of faith (Cause xxiv, question 1, *Quotiens*): *Whenever a judgment of faith is brought into discussion, I believe that all our brothers and fellow bishops ought to consult only the authority of St. Peter, and to defer to his name and honor.* The same pope[2] says elsewhere (canon *Majores*, DE BAPTISMO ET EJUS EFFECTU): *He who holds that the more important cases of the Church, especially those concerning articles of faith, must be referred to the see of Peter, will perceive that Peter, when the Lord asked who his disciples said that he was, responded: "You are the Christ, the Son of the living God," and will perceive that the Lord prayed for him that his faith should not fail.* Thus the most blessed JEROME,[3] the scourge of heretics, when he offered the confession of his faith to the judgment of the Supreme Pontiff, said (Cause xxiv, question 1, *Haec est*): *But if this our confession is acknowledged by your episcopal judgment, whoever will condemn me will reveal that he is unlearned, malevolent, or even not a Catholic, but a heretic.*

PART TWO

Now in resting my case upon these truths accepted and approved by the holy Church our Mother, which can only heretically be judged to err, and firmly and clearly drawn from the irrefutable opinions of the holy Fathers, I proceed more precisely to our subject. In doing so, I

---

[1] Innocent I (402–417).
[2] Historical error. This canon is drawn from a letter of Innocent III (1198–1216) to the Archbishop of Arles.
[3] See p. 337.

positiones factum depositionis domini Dietheri de Isenburg, quondam
electi et^a confirmatae^a ecclesiae Moguntinae, et provisionis reverendissimi in Christo Patris et Domini, domini Adolphi de Nassau, electi et
confirmati jam dictae ecclesiae Moguntinae, concernentes.

5   Pro quorum intellectu clariori praesuppono factum firme^b omnibus
volentibus scire notum, quo^c sanctissimus dominus noster Pius, papa
dominus^d, de fratrum suorum dominorum cardinalium consilio, dictum
dominum Dietherum propter certas notorias transgressiones et crimina,
non vocatum et indefensum, omni jure, quod sibi in dicta ecclesia
10 competere potuisset^e, privavit, et privatum ipso jure declaravit, omnesque sibi fidelitate et sacramentis, quomodolibet astrictos, absolvit^f.
Reverendissimum quoque patrem et omnium^g, dominum Adolphum
comitem de Nassau eidem ecclesiae praefecit motu proprio, tamquam
verum et legitimum pastorem, mandans omnibus Christifidelibus et
15 praesertim dictae ecclesiae in temporalibus aut spiritualibus subjectis,
sub interminatione maledictionis aeternae aliisque poenis formidabilibus,
quatenus apostolicis decretis privationis, provisionis et ceteris hanc
causam concernentibus, obedientes domino Diethero privato in nullis
tamquam electo moguntino responderent, sed magis renitentem expel-
20 lerent. Dominum vero Adolphum tamquam verum pastorem ecclesiae
saepe dictae susciperent, introducerent, eique ut tali responderent,
obedirent, adhaererent.

  Consentiente in his invictissimo^h Friderico romanorum imperatore
semper augusto, prout haec et alia multa in bullis papalibus, ac imperiali-
25 bus litteris infraⁱ positisⁱ, per totum paene mundum publicatis, plenius
continentur. Et quod haec de mente sanctitatis suae sufficienter informa-
tae, non praecipitanter, sed velut matura deliberatione digesta, pro-
cessisse non dubitarentur, omnisque non obediendi tolleretur occasio,
non modo secundo, sed iterum atque iterum patentibus bullis et plurifi-
30 catis brevibus missis praelatis, principibus ac communitatibus^j, tam

---

^{a–a} *om. T H*   ^b fame *V*, ferme *T H*   ^c Quomodo *T H*   ^d secundus *T H*   ^e potuit *H*
^f *add.* et *M V*   ^g dominum *T H*   ^h *add.* domino *T H*   ^{i–i} *om. T H*
^j comitatibus *M V*

propose other propositions relating to the deposition of Graf Diether von Isenburg, formerly elected and confirmed to the church of Mainz and relating to the provision of the most reverend in Christ, the Father and the Son, Graf Adolf von Nassau, elected and confirmed to the same church of Mainz.

For the clearer understanding of these things, I presuppose that this affair is well known to all who wish to know. Our most holy lord, Pope Pius II, with the advice of his brothers, the lord cardinals, deposed the said Graf Diether for certain notorious crimes and transgressions, without a summons or a defense, but in all legality. He deprived him of all that he could claim as his in the said church, declared him deposed in all legality, and released all those bound in fealty to him or to his holy office in any manner. He appointed on his own authority the most reverend father of all, Graf Adolf, Count of Nassau, as the true and legitimate pastor, and commanded all Christians, and especially those subject to the said church in spiritual and temporal goods, under the threat of eternal malediction and other formidable penalties in accordance with the papal decrees of privation, provision, and other measures related to this case, to grant obedience in no regard to the deposed Graf Diether as the elected Archbishop of Mainz, but to expel this rebellious man. He ordered them to support and institute Graf Adolf as the true pastor of the said church and regard, obey, and adhere to him as such.

The invincible and always august Frederick, Emperor of the Romans, consents in these things; these and many other matters are discussed in the papal bulls and imperial letters included here and published throughout almost the whole world. So that the intent of his Holiness might not be doubted, so that it might not be questioned that he proceeded sufficiently informed, not hastily, but with mature and considered deliberation and so that every occasion for disobedience might be removed, he declared Diether deposed not only a second time, but again and again in open bulls and in repeated letters sent to prelates, rulers, and cities,

spiritualibus, quam saecularibus declaravit. Sed et oratores suos ad informandum universos de hac ipsa mente, ac de processus causae justitia, necnon ad exsequendum apostolica hujusmodi mandata ceteraque[a] his rebus accomoda, idem Dominus noster sanctissimus
5 delegavit. Quibus sic tamquam notoriis praesuppositis sequitur propositio prima talis.

PROPOSITIO PRIMA

Omnes et singuli Christifideles, mandatis hujusmodi apostolicis sufficienter sibi publicatis, tenentur sub poena aeternae damnationis in his, quae ad se pertinent, obedire.

10 Cum enim in omnibus, quae scripturae sacrae, legi divinae, aut naturali non obviant, summo pontifici tamquam voci Petri ex divino praecepto, de necessitate salutis obedire oportet, ut ex praemissis veritatibus eductum est. Mandata apostolica, de quibus nunc sermo, quoniam scripturae sacrae, legi divinae et naturali non contrariantur, sed con-
15 sonant, ea sine dispendio salutis aeternae transgredi potest nemo. Quod vero legi divinae et naturali, quin immo et positivae[b], dicta mandata sint conformia, patet manifeste.

Nam et lex divina eum qui ecclesiae praelatis obedire contemnit, eici et a fidelium communionibus[c] jubet proici. Ait enim MATTH. xviii:[1]
20 *Si*, inquit[d], *ecclesiam non audierit, sit tibi sicut ethnicus et publicanus.*

Ratio denique naturalis dictat eum officio praeesse non debere, qui sibi vacans negligit quae ad illius executionem officii requiruntur, nec bonum personae, bono communi[e] praeferendum et[e] praeponendum fore, docet PHILOSOPHUS, ii, ETHICORUM.[2]
25 Jus positivum electum in episcopum, qui infra tempus a jure statutum consecrari negligit, ecclesia, ad quam electus est, privari disponit.

---

[a] ceterasque *M V*   [b] positivo *M V*   [c] communione *T H*   [d] *om. T H*   [e-e] *om. T H*

[1] *Matth.* 18, 17.
[2] Cf. Aristoteles, *Opera*, ed. Academia Regia Borussica (Berlin, 1831–1870), *Nico. Eth.*, L. I, c. 1, 1094b.

A DEFENSE OF APOSTOLIC OBEDIENCE

lords spiritual as well as temporal. The same, our most holy lord, dispatched his spokesmen to inform all of his intent and the justice of the case advanced, and took other appropriate steps of this nature as well, to carry out the papal decrees in these matters. My first proposition is based upon the assumption that these actions are public knowledge.

FIRST PROPOSITION

All Christians collectively and individually must obey apostolic mandates of this sort that are sufficiently made known to them, and are bound under the threat of eternal damnation to obey these mandates in those matters which concern them.

For in all matters which are not contrary to Holy Writ, divine law, or natural law, the Supreme Pontiff, as the voice of St. Peter, must be obeyed from divine precept and for salvation, as must be concluded from the foregoing truths. No one may transgress the apostolic mandates that are being discussed without the loss of eternal salvation, since they are not in conflict but rather in agreement with Holy Writ, divine law, and natural law. It is self-evident that these mandates are in real conformity with divine and natural law, and even positive law.

Divine law commands that he who disdains to obey the rulers of the Church be driven out and barred from the sacraments of the faithful. For Christ says (MATTHEW 18): *If he will not listen to the church, you must then treat him as you would a pagan or a taxgatherer.*

Accordingly natural reason dictates that he ought not to possess an office which stands vacant who neglects those things required for the fulfillment of that office. For the welfare of an individual must not be placed above and preferred over the common welfare, as ARISTOTLE teaches (ETHICS, Book II).

Positive law provides that an elected bishop who neglects to be consecrated within the term appointed in law is ousted from the see to which

125

DEFENSORIUM OBEDIENTIAE APOSTOLICAE

Tempus hoc trium mensium curriculo post confirmationem determinatur in cap. i, dist. lxxv,[1] et cap. *Quoniam quidem*, c. dist.[2] Et notatur in GLOSSA *Cum in cunctis* DE ELECTIONE:[3] Quod si ultra quinque menses suam electus consecrationem distulit[a], inhabilis redditur non solum ad
5 ecclesiam, quam tenet, sed etiam[b] aliam quamcumque obtinendam; ut in cap. *Quoniam quidem* supra allegato.[4] Nec mirum de electo in episcopum, cum etiam quisquis ad curam animarum assumptus fuerit, si infra annum se ad sacerdotium promoveri non faciat, etiam ipso[c] jure pastorali officio est privatus, sicut expresse habetur in cap. *Licet canon*, DE
10 ELECTIONE, lib. vi, ubi sic dicitur:[5] *Is*[d] *qui ad regimen hujusmodi assumitur, ut gregis sibi crediti diligentius gerere curam possit, infra annum a sibi commissi regiminis tempore numerandum se faciat ad sacerdotium promoveri. Quod si infra idem tempus promotus non fuerit, ecclesia sibi commissa, nulla etiam praemissa monitione, sit praesentis constitu-*
15 *tionis auctoritate privatus.* Qui canon locum habet de electo in episcopum, ut expresse tenet JOANNES ANDREAS in dicto capitulo in GLOSSA verbi *privatus*;[6] et JOANNIS MONACHI ibidem[e] in verbo *quando* incipiet:[7] *Tum quia episcopus vere curatus est habens parochiam videlicet diocesim suam. Capitulum*[f] *loquitur generaliter de assumpto ad regimen*
20 *parochiae. Tum quia eadem, immo major, ratio legis reperitur in episcopo quam in simplici curato. Ratio enim in textu assignatur, "ut gregis sibi crediti diligentius curam gerere possit"; numerosior autem grex episcopo commissa est quam parochiae simplicis curatori.*

---

[a] distulerit *T H*   [b] *add.* ad *T H*   [c] ipse *V*   [d] Ideo *T H*   [e] *om. V*   [f] *add.* autem *T H*

[1] c. 2, D. LXXV (RF I, 265–266).
[2] c. 1, D. C (RF I, 352).
[3] c. 7, X (1,6) (RF II, 51–52); cf. *Decretales Gregorii Noni Pont. Max. cum epitomis, divisionibus, et glossis ordinariis* (Venice, 1567), 72.
[4] c. 1, D. C. (RF I, 352).
[5] c. 14, VI (1,6) (RF II, 954).
[6] Cf. *Liber sextus decretalium d. Bonifacii Papae VIII suae integritati una cum Clementinis et Extravagantes earumque glossis cum glossa J. Andreae* (Paris, 1585), 107.
[7] Non invenitur.

he was elected. In canon law, this period of grace is determined as a period of three months from confirmation (distinction lxxv, canon 1 and distinction c, canon *Quoniam quidem*). It is noted in the gloss to *Cum in cunctis*, DE ELECTIONE, that if an elected prelate postpones his consecration more than five months, he becomes unfit not only for the church which he rules, but also for the rule of any other church he might obtain thereafter, as was asserted in the canon just cited (*Quoniam quidem*). It is not extraordinary that this applies to an elected bishop, since anyone who accepts the cure of souls and is not ordained to the priesthood within one year is also deprived of his office by the same law. This is expressly stated in canon law (canon *Licet canon*, DE ELECTIONE, Book VI) where it is written: *He who is accepted in an office of this sort, so that he may more fruitfully exercise the pastorate of the flock assigned to him, must be ordained a priest within one year reckoned from the time when the office was bestowed upon him. If he is not ordained within this time, he will lose the church assigned to him without advance notice by the authority of the present edict.* This canon also applies to an elected bishop as JOANNES ANDREAS expressly maintains in his gloss on the word *privatus* in this canon; JOANNES MONACHUS, in the same place, glosses the word *quando*: *Moreover, this is because the bishop is a curate who enjoys a parish, namely, his diocese. The canon speaks in general terms concerning one who assumes the rule of a parish. Moreover, this is because the same, indeed greater, interpretation of the law applies to the bishop as to the mere curate. The interpretation is assigned in the text "so that he may more fruitfully exercise the pastorate of the flock assigned to him," since the flock assigned to a bishop is more numerous than that assigned to the curate of a mere parish.*

DEFENSORIUM OBEDIENTIAE APOSTOLICAE

Privat denique constitutio mantuana[1] omnem appellantem contra jura antiqua a summo pontifice ad futurum concilium omni dignitate, si quam habet, ipso facto. Sic excommunicatum, praesertim episcopum, divinis se temere ingerentem et coram eo celebrare[a] facientem gravibus
5 poenis subiciunt, etiam poenae irregularitatis, ut communiter sentiunt doctores in cap. *Si quis episcopus*[2] et sequenti xi, quaest. ii,[3] et in cap. *Illud*, DE CLERICO EXCOMMUNICATO MINISTRANTE,[4] et in cap. *Latore*[b],[5] eodem titulo.

Notorium vero est dominum Dietherum nec sacerdotalem, nec alium
10 sacrum ordinem post electionem suam ante triennium factam suscepisse, nec dispensationem quaesisse, nec impedimentum ante statutum terminum allegasse; quod nec ipse negat, nec sui defensores. Notorium denique est et in scriptis propriis confitetur se appellasse ad futurum concilium, contra constitutionem mantuanam. Manifestum quoque est
15 dictum[c] Dietherum dudum ante sui privationem excommunicationis sententiam incidisse et ut talem in urbe[d] et Colonia publicatum fuisse, et nihilominus se[e] divinis[e] ingessisse officiis, quemadmodum se ingerit temere de praesenti. Quapropter[f] apostolica mandata poenas privationis et alias contra tales a jure taxatas, in[g] Dietherum saepe dictum
20 fulminantia, juribus concordant, et in nullo penitus contradicunt. Alia vero crimina in papalibus bullis objecta, quia gravia sunt et scandalosa, sileo, quoniam infamia[h] nullius[h], conscientia teste, pascor.

Neque tamen processum sanctissimi domini nostri vitiat, quod non vocatum et indefensum privatione[i] damnavit. Nec ab[j] obedientia

---

[a] celebrari *T H*   [b] *Labore V*   [c] *add.* dominum *T H*   [d] orbe *M V*   [e-e] divinis se *T H*
[f] *add.* et *T H*   [g] *add.* dominum *T H*   [h-h] nullius infamia *T H*   [i] privando *T H*
[j] *om. M*

[1] Cf. *Execrabilis*, 18 Jan. 1460, cit. in H. Denzinger et A. Schönmetzer, *Enchiridion symbolorum definitionum et declarationum de rebus fidei et morum*, 33 ed. (Freiburg i. Br., 1965), 345; *Magnum Bullarium Romanum*, 149–150; vide p. 224–226.
[2] c. 6, C. XI, qu. 3 (RF I, 644).
[3] c. 7, C. XI, qu. 3 (RF I, 644–645).
[4] c. 5, X (5,27) (RF II, 828–830).
[5] c. 4, X (5,27) (RF II, 827–828).

A DEFENSE OF APOSTOLIC OBEDIENCE

Finally the Mantuan constitution deprives everyone of office who appeals against age-old laws from the Supreme Pontiff to a future council, by the very nature of such an appeal. By these laws an excommunicated bishop is especially subject to serious penalties, even the penalties for disobedience, when he dares rashly to interfere with the sacraments and causes them to be celebrated in his presence.[1] Upon this the doctors are generally agreed (canon *Siquis episcopus*; the following canon, Cause xi, question 2; canon *Illud*, DE CLERICO EXCOMMUNICATO MINISTRANTE; and the canon, *Latore* under the same title).

It is quite notorious that Graf Diether has not received priestly or other holy orders in the three years that have elapsed since his election;[2] furthermore he has sought no dispensation and has offered no evidence of valid hindrance within the allotted period of time. Neither Diether himself nor his defenders deny these things. It is also notorious that Diether admits in his own writings that he appealed to a future council in defiance of the Mantuan constitution.[3] Furthermore, it is clear that although the said Diether incurred the sentence of excommunication before he was deposed and proclaimed as such in Rome and Cologne, he has nevertheless insisted upon tampering with the celebration of the sacraments and continues presumptuously to do so at the present time. Therefore the apostolic mandates, repeatedly hurling against the said Diether the judgment of deposition and other blows inflicted upon such in law, are in harmony with the canons and do not contradict them in any manner at all. Indeed, I pass over in silence other crimes exposed in the papal bulls that are quite severe and scandalous, since I find no satisfaction in discrediting any man, if I may say so in all good conscience.

Moreover, it does not invalidate the legal procedure of our most holy lord that he condemned Diether to be deposed without a summons or a hearing. The publication of a frivolous appeal cannot absolve anyone

---

[1] See p. 237.
[2] See Introduction, p. 19.
[3] See p. 263.

mandatorum ejusdem sanctissimi domini nostri appellationis frivolae interpositio aliquem absolvere poterit. Sunt namque, qui his duobus innixi apostolicae sedi rebellant, se et alios damnabiliter seducentes, qui non verentur quoad primum verbo et scriptis asserere, quod damnare
5 aliquem non vocatum et indefensum legi divinae contrarium sit, naturali et positivo, et per consequens hujuscemodi sententia liget neminem, eo quod ipso jure divino et humano sit irrita et inanis. Ad sui erroris stabilimentum superaddentes, quod non legitur dominum aliquem, nisi vocatum et defensum, damnavisse, quod vel temerarium est, aut
10 haeresis manifesta. Equidem si ad fugiendum[a] temeritatem dicere volunt, scripturam non commemorare, judicasse quempiam Dominum, quin et judicati vocationem et concessam defensionem commemoret, prout[b] exemplis de protoparente Adam, primogenito suo Cain, ac Sodomitis[c] moliuntur, haeresim asseruerunt[d] manifestam, quia divinae
15 scripturae aperte contrariuntur[e], quod sequentia declarabunt.

Pro quorum intellectu[f] clariori[f] animadvertendum[g] puto, quod de vocatione et defensione dupliciter loqui contingit. Uno modo[h] generaliter satis, ut per vocationem intelligatur vel juris promulgatio, vel ad ejus observantiam exhortatio, vel a transgressione revocatio; et hoc sive fiat
20 praeceptis, exhortationibus, internis inspirationibus, beneficiis sive flagellis, quomodo nos a Domino vocari et multipliciter vocari testatur beatus GREGORIUS, HOMELIA xxxvi[1] et alibi. Sic per defensionem accipi potest ipsa conversio vel paenitentia, quibus defenditur peccator, ne sententiam excipiat dignam factis. Illo modo verum est, quod Dominus
25 non vocatum non condemnat. Sed ille intellectus nihil ad propositum, quoniam sic multipliciter vocatus est dominus Dietherus, sacrorum scilicet canonum constitutionibus, scriptis apostolicis, et missis oratoribus,

---

[a] fingendum *M V*   [b] *add.* etiam *T H*   [c] *add.* ostendere *T H*   [d] asserunt *T H*
[e] contraria *T H*   [f-f] clariori intellectu *T H*   [g] advertendum *T H*   [h] *add.* signat *V*

[1] Cf. *Hom. in evang.*, L. II (*PL* 76, 1270D–1272C).

A DEFENSE OF APOSTOLIC OBEDIENCE

from obeying the decrees of our most holy lord. Those who rebel against the Apostolic See rest their case upon two propositions, thus deceiving themselves and others to their damnation: in the first instance, they do not blush to assert in speech and writing that it is contrary to divine law, natural law, and positive law to condemn anyone without a summons or a hearing, and that consequently a judgment of this sort binds no one to it since it is invalid and void in both human and divine law.[1] They add in further support of their error that it can nowhere be read that the Lord condemned anyone unless summoned and heard, which is a wild assertion, or even overt heresy. Certainly if, in order to avoid the former charge, they contend that Scripture does not relate that the Lord condemned anyone without granting him a summons and a hearing—as they strive to do in the cases of Adam, the parent of mankind, his oldest son, Cain, and the Sodomites[2]—they have embraced overt heresy, for the Holy Scriptures clearly contradict this as the following examples will demonstrate.

For a clearer comprehension of these matters I think that it must be understood that one ought to speak of "summons" and "hearing" in two ways. In one sense, it is generally sufficient to understand "summons" to mean a proclamation of a law, an exhortation to the observance of it, or an appeal to turn from transgression. This summons is accomplished by precepts, exhortations, inner promptings, promised benefits, or calamities; ST. GREGORY suggests in Sermon xxxvi and elsewhere that we are again and again summoned by God in these ways. Thus "hearing" may be understood as conversion and repentance in which the sinner is defended lest he receive the judgment that his sins deserve. In this sense, it is true that the Lord does not condemn one who has not been summoned. But this understanding has no bearing upon the case under consideration, because Graf Diether was repeatedly summoned by the decrees of canon law, papal letters, and dispatched spokesmen. He

---

[1] See p. 275 and Introduction, p. 43.
[2] See p. 299.

131

diligentissime admonitus est, ne clavium potestatem vilipenderet, ne censuras ecclesiasticas sperneret, ne superiori potestati contrairet, ne juramentorum factorum immemor existeret, ne se gravioribus poenis et sententiis innodaret.

5   Aliter vocatio dicit judicialem rei citationem, et defensio judiciales actus, quibus reus ab impetitione actoris[a] suam innocentiam ostendendo vel repellendo actionem se tuetur. Et sic loquendo de vocatione et defensione scriptura frequenter commemorat reos non solum a Domino, sed[b] ab hominibus laudabiliter punitos, de quorum vocatione et con-
10 cessa defensione post admissa crimina mentionem penitus nullam facit[c]. De multis pauca,[d] quae sequuntur, exempla subicio in testimonium praedictorum.

    Adam protoplastus, mox ut mandatum Dei transgressus est, damnationis suae sententiam excepit, scilicet privationem gratiae ac[e] justiciae
15 originalis, moriendi necessitatem, carnis rebellionem, peccati fomitem; ideo verecundia impulsus ad folia confugit, priusquam a Domino non tam ad judicium quam ad paenitentiam vocaretur, ut vult GLOSSA beati GREGORII,[1] GEN. iii super illud *Adam ubi es?*[2] *Dum vocat,* inquit, *significat, quod ad paenitentiam revocat.*

20   Item diluvio Dominus universum genus humanum usque ad octo animas judicio terribili absorpsit, quod licet justo Noe praenuntiabit[f] GEN. vi et vii[3] atque cxx annos ad paenitendum mundo concessit, nullam tamen peccatorum vocationem aut defensionem praeviam canon prodit. Aedificatores turris Babel per linguarum confusionem corripuit,
25 GEN. xi.[4] Regem Egypti plagis maximis flagellavit GEN. xii.[g][5] Domum

---

[a] actorum *V*   [b] *add.* etiam *T H*   [c] faciet *M*, faciendo *V*   [d] paucis *M*   [e] et *T H*
[f] pronuntiavit *M V*   [g] xiii *V T H*

[1] *Biblie iampridem renovate* . . . , I, f. 42ʳ.
[2] *Gen.* 3, 9.
[3] *Gen.* 6 et 7.
[4] *Gen.* 11, 1–9.
[5] *Gen.* 12, 17.

was urged most diligently not to disdain the power of the keys, not to scorn the censures of the Church, not to resist higher authority, not to forget the vows he had sworn, and not to bring even more serious chastisement and condemnation upon himself.

In another sense, "summons" means the juridical summons of the accused, and "hearing" the juridical procedure in which the accused defends himself against the charge of the plaintiff by demonstrating his innocence or disproving the accusation. Scripture, in discussing "summons" and "hearing" in this way, frequently relates that persons accused were punished in a praiseworthy fashion, not only by the Lord, but by men as well, and absolutely no mention is made of granting a summons or a hearing to them after their crimes were admitted. From the many I could cite, I submit only the few following examples to support what I have just said.

Adam, the first in creation, as soon as he transgressed God's commandment, received the verdict of damnation, namely, the loss of grace and original justice,[1] the sentence of death, the rebellion of the flesh, and the tinder of sin. Indeed, driven by shame, he concealed himself in leaves before he was summoned by the Lord, not so much to judgment as to repentance, as is suggested in the gloss of ST. GREGORY upon the text *Adam, where are you?* (GENESIS 3): *When God summons, it means that he calls back to repentance.*

Likewise, by the flood the Lord drowned the entire human race, with the exception of eight souls, in a terrible judgment. Although he warned the righteous Noah (GENESIS 6 and 7) and permitted the world one hundred and twenty years to repent, Scripture, nevertheless, records no summons or hearing of sinners before the flood. God chastised the builders of the tower of Babel by the confusion of tongues (GENESIS 11). He inflicted the king of Egypt with great plagues (GENESIS 12). He also

---

[1] Cf. Biel's *Commentary on the Sentences*, II, dist. 30–32; see Oberman, *Harvest of Medieval Theology*, pp. 126–131.

quoque Abimelech sterilitate percussit, GEN. xx,[1] propter Sarai[a] uxoris Abraae[b] ablationem. Transeo summersionem, EXOD. xiiii[c],[2] Pharaonis cum curribus et equitibus in mari rubro, plurimas quoque plagas Egypti. Venio ad exitum Israel de Egypto, quotiens correpti sunt a Domino in
5 via deserti. Nam LEVIT. x[3] Nadab et Abium, filii Aaron, qui[d] ignem obtulerunt alienum, igne egresso a Domino sunt consumpti. *Ortum est murmur populi* NUM. xi,[4] *quasi dolentium pro dolore[e], et accensus in eos ignis Domini, devoravit extremam castrorum partem.*

Rursus, NUM. xvi,[5] murmuravit populus contra Moysen et Aaron,
10 et percussi sunt a Domino 14700. Iterum locutus est, NUM. xxi,[6] populus contra Dominum et Moysen, et per ignitos serpentes a Domino sunt puniti. Praevaricatus est. JOSUE vii,[7] Achan filius Carmi accipiens de anathemate Jericho, et percussi sunt de populo xxxvi in perpetrati criminis ultionem. Propheta quidam[f] III REG. xiii[8] contra Domini
15 praeceptum levi credulitate[g] deceptus, comedit panem in Bethel, mox sententian Domini a propheta, qui eum deceperat, audivit, et in via rediens a leone percussus interiit. Senacherib, rex assyriorum, per nuntios blasphemiam locutus est, IIII REG. xix,[9] in Dominum, et occisi sunt de exercitu ejus nocte una per angelum Domini 185000.

20 Longum esset enarrare singula. In his omnibus punitos legimus peccatores, quorum judicialem vocationem et defensionem penitus scripta[h] silent[i]. Nec solum haec a Domino, sed ab hominibus laudabiliter facta[j] legimus, inspirante Domino, jubente, vel admittente. Numquid

---

[a] Saram *M*, Sara *V*   [b] Abrahae *M V*   [c] xviii *M*   [d] quia *T H*   [e] labore *T H*
[f] quidem *V*   [g] crudelitate *V*   [h] scriptura *T H*   [i] silet *T H*   [j] om. *M*

---

[1] *Gen.* 20, 18.
[2] *Exod.* 14, 26–28; *Exod.* 7–11.
[3] *Levit.* 10, 1–2.
[4] *Num.* 11, 1.
[5] *Num.* 16, 41–50.
[6] *Num.* 21, 6–9.
[7] *Josue* 7, 1–5.
[8] *III Reg.* 13, 1–25.
[9] *IV Reg.* 18, 17–35; 19, 35.

134

A DEFENSE OF APOSTOLIC OBEDIENCE

smote the household of Abimelech with sterility for the abduction of Sarah, the wife of Abraham (GENESIS 20). I merely allude to the drowning of Pharaoh and his horsemen and chariots in the Red Sea (EXODUS 14) and to the many plagues of Egypt. I come to the exodus of the children of Israel from Egypt and the repeated occasions when they were chastened by the Lord during their wanderings in the desert. Again Nadab and Abihu, the sons of Aaron, who offered unholy fire before the Lord, were devoured by fire which came forth from the Lord's presence (LEVITICUS 10). *The murmuring of the people rose as the wailing of mourners and the kindled fire of the Lord burned among them and consumed the outlying part of the camp* (NUMBERS 11).

Again when the people murmured against Moses and Aaron, 14,700 persons were struck down by the Lord (NUMBERS 16). It is written elsewhere (NUMBERS 21) that the people murmuring against the Lord and Moses were even punished by fiery serpents sent by the Lord. Achan, the son of Carmi, sinned when he took some of the accursed things from Jericho for himself; 36 were smitten to punish this crime. A certain prophet, beguiled by his own credulity to sin against the Lord's commandment, ate bread in Bethel; soon after he heard the judgment of the Lord from the prophet who had deceived him, and on his way home he was torn to pieces by a lion (I KINGS 13). Sennacherib, king of the Assyrians, uttered blasphemy against the Lord through his messengers, and in one night 185,000 men of his army were slain by the angel of the Lord (II KINGS 19).

It would be too time-consuming to recount every instance. In all these cases, sinners were punished and absolutely nothing is said about any juridical summons or hearing. Moreover, we read that these things were done not only by the Lord, but also by men, worthily, and with the Lord's inspiration, approval, and permission. Moses, the Lord's servant,

non Moyses, famulus Domini, in ultionem idolatriae in vituli adoratione commissae, vocato quidem Aaron, sed non populo, *EXO.* xxxii,[1] percussit ex idolatris[a] 23000. Et cum initiati sunt Beelphegor, jussu Domini principes suspendit in patibulis, percussit[b] de populo, NUM. xxv,[2]
5 24000.

Sed et Phineus, zelo Domini permotus, Zambri filium Salu, et Cozbi filiam Sur principis Madian confornicantes pugione pariter[c] transfodit, propter quod et Dominus placatus est, et Phineus non parum a Domino commendatus, ibidem.[3] Similiter Matathias, zelo legis accensus, I
10 MACHAB, ii,[4] israeliticam[d] idolo sacrificantem, in altari trucidavit, et regis nuntium, qui immolare compulit, interfecit. Sic populus Israel tribum Benjamin, JUDIC. xx,[5] in ultionem stupri jussu Dei paene extinxerat. Sic denique idem[e] filii Israel Madianitas[f], NUM. xxxi,[6] sic Chananeos[g], JOSUE per totum[h],[7] sic Saul Amalech, I REG. xv.[8]
15 Alios quoque plurimos demoliti sunt Domini ex mandato. Sic Paulus Spiritu Sancto repletus, ACT. xiii,[9] Elimam magum[i] verbis durissimis infamavit et corporaliter excaecavit. Corinthum publicum fornicatorem absentem excommunicavit, I COR. v,[10] ac Satanae tradidit in interitum carnis, ut spiritus salvus fiat. Sed[j] et scribens TIMOTHEO[11] quia dixerat
20 nihil faciendum sine praejudicio statim determinans ubi hujusmodi praejudicium, id est examen esset necessarium et ubi non, dividit mala in manifesta et occulta, ut ostendet in manifestis non esse opus examine,

---

[a] ydolatriis *M* [b] percussis *M* [c] parire *M* [d] israelitam *T H* [e] eidem *T H*
[f] Madianitis *V* [g] *om. M V* [h] *add.* Cananeos *M V* [i] magnis *M V* [j] *om. M V*

[1] *Exod.* 32, 15–29.
[2] *Num.* 25, 1–9.
[3] *Num.* 25 ,24.
[4] *I Machab.* 2, 23–26.
[5] *Jud.* 20, 47–48.
[6] *Num.* 31, 1–12.
[7] *Josue,* passim.
[8] *I Reg.* 15, 7–9.
[9] *Act.* 13, 6–11.
[10] *I Cor.* 5, 3–5.**
[11] Cf. *I Tim.* 5, 21.

A DEFENSE OF APOSTOLIC OBEDIENCE

in exacting judgment for the idolatrous worship of the golden calf, struck down 23,000 idolaters; although he summoned Aaron, he did not summon the people (EXODUS 32). Also when the children of Israel were initiated to Baalphegor, by the Lord's command Moses hanged the leaders of the people on gallows and struck down 24,000 souls (NUMBERS 25).

Furthermore, Phinehas, moved by the zeal of the Lord, stabbed to death both Zimri, the son of Salu, and Cozbi, daughter of Zur, a prince of Midian, with the same spear-thrust as they lay together. The Lord was pleased by this deed and warmly commended Phinehas. Likewise Matathias, burning with zeal for the law (I MACCABEES 2) butchered the Israelite offering a sacrifice to an idol upon an altar and slew the king's officer who compelled the Israelites to sacrifice. Thus the people of Israel by the Lord's command almost annihilated the tribe of Benjamin to avenge their disgrace (JUDGES 20). Thus in the same fashion the children of Israel smote the Midianites (NUMBERS 31) and the Canaanites (throughout the book of JOSHUA), and thus Saul smote the Amalekites (I SAMUEL 15).

Many others have been slaughtered by the Lord's command. Thus St. Paul, filled with the Holy Spirit, condemned Elymas the magician with very harsh words and physically blinded him (ACTS 13).[1] He excommunicated the Corinthian living in open sin with his father's wife, although he was absent, and delivered him over to Satan for the destruction of the flesh, that his spirit might be saved. Moreover, St. Paul, writing to TIMOTHY, insisted that nothing should be done without previous judgment and immediately determined when, and when not, such previous judgment or examination might be necessary; hence he divides sins into those which are manifest and those which are secret so that he may indicate that no investigation is needed where sins are

---

[1] See p. 301.

137

in occultis autem sine praeexaminatione non posse fieri judicium. Ait
ergo I TIM. v:[1] *Quorundam hominum peccata manifesta sunt praecedentia
ad judicium, quorundam autem et subsequuntur.* Ubi NICOLAUS DE
LYRA ait:[2] *Manifestat apostolus quoddam superius dictum. Dixerat*
5 *enim quod Timotheus nihil ageret sine diligenti examinatione praevia. Ideo
declarat quae sint illa quae indigent tali discussione dici.* "*Quorundam
hominum peccata manifesta sunt*" *ex evidentia facti et talia non indigent
actione, testificatione, seu examinatione. Ideo subditur:* "*praecedentia ad
judicium,*" *id est examinationem, quia per se sunt notoria, et sic punienda*
10 *sine discussione.* Haec Lyra[a].

Sed et salvator noster Christus ementes in templo et vendentes, JOAN.
ii[3] et MATTH. xxi,[4] verbis corripiens et flagello, de domo Domini
eiciens castigavit. In quibus omnibus aliisque quampluribus[b] punitiones
fore facientium legimus nullam vero judicialem punitorum vocationem,
15 nullam[c] eorundem concessam defensionem[d] legimus praccessisse. Sic
etiam secundum legem, NUM. xxxv:[5] Ultor proximi sanguis effusi
homicidam extra urbem refugii, priusquam summus pontifex moreretur,
casualiter inventum occidere poterat sine culpa. Nec refert, quod
quidam ex supradictis puniti sunt non vocati et indefensi, quia in crimine
20 actu deprehensi, sufficit enim quod in aliquo casu puniri potest laudabiliter non vocatus nec defensus, et ita, saltem in illo casu, nullo juri
obviat, cujus contrarium rebelles clamant.

Quod si causam sciscitari[e] placuerit, cur liceat taliter deprehensum in
crimine punire indefensum, credo, quod alia efficacior causa, si veritas
25 colitur, assignari non valet, nisi quia in hujusmodi deprehenso crimine
notorium est, et nulla potest tergiversatione celari. Quod[f] si verum est,

---

[a] *om. M V*   [b] compluribus *T H*   [c] *add.* de *T H*   [d] devotionem *M*   [e] suscitari *M*
[f] Quis *M*

[1] *I Tim.* 5, 24.
[2] *Biblie iampridem renovate* . . . , VI, f. 221[r].
[3] *Joan.* 2, 13–17.
[4] *Matth.* 21, 12–13.
[5] *Num.* 35, 26–28.

manifest. Judgment cannot be handed down upon secret sins without previous examination. Therefore St. Paul writes (I TIMOTHY 5): *There are people whose offenses have not yet overtaken them.* NICHOLAS OF LYRA glosses this text: *The apostle clarifies what he said previously. For he said that Timothy should do nothing without a thorough previous examination. Therefore he makes clear what matters require such examination: "There are men whose sins are so obvious" from the evidence of the case that they require no formal accusation, testimony, or examination. So he can add: "they run before them into court," or anticipate an examination, because such sins are so notorious that they ought to be punished without formal discussion.*

Moreover, Christ, our Savior, chastened those who bought and sold in the temple with words and a whip and ousted them from the house of God (JOHN 2 and MATTHEW 21). In all these instances and a host of others we read that punishments were inflicted without any real juridical summons of those punished and without any real hearing granted them preceding their condemnation. Thus according to the Mosaic law (NUMBERS 35) the man who avenged the blood of a neighbor could slay the murderer without guilt if he found him outside his city of refuge before the death of the high priest. It does not matter that some of the persons just mentioned were punished without a summons or a hearing, since they were apprehended in their crime; for it is permissible, even praiseworthy, in certain instances to punish one without a summons or without a hearing. Thus, at least in instances of this sort, no law is opposed no matter what the rebels cry out to the contrary.

But if someone asks why it is permissible to punish anyone apprehended thus in a crime without a defense, I believe no more effective reason can be given, if truth is cherished, than this: it is common knowledge that when one is apprehended in a crime of this sort it cannot be hidden by any evasion. If this is true, whenever a crime is sufficiently notorious so that

immo quia verum est, ergo ubicumque crimen sufficienter notorium est, ita ut nulla possit tergiversatione celari nec excusari, similiter non requiritur ad justam condemnationem vocatio criminosi, et concessio defensionis, cum ubi causa est eadem, idem just dicatur DE[a] CONSTITU-
5 TIONIBUS *Translato sacordotio*,[1] in GLOSSA,[2] tametsi in mere positivis, eo quod odia sunt constringenda, non oportet esse, sed potest esse idem jus ubi videtur esse eadem causa[a].

Ex quibus clare patet, quod dicere "quia nusquam legitur[b] Dominum punivisse peccatores nisi vocatos et defensos, secundum scripturae
10 testimonium"[3] scripturae divinae contrariatur aperte et per consequens est haeresis manifesta. Si vero quis dicat: Licet scriptura in praemissis exemplis punitorum vocationem et defensionem taceat praecessere, tamen temerarium est asserere, quod nulla scripturarum auctoritate ostendi poterit, nec probabili ratione. Quod iterum juri naturali non
15 obviet, immo consonet damnare criminosum notorie sine vocatione. Ex eo manifestum est, quoniam Deus et natura, secundum PHILO-SOPHUM,[4] nihil[c] faciunt[d] frustra; idea nec ratio naturalis dictat aliquid fieri debere frustra; immo oppositum dictat, nihil, scilicet frustra debere fieri. Sed frustra servatur judiciarius ordo in crimine sufficienter notorio,
20 quantum ad illam causam pertinet, quoniam ad hoc requiritur judiciarius ordo, cujus partes sunt vocatio et defensio rei, ut veritas causae inno-tescat judici et his, quorum interest, cognoscere; qua certe cognita, judex partibus reddat justiciae complementum, quoniam secundum PHILOSOPHUM, I ETHICORUM:[5] *Unusquisque bene judicat, quae*
25 *cognoscit; et horum est bonus judex.* Et in PROV. cap. xii dicitur:[6] *Judex, qui judicat, quod novit, judex justiciae est.* Dum ergo causa sufficienter

---

[a–a] *om.* M V   [b] legimus T H   [c] nil H   [d] facuit M

[1] c. 3, X (1,2) (RF II, 8).
[2] Cf. *Decretales Gregorii Noni Pont. Max.* . . . , 10.
[3] Cf. p. 130.
[4] Cf. Aristoteles, *Opera, Phys.*, L. II, c. 4, 196a; L. II, c. 8, 199a.
[5] Aristoteles, *Opera, Nico. Eth.*, L. I, c. 3, 1094b–1095a.
[6] *Prov.* 12, 17.**

it may not be hidden or excused by any evasion, in like fashion the summoning of the guilty man is not necessary for an equitable condemnation. Neither must a hearing be granted. Where the case is the same, the same law applies (*Translato sacerdotio*, DE CONSTITUTIONIBUS and its gloss; but in positive law notoriety is not necessary, since the same law applies in emergencies when that law only appears to be involved).

From these examples, it is quite clear that the assertion "because it has never been proven from Scripture that the Lord punished sinners without a summons and a hearing" is openly contradicted in Holy Scripture and is consequently overt heresy. If perchance someone objects: granted that Scripture in the preceding examples says nothing of any summons or hearing before their condemnation, nevertheless it is foolhardy to assert that this position cannot be demonstrated by any scriptural authority or any probable reason. Once more this position does not contradict natural law; indeed, natural law agrees in condemning a notorious criminal without a summons. Thus it is evident that since God and nature do nothing in vain, according to ARISTOTLE, so natural reason does not dictate that anything must be done in vain; indeed it dictates the contrary, namely, that nothing must be done in vain. But due process is observed in vain when a crime sufficiently notorious is involved. For the due process which includes the summons and hearing of the accused is only required so that the truth of the case may become known to the judge and those the case concerns; thus the judge renders full justice to all parties in the case, because in the words of ARISTOTLE (Book I, ETHICS): *Each man judges well those matters with which he is acquainted; it is of these that he is a competent judge.* It is written in Scripture (PROVERBS 12): *The judge who judges what he knows is a just judge.* When, therefore, the facts of a case are sufficiently known to the

nota est judici et partibus ac ceteris, quorum interest, frustra adhuc inquireretur. Alioquin post partis confessionem aut testium sufficientem depositionem, adjuc oporteret inquirere, quod absurdum reputatur, pariter et ridiculosum.

5 De jure autem positivo non oportet prolongare sermonem, cum jus pure positivum summum pontificem non astringit. Quoniam, ut habetur xxv, quaest. i *Ideo*[a] *permittente*, sect. *sacrosancta*:[1] *Sacrosancta romana ecclesia jus et auctoritatem sacris canonibus impartit*[b], *sed non eis alligatur*[c]. *Habet enim jus condendi canones, utpote quae caput est et cardo omnium* 10 *ecclesiarum, a cujus regula nemini dissentire licet. Ita ergo canonibus auctoritatem praestat, ut seipsam non subiciat eis, et cetera quae sequuntur.* Ideoque si ex certa scientia summus pontifex aliter vel contra jus positivum diffinit, praecipit[d] vel agit, omni cum reverentia hujuscemodi obtemperandum est diffinitionibus et mandatis. Verumtamen jus 15 positivum clarissime decernit in plerisque locis sufficienter[e] notoriis, ordinem judiciarium servare non oportere, notoria quoque examinata esse iterum[f] non[f] examinanda, propter quod etiam processus in notoriis sine judiciario ordine habiti, contra multos imperatores, reges, archiepiscopos, et episcopos sine vocatione privatos et depositos, in regulam 20 et exemplum futurorum, corpori sacrorum canonum sunt inserti, quorum prolixiorem recitationem transeo, favens brevitati. Loca tamen quaedam signo[g], ut qui vult legat ipse: ii, quaest. i, *Manifesta*,[2] et cap. sequenti[3] et cap. *Scelus* eadem quaestione et causa,[4] cap. *Romana*, DE CENSIBUS, Libro Sexto[5] in versis [sic] *notoria* in textu et in glossis;[6] *Ad nostram* iii,

---

[a] *om. M V*   [b] impartitur *T H*   [c] obligatur *V*   [d] sapit *T H*   [e] insufficienter *T H*
[f-f] non iterum *T H*   [g] designo *T H*

---

[1] c. 16, C. XXV, qu. 1 (RF I, 1011).
[2] c. 15, C. II, qu. 1 (RF I, 445).
[3] c. 16, C. II, qu. 1 (RF I, 445).
[4] c. 21, C. II, qu. 1 (RF I, 449).
[5] c. 1, VI (3,20) (RF II, 1056–1057).
[6] *Liber sextus decretalium d. Bonifacii Papae VIII* . . . , 386–389.

A DEFENSE OF APOSTOLIC OBEDIENCE

judge, the litigants, and others concerned in the case, further inquiry would be in vain. To require further inquiry after the confession of the accused and sufficient testimony of witnesses may be regarded as ridiculous and absurd.

I need not, however, labor my discussion of positive law, since positive law does not bind the Supreme Pontiff. As it is written in canon law (Cause xxv, question 1, *Ideo permittente* under the section *sacrosancta*): *The most holy Roman Church imparts power and authority to the sacred canons but it is not bound by them. For it has the authority to establish canons since it is the head and hinge of all the churches, from whose rule none may deviate. Therefore it bestows authority to the canons so that it does not subject itself to them, and so forth.* Hence, if the Supreme Pontiff defines, orders, or acts beyond or against positive law from certain knowledge, all definitions and commands of this sort must be obeyed with the utmost respect. Nevertheless, positive law does state with utter clarity, in many instances sufficiently well known, that there is no need to preserve due process and that notorious crimes already investigated ought not to be considered again. There are legal proceedings recorded in canon law which were conducted in instances of notoriety, without following due process, against many emperors, kings, archbishops, and bishops who were removed and deposed without a summons as a rule and example for their successors. For the sake of brevity, I will not recite these at length. But I will designate certain instances so that those who wish may consult them: Cause xi, question 1, *Manifesta*, and the following canon; canon *Scelus* in the same question and cause; canon *Romana*, DE CENSIBUS, in the DECRETALS under the word *notoria* in the text and its gloss; canon *Ad nostram*, title iii, DE JUREJURANDO; canon *Bonae*, DE

DEFENSORIUM OBEDIENTIAE APOSTOLICAE

DE JUREJURANDO,[1] cap. *Bonae*, primo DE ELECTIONE,[2] cap. *Illud*, DE CLERICO EXCOMMUNICATO MINISTRANTE;[3] *Ad apostolicae*, DE SENTENTIA ET[a] RE JUDICATA[b], Libro Sexto,[4] xxi dist. *In tantum*[5] et in aliis pluribus locis.

5 Placuit[c] nihilominus verbum beati BERNARDI ad propositum nostrum apertissime loquentis inserere, quod in canonicae scripturae auctoritate fundans, ad Eugenium papam, lib. I, DE CONSIDERA-TIONE, ita scribit:[6] *Aliis alias multas causas poteris committere termi-nandas, quamplures ne[d] audientia dignas judicare. Quid enim opus est* 10 *admittere illos, "quorum peccata manifesta sunt praecedentia ad judi-cium."*[7] Et sequitur:[8] *Si Christi discipulus es, ignoscat [sic] zelus tuus, exurgat auctoritas adversus impudentiam hanc. Intuere magistrum sic facientem, et audi dicentem:*[9] *"Qui mihi ministrat, me sequatur." Non parat aures, ut audiat, sed flagellum, quo feriat. Verba nec facit, nec recipit.* 15 *Nec enim sedet judicans, sed insequitur puniens. Causam tamen non tacet, quod videlicet domum orationis negotiationis fecissent; ergo "et tu fac similiter."*[10] Haec BERNARDUS[c].

Ex quibus ad supradictorum confirmationem irrefragabilem patet, quod dicere, quod damnare sufficienter notorium non[e] vocatum[e] et inde-20 fensum obviat legi divinae et naturali, et ideo injustum est[f], sapit haere-sim manifestam. Cum etenim romanorum pontificum et universalium conciliorum decretis, corpori juris insertis, et per consequens ab uni-versali ecclesia approbatis, sancitum est, licite et juste, sufficienter

---

[a] *add.* DE *M V*   [b] in *M*, iii *V*   [c-c] *om. M V*   [d] vero   [e-e] *om. M V*   [f] *add.* et *T H*

[1] c. 21, X (2,24) (RF II, 367).
[2] c. 23, X (1,6) (RF II, 66–68).
[3] c. 5, X (5,77) (RF II, 828–830).
[4] c. 2, VI (2,14) (RF II, 1008–1011).
[5] c. 9, D. XXI (RF I, 72).
[6] c. 10 (*PL* 182, 741A).
[7] *I Tim.* 5, 24.
[8] c. 11 (*PL* 182, 741B–742A).
[9] *Joan.* 12, 26.*
[10] *Luc.* 10, 37.

A DEFENSE OF APOSTOLIC OBEDIENCE

ELECTIONE; canon *Illud,* DE CLERICO EXCOMMUNICATO MINISTRANTE; canon *Ad apostolicae,* DE SENTENTIA ET RE JUDICATA, in the DECRE-TALS; distinction xxi, canon *In tantum;* and many others as well.

Nonetheless, we may include the words of ST. BERNARD, founded in the authority of canonical Scripture, who speaks most directly to our problem when he writes to Pope Eugenius (DE CONSIDERATIONE, Book I): *You can entrust many cases to subordinates for settlement; a great many, those "whose offenses are so obvious that they run before them into court," do not merit a hearing.* He continues: *If you are a true disciple of Christ, let your zeal be kindled and your authority exerted against this impudence. Consider the deeds of the Master and hear him when he says: "Anyone who serves me must follow me." He does not open his ears that he may hear but he seizes a whip that he may scourge them out of the temple. He does not banter words back and forth, for he does not sit to judge their case but pursues them to chastise them. Nevertheless, he did not conceal the cause of his wrath, telling them that they had made the house of prayer into a market-place. Therefore, "go and do as he did."*

From this evidence, which presents indisputable verification of what we have asserted, it is clear that it is overt heresy to assert that the condemnation of one sufficiently notorious without a summons and without a

145

DEFENSORIUM OBEDIENTIAE APOSTOLICAE

notorium sine vocatione et concessa defensione condemnari posse. Si id
injustum est et legi[a] divinae et naturali contrarium, sequitur universalem ecclesiam in his, quae fidei sunt et morum, errasse, quod articulo
symboli, *Et unam sanctam ecclesiam*[b] *catholicam et apostolicam ecclesiam,*
5 ut supra deductum est,[1] contradicit.

    Et mirum satis est, quomodo audeant[c] damnationem indefensi notorii
velut rem novam coram simplicibus admirari, cum tamen frequenter et
apud clericos et apud laicos hujusmodi practicantur. Si nempe beneficia-
tus[d] aut ad dignitatem quamlibet etiam episcopalem vel archiepiscopa-
10 lem electus et assumptus contrahit publice matrimonium, statim sine
ejus vocatione, ad beneficium vel dignitatem quam possedit, alius
promovetur. Sic habens curatum beneficium si aliud curatum acceptat,
incompatibile primo, sine dispensatione collator primi beneficii alteri id
confert, possessore priore non vocato. Sic[e] si ad parochiam promotus
15 infra annum se ad sacerdotium non faciat promoveri, clara sunt jura.
Sic quoad laicos, si subditi tributa in termino constituto suis dominis
aut communitatibus, quibus subsunt, non solvunt, eis nec vocatis nec
defensis de habitationibus suis, aliquando etiam effractis seris, pignora
efferuntur[f]. Sic qui vocati ad communia servitia venire negligunt,
20 indefensi puniuntur, secundum consuetudinem multarum regionum,
civitatum, et villarum. Solent quoque domini feudorum, si vasalli infra
terminum certum a lege vel consuetudine statutum homagium facere,
et feudum ab eo acceptare contemnunt, lapso termino, istis non vocatis,
alios infeudare. Similia multa ad propositum adduci possent.

---

[a] lege *T H* [b] *om. T H* [c] audiant *T* [d] beneficiatu *M*, beneficiatum *V*
[e] Si *M* [f] efferentur *M*

[1] Vide p. 70.

hearing is contrary to divine and natural law and henceforth unjust. A sufficiently notorious wrongdoer may be condemned without granting a summons or a hearing, because it is correctly established in the decree of Roman pontiffs and general councils included in the body of canon law and consequently approved by the Church Universal. If such a condemnation is unjust and opposed to divine and natural law, it follows that the Church Universal has erred in those matters which concern faith and morals. But this contradicts the article of the Creed, *one holy Catholic and Apostolic Church*, as we have previously demonstrated.

It is quite extraordinary, since this sort of procedure is frequently employed among the clergy and the laity, that these men dare to express amazement at the condemnation of a notorious wrongdoer without a defense as if it were a novelty introduced among simple folk. Assuredly if one who enjoys a benefice or one who has been elected and elevated to the see of a bishop or an archbishop openly marries, another is immediately appointed to the benefice or see which the former occupied without summoning him to account. Thus if the holder of a benefice involving the cure of souls accepts another cure incompatible with the first, the collator of the first benefice confers it without any thought upon another and does not summon the previous occupant to defend himself. So too the laws are clear with respect to one named to a parish who does not take priestly orders without one year's time. With regard to the laity, if subjects do not pay taxes within the allotted period of time to their lords or the officials of the city to which they are subject, security for the unpaid taxes is confiscated from the subjects' homes without any summons or hearing—sometimes even if locks must be broken. Those who when called fail to fulfill their feudal military obligation are punished without a defense according to the customary law of many regions, cities, and fiefs. Many feudal lords are also accustomed, if their vassals do not render homage within a certain time fixed by law or custom, and if they neglect to receive their fiefs from them when the fixed time has passed, to grant these fiefs to others without summoning the former occupants. Many similar instances could be cited for my purposes.

147

DEFENSORIUM OBEDIENTIAE APOSTOLICAE

Appellatio perinde[a], ut dicitur per dominum Dietherum "ad papam melius informandum" interposita nullum ab obedientia processum apostolicorum poterit excusare. Tum quia a notorio appellari[b] canones sacri prohibent, neque deferendum fore tradunt, ut in cap. *Consuluit*, 5 primo,[c] DE APPELLATIONIBUS,[1] et cap. *Cum speciali*,[2] et cap. *Cum sit*, sect. ii[3] et cap. *Pervenit*, eodem titulo.[4] Tum quia ab appellatione recessit per contrarios actus, dum publico edicto contumacissimo pariter et crudelissimo, sub poenis ultimis litteras et mandata serenissimi[d] domini nostri, ad quem appellavit, recipi prohibuit, nuntios capi, atque 10 captos suis demandavit vinculis praesentari, dumque juris viam deserens[e], viam facti assumpsit, violenter obedientes ecclesiae armis invasit, sicut et facere non desinit de praesenti; ideo beneficio apostolicae sedis se[f] reddidit indignum ut[g] in cap.[g] *An sit*, DE APPELLATIONIBUS[5] et cap. *Quia frustra*, DE USURIS.[6] Cum praeterea per appellationem, quam 15 interponit excommunicatus, nequaquam ab excommunicatione, quam prius inciderat, absolvitur, siquidem appellatio legitime interposita ab excommunicatione, quae post appellationem legitimam fertur, defendit appellantem, non ab ea, quam prius inciderat; ut in cap. *Per tuas*, DE SENTENTIA EXCOMMUNICATIONIS.[7] Notorium quoque sit dominum 20 Dietherum dudum ante appellationem suam excommunicatum et denuntiatum in urbe et in partibus extitisse, et a nonnullis longe priusquam privaretur tamquam excommunicatus vitatum fuisse, quomodo usque hodie non absolutus esse[h] divinis ingerit, profanus quoque clerus suus inexcusabiliter sibi communicat temere et damnabiliter in divinis.

---

[a] proinde *M T H* [b] appellare *M V* [c] id est *T H* [d] sanctissimi *V* [e] deserans *V*
[f] *om. T H* [g-g] *om. T H* [h] se *T H*

[1] c. 18, X (2,28) (RF II, 415).
[2] c. 61, X (2,28) (RF II, 437–438).
[3] c. 5, X (2,28) (RF II, 411).
[4] c. 13, X (2,28) (RF II, 413–414).
[5] c. 11, X (2,28) (RF II, 425).
[6] c. 14, X (5,19) (RF II, 815).
[7] c. 40, X (5,39) (RF II, 906–907).

A DEFENSE OF APOSTOLIC OBEDIENCE

Therefore the appeal which Graf Diether terms an appeal "to a pope better informed" can excuse no one from obeying papal decisions. Furthermore, the sacred canons do not permit a notorious wrongdoer to appeal nor do they state that such an appeal must be respected (canon *Consuluit*, DE APPELLATIONIBUS; canon *Cum speciali*; canon *Cum sit*, section 2, and canon *Pervenit* under the same title). Moreover, he has compromised his appeal by deeds which contradict the appeal. He has forbidden under the threat of death the letters and decrees of his Most Serene Highness, our lord, to whom he appealed to be delivered in an extremely insolent and savage public edict; he has ordered the Pope's messengers to be seized and presented before him in chains; and, abandoning the path of justice, he has taken the path of action and has violently invaded with armed force the lands of those loyal to the Church and does not cease to do so at the present time. Therefore he has rendered himself unworthy of the favor of the Apostolic See as canon law attests (canon *An sit*, DE APPELLATIONIBUS, and canon *Quia frustra*, DE USURIS). Moreover, because one who has been excommunicated is in no respect released through any appeal which he makes from that excommunication, an appeal legally made from a sentence of excommunication incurred after a legal appeal does not indeed protect the appellant from those penalties which he previously incurred (canon *Per tuas*, DE SENTENTIA EXCOMMUNICATIONIS). It is also notorious that Graf Diether long before his appeal was publicly excommunicated and denounced in Rome and elsewhere, and that long before he was deposed, he was avoided by some as one excommunicated. It is also notorious that until the present, although not absolved, he tampers with the sacraments and his impious clergy inexcusably celebrate the sacraments in his

DEFENSORIUM OBEDIENTIAE APOSTOLICAE

In quo manifesta rebellio apparet, non juridica prosecutio interpositae appellationis.

Se denique meritum causae secundum regulam legis divinae rimemur, invenire non possumus, in quo apostolica sedes dominum Dietherum
5 gravarit, quam enim ei intulit injuriam, cum ea[a] quae notoria sunt in publicum deduxit? De manifestis autem, secundum sententiam venerabilis BEDAE,[1] nedum sedi apostolicae, sed cuilibet licet proximum judicare. Privavitque archiepiscopatu[b], qui nedum archiepiscopos[c], sed et archiepiscopatus instituere habet et revocare. Et quid egit? ab
10 onere grandi, cura gravi, periculo formidabili absolvit, ad quod aspirare stultum est, sine vocatione accedere praesumptio damnabilis, contra superioris voluntatem tenere argumentam nimiae temeritatis. Nam teste AUGUSTINO, lib. XIX DE CIVITATE DEI, cap. xix:[2] *Locus superior[d], sine quo regi populus non potest, etsi ita teneatur[e] atque administretur, ut*
15 *decet, indecenter tamen appetitur. Quamobrem otium sanctum quaerit caritas veritatis. Negotium justum suscipit necessitas caritatis. Quam sarcinam si nullus imponit, percipiendae atque intuendae vacandum est veritati. Si autem imponitur, suscipienda est[f] propter caritatis necessitatem.*

Sed forte dicis: Non hic de episcopali opere agitur, sed de principatu.
20 de[g] honore, de dominio, de terrarum possessione. Cui e regione respondeo, quisquis haec quaerit, et adepta temere tenet, opes, scilicet non episcopale opus, eo ipso indignus est episcopo, longe talis est a viro secundum cor Dei,[3] David loquor, qui egressus regiam civitatem Hierusalem fugiens Absalon filium suum, patris regnum injuste sibi usurpare molientem, ait
25 I REG. xiii:[4] *Si invenero gratiam in oculis Domini, reducet me. Si autem dixerit: "Non places," praesto.* Sed Saul ita est Saulis imitator,[5] qui et

---

[a] *om. M V*   [b] aut episcopatu *M V*   [c] aut episcopos *M V*   [d] superioris *M V*
[e] tenatur *V*   [f] *om. M V*   [g] *om. M V*

[1] Cf. c. 31, C. II, qu. 7 (RF I, 492–493).
[2] *CCh* 48, 687; *CSEL* 40², 407; *PL* 41, 647–648.
[3] Cf. *I Reg.* 13, 14.
[4] *II Reg.* 15, 25–26.
[5] Cf. *Act.* 9, 1–2; *Gal.* 1, 13.

presence in a rash and condemnable manner. In this sort of activity open rebellion is apparent, not the juridical prosecution of an appeal.

If finally we reconsider the merits of the case according to the standard of divine law, we cannot discover how the Apostolic See has wronged Graf Diether. What injury did it do him, since those crimes which he has openly committed are notorious? Yet when sins are evident, according to the view of the VENERABLE BEDE, not only the Apostolic See, but anyone may judge his neighbor. He deposed him from his episcopal throne who has not only the authority to elevate and recall archbishops, but to create and abolish their sees as well. What did the Pope do? He released him from a heavy burden, a serious concern, and a terrible danger which to aspire to is foolish, to approach without a calling is damnable presumption, and to sustain contrary to the will of one's superior is evidence of exceeding foolhardiness. For ST. AUGUSTINE declares (Book XIX, DE CIVITATE DEI, chapter 19): *The higher position required for governing the people, although it is held and administered in a proper manner, is improperly sought. Therefore the love of truth seeks holy leisure. The necessity of love undertakes a necessary burden. If no one imposes this burden, one has leisure for the pursuit and contemplation of truth. But if it is imposed, it must be undertaken for the necessity of love.*

But you may say: this does not concern episcopal office but secular rule, honor, dominion, and the possession of lands. To such I directly respond that whoever seeks these things and boldly defends such power once attained—I do not refer to the episcopal office, but secular authority —is thus unworthy to be a bishop, for such is far from being a man after the Lord's heart. I refer to David, who, when he abandoned the royal city of Jerusalem in his flight from his son, Absalom, who unjustly attempted to usurp his father's kingdom, said (II SAMUEL 15): *If I find favor in the eyes of the Lord, he will bring me back. But if he says, "I have no pleasure in you," here I am.* But Diether is the imitator of Saul,

DEFENSORIUM OBEDIENTIAE APOSTOLICAE

ipse per Dominum a regno depositus non recessit[a], magis autem in armorum potentia confisus persequebatur eum, quem Dominus elegerat; ideo sceleris proprii saevissimus ultor seipsum interficiens interiit, morte miserabili consummatus, I REG, ultimo.[1]

5   Ostenditur nihilominus propositio principalis ex alio principio sic breviter. In dubiis sedi apostolicae obediendum fore supra ostensum est.[2] Sed processum sedis apostolicae contra dominum Dietherum non esse injustum certum est cuilibet ejus notitiam habenti, vel ad minus esse injustum dubium est. Siquidem nullus quantumlibet simplex ac
10 rudis fuerit, potest rationabiliter non dubitare immo[b] non presumere[b] de justicia processus domini papae, si eam certam non habeat, pro qua semper praesumendum est, sicut et de justicia judicis inferioris—sicut tradit jus in cap. *Sicut*[c], DE SENTENTIA ET RE JUDICATA[3] et in[d] cap. *In praesentia*, DE RENUNCIATIONE[4]—etiam quantumcumque oblatret pars
15 domini Dietheri injuriam pertulisse. Tum quia plurimi in utroque jure periti, divino pariter et humano, viri bonae famae et opinionis, religiosi denique, observantiae sanctae cultores, cum dispendio rerum et corporis periculo, nulla spe terrenae remunerationis ducti, processibus apostolicis obediunt, dominum[e] Dietherum[e] cum sibi adhaerentibus tamquam
20 excommunicatos vitantes. De quorum numero sunt fratres Carthusienses, Benedictini, Cistercienses, regulares canonici, Carmelitae, Praedicatores, fratres beati[f] Francisci, etiam in terris ac dominiis rebellium commorantes. Quorum nonnulli monasteria, beneficia, domus[g], possessiones, et omnia temporalia relinquentes, exulare[h] magis elegerunt,
25 quam cum inobedientia ac apostolicorum transgressione mandatorum suis in pace frui, de quibus omnino praesumi non potest, quod ignorantia, levitate, aliave sinistra occasione permoti a juris veritatisque tramite

---

[a] cessit *T H*   [b-b] *om. T H*   [c] *Sic T H*   [d] *om. T H*   [e-e] domino Diethero *T H*
[f] *add.* beati *V*   [g] domos *V*   [h] exultare *T H*

---

[1] *I Reg.* 31, 4–5.
[2] Vide p. 118.
[3] c. 16, X (2,27) (RF II, 401).
[4] c. 6, X (1,9) (RF II, 104–106).

152

who, deposed from his kingdom by the Lord, confident in his armed strength, persecuted him whom the Lord had chosen. Therefore as a most terrible avenger of his own crime he committed suicide, thus ending his wretched life in a miserable death (I SAMUEL 31).

Nevertheless, my principal proposition may be briefly demonstrated upon other grounds. We have previously shown that the Apostolic See must be obeyed when there is occasion for doubt. But the proceedings of the Apostolic See against Graf Diether are clearly not unjust to any who know him or, at least, it is doubtful that they are unjust. Indeed none, no matter how naive and ignorant he may be, can reasonably question or form his own conclusions concerning the justice of the proceedings of our lord, the Pope, if he lacks full knowledge—which ought always to be assumed just as one regards the justice of an inferior judge with reserve, as canon law states (canon *Sicut*, DE SENTENTIA ET RE JUDICATA and canon *In praesentia*, DE RENUNCIATIONE)—no matter how loudly the faction of Diether snarls that he has suffered an injustice. Furthermore, many who are skilled in canon law and civil law, men of good character and sound judgment, clergy who seek to observe a strict ecclesiastical rule, although led by no hope of earthly reward and threatened with loss of their goods and with peril to their bodies, obey the papal decrees and avoid Graf Diether and his adherents as excommunicate. These include Carthusians, Benedictines, Cistercians, canons regular, Carmelites, Dominicans, and Franciscans who remain in the lands and domains of the rebels. Some of these have abandoned their monasteries, benefices, homes, possessions, and all temporal goods, and have chosen exile rather than peaceful enjoyment of their property through the disobedience and transgression of papal mandates. It cannot be presumed that all these, led by ignorance, shallowness, or other wrong causes, deviated from the path of truth and justice. However, there are

DEFENSORIUM OBEDIENTIAE APOSTOLICAE

deviarent; pauci vero, si tamen aliqui in parte Dietheri inveniantur, quod elatio, cupiditas, carnalis propinquitas vel affectio, aut improbum temporale corporis commodum in rebellionem sedis apostolicae irretivit. Sed et archiepiscopi et episcopi, quorum multi extra hanc causam
5 domino Diethero favebant plurimum, obedientiam apostolicae sedis, sicut tenentur, in dicta privatione Dietheri affectioni praeferunt et favori. Quin immo universitates in dominio rebellium constitutae, licet a quibusdam poenis in processibus apostolicis contentis[a] appellarunt, protestantur tamen aperte et fatentur, quod sententia privationis
10 domini Dietheri, et provisionis[b] domini Adolphi ab inferioribus judicanda non sit, sed magis ei devote et humiliter obtemperandum, ut in forma appellationis Heidelbergensium, et Erfordensium[c,1] clare patet[d]. Quae omnia et similia multa etiam indoctis[e] probabile dubium inducunt, verius vehementem praesumptionem de justicia actorum[f] per apostoli-
15 cam sedem, quo dubio stante de necessitate salutis tenentur omnes sic probabiliter dubitantes sedi apostolicae obedire.

PROPOSITIO SECUNDA

Quicumque dominum Dietherum post sufficientem[g] agnitam ejus privationem tamquam electum et confirmatum moguntinum verbo vel facto venerantur, et in sua rebellionis pertinacia defendunt[h], adhaerent,
20 fovent, assistunt, aut quomodolibet[i] consentiunt, tamquam ecclesiasticae postestatis et ordinationis divinae contemptores culpabiliter peccant, secumque eisdem censuris et maledictionibus illigantur.

Scientes[j] namque[k] dominum Dietherum et credentes privatum, et tamen ob metum vel favorem blandiendo, verbo vel facto talem asserunt,
25 qualem non esse credunt, perniciose mentiuntur, in scandalum videlicet

---

[a] concessus *V* [b] provisionum *M* [c] *om. T H* [d] *add.* cujus tenorem hic inserere non oportet *T H* [e] in doctis *V* [f] actoris *T H* [g] sufficienter *T H* [h] *om. V* [i] *om. T H* [j] scientetes *V* [k] namquam *M*

[1] Vide Gerhard Ritter, *Die Heidelberger Universität* (Heidelberg, 1936) I, 366–368; Ritter citat U.A. I, 3 f. 88ᵛ–90ʳ; U.B. II, 417; et Cod. Germ. Monac. 975, f. 181ᵛ–188ʳ.

few in Diether's faction, if indeed any can be found, whom pride, avarice, ties of blood and affection, or dishonest, temporal indulgence of the flesh have not ensnared into rebellion against the Apostolic See. Moreover, both bishops and archbishops, many of whom were exceedingly well disposed to Graf Diether before this conflict, prefer, in the deposition of Diether, the obedience of the Apostolic See, as they should, to Diether's affection and favor. And the universities situated in the lands of the rebels, although they have appealed against certain penalties included in the papal proceedings, avow publicly and acknowledge that the papal decision to depose Graf Diether and to elevate Graf Adolf should not be judged by more lowly folk, but rather should be heeded devoutly and humbly—as is quite evident in the appeals of Heidelberg and Erfurt.[1] All these considerations, or rather strong feelings, may cause doubt in the uninformed about the justice of the acts of the Apostolic See; but all who entertain such doubts are obligated for their salvation to obey the Apostolic See.

SECOND PROPOSITION

Those sufficiently informed of Graf Diether's deposition who do homage to him as the elected and confirmed occupant of the see of Mainz in word or deed, and who defend, support, sustain, aid him, or approve in any manner his stubborn revolt, sin criminally as people who scorn church authority and providential order and are included with him in the same censures and curses.

For those who know and admit that Graf Diether is deposed but nevertheless, because of fear or the desire to court favor, assert in word or deed that he is what they do not believe him to be, lie perniciously and

---

[1] See Introduction, p. 36.

155

DEFENSORIUM OBEDIENTIAE APOSTOLICAE

proximi, et damnum domini Adolphi, et per consequens contra legem divinam damnabiliter peccant, secundum illud PSAL.:[1] *Perdes omnes, qui loquuntur mendacium.* Quod si consentiunt[a] eum in sua rebellione fovendo aut defendendo pari poena puniendi, teste apostolo ROM. 1, qui

5 cum inobedientiam et plurima crimina, Romanis scribens, enumerasset, addidit[b]:[2] *Qui talis agunt digni sunt morte, non solum qui ea faciunt[c], sed qui consentiunt facientibus.* Cui concordat beatus ISIDORUS dicens:[3] *Qui consentiunt peccantibus, et defendit alium delinquentem, maledictus erit apud Deum et homines, et corripietur increpatione severissima. Hinc*

10 *etiam quidam sanctissimus pater ait:* "*Si quis peccantem defendit, acrius quam ille, qui peccavit[d], coerceatur.*" *Hinc etiam alius pater ait[e]:* "*Si qui alterius errori consentit, sciat se cum illo simili modo culpabilem judicandum,* xi[f], quaest. iii, *Qui consentit,* addit GLOSSA:[4] *Per cooperationem et auctoritatem[f].* Participans denique excommunicato in crimine

15 eidem sententiae innodatur, eo quod facientem et consentientem par poena constringat, ut dicit lex in cap. *Nuper,* DE SENTENTIA EXCOMMUNICATIONIS[5] et cap. *Si concubinae* eodem titulo.[6]

PROPOSITIO TERTIA

Sacerdotes et clerici saeculares aut regulares, dicto privato aut suis complicibus adhaerentes, in locis interdictis et coram excommunicatis,

20 ipsi excommunicati celebrantes, irregulares sunt et profani, populumque Dei perniciose decipiunt, et divina contaminant sacramenta.

---

[a] *add.* efficaciter per cooperationem et auctoritatem *T H* [b] addit *V* [c] facuit *M*
[d] peccat *M V* [e] *om. M V* [f–f] *om. M V*

---

[1] *Psal.* 5, 7.
[2] *Rom.* 1, 32.
[3] c. 100, C. XI, qu. 3 (RF I, 671).
[4] *Gratiani Decreta cum glossis,* f. 324[r].
[5] c. 29, X (5,39) (RF II, 900–901).
[6] c. 55, X (5,39) (RF II, 912).

become a stumbling block to their neighbors and a source of harm to Graf Adolf. Consequently they sin damnably against the divine law, in the words of the Psalmist: *Thou destroyest those who speak lies.* For those who lend him approval by fostering and defending his rebellion must be punished equally with him, as the apostle declared when he wrote to the Romans and listed disobedience and many other faults (ROMANS 1): *Those who do such things deserve to die, not only these, but those who applaud them.* ST. ISIDORE agrees with St. Paul: *He who approves sinners and defends another in transgressions will be accursed in the presence of God and men and will be reproached with the harshest rebuke. A certain most holy Father said, "If anyone defends one who sins, let him be chastised more severely than the sinner." Another Father says, "If anyone consents to the error of another, let him understand that he must be judged guilty to an equal extent."* The GLOSS adds: *He consents through sanction and support.* Finally, he who abets one who has been excommunicated in his wrongdoing falls under the same sentence, since in canon law an equal punishment falls upon the one who acts and the one who consents (canon *Nuper*, DE SENTENTIA EXCOMMUNICATIONIS, and canon *Si concubinae* under the same title).

THIRD PROPOSITION

Those priests and members of the secular and regular clergy who adhere to the deposed Diether and his allies and who, excommunicated themselves, celebrate the sacraments in forbidden places and in the presence of those excommunicate, are impious and disobedient to their rule; they deceive the people of God perniciously and defile the holy sacraments.[1]

---

[1] Cf. "Biel's Letter to the Church at Mainz under Interdict," Oberman, *Harvest of Medieval Theology*, pp. 26–29.

DEFENSORIUM OBEDIENTIAE APOSTOLICAE

Quid execrabilius ac blasphemum magis quam sacramentum unitatis ecclesiae tractari extra ecclesiae unitatem, DE CONSECRATIONE, dist. ii, *Hoc sacramentum.*[1] Ac summae sacrificium obedientiae—de quo apostolus AD PHIL. ii:[2] *Factus est obediens patri usque ad mortem, mortem*
5 *autem crucis*—contumaci rebellione contra sacrorum instituta canonum tractare, propter quod sine dubio apostolicam incidunt sententiam, contra[a] indigne sumentes eucharistiam, aeterno dignos judicio, I COR. xi,[3] et reos corporis Domini et sanguinis condemnavit[b]. *Neque,* ait[c] idem apostolus[d], *calicem Domini bibere potestis et calicem demoniorum, non*
10 *potestis mensae domini participes esse et mensae demoniorum,* I COR. x.[4] Quis autem magis mensam demoniorum participat, nisi qui per inobedientiam contra superiores et maxime caput ecclesiae superbiens censuras contemnit, divisionem[e] facit, schismata generat, pacem corporis Christi ac conexionem membrorum cum capite, quantum in eo est,
15 violat atque rumpit? Quod beatus AUGUSTINUS in DE VERBIS APOSTOLI, sermone lxxviii, et habetur xi, quaest. iii, *Omnis,*[5] innuit, cum dicit: *Omnis christianus, dilectissimi, qui a sacerdotibus excommunicatur, Satanae traditur. Quomodo? quia, scilicet extra ecclesiam est diabolus, sicut in ecclesia Christus. Ac per hoc quasi diabolo traditur, qui ab ecclesiae*
20 *communione removetur. Unde illos quos apostolus Satanae esse traditos praedicat, a se excommunicatos esse demonstrat.*

Quae excommunicatio, quantum sit cuilibet fideli timenda, idem SUPER JOANNEM[f] scribens ait:[6] *Nihil sic debet formidare christianus[g] quam separari a corpore Christi. Si enim separatur a corpore Christi, non*
25 *est membrum ejus. Si non est membrum ejus, non vegetatur spiritu ejus.*

---

[a] qua *T H*   [b] *add.* Sed *T H*   [c] ut *T H*   [d] *add.* inquit *T H*   [e] divisiones *T H*
[f] AUGUSTINUS *V*   [g] *om. V T H*

[1] c. 63, D. II, *De cons.* (RF I, 1337).
[2] *Phil.* 2, 8.*
[3] *I Cor.* 11, 27.
[4] *I Cor.* 10, 21.*
[5] c. 32, C. XI, qu. 3 (RF I, 653), non invenitur in Augustino.
[6] c. 33, C. XI, qu. 3 (RF I, 653); *Tract. 27 in Joan. evang.,* §6 (CCh 6, 272–273; PL 35, 1618).

A DEFENSE OF APOSTOLIC OBEDIENCE

What can be more execrable or greater blasphemy than the celebration of the sacrament that signifies ecclesiastical unity outside the unity of the Church (DE CONSECRATIONE, distinction ii, *Hoc sacramentum*). In celebrating the sacrifice of ultimate obedience—of which the Apostle wrote (PHILIPPIANS 2): *He became obedient to the Father unto death, even death on a cross*—in stiff-necked revolt against the instructions of canon law, without a doubt they incur the sentence of the Apostle against those who unworthily receive the Eucharist; Paul regarded such celebration as worthy of eternal damnation and as desecration of the body and blood of the Lord (I CORINTHIANS 11). Paul also insisted (I CORINTHIANS 10): *You cannot drink the cup of the Lord and the cup of demons. You cannot partake of the Lord's table and the table of demons.* But who partakes more of the table of demons than he who through disobedience to his superiors and especially the head of the Church defies censures, creates division, fosters schisms, and violates and breaks the peace of the body of Christ and the union of the head and members, to the limit of his power? ST. AUGUSTINE suggested this when he wrote (DE VERBIS APOSTOLI, Sermon lxxviii, which is found in canon law, Cause xi, question 3, *Omnis*): *Every Christian, dearly beloved, who is excommunicated by the priests is consigned to Satan. How can this be? Because the Devil is plainly outside the Church as Christ is within the Church. Thus he who is removed from the communion of the Church is consigned to the Devil. Therefore, the Apostle demonstrates that those who he declares are consigned to Satan are excommunicated from the Church.*

ST. AUGUSTINE suggests how much every devout Christian must fear this excommunication in his *Commentary on the Gospel of John: A Christian ought to fear nothing more than separation from the body of Christ. If he is separated from the body of Christ, he is not a member of Christ. If he is not a member of Christ, he is not quickened by the Spirit of Christ. For the*

159

DEFENSORIUM OBEDIENTIAE APOSTOLICAE

"Quisquis autem," inquit apostolus ROM. viii,[1] *"spiritum Christi non habet, hic non est ejus."* Et CHRYSOSTOMUS SUPER MATTHEUM xi, quaest. iii, *Nemo:*[2] *Nemo contemnat vincula ecclesiastica. Non enim homo est, qui ligat, sed Christus, qui hanc potestatem dedit, et dominos*[a]
5 *fecit homines esse tanti honoris.*

Audiant denique cum tanto contemptu sacramenta[b] sumentes prophetam dicentem JERE. xi,[3] AGGEI ii:[4] *Numquid carnes sanctae auferent a te malitiam tuam, in quibus gloriata es?* Si[c] anima polluta edens ex carnibus hostiae pacificorum divina sententia jussa est exterminari
10 de populo, LEVIT. vii,[5] quid fiet de anima excommunicata, a sacramentorum communione separata, quae manducat de hac hostia, *per quam pacificata sunt omnia, et quae in caelis sunt et quae super terram,* AD COL. i.[6] Timeant necesse est, ne justo Dei judicio patiantur in anima, incendium ignis inextinguibilis, quod passi sunt Chore et congregatio
15 sua ccl viri[d], dum eos imitantes sicut illi, ut habetur NUM. vi[e],[7] in officio sibi indebito non[f] desinunt[f] sacra[g] profanare. Statuit[h] quoque universalis ecclesia in concilio Martini papae[h]:[8] *Si quis episcopus in concilio excommunicatus fuerit, sive presbyter aut diaconus a suo episcopo, et post excommunicationem praesumpserit*[i]—*sive episcopus ille aut presbyter vel*
20 *diaconus—facere oblationem, vel matutinum vel vespertinum sacrificium quasi in officio sua agere sicut prius, non liceat*[j] *ei*[k] *nec in alio concilio* [sic] *spem reconciliationis habere, nec ultra reconciliari. Sed etiam eos qui*

---

[a] Dominus *T H,* dignos *V*   [b] sacra *T H*   [c] *add.* vero *T H*   [d] *om. M V*
[e] *add.* non desinunt *T H*   [f-f] *om. T H*   [g] *om. M V*
[h-h] Item ex consilio Martini papae, xi, quaest. iii *T H*   [i] praesumptionem *M V*
[j] licet *V*   [k] *om. M V*

---

[1] *Rom.* 8, 9.
[2] c. 31, C. XI, qu. 3 (RF I, 653); *Hom. 4 in epist. ad Hebraeos,* §6 (*PG* 63, 45).
[3] *Jerem.* 11, 15.
[4] *Aggeus* 2, 14.
[5] *Levit.* 7, 20.
[6] *Colos.* 1, 20.**
[7] *Num.* 16, 35.
[8] c. 7, C. XI, qu. 3 (RF I, 644–645).

A DEFENSE OF APOSTOLIC OBEDIENCE

Apostle says (*ROMANS 8*): "*A man who does not possess the Spirit of Christ is no member of Christ.*" ST. CHRYSOSTOM also writes in his *Commentary on St. Matthew* (Cause xi, question 3, *Nemo*): *Let no man disregard the bonds of the Church. For it is not man who binds, but Christ who has given this authority and has placed men in such high estate.*

Therefore, let those who partake of the sacraments with such scorn hear the words of the prophet (JEREMIAH 11; HAGGAI 2): *Shall the sacrificial flesh remove from you the crime in which you exulted?* If an unclean soul eating of the flesh of the peace offerings was ordered banished from his people by the Lord's command (LEVITICUS 7), what should be done with the excommunicate, separated from the communion of the sacraments, who eats of this sacrificial offering *through whom all things were given peace, whether on earth or in heaven?* They should fear lest they experience the merited wrath of God in their souls, the unquenchable conflagration that consumed Korah and two hundred and fifty of his supporters (NUMBERS 6), when they follow Korah's example and continue to desecrate what is holy in an office not properly theirs. The Church Universal declared in a council under Pope Martin:[1] *If a bishop who is excommunicated by a council—or a presbyter or deacon excommunicated by his bishop—defiantly celebrates mass after his excommunication or takes part in morning and evening services and functions in his office as he did before he was excommunicated, he may not hope to be reconciled at*

---

[1] Martin I (649–655) actually convoked only a synod of 20 canons in the Lateran to deal with the Monothelite heresy.

ei communicaverint omnes ab ecclesia respui, maxime eos[a] *qui sciebant eum esse dejectum. Si autem permanserit turbans et concitans ecclesiam per forinsecam potestatem, oportet eum quasi seditionarium ab omni plebe expelli.*

5   Poenam etiam irregularitatis et depositionis incurrere, hujusmodi canon expressius depromit in cap. *Latores*, DE CLERICO EXCOMMUNICATO MINISTRANTE[1] et cap. *Postulastis*, eodem titulo[2] in textu et in GLOSSA.[3]

Non autem solum seipsos, sed et populum perniciose decipiunt, suis sceleribus facientes participare et execrandis suis ministeriis interesse.
10 Execranda eorum dicuntur ministeria, non quod immunda[b], polluta[b], aut non vera sint sacramenta, quae ministrant, excepto solo paenitentiae sacramento, quod excommunicatus aut suspensus eo, quod materia debita—quae est peccator subditus—sibi subtracta est, ministrare non potest, etiamsi attemptet de facto. Quoniam quidem sacerdos aut
15 episcopus quantumcumque suspensus fuerit, excommunicatus[c] vel depositus, si intentione debita et in forma ecclesiae baptizat, celebrat, confirmat[d] aut ordinat, licet sibi ad judicium, vere tamen facit quod attemptat.[4] Siquidem, AUGUSTINO in libro DE CORPORE DOMINI teste, *intra catholicam ecclesiam in mysterio*[e] *corporis et sanguinis Domini*
20 *nihil a bono magis, nihil a malo minus conficitur sacerdote, quia non in merito consecrantis, sed in verbo perficitur creatoris, et virtute Spiritus Sancti,* i, quaest. i, *Intra catholicam.*[5] Et AD DONATISTAS[f] scribens ait:[6] *Deus adest sacramentis et verbis suis, per quoslibet administrentur,*

---

[a] *om. M V*   [b–b] publuta aut immunda *M V*   [c] excommunicationibus *M V*
[d] conformat *M*   [e] ministerio *M V*   [f] DONASTICAS *T*

---

[1] c. 4, X (5,27) (RF II, 827–828).
[2] c. 7, X (5,27) (RF II, 830–831).
[3] *Decretales Gregorii Noni Pont. Max.* . . . , 1037–1038.
[4] Cf. *Canonis misse expositio Gabrielis Biel,* ed. H. A. Oberman and W. J. Courtenay (Wiesbaden, 1963–1967), vol. I, Lect. XXVI G, 244–245.
[5] c. 77, C. I, qu. 1 (RF I, 385); S. Paschasii Radberti, *De corp. et sang. Domini* (*PL* 120, 1310).
[6] c. 32, C. I, qu. 1 (RF I, 372); *De baptismo contra Donatistas,* L. V, c. 20 (*PL* 43, 190).

another council or at some later date. Moreover, all those who associate with
him, particularly those who know that he was condemned, must be cast out
of the Church. If he persists in disturbing and troubling the Church through
physical force, all the faithful should reject him as subversive.

Canon law declares even more clearly that men of this sort incur the
penalty of irregularity and deposition (canon *Latores*, DE CLERICO EX-
COMMUNICATO MINISTRANTE;[1] canon *Postulastis* under the same title
in both text and gloss).[2]

Such men perniciously deceive not only themselves but the people in
making them abet their crimes and participate in their accursed ministry.
Their ministry is termed accursed not because the sacraments which
they administer are unclean, defiled, or false, if one excepts the sacrament
of penance, but because he who has been excommunicated or suspended
cannot minister, although he attempts to do so, since the requisite conditions—the contrition of a sinner—have been withdrawn from him.
Therefore if a priest or bishop baptizes, celebrates mass, confirms, or
ordains with the proper intent and in due church form although he is
suspended, excommunicated, or deposed, and although he does so to his
own damnation, nevertheless he truly accomplishes what he attempts.
ST. AUGUSTINE bears witness to this in his book DE CORPORE
DOMINI (Cause i, question 1, *Intra catholicam*): *Within the Catholic*
Church in the mystery of the body and blood of the Lord nothing more is
accomplished by a good priest, and nothing less by a bad priest, because the
sacrament is perfected not by the merit of the one who consecrates, but through
the word of the Creator and through the power of the Holy Spirit. ST.
AUGUSTINE also wrote to the Donatists: *God is present in his words and*
sacraments. The sacraments and God's words remain efficacious no matter

---

[1] This canon is drawn from a letter of Alexander III (1159–1181) to the Archbishop of
Toledo which commands that an excommunicate celebrating mass under interdict be
deposed.

[2] This canon is drawn from a letter of Innocent III (1198–1216) to the dean and prior of
Cologne that declares that any cleric who celebrates the sacraments under interdict
loses his benefice.

DEFENSORIUM OBEDIENTIAE APOSTOLICAE

quorum sacramenta et verba recta sunt. Et beatus GREGORIUS pulchre
ad idem loquitur in cap. *Multi*, ubi supra, i, quaest, i.[1] Neque sacramenta
atque Dei dona in se per ministrorum malitiam contaminari valent aut
pollui, sicut AUGUSTINUS dicit et habetur ibidem cap. *Si justus*, cum
5 inquit:[2] *Qui superbus minister fuerit, cum zabulo computatur, sed non
contaminantur dona Christi per illum purus fluvius transit, et venit ad
fertilem terram. Scio*[a] *quia lapis ex aqua*[a] *fructum ferre non potest, et*[b] *per
lapideos canales transit aqua ad areolas*[c]*, et in canali lapideo nihil generatur,
sed ortus*[d] *plurimum fructum affert. Spiritualis enim*[e] *virtus sacramenti, ut*
10 *lux pura ab illuminandis excipitur, sed per immundos transiens non
inquinatur.* Et iterum ait ibidem, *Nec foris:*[3] *Nec foris, ergo nec intus
quisquam, qui ex parte diaboli est, potest in se vel in quolibet maculare
sacramentum, quod Christi est.*

Dicuntur tamen pollui et contaminari sacramenta in se semper munda
15 per malos ministros, quantum est ex parte ministrorum pro quanto ea
polluta conscientia, in peccatis mortalibus, irreverenter, indigne, et
contra ecclesiae prohibitionem, quasi rem vilam et immundam, tractant
et ministrant, quomodo MALACH. i,[4] per prophetam Dominus dicit de
malis sacerdotibus: *Offertis super altare meum panem pollutum.* Et
20 infra:[5] *Nomen meum magnum in gentibus, et vos polluistis illud.* Et
beatus HIERONYMUS SUPER AGGEUM, i, quaest. i, *Sic populus:*[6]
Sacrificia, ait, *quamvis sancta videantur specie sua, qua offeruntur, tamen
quia tractata sunt ab illo, qui pollutus est in anima, polluuntur omnia.* Et
GREGORIUS, i, quaest. i, *Multi*, ubi supra:[7] *Polluimus itaque panem, id*
25 *est corpus Christi, quando indigni accedimus ad altare, et sordidi sanguinem*

[a-a] Scioque ex aqua lapis *M V*   [b] sed *M V*   [c] aureolas *M T*   [d] hortus *H*
[e] vero *M V*

---

[1] c. 84, C. I, qu. 1 (RF I, 387–388).
[2] c. 30, C. I, qu. 1 (RF I, 371); *Tract. 5 in Joan. evang.*, §15 (*CCh* 36, 49–50; *PL* 35, 1422).
[3] c. 34, C. I, qu. 1 (RF I, 372).
[4] *Malach.* 1, 7.
[5] *Malach.* 1, 11–12.
[6] c. 61, C. I, qu. 1 (RF I, 381); *Comm. in Aggaeum*, c. 2 (*PL* 25, 1477C).
[7] c. 84, C. I, qu. 1 (RF I, 388).

who administers them. ST. GREGORY eloquently expresses the same truth (canon *Multi*, Cause i, question 1). The sacraments and the gifts of God can in themselves be neither defiled nor corrupted through the wickedness of those who administer them, as ST. AUGUSTINE says (Cause i, question 1, canon *Si justus*): *He who is an arrogant minister is considered to be with the Devil, but the gifts of Christ are not corrupted for they flow through him as a pure river and come to the fertile earth. I know that a watered stone cannot bear fruit, but through stony channels the water flows to garden plots. The water causes nothing to grow in the stony channel, but it brings much fruit to the gardens. For the spiritual virtue of the sacrament is like light which is received pure by those to be enlightened but which passes through the impure unstained.* Again ST. AUGUSTINE says (canon *Nec foris*): *No one within or without who is of the party of the Devil can stain in any manner the sacrament of Christ.*

Yet the sacraments, in themselves always pure, can be said to be corrupted and defiled by wicked ministers because these ministers celebrate and administer the sacraments with an unclean conscience, in mortal sin, irreverently, unworthily, and contrary to the Church's ban, as if the ban were a vile and impure thing. The Lord spoke through the prophet in this manner concerning wicked priests (MALACHI 1): *You offer polluted food upon my altar. My name is great among the nations, but you profane it.* ST. JEROME writes in his *Commentary on Haggai* (Cause i, question 1, *Sic populus*): *Although the holy sacrifices appear in the visible form in which they are offered, nevertheless, because they are celebrated by one defiled in soul, they are completely defiled.* ST. GREGORY writes (Cause i, question 1, *Multi*): *Accordingly, we defile the bread, the body of Christ, when we unworthily approach the altar and foully drink his pure*

mundum bibimus. Et quoniam talibus sacrificiis immundi Deum non placant, sed magis offendunt, merito execranda eorum ministeria tamquam offensiva Domini dici possunt.

PROPOSITIO QUARTA[a]

Cavendi sunt profani sacerdotes tamquam rapaces lupi, a quibus nec
5 divina audienda, nec quaecumque sacramenta excepto baptismate solo in necessitatis articulo aliquatenus sunt sumenda.

Quos per lupos designavi rapaces, fures dicere potui et latrones, secundum verbum Christi, JOAN.:[1] *Qui non intrat per ostium in ovile ovium sed aliunde, fur est atque latro.* In ovile ovium, quod est sancta
10 ecclesia catholica, *non intrat per ostium humile,* Christum videlicet[b], secundum AUGUSTINUM, homelia xlv SUPER JOANNEM,[2] qui suam, non Christi gloriam quaerit, qui se non humiliat per obedientiam, sed extollit per rebellionis superbiam, hic aliunde, id est per maceriam ascendit, exaltatus[c] ideo, ut cadat. Maluissem dicere *mercennarios,* si
15 *mercenariorum* limitibus se arcerent, qui, ut ibidem homelia xlvi AUGU-STINI SUPER JOANNEM ait,[3] ne perdant, quod sectantur, humanae amicitiae gaudium[d], et inimicitiarum incurrant molestiam, eum qui corrigendus est, qui excommunicandus est[e], si excommunicatus inimicus erit, si insidiabitur, si nocebit, non corrigunt, tacent, non vitant; nunc
20 autem quia metas has transcendunt, nam et ipsi, quod luporum est, oves Christi dispergunt, ab obedientia romanae ecclesiae seducentes lacerant et occidunt, in ejusdem suae pertinaciae foveam ac damnationis barathrum contrahentes modestius rapaces dico lupos. An lupi non sunt qui simplici populo quasi ovibus insidiantur, et universa, quae pastor

---

[a] *add.* TALIS EST *M V* [b] scilicet *V* [c] exultatus *V* [d] commodum *T H* [e] *om. V*

[1] *Joan.* 10, 1.
[2] *Tract. 45 in Joan. evang.,* §5 (*CCh* 36, 390; *PL* 35, 1721).
[3] *Tract. 46 in Joan. evang.,* §8 (*CCh* 36, 402–403; *PL* 35, 1732).

166

blood. Since the impure do not please but rather offend God with such sacrifices, their ministries can be justly said to be detestable, as well as offensive before God.

FOURTH PROPOSITION

Impious priests must be avoided as savage wolves, and divine services conducted by them must not be heard nor sacraments received from them, with the sole exception of baptism in a grave emergency.[1]

Those whom I call savage wolves I could have termed thieves and robbers, according to the word of Christ (JOHN 10): *The man who dares not enter the sheepfold by the door, but by some other way, is a thief and a robber. The sheepfold* is the holy Catholic Church; *the humble door* refers to Christ, according to ST. AUGUSTINE (*Tractate 45 on the Gospel of John*). He who seeks his own glory and not the glory of Christ, and who does not humble himself through obedience but exalts himself through arrogant rebellion, climbs up another way over the wall. Therefore he is exalted that he may fall. I would rather have said *hirelings*, if one includes in the term *hireling* those who, as ST. AUGUSTINE says (*Tractate 46 on the Gospel of John*), remain silent and do not rebuke or avoid the evildoer who ought to be rebuked and excommunicated. Such men fear that they may lose what they pursue, the comfort of human friendship, and that they may incur the discomfort of human enmity because the evildoer, once he is excommunicated, may become an enemy and contrive to do them harm. Now, moreover, because such men overstep their bounds and act as wolves, they scatter the sheep of Christ; leading astray Christ's sheep from the obedience of the Roman church, they persecute and destroy them; moreover, they draw the sheep with them into the snare of their obstinacy and into the abyss of damnation—to term them savage wolves is almost an understatement. They are indeed wolves who lay snares for the simple folk as for sheep and direct to perdition the whole

---

[1] Cf. "Biel's Letter to the Church at Mainz under Interdict," Oberman, *Harvest of Medieval Theology*, p. 27.

bonus contulit ad salutem, vertunt in perniciem, dum damnabiliter sacramenta ministrando, paenitentiam in culpam, vitae cibum in venenum[a], infirmorum unctionem in mortis occasionem, doctrinam in errorem, exemplo pariter et verbo, malum bonum, bonum dicentes malum,
5 commutatione sceleratissima transformant[b], eligentes magis innumerabiles christianorum animas perpetuo illigari exitio quam universalium[c] bonorum hujus temporis incommoda sustinere.

Cavendi ergo sunt tamquam saevissimi non corporum, sed animarum inimici. Cavendi, inquam, ut nulla cum eis sacramentalis communio
10 habeatur, nisi inevitabilis cogeret necessitas, quantum ad baptismi sacramentum, quae tunc immineret, dum ad baptizandum in mortis articulo constitutum, nullius hominis non excommunicati baptizare potentis, scientis, et volentis copia haberi possit[d]. Si vero assit laicus non excommunicatus, sive vir, sive mulier, etiamsi parens fuerit contempto[e]
15 baptizandi, sacerdote excommunicato[f], laicus ipse baptizet. Cetera vero sacramenta: paenitentiae scilicet, eucharistiae, unctionis, aut[g] etiam in mortis articulo ab excommunicato recipi non debent. Sed si alium moriturus habere nequit, contritus coram Domino cum proposito firmo ac voluntate confitendi ac cetera sacramenta, suscipiendi, si habere
20 posset ministrum idoneum, sacerdotem, scilicet, non excommunicatum, securus in Domino morietur. Haec omnia aperte probantur in canone DE PAENITENTIA, dist. vi, cap. i, sect. *ideoque*, ubi dicitur:[1] *Nemo digne paenitere potest, quem non sustineat unitas ecclesiae. Ideoque non petat sacerdotes per aliquam culpam ab unitate ecclesiae divisos*, et addit GLOS-
25 SA:[2] *Etiam in necessitate. Judas enim*[h] *paenitens ivit ad Phariseos, relinquens apostolos, nihil invenit auxilii sed*[i] *augmentum*[j] *desperationis*[k] et xxxii dist. *Praeter haec*, sect. *sciendum*, URBANUS papa causam assignans quare a praesciso ab ecclesia in necessitate suscipi debeat[m] baptisma

---

[a] venuum *V* [b] transformantes *V* [c] vilium *M V* [d] posset *T H* [e] *om. T H*
[f] *add.* dimisso *T H* [g] *om. T H* [h] *add.* qui *M V* [i] nisi *T H* [j] argumentum *T H*
[k] *add.* et cetera *T H* [m] debet *T H*

[1] c. 1, D. VI *De paen.* (RF I, 1243).
[2] *Gratiani decreta cum glossis*, f. 613^r.

A DEFENSE OF APOSTOLIC OBEDIENCE

flock which the good shepherd gathered for its salvation; they are wolves when in administering the sacraments damnably they transform, through a diabolic transubstantiation, repentance into guilt, the bread of life into poison, the anointment of the ill into a cause of death, true teaching into error, by both word and example, and good into evil, since they call good evil. Such wicked men elect rather to ensnare countless Christian souls in eternal perdition than to endure the misfortunes of all good men in this age.

Therefore they must be shunned as raging enemies of the soul and not the body. They must be shunned in that no one may partake with them in the sacraments except in unavoidable necessity. Such need arises only when baptism must be performed for someone on the verge of death and no man who is not excommunicated and who possesses the ability, knowledge, and desire to baptize is available. Indeed, in such need, a layman who has not been excommunicated—whether man, woman, or even parent—may himself perform the baptism disregarding a priest who has been excommunicated. Certainly the other sacraments— penance, the Eucharist, and extreme unction—must not, even on the verge of death, be received from one who has been excommunicated. But if a dying man can have no one else, and he dies contrite before God with a firm intent and desire to confess and receive the sacrament if he could have had a suitable minister or priest, in other words one who has not been excommunicated, he dies secure in the Lord. All this is clearly examined in canon law where it is written (DE PAENITENTIA, distinction vi, canon 1, section *Ideoque*): *No one can worthily do penance for any fault who is not sustained by the unity of the Church.* The GLOSS to the words *even in necessity* adds: *For when Judas repented he went to the Pharisees; abandoning the apostles, he found no comfort, but only increased despair.* Pope URBAN,[1] giving the reason baptism must be received in necessity from one separated from the Church, but not the other sacraments, says:

---

[1] This canon is attributed to Alexander II (1061–1073).

169

DEFENSORIUM OBEDIENTIAE APOSTOLICAE

non autem cetera sacramenta, ait:[1] *Alia in baptismo, alia in reliquis sacramentis consideratio est, quippe cum et ordine prior et necessarior sit. Subito enim morituro baptismate* [sic] *prius quam dominici corporis communione vel aliis sacramentis consulitur. Et dum forte catholicus non in-*
5 *venitur, sanctius est ab heretico baptismi sacramentum sumere, quam in aeternum perire.* Ad idem expresse facit cap. *Subdiaconus*, sect. *sciendum*, xxiiii, quaest. i in textu[2] et in GLOSSA[3] et cap. sequenti *Si forte*,[4] et canon beati GREGORII, *Cepit Hermigildus* eadem causa et quaestione,[5] ubi commendatur beatus Hermigildus, propter hoc martyrii coronam
10 assecutus, quia magis mori elegit quam ab episcopo haeretico sumere eucharistiae sacramentum. Concordat beatus THOMAS in iiii SCRIPTO, dist. xiii,[6] et JOANNES in SUMMA, lib. iii, tit. xxiiii, quaest. xliiii.[7]

PROPOSITIO QUINTA[a]

Ad defensionem obedientium ecclesiae filiorum contra perversorum impugnationem, ad inobedientiam vi, armis, vel fraude compellentium,
15 tenetur de necessitate salutis secundum modum sibi possibilem pro tempore et loco, debitis servatis circumstantiis, omnis vere catholicus et fidelis.

Defensio ista contra impugnantes multipliciter fieri potest, quandoque armis violentiae resistendo, quandoque injuriam passos in loco tuto
20 recipiendo, vel ab impugnatoribus abscondendo, quandoque subsidia in

---

[a] *add.* TALIS EST *M V*

[1] c. 6, D. XXXII (RF I, 119).
[2] c. 39, C. XXIV, qu. 1 (RF I, 982).
[3] *Gratiani decreta cum glossis*, f. 478[r].
[4] c. 40, C. XXIV, qu. 1 (RF I, 982–983).
[5] c. 42, C. XXIV, qu. 1 (RF I, 983).
[6] *Sent.*, L. IV, d. 13, qu. 1, a. 1 (Moos, IV, 549–550).
[7] Joannes Runsic Friburgensis, *Summa Confessorum* (Lyons, 1518), L. III, t. 24, qu. 22–23 (120[r]), qu. 124 (126[v]).

A DEFENSE OF APOSTOLIC OBEDIENCE

There is a difference between baptism and the other sacraments, especially since baptism precedes the other sacraments in order and is more indispensable. For one who is about to die must be baptized before he is consoled by the communion of the Lord's body and the other sacraments. And when perchance no Catholic is available, it is better to receive the sacrament of baptism from a heretic than to perish eternally. Other canons expressly declare the same teaching (canon *Subdiaconus*, section *Sciendum*, Cause xxiv, question 1 in the text and its gloss; the following canon, *Si forte*, and the canon of ST. GREGORY, *Cepit hermigildus*, in the same cause and question). In the last canon cited, St. Hermengild is commended because he chose, in pursuing the crown of martyrdom, to die rather than receive the sacrament of the Eucharist from a heretical bishop. ST. THOMAS AQUINAS agrees in his *Commentary on the Sentences* (Book IV, distinction xiii) as does JOHN RUNSIC OF FREIBURG in his SUMMA (Book III, title xxiv, question 44).

FIFTH PROPOSITION

Every faithful Catholic is rightly bound for his salvation to defend the obedience of the Church according to the means possible for him, taking time, place, and circumstances into account, against the assault of her wicked sons who compel others to disobedience by force, warfare, and deceit.

The defense of the Church against her assailants can be accomplished in many ways: sometimes in opposing violence with arms; sometimes in offering a refuge to those who have suffered injury or in concealing such fugitives from their assailants; sometimes in dispatching assistance in

DEFENSORIUM OBEDIENTIAE APOSTOLICAE

armis, pecuniis, victualibus, et similibus, quibus resistere[a] valeant,
impendendo, quandoque fraudes inimicorum sive impugnantium avisa-
mentis congruis detegendo, quandoque prohibitionibus, praeceptis, exhortationibus, supplicationibus, impugnatores a violentia reprimendo,
5 aliquando orationibus devotis divinam assistentiam obedientibus im-
petrando. Qui modi aliique consimiles, quia non omnibus omnes conveniunt, quilibet secundum modum sibi possibilem unum vel plures
obligatus est lege caritatis defendere innocentes. Non quidem semper,
sed pro loco et tempore[b], debitis circumstantiis observatis, dum, scilicet,
10 noscitur defensionis urgens et evidens necessitas, nec apparet alius, qui
possit et velit defendere. Et[c] verisimiliter praesumitur sua defensio
secundum modum sibi possibilem, plus defendendo pro futura[d], quam
defendenti nocitura[e], etsi quae sunt[f], circumstantiae attendendae. In
tali namque casu qui defensionem negat, mortaliter peccat. Quod multis
15 viis ostenditur. Ex debito, scilicet, caritatis Dei et proximi, ex[g] amore
justiciae, et ex odio vitiorum.

Ex amore Dei sic: Debitum est honorem et bonum Christi Jesu,
Domini Dei nostri, procurare et defendere. Siquidem minime amat, qui
amatum non defendit, cum potest, quoniam ejusdem virtutis est agere
20 virtutis actum et repellere contrarium. Eapropter beatus AUGUSTINUS
tractans illud PSAL.:[1] *Eripite pauperem et egenum, de manu peccatoris
liberate*, ait, xxiii, quaest. iii, cap. ultimo:[2] *Ostendit propheta nec illos
immunes a scelere, qui permiserunt principibus Christum crucifigere et
interficere, cum pro multitudine timerent, et possent illos a facto, et se a
25 consensu liberare.* Christo autem, quia[h] caput est corporis mystici, quod
est ecclesia, propter capitis et membrorum conexionem, defensio im-
penditur, quotiens membrum ejus defenditur. Et ab eo defensio negatur,
quotiens membris[i] ejus negatur. Quod ipsemet testatur, cum ait:[3] *Amen,*

---

[a] insistere *V*   [b] *add.* et *T H*   [c] *add.* dum *T H*   [d] futurum *V*   [e] nocituram *M V*
[f] *add.* aliae *T H*   [g] *om. T H*   [h] qui *V*   [i] membrum *M V*

---

[1] *Psal.* 81, 4.
[2] c. 11, C. XXIII, qu. 3 (RF I, 898); cf. *Enarratio in Psalmum lxxxi (PL* 37, 1049).
[3] *Matth.* 25, 40.

arms, funds, supplies of food, and other things useful in resisting the Church's assailants; sometimes in detecting the deceits of the enemy or similar deliberations of the assailants; sometimes in restraining them from violence by bans, precepts, exhortations, and entreaties; and sometimes in securing divine aid for the obedient through devout prayers. Everyone is bound by the law of love to defend the innocent in these ways and others like them—since all these means are not applicable to everyone—according to the one or more means possible for him. This obligation, of course, is not always in force, but when, taking time, place, and circumstances into account, the urgent and evident necessity of defense is recognized and no one else appears who is able and willing to assume the defense. Likewise, it is assumed that each man's defense will take the form possible for him; each assumes such defense more for his own future good than for the defense of the injured party, although the particular circumstances must be considered. For in such a case he who refuses to offer assistance in defending the innocent sins mortally. This may be demonstrated in many ways—from the obligation to love God and one's neighbor, from the love of justice and the hatred of vice.

Such is the obligation to love God; we are bound to defend and attend to the honor and advantage of Jesus Christ, our Lord. He indeed loves little who does not defend his beloved when he is able to do so, because it is equally meritorious to perform a virtuous deed and to prevent a wicked one. Therefore ST. AUGUSTINE, when he expounds the words of the PSALMIST, *Rescue the poor and the needy; deliver them from the hand of sinners,* says (Cause xxiii, question 3, the final canon): *The prophet declares that they were not innocent of evil who permitted the rulers to crucify Christ and to put him to death, since the rulers feared the multitude, which could have prevented the deed if it had so willed.* Whenever a member of Christ is defended, Christ is defended, for he is the head of the mystical body which is the Church, because of the union of the head and members. Whenever a defense is denied the members of Christ, a defense is denied Christ. Christ himself bears witness to this, when he says: *I tell you this:*

dico vobis, quamdiu fecistis uni de his fratribus meis minimis, mihi feci-
stis, MATT. xxv. Et sequitur:[1] *Quamdiu non fecistis uni de minoribus his,*
nec mihi fecistis. Et Saulo persequenti ecclesiam, ait ACT. ix:[2] *Saule,*
Saule, quid me persequeris membrorum suorum persecutionem[a] deputans.
5 Itaque[b] membra Christi in necessitate defendit[c], quisquis Christum diligit. Cujus omissio, sicut ceterorum misericordiae operum negligentes,
damnat, ut MATT. xxv,[3] Dominus contestatur. Denique LUC. xi:[4] *Qui*
non est mecum, ait, *ipse contra me est.* Cum Christo non est, qui membra
sua defendere negligit, et ita sibi contrarius convincitur, quod delictum
10 culpabile non evadit.

Ex amore proximi[d] injuriam patientis[e] idem ostenditur. Ad fraternam
pertinet caritatem proximo in cunctis necessitatibus[f] subvenire, si[g]
potest[g], non solum lingua, sed opere et veritate; teste Joannis, qui ait, I
JOAN. iii:[5] *Qui habet substantiam mundi hujus, et viderit[h] fratrem suam*
15 *necessitatem habere, et clauserit viscera sua ab eo, quomodo caritas Dei manet*
in eo? quasi dicere[i] nullo modo. Ideo subdit:[6] *Non diligamus verbo, neque*
lingua, sed opere et veritate. Quod maxime verum est, dum quis sine
culpa, immo pro justicia conservanda, necessitatem hanc incidit. Tunc
enim locum habet lex illa naturalis, quam in evangelio Dominus com-
20 memorat, LUC. vi:[7] *Prout[j] vultis ut faciant vobis homines, hoc[k] facite illis.*
Vult autem rationabiliter quilibet in justicia foveri et juvari. Et cum
ad eundem spectat malum proximi removere, ad quem spectat bonum
ejus procurare, sequitur manifeste, quod quilibet tenetur malum ab injuriam patiente possetenus removere, quod est ipsum ab impugnantibus

---

[a] *add.* suam *T H*   [b] Quare *M V*   [c] *add.* si potest *T H*   [d] christi *M V*   [e] patientes *T H*
[f] *add.* possetenus *T H*   [g-g] *om. T H*   [h] videt *M V*   [i] diceret *M*   [j] Quae *T H*
[k] haec *T H*

---

[1] *Matth.* 25, 45.
[2] *Act.* 9, 4.
[3] *Matth.* 25, 41–46.
[4] *Luc.* 11, 23.
[5] *I Joan.* 3, 17.
[6] *I Joan.* 3, 18.
[7] *Luc.* 6, 31.**

anything you did for one of my brothers, however humble, you did for me (MATTHEW 25). He adds, *anything you did not do for one of these, however humble, you did not do for me.* Christ spoke to Saul who was persecuting his Church (ACTS 9): *Saul, Saul, why do you persecute me?* Thus he condemned the persecution of his members. Therefore everyone who loves Christ defends the members of Christ in case of need. The Lord condemns the neglect of such defense just as the neglect of other works of mercy, as he bears witness in MATTHEW 25. Finally the Lord says (LUKE 11): *He who is not with me is against me.* He is not with Christ who fails to defend his members; thus he convicts himself of hostility and does not escape grave transgression.

The same duty to love one's neighbor applies to one who has suffered a wrong. It is characteristic of brotherly love to come to the assistance of one's neighbor in all his needs if this is possible. Such love not only manifests itself in talk, but is genuine and shows itself in action. ST. JOHN supports this when he writes (I JOHN 3): *If a man possesses worldly goods, and yet when he sees his brother in need shuts up his heart against him, how can it be said that divine love dwells in him?* That is to say, it cannot dwell in him in any way. Therefore he adds: *Love must not be a matter of words or talk; it must be genuine and show itself in action.* This is particularly true when one encounters need for which one is not responsible—indeed, even more so when justice is involved. For in such instances the natural law applies, as the Lord calls it to our memory in the Gospel (LUKE 6): *Treat others as you would like them to treat you.* But he, in accord with reason, wishes all to be fostered and supported in justice. Since to right one's neighbor's misfortune is equally to secure his good, it clearly follows that everyone is obligated to right the wrong of one who suffers an injustice as far as possible—in other words, everyone must defend him from his assailants. Indeed, the obligation to defend a

DEFENSORIUM OBEDIENTIAE APOSTOLICAE

defensare. Et quidem non minus indigeret[a] in periculo constitutus contra injuriantem defendi, quam esuriens cibari. Ait autem AMBROSIUS in libro DE OFFICIIS, dist. lxxxvi, *Pasce:*[1] *Pasce fame morientem, quos enim pascendo homines servare poteris, si non paveris*
5 *occidisti*[b]. Sicut etiam naturale est omnibus sanis membris compati infirmo ejusdem corporis membro, ita secundum apostolum I COR. xii,[2] membra sana corporis Christi mystici compatiuntur membris in periculo constitutis. Qui vero compatitur miseriae alterius, ab ea liberat, si potest, alioquin simulata non vera compassio probaretur. Rursus
10 Salomon PROV. xxiiii: [3]*Erue, inquit, eos qui ducuntur ad mortem, et qui trahuntur ad interitum, liberare non cesses.* Cui consonant beatus AMBROSIUS:[4] *Si tempore periculo, quo rapiatur ad mortem, plus apud te pecunia tua valeat, quam vita morituri, non leve peccatum est.* Ad idem pulchre loquitur AUGUSTINUS in epistola AD BONIFACIUM, xxiii,
15 c. xxiiii, *Ipsa pietas,*[5] ostendens quod a periculo tenemur liberare[c] etiam invitos, id est, qui liberari nollent. Similiter si propter unius liberationem multi alii se occidere vellent, nihilominus ille liberandus esset, quanto magis tenemur ad defensionem eorum, qui defensionem ab injuriantibus petunt.
20 Adhuc quilibet de necessiatate salutis tenetur cavere damnum proximi, dum potest; ideo lex divina praecipit EXO. xxi,[6] quod fodiens cisternam operiret eam, quia ipsa non operta[d] poterat asinus vel bos incidere in eam; propter hoc etiam mandatur ibidem,[7] ut dominus bovis, quem novit cornupetam, recludat eum, ne virum vel mulierem occideret; quod si
25 propter non reclusionem sequebatur homicidium, jussus est dominus

---

[a] indiget *T H*   [b] occididi *T H*   [c] *add.* liberare *V*   [d] aperta *V*

[1] c. 21, D. LXXXVI (RF I, 302); non invenitur in Ambrosio.
[2] *I Cor.* 12, 26.
[3] *Prov.* 24, 11.
[4] *De officiis,* L. I, c. 30 (*PL* 16, 72A); c. 7, C. XXIII, qu. 3 (RF I, 897–898).
[5] c. 24, C. XXIII, qu. 4 (RF I, 909–910); *Epist.* 185, c. 8 (*PL* 32, 808).
[6] *Exod.* 21, 33–34.
[7] *Exod.* 21, 28–32.

man in peril against the one who wrongs him is no lighter than the duty to feed the hungry. Moreover ST. AMBROSE writes in his book, DE OFFICIIS (in canon law, distinction lxxxvi, *Pasce*): *Feed anyone who is dying from hunger; for in feeding men you can save them. If you do not heed their starvation, you kill them.* As it is natural for all the healthy members to suffer with a diseased member of the same body, so, according to the Apostle (I CORINTHIANS 12), the healthy members of the mystical body of Christ suffer together with the members placed in peril. He who truly suffers the misfortune of another releases him if possible; otherwise compassion is proven false and feigned. Again Solomon declared (PROVERBS 24): *Rescue those who are being taken away to death; liberate those who are drawn to destruction.* ST. AMBROSE is in agreement: *If in the time of danger when a man is dying your money is worth more to you than his life, it is no light sin.* ST. AUGUSTINE speaks eloquently to the same effect in a letter to Boniface (Cause xxiii, canon 24, *Ipsa pietas*) showing that we must release from peril even those who are unwilling, in other words those who do not wish to be released. Likewise, if because of the release of one many others wish to commit suicide, and nevertheless he must be released, how much more are we obligated to defend those who seek defense from assailants.

Besides everyone is bound for his salvation to avoid harming his neighbor if possible. Therefore divine law teaches (EXODUS 21) that he who digs a pit should cover it, for an ox or ass could fall into it if it were not covered. For this reason it is also ordered there that the owner of an ox which he knows to be dangerous should keep it shut up lest it kill some man or woman; if someone is killed because the ox has not been shut up, the owner of the ox is ordered to be killed. From these examples it

bovis occidi. Ex quibus colligitur, quod de necessitate salutis tenetur
homo facere ea, quibus omissis, potest damnum[a] verisimiliter vel jactura
proximo provenire. Tenetur ergo proximum defendere, dum sua defensione potest ab impugnatoris injuria liberari. Iterum lex divina sancivit,
5 EXO. xxiii:[1] *Si occurreris bovi inimici tui aut asino erranti, reduc ad eum.*
Item si videris asinum odientis te jacere sub onere, non pertransibis, sed
levabis cum eo. Sed nemo nisi insanus dubitat, quin[b] majori debito
defendus sit[c] homo pro justitia impugnatus quam inimici asinus re-
ducendus vel sublevandus.

10 Ex amore quoque injustae[d] impugnantis idem sic ostenditur. Nam qui
injuriatur alteri[e] spiritualiter, perit secundum animam, sed pereunti
spiritualiter succurrendum est, multo magis quam[f] pereunti corporaliter[g], sicut AUGUSTINUS, AD BONIFACIUM, innuit xxiii, quaest. iiii,
Ipsa pietas, cum dicit:[2] *Quid de opere misericordiae, quod pro vita aeterna*
15 *adipiscenda et poena aeterna vitanda hominibus debemus impendere,*
judicandum est, cum pro salute corporis non solum temporali sed etiam brevi
et ad tempus exiguum liberanda sic non subvenire omnibus ratio vera et
benigna compellit? ANACLETUS etiam ad idem sic ait, xxiiii, quaest. iii,
Tam sacerdotes:[3] *Tam sacerdotes quam fideles reliqui*[h] *omnes sanam debent*
20 *habere curam de his, qui pereunt.* Cui consonat scripturae auctoritas:
Unicuique mandavit Deus de proximo, ECCLE. xvii.[4] Subveniamus
autem injurianti, eum ab injuria prohibendo. Nam secundum HIERO-
NYMUM SUPER SOPHONIAM[i] xxiii, quaest. iii, *Si quis:*[5] *Si quis forti-*
tudinem latronis enervat aut piratae, et infirmos reddit, prodest illis sua in-
25 *firmitas. Debilitata enim membra, quibus*[j] *prius non bene*[k] *utebantur, a malo*
opere cessabunt.

---

[a] damnari *M V*   [b] *om. M V*   [c] fore *M V*   [d] justitiae *M V*   [e] alicui *T H*   [f] *om. V*
[g] corporali *M*   [h] reliquae *M*   [i] SOPHONIAS *M T H*   [j] qui *V*   [k] tamen *T H*

[1] *Exod.* 23, 4–5.*
[2] c. 24, C. XXIII, qu. 4 (RF I, 910); *Epist.* 185 (*PL* 32, 808).
[3] c. 14, C. XXIV, qu. 3 (RF I, 994).
[4] *Eccle.* 17, 12.*
[5] c. 6, C. XXIII, qu. 3 (RF I, 897); *Comm. in Sophoniam,* c. 1 (*PL* 25, 1417A).

may be gathered that a man for his salvation must do those things that undone could cause harm and likewise loss to one's neighbor. Therefore he is bound to defend his neighbor when his defense can free him from the blows of his assailant. In turn, the divine law ordained (EXODUS 23): *If you meet your enemy's ox or ass wandering astray, bring it back to him. If you see the ass of one who hates you lying under its burden, you shall not pass by but shall help him to lift it up.* But no one except a madman doubts that the obligation to defend a man assailed for justice is greater than the duty to return an enemy's ass or to lift it up when it lies beneath its burden.

Love of the unjust assailant is also thus demonstrated. For he who wounds another spiritually loses his soul; and he who perishes spiritually must be aided far more than he who perishes physically. ST. AUGUSTINE signified this in his letter to Boniface when he said (Cause xxiii, question 4, *Ipsa pietas*): *How should we consider the work of mercy to which we ought to apply ourselves so that men may attain everlasting life and escape eternal perdition, since true reason and benevolence compel us to give such aid to all men to secure a physical safety which is only temporal and very short in duration?* POPE ANACLETUS addresses himself to the same matter (Cause xxiv, question 3, *Tam sacerdotes*): *Priests as well as all the rest of the faithful should entertain deep concern for those who perish.* The authority of Scripture concurs: *God commanded each of them concerning his neighbors* (ECCLESIASTICUS 17). We benefit the one who does wrong by forbidding him to do evil. For ST. JEROME writes in his *Commentary on Zephaniah* (Cause xxiii, question 3, *Si quis*): *If someone saps the strength of a pirate or a robber and weakens them, their weakness is for their own good. For the weakened members which formerly were used for no good purpose cease to do evil.*

DEFENSORIUM OBEDIENTIAE APOSTOLICAE

Subvenimus etiam corrigendo. Hic[a] est illa fraterna correctio,[1] qua[b] tenetur quilibet fidelis proximo impendere, secundum praeceptum evangelicum MATT. xviii,[2] dum probabiliter putat[c], hujusmodi correctione fratrem a peccato posse retrahere, quae[d] tantum[e] obligat
5 quemlibet fidelem secundum beatum THOMAM, ii, ii, quaest. xxxiii, art. iii,[3] quod si in casu posito praetermittatur propter timorem cruciationis carnis vel interemptionis aut cupiditatem, mortale incurritur; et est sententia beati AUGUSTINI, lib. I, DE CIVITATE DEI, cap. ix,[4] originaliter. Est enim haec correctio actus caritatis pertinens ad un-
10 umquemque respectu cujuslibet personae, ad quam caritatem tenetur habere, si in eo aliquid corrigibile inveniatur. Loquitur ad idem AUGUSTINUS in cap. *Duo*, xxiii, quaest. iiii.[5] Dum autem impugnatur injurians aut corrigitur, passus injuriam liberatur.

Ex amore virtutis idem breviter deducitur, quoniam secundum beatum
15 AMBROSIUM, libro DE OFFICIIS, xxiii, quaest. iii, *Fortitudo*:[6] *Fortitudo, quae bello tuetur patriam a barbaris, vel domi defendit infirmos, vel a latronibus socios[f], plena justitia est.* Et iterum *Non[g] inferenda,*[7] ibidem ait[g]: *Non inferenda, sed vi depellenda injuria lex virtutis est.* Ideoque ab injuria, si potest, proximum defendit, quicumque justitiam
20 diligit et virtutem.

Demum ex odio vitiorum propositio[h] nostra[h] sic probatur: Nam qui odit vitia—quod justorum est, secundum illud PSAL.:[8] *Omnem viam iniquam odio habui*—secundum modum sibi possibilem et congruentem ea persequitur, alioquin non odisse probatur. Quippe sicut teste

---

[a] Hinc *M V*   [b] quam *M*   [c] *add.* aut putare debet *T H*   [d] quem *V*   [e] tuum *M V*
[f] socius *T H*   [g-g] *om. V*   [h-h] idem *T H*

[1] Cf. *Canonis misse expositio*, Vol. III, Lect. LXXIV, 217–240.
[2] *Matth.* 18, 15–18.
[3] *Summa theol.*, P. II, II, qu. 33, a. 2 (Moos, 1602a–1602b; Parma III, 136).
[4] *CCh* 47, 9–10; *CSEL* 40, 16–18; *PL* 41, 22–23.
[5] c. 35, C. XXIII, qu. 4 (RF I, 915–916).
[6] c. 5, C. XXIII, qu. 3 (RF I, 897); L. I, c. 27 (*PL* 16, 66B).
[7] c. 7, C. XXIII, qu. 3 (RF I, 897–898); L. I, c. 36 (*PL* 16, 81C).
[8] *Psal.* 118. 128.

A DEFENSE OF APOSTOLIC OBEDIENCE

We assist our neighbor even in correcting him. This is the fraternal correction that every Christian is obligated to give his neighbor, according to the teaching of the gospel (MATTHEW 18), when he recognizes an opportunity to rescue a brother from sin by correction of this sort. Every Christian has this duty to such an extent, according to ST. THOMAS AQUINAS (II, II, question xxxiii, article 3), that to neglect such an opportunity for fear of bodily pain or death or for self-interest is to incur mortal sin. This opinion is founded upon that of ST. AUGUSTINE (Book I, DE CIVITATE DEI, chapter 9). For such correction is an act of love that extends in every instance to all persons to whom love is owed if there is anything in their characters which ought to be corrected. ST. AUGUSTINE discusses this in canon law (canon *Duo*, Cause xxiii, question 4). When the one who inflicts a wrong is opposed or corrected, the one who suffers the wrong is benefited.

The obligation to defend the innocent is briefly concluded from the love of virtue, since ST. AMBROSE writes in his book DE OFFICIIS (Cause xxiii, question 3, *Fortitudo*): *Courage, which in war defends one's household from barbarians or in the home defends the weak or comrades from thieves, is completely just.* The same author adds (canon *Non inferenda*, Cause xxiii, question 3): *The law of courage is put into practice not in inflicting wrong, but in driving out wrong.* Therefore anyone who loves justice and virtue defends his neighbor from a wrong if he is able to do so.

Finally this obligation is proved from the hatred of evil deeds. For he who hates evil deeds—such hatred characterizes the just, in the words of the PSALMIST: *I hated every path of wickedness*—pursues them in every way he finds possible and appropriate. Otherwise he proves that he does

DEFENSORIUM OBEDIENTIAE APOSTOLICAE

GREGORIO, HOMELIA xxx.[1] *Caritas operatur magna, si est; si operari desinit, caritas non est.* Ita pariformiter de odio sancto vitiorum: si est, otiosum non est, sed ea persequitur, reprobat, corrigit, detestatur. Alioquin, ut JOANNES papa octavus lxxxvi dist., i, *Facientis* ait:[2]
5 *Facientis proculdubio culpam habet, qui quod potest corripere, negligit obviare.* Et eodem teste, xxiii, quaest. viii, *Praeterea:*[3] *Crimina quae potest emendare, qui non corrigit, ipse committit.* Et INNOCENTIUS papa, lxxxiii dist. *Error:*[4] *Error cui non resistitur, approbatur et fides cum minime defenditur, opprimitur.* ANASTASIUS quoque et DAMASUS
10 papa xxiii, quaest. iii, *Qui potest:*[5] *Qui potest obviare et perturbare perversos, et non facit, nihil aliud est, quam favere impietati eorum. Nec caret scrupulo societatis occultae, qui manifesto crimini non desinit obviare.* Et multa talia ad propositum patres sancti tradiderunt. Ex quibus patet luculenter, quam multipliciter tenentur fideles singuli defendere passos
15 injuriam, secundum moderationem praedictorum.

PROPOSITIO SEXTA[a]

Summo pontifici eidemque obedientibus[b] detrahentes, bonam eorum opinionem denigrando, delinquunt damnabiliter et sine spe veniae, nisi possetenus restituant laesam famam.

Ex priori propositione per locum a majori sequitur ista. Si enim non
20 defendens peccat, magis probatur delinquere, qui offendit. Cum[c] denique detractio respectu cujuslibet cum famae denigratione sit peccatum mortale gravius furto, quanto fama melior est divitiis. *Siquidem melius*

---

[a] *add.* EST HAEC *M V*   [b] obedientes *V*   [c] Cumque *M V*

[1] *PL* 76, 1221B.**
[2] c. 3, D. LXXXVI (RF I, 298).
[3] c. 12, C. XXIII, qu. 8 (RF I, 955–956).
[4] c. 3, D. LXXXIII (RF I, 293–294).
[5] c. 8, C. XXIII, qu. 3 (RF I, 898).

not hate evil deeds. Indeed, as ST. GREGORY bears witness in *Sermon 30 on the Gospels*: *Love is very active; if love ceases to be active, it is not love.* The same is applicable to the devout hatred of evil deeds; where such hatred is found it is not idle but pursues, reproves, corrects, and detests evil deeds. Otherwise, as Pope JOHN VIII says (distinction lxxxvi, canon *Facientis*): *Without a doubt, he who fails to oppose what he is able to correct shares the guilt of the wrongdoer.* The same pope says (Cause xxiii, question 8, *Praeterea*): *He who does not correct crimes which he can amend commits them himself.* Pope INNOCENT[1] says (distinction lxxxiii, *Error*): *Error that is not resisted is approved; and faith is oppressed when it is feebly defended.* Pope ANASTASIUS and Pope DAMASUS agree (Cause xxiii, question 3, *Qui potest*): *He who is able to oppose and confound the wicked and does not do so does nothing other than to foster their ungodliness. He who ceases to oppose manifest wrong assumes the guilt of joining a secret organization.* The holy Fathers taught many similar things concerning this obligation. From this evidence it is quite clear that all the faithful are obligated in many ways to defend those who suffer a wrong as we have just expounded.

SIXTH PROPOSITION

Those who revile the Supreme Pontiff and the obedient faithful slander their own good names and sin damnably and without hope of mercy unless they make good their slander as far as possible.

This proposition follows in logic from the one just preceding. For if one sins in not defending one who suffers a wrong, the one who inflicts the wrong is proven to sin even more. This is because to disparage anyone by slandering his reputation is a mortal sin more serious than theft to the extent that reputation is above wealth. *Indeed, a good name is*

---

[1] Innocent I (402–417).

DEFENSORIUM OBEDIENTIAE APOSTOLICAE

est nomen bonum quam divitiae multae, PROV. xxiii.[1] Hinc ANTERUS
papa, vi, quaest. i, *Ex merito:*[2] *Deteriores sunt, qui vitam moresque
bonorum corrumpunt, quam hi, qui substantias aliorumque praedia
diripiunt;* et AUGUSTINUS, xi, quaest. iii, *Nemo:*[3] *Nemo peritorum*[a]
5 *aut prudentium putet, quod minus sit periculi in verbis lingua mentiendo,
quam manibus sanguinem fundendo. Melius est enim pro veritate supplicium
pati, quam pro adulatione beneficium.* Gravior tamen est si contra sacerdotes committitur et rectores, eo quod haec detractionis species a
Domino specialiter, EXOD. xxii,[4] prohibetur: *Diis,* inquit, *non detrahes;*
10 ubi GLOSSA INTERLINEARIS:[5] *Diis, id est, sacerdotibus et doctoribus
qui ecclesiae principantur. Cum enim omnis detractio perniciosa sit, in
illis est perniciosior.* Haec GLOSSA. Hinc[b] ANACLETUS papa ait, ii,
quaest. vii, *Accusatio primum:*[6] *Si detractores*[c] *quorumcumque graviter
judicantur et in perditionis laqueum cadunt, multo magis laceratores et*
15 *detractores famulorum Dei damnantur, et in barathrum—nisi*[d] *correxerint
et per eorum satisfactionem condignam egerint paenitentiam—indubitanter
cadunt, et vindicibus flammis exuruntur.* Et infra:[7] *quoniam injuria eorum
ad Christum pertinet, cujus legatione funguntur.* Ideo per prophetam
ZACH. ii Dominus ait:[8] *Qui vos tangit, tangit pupillam oculi mei.* Et
20 iterum:[9] *Nolite tangere christos meos.* Gravissima vero est detractio, si
fiat contra summum pontificem, Christi supremum in terris vicarium.
Hinc beatus CLEMENS, ii, quaest. vii, *Qualis:*[10] *Qualis,* inquit, *damnatio
eis immineat, qui in patres peccant, divina scriptura ostendit. Si enim*

---

[a] *peccatorum M V*   [b] *add.* beatus *T H*   [c] detractoribus *M V*   [d] *add.* se *T H*

[1] *Prov.* 22, 1.
[2] c. 13, C. VI, qu. 1 (RF I, 557).
[3] c. 81, C. XI, qu. 3 (RF I, 665).
[4] *Exod.* 22, 28.
[5] *Biblie iampridem renovate* . . . , I, f. 171ʳ.
[6] c. 15, C. II, qu. 7 (RF I, 486).
[7] *Ibid.*
[8] *Zach.* 2, 8.*
[9] *Psal.* 104, 15.
[10] c. 9, C. II, qu. 7 (RF I, 484–485).

A DEFENSE OF APOSTOLIC OBEDIENCE

better than great riches (PROVERBS 23). Pope ANTERUS discusses this (Cause vi, question 1, *Ex merito*): *Those who corrupt the life and morals of good men are far worse than those who plunder their goods and property.* So also ST. AUGUSTINE (Cause xi, question 3, *Nemo*):[1] *Let no man who has learning or prudence declare that there is less danger in the words of a tongue which speaks lies than in hands which shed blood. For it is better to suffer for the truth than to enjoy comfort for false flattery.* It is still more serious if such slander is aired against priests and rulers, since this sort of defamation is expressly forbidden by the Lord (EXODUS 22): *You shall not revile the gods.* The INTERLINEAR GLOSS to this passage reads: *The gods, namely, the priests and doctors who rule the Church. For although all defamation is pernicious, against these it is more pernicious.* POPE ANACLETUS says on this account (Cause ii, question 7, *Accusatio primum*): *If slanderers of every sort are severely judged and fall into the jaws of destruction, how much more those who persecute and revile the servants of God—unless they will make amends and do penance through genuine satisfaction—without a doubt fall into the abyss and are consumed in the flames of judgment.* He continues: *because their wrong applies to Christ, whose service they discharge.* Therefore the Lord speaks through the prophet (ZECHARIAH 2): *He who touches you touches the apple of my eye.* Elsewhere the Lord says: *Touch not my anointed ones.* That defamation is most serious if it is aired against the Supreme Pontiff, the chief vicar of Christ on earth. ST. CLEMENT says (Cause ii, question 7, *Qualis*): *Holy Scripture reveals that destruction threatens those who sin*

---

[1] This canon is attributed to Isidore.

DEFENSORIUM OBEDIENTIAE APOSTOLICAE

Cham quia non pudenda patris operuit, maledictus[a] *est*[a] *GEN. ix,*[1] *multo ampliori condemnatione sunt digni, qui patribus legatione Dei fungentibus contumeliam inferunt.* Et Dominus in EXOD. cap. xxii:[2] *Principi populi tui ne maledicas.* Augetur namque[b] crimen dignitate propositi.

5 Quod autem sine spe veniae hujusmodi detractor peccat, nisi famam restituat dicta retractando secundum detractionis modum, si potest, patet quia secundum[c] AUGUSTINUM, epistola ii AD MACEDONIUM:[3] *Non dimittitur peccatum, nisi restituatur ablatum, si restitui potest.* Et cum hoc verum sit in bonis fortunae ablatis, magis locum habebit in
10 bonis famae. Cujus sententiae est beatus THOMAS,[4] SCOTUS[5] et communiter omnes doctores in dist. xv, lib. IIII SENTENTIARUM.[6]

Nec solum detrahentes, sed etiam detractiones delectabiliter audientes, crimen damnabiliter[d] sibi agerant[e], quoniam praestantes audientiam detrahentibus consentire judicantur. Hinc Salomon ait, PROV. xxiiii:[7]
15 *Cum detractoribus ne commiscearis;* et ECCLE. xxviii:[8] *Saepe aures tuas spinis et noli*[f] *audire linguam nequam.* Hinc etiam ANTERUS papa, vi, quaest. i *Ex merito:*[9] *Caveat,* inquit, *unusquisque, ne aut linguam aut aures prurientes, id est ne aut aliis ipse detrahat, aut alios detrahentes audiat.* Et xi, quaest. iii, *Non solum*[g] dicitur:[10] *Non solum, ille reus est,*
20 *qui falsum de alio profert, sed is, qui aurem cito criminibus praebet.*

[a–a] maledictione *M V* [b] nempe *T H* [c] add. beatum *T H* [d] damnabile *T H*
[e] exaggerant *T H* [f] non *M* [g] add. et *V*

---

[1] *Gen.* 9, 22–24.
[2] *Exod.* 22, 28.
[3] *Epist.* 153, c. 6 *PL* 33, 662).
[4] *Sent. Comm.*, dist. 15, qu. i, a. 5 (Parma VII², 713–715).
[5] *Sent. Comm.*, dist. 15, qu. 2 (Wadding XVIII, 350–353).
[6] *PL* 192, 873; Gabriele Biel, *Collectorium in quattuor libros sententiarum* (Basel, 1512), L. IV, dist. XV, qu. 2, f. Mv.ᵛ.
[7] *Prov.* 24, 21.
[8] *Eccle.* 28, 28.
[9] c. 13, C. VI, qu. 1 (RF I, 557).
[10] c. 77, C. XI, qu. 3 (RF I, 664).

against their fathers. For if Shem was cursed because he did not cover the nakedness of his father (GENESIS 9), how much more worthy of condemnation are those who heap scorn upon their fathers who carry out God's bidding. The Lord said (EXODUS 22): *You shall not curse a ruler of your people.* For the crime is increased according to the dignity of him who is reviled.

This sort of slanderer sins without the hope of mercy unless he repairs his wrong, if possible, by retracting what he has said according to the nature of the insult. ST. AUGUSTINE makes this clear in his second letter to Macedonius: *The sin is not forgiven unless what has been stolen is restored, if restitution is possible.* Although this is true of ordinary stolen goods, it concerns much more the goods of reputation. ST. THOMAS AQUINAS, SCOTUS, and by and large all the doctors in their commentaries upon the SENTENCES, Book IV, distinction 15, agree.

Not only those who revile but also those who hear such slander with delight sin damnably against the same, since they who grant a hearing to slanderers are deemed to consent to their insults. In this regard Solomon says (PROVERBS 24): *Have nothing to do with slanderers.* It is written in ECCLESIASTICUS 28: *Hedge in your ears with thorns; hear not a wicked tongue.* Pope ANTERUS also speaks to this effect (Cause vi, question 1, *Ex merito*): *Let everyone beware that he has neither an itching tongue nor itching ears, that is to say, that he neither slanders others or gives ear to the slanders of others.* It is said elsewhere (Cause xi, question 3, *Non solum*): *Not only is he guilty who invents lies about another, but also he who quickly lends ear to accusations.*

DEFENSORIUM OBEDIENTIAE APOSTOLICAE

PROPOSITIO SEPTIMA

Christiani[a] nomine, sed opere rebelles, obedientium sedi apostolicae invasores, periculosiores sunt, quam tyranni infideles palam Christi famulos persequentes.

Eo utique periculosiores, quo christianum nomen participantes re-
5 ligionis putantur amici. Nam teste BOETHIO:[1] *Nulla pestis efficatior ad nocendum quam familiaris inimicus.* Nec est hostis deterior quam fictus amicus. De hoc sufficiat auctoritas beatissimi Petri apostoli in ordinatione beati Clementis xciii dist., *Si inimicus est,* ita populum alloquentis:[2] *Si inimicus est Clemens iste alicui pro actibus suis[b], nolite expectare, ut ipse*
10 *vobis dicat cum illo nolite amici esse, sed prudenter observare debetis et voluntati ejus sine communione obsecundare, et avertere vos ab eo, cui ipsum sentitis adversum. Sed nec loqui his, quibus ipse non loquitur, ut[c] unusquisque, qui in culpa est, dum cupit omnium vestrum amicitias habere, festinet citius reconciliari ei, qui omnibus praeest, et per hoc redeat ad*
15 *salutem, cum obedire ceperit monitis praesidentis. Si quis vero amicus fuerit his, quibus ipse non loquitur, unus est ipse ex illis, qui exterminare ecclesiam Dei volunt. Et cum corpore videatur esse vobiscum[d], mente tamen et animo contra vos[e] est et est multo nequior hostis hic, quam illi, qui foris sunt, et evidenter inimicantur. Hic etenim per amicitiarum speciem, quae*
20 *inimica sunt[f], gerit, et ecclesiam dispergit et vastat. Ideoque hujusmodi apostolicis institutis vos monentes instruimus, ut effecta sollicitior caritas vestra certiora gerere satagat, et cautius, ne perversi et infideles homines, laedendi fideles et benivolos habeant facultatem.*

---

[a] *add.* tantum *T H*   [b] *add.* pravis *T H*   [c] et *M V*   [d] nobiscum *M T H*   [e] nos *T H*
[f] *om. V*

---

[1] *De cons. phil.,* L. III (*CCh* 94, 45; *CSEL* 67, 55; *PL* 63, 743).*
[2] c. 1, D. XCIII (RF I, 320).

A DEFENSE OF APOSTOLIC OBEDIENCE

SEVENTH PROPOSITION

Those who persecute the servants of Christ are Christians in name but rebels in deed, and assailants of those loyal to the Apostolic See; they are more dangerous than pagan tyrants.

Assuredly, therefore, such men are very dangerous, because those who are called Christians are considered friends of religion. For BOETHIUS bears witness: *What plague is more deadly than an intimate enemy?* No enemy is worse than a false friend. This is sufficiently demonstrated by the most blessed apostle Peter when he thus addressed the people in ordaining St. Clement (distinction xciii, *Si inimicus est*): *If Clement spurns anyone on account of his actions, do not wait for him to tell you to avoid the friendship of such. On the contrary, you ought to note his will and support it without an express command. Separate yourselves from anyone whom you see he opposes. Do not speak to those to whom he does not speak, so that anyone who is at fault (since he desires to possess the friendship of you all) may hasten all the more to be reconciled with him who rules over all and thus return to spiritual health and obedience to the admonition of him who rules. However if anyone befriends those with whom he does not speak, he must be regarded as one of those who wish to destroy the Church of God. Although such a man seems to be with you in body, he is against you in heart and mind. He is a much more dangerous foe than those who are outside the Church and openly hostile. For this man under the guise of friendship acts as an enemy who scatters and ruins the Church. Therefore through apostolic instructions of this sort we warn and teach you, so that your strengthened love may concern itself to act with greater care and caution, and so that wicked, faithless men may not be able to harm the faithful and the well disposed.*

DEFENSORIUM OBEDIENTIAE APOSTOLICAE

PROPOSITIO OCTAVA[a]

Vasalli, familiares et subditi, dominos suos ad invadendum res aut[b] personas obedientium christianorum sequentes, consilio et auxilio cooperantes, aeternae damnationi se exponunt, nisi invincibili ignorantia laborarent.

5 Cum enim *Deo magis quam hominibus obedire oportet,*[1] lex quoque divina et naturalis prohibet proximum fratrem sine culpa damnificare, obedire autem sedi apostolicae culpa non est, sed lege divina debitum sanctum et justum; manifestum est, quod contra hujusmodi legem nemo debet homini obedire. De quo beatus HIERONYMUS SUPER 10 EPISTOLAM AD EPHESIOS, xi, quaest. iii, *Si dominus:*[2] *Si dominus,* inquit, *jubet ea, quae non sunt contraria vel adversa sacris scripturis, subiciatur domino servus. Si vero contraria praecipit, magis obediat Christo Domino*[c]. *Et infra. Si bonum est quod precipit imperator, jubentis exsequere voluntatem. Si malum, responde:*[3] "*Oportet magis obedire Deo,* 15 *quam hominibus.*"

Et beatus AUGUSTINUS:[4] *Si illud jubeat potestas quod non debes facere? Hic*[d] *sane contemne potestatem, et infra:*[5] *Si aliquid imperator et aliud jusserit Deus quid judicatis major est potestas Deus. O, imperator, da veniam, tu carcerem et ille minatur gehennam*[d]. *Hic jam tibi assumenda est* 20 "*fides tua tamquam scutum, in quo possis omnia ignita jacula inimici extinguere.*"[6] Sanctus AMBROSIUS quoque de eodem dist. xi, quaest. iii, *Julianus:*[7] *Julianus quamvis imperator esset apostata, habuit tamen*

---

[a] *add.* EST TALIS *M V*   [b] et *T H*   [c] *add.* ut supra etiam tactum fuit *T H*
[d-d] et cetera, ut supra in veritate octava tactum fuit *T H*

---

[1] *Act.* 5, 29.
[2] c. 93, C. XI, qu. 3 (RF I, 669); *Comm. in epist. ad Titum,* c. 2 (*PL* 26, 619C et 626C).
[3] *Act.* 5, 29.
[4] c. 97, C. XI, qu. 3 (RF I, 670); *Serm.* 62, c. 8 (*PL* 38, 421).
[5] *Ibid.*
[6] Cf. *Ephes.* 6, 16.
[7] c. 94, C. XI, qu. 3 (RF I, 669); cf. Aug., *Enarratio in Psalmum cxxiv* (*PL* 37, 1654; *CCh* 40, 1841–1842).

A DEFENSE OF APOSTOLIC OBEDIENCE

EIGHTH PROPOSITION

Vassals, servants, and subjects who follow their lords in molesting the property or persons of loyal Christians and give them aid through counsel and military support expose themselves to eternal damnation unless they do so in invincible ignorance.

For although *God must be obeyed rather than men*, and although divine law forbids the infliction of punishment upon a neighbor without fault, it is no fault to obey the Apostolic See but a holy and just obligation under divine law; it is evident that no one ought to obey man against a law of this sort. ST. JEROME discusses this in his *Commentary upon the Epistle to the Ephesians* (Cause xi, question 3, *Si dominus*):[1] *If a master orders things that are not contrary to or opposed to Holy Scripture, the servant ought to be subject to his master. If, however, he orders what is opposed to Holy Scripture, the servant ought rather to obey Christ the Lord. Moreover if the emperor orders what is good, fulfill his will; if evil, respond: "God must be obeyed rather than men."*

ST. AUGUSTINE states: *What if that authority commands what you ought not to do? In this event, by all means disregard that authority. How should one decide if the emperor enjoins one thing, and God another? God is the greater authority. O emperor, with your indulgence, you threaten prison, but he threatens Hell! In such a dilemma you must at once assume "the shield of faith with which you will be able to quench all the flaming arrows of the evil one."* ST. AMBROSE also writes (Cause xi, question 3, *Julianus*): *The emperor Julian, although he was an apostate, had under him Christian*

---

[1] See p. 115.

191

DEFENSORIUM OBEDIENTIAE APOSTOLICAE

sub se christianos milites, quibus cum dicebat: producite aciem pro defensione rei publicae; obediebant ei. Cum autem diceret eis: producite arma in christianos, tunc cognoscebant imperatorem caeli. Item ISIDORUS, xi, quaest. iii, *Si is, qui praeest:*[1] *Si quis prohibet vobis*[a], *quod a Domino*
5 *praeceptum est, vel rursus imperat fieri, quod Dominus fieri prohibet, execrabilis sit omnibus, qui diligunt Deum*[b]. Et FABIANUS papa, xi, quaest. iii, *Qui omnipotentem:*[2] *Qui omnipotentem Deum*[c] *metuit, non contra evangelii nec*[d] *contra apostolos*[d]*, nec contra prophetas vel sanctorum patrum statuta agere ullo*[e] *modo consentit.* Nec excusare poterunt subditos
10 juramenta fidelitatis, confederationis ligae aut vinculum qualecumque. Tum[f] quia juramentum, vinculum[f] iniquitatis esse non debet—ut dicit AUGUSTINUS AD SEVERINUM, militanum episcopum;[3] et DE JUREJURANDO, *Quanto personam tuam.*[4] Item xxii, quaest. iii, *Inter.*[5] Tumb uia contra praeceptum Dei nulla hominum liga est
15 servanda, teste URBANO papa, qui, xv, quaest. vi, cap. ultimo, ait:[6] *Fidelitatem quamchristiano principi juraverunt, Deo ejusque sanctis adversanti et eorum praecepta calcanti, nulla cohibentur auctoritate persolvere.* Sola ergo[g] ignorantia invincibilis, hoc est quae manet post diligentiam debitam factam, excusat, ut vult AUGUSTINUS in auctori-
20 tate allegata supra veritate nona.[7]

PROPOSITIO NONA

Consules potestatum et principum et[h] ad persequendum innocentes, suadendo, hortando, suggerendo, vel aliter inducentes, inexcusabiles

---

[a] nobis *M V*   [b] *add.* Dominum *M V*   [c] Dominum *M V*   [d–d] *om. M V*   [e] nullo *M*
[f–f] *om. M V*   [g] autem *T H*   [h] *om. V*

---

[1] c. 101, C. XI, qu. 3 (RF I, 671–672); cf. Basilii, *Regulae brevius tractatae*, c. 114 et 303 (*PG* 31, 1159A–D et 31, 1297D–1298D).
[2] c. 95, C. XI, qu. 3 (RF I, 669).
[3] *Epist.* 32 (*PL* 33, 194–195).
[4] c. 18, X (2,24) (RF II, 365–366).
[5] c. 22, C. XXII, qu. 4 (RF I, 880–881).
[6] c. 5, C. XV, qu. 6 (RF I, 756).
[7] Vide 118.

soldiers who obeyed him when he ordered them to engage in battle for the defense of the empire. However, when he ordered them to bear arms against Christians, they recognized only the emperor of heaven. ISIDORE writes thus (Cause xi, question 3, *Si is, qui praeest*): *If anyone forbids you to do what has been enjoined by the Lord or again orders done what the Lord forbids, let him be accursed by all who love God.* Pope FABIAN declares (Cause xi, question 3, *Qui omnipotentem*): *He who fears God Almighty agrees in no way to do anything contrary to the gospel or contrary to the prophets or the teachings of the holy Fathers.* Oaths of fealty, systems of alliance, or any bond whatsoever cannot excuse subjects, because an oath must never be a bond of wickedness, as ST. AUGUSTINE says in a letter to Severinus, Bishop of Mileum. This is also echoed in canon law (DE JUREJURANDO, *Quanto personam tuam;* Cause xxii, question 4, *Inter*). A human alliance must never be observed when it is contrary to the Lord's command, as Pope URBAN[1] witnesses when he says (Cause xv, question 6, canon 5): *Those who have sworn fealty to a Christian ruler are bound by no authority to observe their oath if the ruler opposes God and the saints and despises their precepts.* Therefore only invincible ignorance that persists after all suitable instruction has been given may excuse, as ST. AUGUSTINE declares in the passage previously cited in the Ninth Truth.

NINTH PROPOSITION

Counselors of rulers and leaders who persuade, exhort, urge, or otherwise induce them to persecute the innocent cannot be excused; they

---

[1] Urban II (1088–1099).

sunt^a et^a dominis suis infideles et saepe manu persequentibus sunt
pejores^b.

Nam cum sicut ex supradictis patet, non solum consentiens^c crimini,
sed et non resistens^d, dum potest^e, eidem damnabiliter participare
5 censentur, quanto magis hi, quorum consilio et dolosis persuasionibus
corda principum seducuntur ad criminum executionem. Siquidem
magis favet crimini committens quam omittens. Nec excusari possunt
consiliarii ignorantia, quoniam ad persequendum homines et damnifican-
dum in rebus, fama et persona, in quibus graviter offenditur Deus.
10 Injuste laeditur proximus, si innocens fuerit; nullus debet persuadere,
nisi fuerit nedum conjectura, sed sufficienti certitudine certus, quod
expugnandi injusti sint, et persecutionem hujusmodi meruerunt. Ideo
tyranni sanctorum martyrum persecutores, quamvis ignorabant se
delinquere, quippe secundum Christi dictum^f, JOAN. xvi^f,[1] *arbitra-*
15 *bantur se obsequium praestare Deo.* Et Paulus AD ROM. x[2] *testimonium*
perhibuit, quia zelum Dei habuere, licet non secundum scientiam, tamen^g
propter hoc non veniunt excusandi, quin damnabiliter peccarunt. Nam
etsi ignorantia facti quandoque excuset, non tamen ignorantia juris,
illius maxime, quod quis scire tenetur. Sicut etiam nec Saraceni nec
20 Judei nec haeretici, persequentes fideles, excusantur, licet se malefacere
ignorent. Etsi non excuset ignorantia, multominus mundanus timor,
aut propriorum cupiditas commodorum. Ab horum consilio summopere
principibus est cavendum, secundum verbum sapientis ECCLE. viii:[3]
Cum fatuis ne consilium habeas, non enim poterunt diligere, nisi quod
25 *ipsis placet. Fatuos* appellat, non defectu^h rationis et ingenii, sed virtutum
et probitatis. Et iterum ECCLE. xxxvii:[4] *A malo consiliario serva*ⁱ
animam tuam. Consiliarius malus est, qui in dandis consiliis non Dei

---

^{a–a} *om.* M V   ^b *add.* et V   ^c consentientes V   ^d resistentes V   ^e possunt V
^{f–f} prophetiam M V   ^g *add.* non V   ^h de facto M V   ⁱ conserva M T H

[1] *Joan.* 16, 2.
[2] *Rom.* 10, 2.**
[3] *Eccle.* 8, 20.
[4] *Eccle.* 37, 9.*

are unfaithful to their lords and frequently worse than those who violently persecute the innocent.

Because it has been demonstrated previously that not only the one who consents to a crime but also he who does not oppose a crime when it is possible to do so is considered to participate in it damnably, how much more guilty are those who mislead the hearts of rulers by their advice and false opinions? Indeed, they foster the commission of crime rather than its prevention. Counselors cannot be excused on the grounds of ignorance, since they urge the persecution of men and harsh measures against their property, reputation, and persons; such things clearly offend God. A neighbor is afflicted wrongly if he is innocent; no one should urge persecution unless not only conjecture but sufficiently established certainty exists that the unjust should be persecuted and that they have merited such persecution. Therefore tyrants were persecutors of the holy martyrs, although they were not aware of their sin; in the words of Christ (JOHN 16), *they supposed that they were performing a religious duty*. And PAUL *testified to the Jews' zeal for God, although it was ill-informed* (ROMANS 10); nevertheless they were not consequently excused but sinned damnably. For although ignorance of fact sometimes excuses, ignorance of the law, especially what anyone is obligated to know, does not excuse. Thus neither Saracens, Jews, nor heretics who persecute the faithful are excused, although they are not aware of their wickedness. If ignorance may not excuse, worldly timidity or concern for personal convenience are even less excusable. Rulers must especially avoid such advice, in the words of the wise man [Jesus Sirach] (ECCLE-SIASTICUS 8): *Do not consult fools, for they cannot love but what pleases them*. He terms them *fools*, not for a lack of reason and intellect, but for a lack of virtue and goodness. He later says (ECCLESIASTICUS 37): *Be wary of an evil counselor*. A counselor is evil who, when he gives advice,

honorem et timorem ambitioni[a], non animae salutem corpori, non
honestum utili, non veritatem justitiae beneplacito, non bonum commune proprio, non honorem principis ac patriae suo commodo, ante-
ponit[b]. Sane consiliarii tales suis dominis perniciosi sunt et infideles,
5 proprios honores, divitias, voluptates corporis, et generaliter quae[c] sua
sunt, magis quam domini sui salutem amantes et honorem, alioquin
quomodo a justitia ad iniquitatem, a veritate ad dolum, et per consequens a vita ad mortem, ab honore ad diffamiam, venenatis suis persuasionibus pervertere principes molirentur; unde non tam principum
10 consiliarii quam principum homicidae sunt censendi, teste AUGUSTINO,
DE PAENITENTIA, dist. i, *Noli :*[1] *Noli,* inquit, *non te homicidam putare,*
quando fratri tuo mala persuades[d]. *Si fratri tuo mala persuades, occidis.*
Et ut scias, quia occidis, audi PSALMUM[e]*:*[2] *"Filii hominum dentes*
eorum, arma et sagittae, et lingua eorum gladius acutus." Et quomodo
15 domini sui verum bonum et honorem procurarent, qui suum parvipen-
dunt. De quo beatus AMBROSIUS, lib. ii, DE OFFICIIS,[3] simul
ostendens, qualis esse debet consiliarius, et[f] ita dicit: *In acquirendis*
consiliis plurimum adjungit vitae probitas, virtutum praerogativa, benivo-
lentiae usus. Quis enim in caeno fontem requirat? Quis exturbatam aquam
20 *potat? Ubi luxuria est, ubi intemperantia, ubi vitiorum confusio, quis non*
horrendum existimet? quis non despiciet morum colluvionem? quis utilem
alienae causae judicet, quem videt inutilem suae vitae? Haec ille. Cui
consonat illud[g] ECCLE. cap. xiiii:[4] *Qui sibi nequam est, cui alii bonus*
erit? Utinam nostri temporis principes attenderent, factoque imitaren-
25 tur, quod de Constantio patre Constantini in TRIPARTITA HISTORIA,
lib. I, cap. vii recitatur:[5] *Cum persecutiones diversas ecclesiae in alio*

---

[a] ambitionem *M V*   [b] anteponunt *M V*   [c] qua *M T H*   [d] persuadens *T H*
[e] *add.* et *M*   [f] *om. V*   [g] *add.* illud *V*

---

[1] c. 27, D. I *De paen.* (RF I, 1164).
[2] *Psal.* 56, 5.
[3] c. 12 (*PL* 16, 126A–B).
[4] *Eccle.* 14, 5.
[5] Cassiodori (*CSEL* 71, 21; *PL* 69, 890B–C).

does not prefer the honor and fear of the Lord to his own ambition, the health of his soul to that of his body, the right thing to the expedient one, true justice to his own inclination, the common welfare to his own, and the honor of the ruler and nation to his own convenience. Surely such counselors prove most destructive and faithless to their lords, for they love their own honor, wealth, physical comfort, and their own interests in general more than the honor and welfare of their lords. Moreover with their poisoned pleas they strive to turn rulers from justice to wickedness, from honor to defamation, from truth to falsehood, and consequently from life to death; therefore such men ought not be termed counselors of rulers but the assassins of rulers, as ST. AUGUSTINE bears witness (DE PAENITENTIA, distinction i, *Noli*): *Do not think that you are not a murderer when you entice your brother to evil. If you entice your brother to evil, you murder him. To learn that you murder him, listen to the PSALMIST: "The teeth of the sons of men are spears and arrows and their tongues sharp swords."* How may they concern themselves with the true welfare and honor of their lord who disregard their own? ST. AMBROSE discusses this and indicates what a counselor should be when he says (Book II, DE OFFICIIS): *In seeking counsel, one considers especially uprightness of life, exceptional virtue, and evidences of good-will. For who seeks a fountain in filth? Who drinks muddy water? Who will not abhor a place where there is riotous living, excess, and an assortment of vices? Who does not despise a foul life? Who will consider a man useful to another man who is seen to be useless in his own life?* The words of ECCLE-SIASTICUS (chapter 14) agree: *If a man is worthless to himself, for whom can he have any worth?* Oh, that rulers of our age would heed and follow in practice the example of Constantius, the father of Constantine, which is recited in the HISTORIA TRIPARTITA, Book I, chapter 7: *When the churches were suffering persecution in other parts of the world, Constantius*

DEFENSORIUM OBEDIENTIAE APOSTOLICAE

terrarum orbe paterentur, solus Constantius Constantini pater, licentiam
christianis in sua consistere religione concessit. Denique probare volens,
quosdam in suo palatio christianos, si boni et solidi essent viri, evocans
universos, praecepit dicens, ut siquidem venirent ad sacrificandum et
5 *ejus colerent deos*[a] *circa eum essent et in suo cingulo permanerent. Si vero*
refugerent, egrederentur de palatio, gratias agentes, quod minime puniren-
tur. Cumque in utroque apparuissent, alii quidem religionis desertores, alii
vero divina praesentibus praeponentes, deliberavit eos amicos et consiliarios
uti, qui in melioribus fideles constantioresque permanserant. Alios autem
10 *velut*[b] *effeminatos aversatus*[c] *expulit a suo colloquio, credens numquam*
circa principem devotos fore, qui fuerint[d] *Dei sui sic paratissimi prodi-*
tores. Illi ergo sunt stabiles consiliarii hominis, qui sunt veri amatores
veritatis. Hinc sapiens ECCLE. xxxvii, dum multiplices repudiandos
consiliarios enumerasset, quorum consilium amplectendum foret,
15 adjecit:[1] *Cum viro sancto maxime assiduus esto, quemcumque cognoveris*
observare timorem Dei. Et sequitur:[2] *Anima viri sancti annunciat ali-*
quando vera plus quam septem circumspectores, qui sedent in excelso ad
speculandum.

Quod vero in fine propositionis additur:[3] *Saepe persuasor pejor est, eo*
20 *qui crimen*[e] *consummat,* tunc veritatem habet, quando mali consiliarii
simplicia et recta principum corda corrumpunt, et ita ad[f] innocentum
persecutionem injustam[g] inducunt. Tunc enim locum habet GLOSSA[4]
super verbo *suades*[h], DE PAENITENTIA, dist. i, *Noli,*[5] quae dicit: *Plus est*
suadere quam facere. Et ideo majus[i] fuisse peccatum Judaeorum, pec-
25 cato Pilati, Dominus ipse testatur JOAN. xix:[6] *Qui,* inquit, *tradidit me*

---

[a] *add.* et *T H*   [b] *om. T H*   [c] adversatos *M,* aversatos *V*   [d] fuerunt *T H*
[e] *add.* manu *T H*   [f] *add.* injustam *T H*   [g] *om. T H*   [h] suade *M V*   [i] magis *M*

[1] *Eccle.* 37, 15.
[2] *Eccle.* 37, 18.
[3] Vide 194.**
[4] *Gratiani decreta cum glossis,* f. 567ᵛ.
[5] c. 27, D. I *De paen.* (RF I, 1164).
[6] *Joan.* 19, 11.

alone, the father of Constantine, accorded the Christians permission to practice their faith. At length, wishing to discover whether certain Christians in his palace were honest and true, he called them all together and told them that if they would sacrifice to his gods and worship them, they might stay at court and remain in his service; but if they refused they would be ousted from the palace, grateful that they were so lightly chastised. When dissension arose among them, some abandoning their faith and others preferring God's honor to present comforts, the emperor determined to retain those as his friends and counselors who had remained faithful and more constant in more noble things. But he in disgust drove away the others from his presence as cowards, judging that those who were so ready to betray their God would never be true to their ruler. Therefore reliable human counselors are those who are genuine lovers of truth. Hence the wise man [Jesus Sirach], when he had catalogued the many sorts of counselors who should be disdained, added those whose counsel should be embraced (ECCLESIASTICUS 37): *Stay constantly with a godly man, whom you know to observe the fear of God.* He adds: *The soul of a godly man sometimes keeps him better informed than seven watchmen sitting high on a watchtower.*

Thence the words added at the end of the proposition, *The one who persuades is often worse than he who commits the crime,* are applicable when evil counselors corrupt the simple, upright hearts of rulers and thus persuade them to persecute the innocent unjustly. For them the GLOSS upon the word *suades* (DE PAENITENTIA, distinction i, *Noli*) is relevant: *It is more serious to persuade than to act.* Therefore the Lord himself witnesses that the sin of the Jews was greater than the sin of Pilate (JOHN 19): *He who delivered me to you has the greater sin.* Finally

DEFENSORIUM OBEDIENTIAE APOSTOLICAE

tibi, majus peccatum habet. Et beatus AUGUSTINUS, DE PAENI-
TENTIA, dist. i, *Periculose:*[1] *Periculose se decipiunt, qui existimant eos
tantum homicidas esse, qui manibus hominem*[a] *occidunt et non potius eos,
per quorum consilium, fraudem et exhortationem homines extinguuntur.*
5 *Nam Judaei Dominum nequaquam propriis manibus occiderunt, sicut
scriptum est:*[2] *"Nobis non licet interficere quemquam." Sed tamen illis
mors Domini imputatur, quia ipsi eum lingua interfecerunt, dicentes:*[3]
"Crucifige, crucifige eum."

PROPOSITIO DECIMA

Utrumque praedicatorum apud Dominum, licet differenter, reum
10 mortalis culpa tenet; et qui errorem seminando a sedis apostolicae
obedientia populum seducit, et qui veritatem tacendo, fideles in praecipitium trahi sinit.

Haec propositio est de mente beati AUGUSTINI AD CASULANUM
dicentis[b], xi, quaest. iii, *Quisquis:*[4] *Quisquis metu cujuslibet potestatis
15 veritatem occultat iram Dei super se provocat, quia magis timet hominem
quam Deum.* Et post pauca: *Uterque reus est, et qui veritatem occultat, et
qui mendacium dicit; et*[c] *quia ille prodesse non vult, et iste nocere desiderat.*
Cui consonat CHRYSTOMUS, xi, quaest. iii, *Nolite:*[5] *Non solum,* inquit,
*ille proditor est veritatis, qui transgrediens veritatem, palam pro veritate
20 mendacium loquitur, sed etiam ille, qui non libere pronunciat veritatem,
quam libere annunciare oportet, aut non libere veritatem defendit, quam
libere defendere convenit, proditor est veritatis.* Et licet gravius peccet, qui
mendaci doctrina populum Dei pervertit, siquidem *hoc mendacii genus in
doctrina, scilicet religionis, gravissimum est, et longe fugiendum,* secundum

---

[a] homines *T H*   [b] dicente *M T H*   [c] om. *M V*

---

[1] c. 23, D. I *De paen.* (RF I, 1163).
[2] *Joan.* 18, 31.
[3] *Luc.* 23, 21.
[4] c. 80, C. XI, qu. 3 (RF I, 665); non invenitur in Augustino.
[5] c. 86, C. XI, qu. 3 (RF I, 667); Pseudo-Chrys., *Hom. 25 in Matthaeum* (*PG* 56, 762).

A DEFENSE OF APOSTOLIC OBEDIENCE

ST. AUGUSTINE declares (DE PAENITENTIA, distinction i, *Periculose*): *They dangerously deceive themselves who consider only those to be murderers who kill a man with their hands, and not those who destroy men by their counsel, deceit, and encouragement. For the Jews certainly did not kill the Lord with their own hands, as it is written: "We are not allowed to put any man to death." Nevertheless they bear the guilt of the Lord's death since they killed him with their tongues, crying: "Crucify him, crucify him!"*

TENTH PROPOSITION

All preachers, although they differ in other respects, are guilty of mortal sin before the Lord when they draw their flocks from obedience to the Apostolic See and, by not speaking the truth, permit the faithful to be drawn into the abyss.

This proposition is drawn from ST. AUGUSTINE who wrote to Casulanus (Cause xi, question 3, *Quisquis*): *Anyone who conceals the truth for fear of some authority calls down the wrath of God upon himself, because he fears men more than God.* Somewhat later he adds: *Both are guilty: he who conceals the truth and he who speaks falsehood, because the former does not wish to make the truth known and the latter desires to refute it.* ST. CHRYSOSTOM agrees (Cause xi, question 3, *Nolite*): *Not only does he betray the truth who transgresses against the truth by openly speaking falsehood and not the truth, but he also betrays it who does not openly speak the truth, which must be openly proclaimed, or does not boldly defend it when it must be boldly defended.* Yet one sins all the more when one corrupts

DEFENSORIUM OBEDIENTIAE APOSTOLICAE

AUGUSTINUM, libro DE MENDACIO.[1] Talibus enim Dominus ve multiplex imprecatur, ISAI. v,[2] pro eo quod *dicunt malum bonum et lucem tenebras, ponentes amarum dulce et dulce amarum, qui justificant impium pro muneribus, et justitiam justi auferunt ab eo,* quibus etiam per
5 JERE., cap. xxiii, ait:[3] *Dabo vos in approbrium sempiternum et ignominiam aeternam, quae numquam oblivione delebitur.* Et iterum JERE. xiiii:[4] *Gladio et fame consumentur prophetae illi, et populi, quibus prophetant.* A quibus denique diligenter cavere docuit ore veritatis. *Attendite,* inquit,[5] *a falsis prophetis, qui veniunt ad vos in vestimentis ovium, intrin-*
10 *secus autem sunt lupi rapaces.* Et sequitur:[6] *A fructibus eorum cognoscetis eos.* Similibus plena est scriptura.

Peccant nihilominus damnabiliter praedicatores, qui, dum vident populum seduci et in errorem prolabi, metu vel favore tacent, et catholica doctrina eos revocare non satagunt, nec contra imminentia eos pericula
15 verbo[a] veritatis munire curant; hi velut canes non latrantes,[7] et mercenarii veniente lupo fugientes, multiplex praeceptum Domini transgrediuntur. Ait enim per ISAI., cap. lviii:[8] *Clama, ne cesses[b], quasi tuba exalta vocem tuam.* Per EZECHIELEM quoque talibus ait cap. xiii:[9] *Non ascendistis ex adverso, nec opposuistis vos murum pro domo Israel, ut*
20 *staretis in praelio in die Domini.* Quae exponens[c] GREGORIUS in PASTORALI ait, dist. xliii, *Sit rector:*[10] *"Ex adverso ascendere" est pro defensione gregis voce libera hujus mundi potestatibus contraire. Et "in die Domini in praelio stare," est pravis decertantibus ex justitiae amore*

---

[a] *om. M V*   [b] *add. et M V*   [c] *add. beatus T H*

---

[1] c. 14 (*PL* 40, 505); c. 8, C. XXII, qu. 2 (RF I, 869).**
[2] *Isai.* 5, 20–23.**
[3] *Jerem.* 23, 40.
[4] *Jerem.* 14, 15–16.
[5] *Matth.* 7, 15.
[6] *Matth.* 7, 16.
[7] Cf. *Isai.* 56, 10.
[8] *Isai.* 58, 1.
[9] *Ezech.* 13, 5.
[10] c. 1, D. XLIII (RF I, 153–154); part. II, c. 4 (*PL* 77, 30B–D).

the people of God with false teaching; indeed ST. AUGUSTINE declares in his book DE MENDACIO: *This sort of falsehood, namely, that in religious instruction, is most serious and must be avoided to the utmost extent.* For the Lord vents his wrath in many ways upon such men (ISAIAH 5), because *they call evil good and light darkness; they put bitter for sweet and sweet for bitter. They acquit the guilty for a bribe and deprive the innocent of his right.* The Lord also addresses such men through JEREMIAH (chapter 23): *I will bring upon you everlasting reproach and perpetual shame, which shall not be forgotten.* Again he declares in JEREMIAH 14: *By sword and famine shall those prophets be consumed and the people to whom they prophesy.* Finally he instructed us to avoid those who only seem to speak the truth: *Beware of false prophets, men who come to you dressed up as sheep while underneath they are savage wolves.* He adds: *You will recognize them by the fruits they bear.* Scripture is filled with such statements.

Preachers sin no less damnably who, when they see their flock misled or falling into error, are silent because of fear or desire for goodwill, who do not attempt to recall their flock to Catholic teaching, and who are not concerned to fortify it with the word of truth against imminent dangers. They are like watchdogs that do not bark and hirelings who flee when the wolf comes; they transgress the Lord's commandment in many ways. For he declared through ISAIAH (chapter 58): *Cry aloud, spare not, lift up your voice like a trumpet.* He also addressed such men through EZEKIEL (chapter 13): *You have not gone up into the breach, or built up a wall for the house of Israel, that it might stand in battle in the day of the Lord.* ST. GREGORY, expounding this verse in his PASTORAL RULE, says (distinction xliii, *Sit rector*): "*To go up into the breach against the enemy*" *is to defend the flock against the powers of this world with a bold voice.* "*To stand in battle in the day of the Lord*" *is to resist the wicked who oppose us out of our love for justice. For does a shepherd who fears to say what is right*

resistere. Pastorem[a] *enim recta timuisse dicere, quid est aliud quam tacendo terga praebuisse? Qui nimirum si pro grege se obicit, murum pro domo Israel hostibus opponit. Hinc delinquenti populo dicitur in Jeremia THREN. iii:*[1] *"Prophetae tui viderunt tibi falsa et stulta; nec aperiebant*
5 *iniquitatem tuam, ut te ad paenitentiam provocarent." Prophetae quippe in sacro eloquio nonnumquam doctores vocantur, qui, dum fugitiva esse praesentia indicant, quae ventura*[b] *sunt, manifestant, quos*[c] *divinus sermo falsa videre redarguit, quia dum culpas corripere metuunt, incassum delinquentibus promissa securitate blandiuntur, qui iniquitatem peccantium*
10 *nequaquam aperiunt*[d]*, quia ab increpationis voce conticescunt. Clavis quippe apertionis est sermo correctionis, quia increpando detegit culpam, quam saepe nescit ipse, qui peccavit.* Talibus rursus per EZECHIELEM minatur[e] Dominus cap. xxxiii:[2] *Si speculator, inquit, viderit gladium venientem, et non insonuerit bucinam*[f]*, et populus se non custodierit,*
15 *veneritque gladius et tulerit animam de his; ille quidem in iniquitate sua*[g] *captus est, sanguinem autem*[h] *ejus de manu speculatoris requiram.* Hinc GREGORIUS, HOMELIA xi IN EZECHIELEM in persona praedicatorum ait:[3] *Tot occidimus, quot ad mortem ire cottidie tepidi*[i] *et tacentes videmus. Quia dum increpare delinquentes noluerit, eos proculdubio*
20 *tacendo pastor occidit;* inquit idem in epistola AD VENANTIUM episcopum.[4]

PROPOSITIO UNDECIMA

A romanae sedis obedientia vi, dolo, et armis trahere nitentibus, fideles ecclesiae filii nequaquam debent cedere, sed tamquam inimicis crucis Christi fortiter usque ad mortem imperterriti repugnare.

---

[a] pastoribus *M V*   [b] futatur *T H*   [c] quod *M*   [d] aperiant *T H*   [e] comminatur *T H*
[f] bucina *V T H*   [g] om. *T H*   [h] om. *M V*   [i] tepide *M V*

---

[1] *Thren.* 2, 14.
[2] *Ezech.* 33, 6.
[3] *PL* 76, 910.
[4] L. I, *Epist.* 34 (*PL* 77, 487B).

do anything in keeping silent besides turn his back upon the truth? Surely he who places himself before his flock builds a wall for the house of Israel against her enemies. Hence it is said to the sinful people in the *LAMEN-TATIONS of Jeremiah (chapter 3): "Your prophets have seen false and foolish visions for you; they have not exposed your wickedness to recall you to repentance."* Indeed, prophets are sometimes called teachers in sacred usage, since by pointing out the fleeting quality of the present they make manifest the things that are to come. The words of the Lord insist that such men see false things, because they vainly flatter wrongdoers with promised security when they are afraid to correct their faults; they do not expose the wickedness of sinners at all because they refrain from rebuking them. Indeed, the word of correction is the key of exposure, because by rebuke it discloses a fault which is often unknown to the one who has committed the fault. The Lord again threatens such teachers through the mouth of EZEKIEL (chapter 23): *If the watchman sees the sword coming and does not blow the trumpet, so that the people are not warned, and the sword comes and takes any one of them, that man is taken away in his iniquity, but his blood I will require at the watchman's hand.* Hence ST. GREGORY says in *Sermon 11 on Ezekiel* concerning the office of preachers: *We slay all those whom every day we indifferently and silently watch risking mortal wrath.* ST. GREG-ORY declares in a letter to Bishop Venantius: *For when the pastor refuses to rebuke those that sin, there is no doubt that in silence he slays them.*

ELEVENTH PROPOSITION

The faithful sons of the Church ought never to yield to those who seek to lure them from obedience to the Roman see by force, deceit, and arms, but undaunted in the face of death should repulse them as enemies of the cross of Christ.

DEFENSORIUM OBEDIENTIAE APOSTOLICAE

Quoniam quidem impellenti ad mortale peccatum, quale est inobedientia sedis apostolicae ex supradictis, nequaquam cedendum est, nec propter quemcumque metum etiam ademptionem vitae corporalis consentiendum, ut mortale peccatum committatur, per quod anima
5 spiritualiter moritur. Siquidem corpus animae, vita temporalis perpetuae, bonum commutabile incommutabili bono est nullatenus praeferendum. Hinc NICOLAUS papa ait, xxxi, quaest. ii, *Lotharius*:[1] *Nec etiam occisores corporis sunt timendi contra justitiam hominem impellentes.* Dicente salvatore nostro MATT. x:[2] *Nolite timere eos, qui corpus*
10 *occidunt, animam autem occidere non possunt. Sicut denique sacerdos debitor est*, ait JOANNES CHRYSOSTOMUS SUPER MATTHEUM xi, quaest. iii, *Nolite*,[3] *ut veritatem quam audivit a Deo, libere praedicet, sicut*[a] *laicus debitor est, ut veritatem, quam audivit a sacerdote, probatam quidem ex scripturis, defendat fiducialiter. Quod si non fecerit, prodit*
15 *veritatem:*[4] *"Corde enim creditur ad justitiam, ore autem confessio fit ad salutem."*

Est autem resistendum invasoribus obedientium tamquam inimicis crucis Christi, quoniam et evacuare crucis Christi fructum, et impellere[b] ad negandum crucifixum, viribus omnibus elaborant. Qui enim non tam
20 corpus perdere quam animam in culpae praecipitium trahere satagit, quomodo facit quicumque ad culpam inobedientiae homines impellit, quantum ad hos passionis Christi fructum evacuat, quos magis vult esse filios gehennae per rebellionem, ad quam cogit, quam vitae per crucem Christi[c] acquisitae per justitiam, quam[d] relinquere compellit.
25 Qui etiam efficaciter vult antecedens, virtualiter vult et consequens, sicut qui unum dicit, dicit et omne, quod sequitur ex eo, argumento[e] xi, quaest. *iii, Existimant.*[5]

---

[a] Sic et *V*, Si *T H*   [b] implere *M V*   [c] om. *V*   [d] quoque *M V*   [e] art. *V T H*

[1] c. 4, C. XXXI, qu. 2 (RF I, 1114).
[2] *Matth.* 10, 28.
[3] c. 86, C. XI, qu. 3 (RF I, 667); pseudo-Chrys., *Hom. 25 in Matthaeum* (*PG* 56, 762).
[4] *Rom.* 10, 10.
[5] c. 84, C. XI, qu. 3 (RF I, 666).

A DEFENSE OF APOSTOLIC OBEDIENCE

Indeed, they must never yield to one who incites them to mortal sin—since we have established that disobedience to the Apostolic See is mortal sin—and must never consent to the commission of a mortal sin that inflicts spiritual death upon the soul on account of any fear, even the loss of life in this world. The body certainly must in no respect be placed before the soul, nor temporal life before life everlasting, nor a transitory good before one that is unchanging. Hence Pope NICHOLAS[1] declares (Cause xxxi, question 2, *Lotharius*): *Not even those who incite a man to oppose justice and who kill the body must be feared.* As our Savior says (MATTHEW 10): *Do not fear those who kill the body but cannot kill the soul.* ST. JOHN CHRYSOSTOM declares (Cause xi, question 3, *Nolite*): *Finally as the priest is bound to proclaim boldly the truth that he received from God, so the layman is bound to defend the truth he received from the priest, indeed, the truth that is founded upon Scripture. If he does not do this, he betrays the truth: "for with the belief of the heart we obtain righteousness, but with the confession of the mouth we obtain salvation."*

But the assailants of the faithful must be resisted as enemies of the cross of Christ, since they strive with all their strength to destroy the fruits of the cross of Christ and to incite the faithful to deny the crucified one. For such men concern themselves not so much with destroying the body as with drawing the soul into the abyss of guilt. He imitates them who incites men to the sin of disobedience and as far as possible destroys the fruit of Christ's passion for them; such a man prefers them to become children of Hell through the rebellion to which he provokes them than to be children of the life acquired by the cross of Christ through the righteousness that he forces them to abandon. He who effectively desires such rebellion virtually desires the consequent loss of righteousness; as he who says one thing says everything that is implied in it, according to the argument of Cause xi, question 3, *Existimant*.

---

[1] Nicholas I (858–867).

DEFENSORIUM OBEDIENTIAE APOSTOLICAE

Eapropter qui vult hominem in peccato[a] in finem vivere, et ita a sua salute deficere, vult etiam hujus salutis pretium, sanquinem Christi pretiosum, jamdudum solutum, jamdudum in cruce fusum, evanescere et frustrari. Rursus quia hujuscemodi pertinaces compellunt negare
5 justitiam, operari[b] iniquitatem, compellunt negare Christum, qui est justitia, sicut sapientia, sicut veritas, sicut virtus, teste apostolo I COR. i:[1] *Factus est nobis a Deo justitia et sanctificatio et redemptio.* Et iterum ibidem:[2] *Praedicamus Christum Dei virtutem et sapientiam.* Sane tota ratio injustitiae et peccati est inobedientia mandatorum, sicut AM-
10 BROSIUS testatur in libro DE PARADISO:[3] *Peccatum est,* inquit, *praevaricatio legis divinae, et caelestium inobedientia mandatorum.* Et AUGUSTINUS, libro DE DUABUS ANIMABUS:[4] *Peccatum est voluntas consequendi vel retinendi, quod justitia vetat:* hoc est dictum[c], peccatum est velle vetitum. Et lib. XXII CONTRA FAUSTUM idem
15 ait:[5] *Peccatum est dictum, factum, vel concupitum contra legem Dei.*

Ecce quomodo per inobedientiam tamquam per[d] formale suum peccatum diffinitur. Itaque recedens ab obedientia, a justitia recedit, per consequens justitiam negat[e]; facto ergo negat Christum, sicut apostolus de illis ait AD TITUM i:[6] *Confitentur se nosse Deum, factis*
20 *autem negant;* de quo et beatus HIERONYMUS dicit, xi, quaest. iii, *Existimant:*[7] *Existimant*[f] *quidem in eo tantum Deum negare* [sic], *si in persecutione quis a gentilitate comprehensus, se confiteri renuerit christianum esse.* Ecce apostolus omnibus, quae perversa sunt factis, Deum asserit negari. Christus sapientia est, justitia et veritas, sanctitas, fortitudo.

---

[a] peccatum *V*   [b] operare *M V*   [c] dictu *T H*   [d] om. *V*   [e] add. et *M*
[f] Existimat *M V*, Estimant *T H*

---

[1] *I Cor.* 1, 30.
[2] *I Cor.* 1, 23–24.
[3] c. 8 (*CSEL* 32,[1] 296; *PL* 14, 309C).
[4] c. 11 (*PL* 42, 105).
[5] c. 27 (*PL* 42, 418).
[6] *Tit.* 1, 16.
[7] c. 84, C. XI, qu. 3 (RF I, 666); *Comm. in epist. ad Titum* (*PL* 26, 611D–612A).

A DEFENSE OF APOSTOLIC OBEDIENCE

Therefore he who desires a man to live in sin until his death and thus forfeit his salvation also desires to debase and devaluate the price of his salvation, the precious blood of Christ, long since shed and poured out upon the cross. This is also true because stiff-necked men force others to deny justice, to do iniquity, and to deny Christ who is justice, wisdom, truth, and virtue, as the Apostle bears witness (I CORINTHIANS 1): *God has made him our righteousness, our sanctification, and our redemption.* Again ST. PAUL declares: *We proclaim Christ, the power of God and the wisdom of God.* Truly the cause of all sin and injustice is the disobedience of commands, as ST. AMBROSE witnesses in his book, DE PARADISO: *Sin is the transgression of the divine law and disobedience of heavenly commands.* ST. AUGUSTINE also declares in his book, DE DUABUS ANIMABUS: *Sin is the will to seek and retain what justice forbids,* that is to say, sin is to desire the forbidden. ST. AUGUSTINE also says in his work, CONTRA FAUSTUM, Book XXII: *Sin is transgression in word, deed, or desire against the law of God.*

Note how sin is defined by disobedience as much as by its particular form. Thus in abandoning obedience, they abandon justice and consequently deny justice; therefore they deny Christ by their actions, as the Apostle says concerning such men (TITUS 1): *They profess to acknowledge God, but deny him by their actions.* ST. JEROME expounds this passage (Cause xi, question 3, *Existimant*): *Some consider that God is denied only when someone who has been arrested by the pagans during a time of persecution refuses to acknowledge that he is a Christian. But note that the Apostle contends that all who do evil deny God. Christ is wisdom, justice, truth, holiness, and strength. Wisdom is denied by folly, justice by*

209

DEFENSORIUM OBEDIENTIAE APOSTOLICAE

Negatur per insipientiam sapientia, per iniquitatem justitia, per menda-
cium veritas, per turpitudinem sanctitas, per imbecillitatem animi forti-
tudo. Quotienscumque vincimur vitiis atque peccatis, totiens Deum negamus;
et econtrario, quotiens bene quid agimus, Deum confitemur; nec arbitrandum
5 *est in die judicii illos tantum a Dei filio denegandos, qui in martyrio*
Christum negaverunt, sed etiam illos omnes, quorum opere vel sermone vel
cogitatione Christus negatur, negat, vel confessus confitetur; de hac puto
confessione, quod discipulis praecepit, dicens:[1] *"Eritis mihi testes in*
Hierusalem et in omni Judea et Samaria et[a] *usque ad terminos terrae."*
10 Haec HIERONYMUS.

Rursus qui non audit, sed spernit, sed temere resistit vicario Christi,
et maxime in his quae ad vicariatus sui officium pertinent, quomodo
pertinere dinoscitur institutio, provisio, ordinatio ministrorum ecclesiae
et ministeriorum, assumptioque eorum in partem sollicitudinis, sicut
15 ex dictis manifestum est, quomodo non Christum spernit, Christo
resistit, cujus ordinationem violat, et ita[b] opere Christum negat? Ipso
dicente, ut supra allegatum est:[2] *Qui vos spernit, me spernit*[c]. Et Paulus:[3]
Qui potestati resistit Dei, ordinationi resistit. Ex quibus aperte colligitur,
quod nihil aliud[d] est dictu[e]: "Nega hunc, quem apostolica sedes juste[f]
20 constituit, confitere illum[g] quem rite privavit, ab illo recede, isti adhaere," quam dicere: "nega Christum, profitere idolum, recede a vicario
Christi, adhaere praecursori antichristi, relinque obedientiam, cole
rebellionem, declina justitiam, operare iniquitatem, separare ab ecclesia,
ordire schisma, egredere arcam salvationis, ingredere Charybdim
25 aeternae damnationis, caelesti cede haereditati, corruptibili contentare
vanitate, vitam perde perpetuam, mortem elige sempiternam."

Unde similiter patet, quod licet principes et potestatem habentes,
moventes arma contra obedientes romano pontifici, crudeles sint[h]

---

[a] *om. M T H*   [b] *iterum M V*   [c] *add.* et cetera *T H*   [d] *om. M V*   [e] *dictum V*   [f] *om. V*
[g] istum *T H*   [h] sunt *M*

---

[1] *Act.* 1, 8.
[2] *Luc.* 10, 16.
[3] *Rom.* 13, 2.

wickedness, truth by falsehood, holiness by filth, and strength by spiritual weakness. Whenever we are vanquished by sins and errors, we deny God; on the other hand, whenever we do what is good, we profess God. One must not suppose that the Son of God will deny in the day of judgment only those who have denied Christ in persecution; but he will also deny all those who deny Christ in thought, word, or deed. Christ will acknowledge him who acknowledges him; in my opinion, this is the acknowledgment that he enjoined upon the disciples, saying: "You will bear witness for me in Jerusalem, and all over Judaea and Samaria, and away to the ends of the earth."

Again does not he who does not heed but rejects and rashly opposes the Vicar of Christ, especially the authority of his office as Vicar—included in this authority are the institution, provision, ordination of the ministers and ministries of the Church, and the responsibility accepted for them, as is clear from what we have said—reject Christ, oppose Christ whose institution he disobeys, and thus in act deny Christ? Christ says, as we have previously noted: *Whoever rejects you, rejects me.* Paul declares: *Anyone who rebels against authority is resisting a divine institution.* From these words one clearly concludes that to say: "Deny this man whom the Apostolic See justly appointed and acknowledge that man whom the Apostolic See solemnly deposed; abandon the former and adhere to the latter" is to say in reality: "Deny Christ, acknowledge an idol, abandon the Vicar of Christ, adhere to the forerunner of the Antichrist,[1] forsake obedience, cleave to rebellion, reject justice, devote yourself to wickedness, separate yourself from the Church, undertake schism, desert the ark of salvation, enter the Charybdis of eternal perdition, exchange a heavenly inheritance for one that perishes, be content with vanity, lose everlasting life, and choose everlasting death."

From this it is evident, in like fashion, that although rulers who enjoy great power and assail those who obey the Roman pontiff are cruel to

---

[1] Cf. Heiko A. Oberman, *The Forerunners of the Reformation* (New York: Holt, Rinehart & Winston, 1966), chap. 1.

inimicis suis innocentibus; crudeliores tamen sunt suis amicis et sub-
ditis, sed crudelissimi sibiipsis. Obedientium quippe etsi res perituras et
corpora invadunt, sed animas nocere non praevalent. Suorum autem
amicorum, auxiliatorum et subditorum, eos ad hujusmodi bellorum
5 excursus sequentium, nedum corpora periculo, sed et animas aeternae
damnationis exponunt judicio. O, horrendam infidelitatem. O, vicem
pessimam: corpus pro domino exponunt subditi, auxiliatores et ministri,
sed versa vice et corpus et animam suorum fidelium dominus tradidit[a]
gehennae, dum magis vult omnes suos a Deo, angelis et[b] beatis perpetuo
10 separari, cumque Diabolo ac damnatis in aeternum cruciari quam suam
superbiam[c] malitiosamque rebellionem, dominandive injustam libidinem
temperare. Sunt tamen tales crudelissimi sibi, in eo quod omnium
suorum damnationem suam efficiunt, seseque tormentis saevissimis
reddunt obnoxios, dum quos regendos a Domino susceperunt ad justi-
15 tiam, compellunt ad injustitiam declinare.

Quibus philosophus[d] in libro SAPIENTIAE loquitur, cap. vi:[1] *A
Domino*, inquit, *data est potestas vobis*[e] *et virtus ab altissimo, qui interro-
gabit opera vestra*[f] *et cogitationes scrutabitur, quoniam cum essetis ministri
regni illius, non recte judicastis, neque custodistis legem justitiae, neque*
20 *secundum voluntatem Dei ambulastis, horrendae et cito apparebit vobis,*[g]
*quoniam judicium durissimum his, qui praesunt, fiet. Exiguo enim, con-
ceditur misericordia, potentes autem potenter tormenta patientur. Non enim
subtrahet personam cujusquam Dominus, neque reverebitur magnitudinem
cujusquam, quoniam pusillum et magnum ipse fecit, et aequalis cura est*
25 *illi de omnibus. Fortioribus autem fortior instat cruciatus.* His ergo
impugnatoribus justitiae debent filii obedientes et salutis aeternae
semper memores fortiter repugnare, nullo pacto[h] eis[i] consentiendo,
dicentes cum beato JOB, cap. xxvi:[2] *Donec deficiam, non recedam ab
innocentia mea. Justitiam meam, quam cepi, non deseram.*

---

[a] tradit *T H*   [b] ac *T H*   [c] superbam *T H*   [d] sapiens *V*   [e] nobis *M*   [f] nostra *M*
[g] nobis *M*   [h] pactu *M*, modo *V*   [i] ejus *M*

[1] *Sap.* 6, 4–9.
[2] *Job* 27, 5–6.*

their innocent foes, they are more cruel to their friends and subjects, and most cruel to themselves. Although they certainly assail the bodies and the perishable goods of the faithful, they have no power over the souls of the faithful. They not only expose to danger the bodies of their friends, allies, and subjects who follow them into warfare of this sort, but they expose their souls, as well, to the threat of eternal condemnation. O monstrous unbelief! O wretched age! Subjects, allies, and officials expose their bodies for their lord, but their lord in turn delivers his subjects' bodies and souls to Hell when he wills them all to be eternally separated from God, the angels, and the saints, and to suffer torment eternally with Satan and the damned rather than curb his arrogance, his wicked rebellion, and his evil lust for power. Yet such rulers are most cruel to themselves, because they effect the loss of all that is theirs and expose themselves to torments of the utmost ferocity when they compel those whom they received from the Lord to rule justly to turn aside into injustice.

The wise man [Solomon] addresses such rulers in the BOOK OF WISDOM (chapter 6): *Your dominion was given you from the Lord and your sovereignty from the Most High, who will search out your works and inquire into your plans. Because as servants of his kingdom you did not rule rightly, nor keep the law of justice, nor walk according to the purpose of God, he will come upon you terribly and swiftly; severe judgment falls on those in high places. For the lowly man may be pardoned in mercy, but mighty men will be mightily tested. For the Lord of all will not stand in awe of anyone, nor show deference to greatness; because he himself made both small and great, and he takes thought for all alike. The mighty incur a mighty chastisement.* Therefore the faithful sons [of the Church] ought to resist the assailants stoutly, always mindful of their eternal salvation; they ought not to consent to any accord with them, declaring with the blessed JOB (chapter 26): *Until I die I will not put away my integrity from me. I will not let go of my righteousness to which I held fast.*

DEFENSORIUM OBEDIENTIAE APOSTOLICAE

Non tamen in sua fortitudine, sed in solo Domino confidant, *apud quem est fortitudo et sapientia, qui novit decipientem et eum, qui decipitur,* JOB xii,[1] *qui adducit consiliarios in stultum finem, et judices in stuporem. Balteum regum dissolvit, et praecingit fune renes eorum.* Quod si impugna-
5 tores secundum terrenam humanamque potentiam fortiores apparent[a], etiamsi reliquus[b] mundus totus assensum praeberet rebellibus et favorem dicendum erit cum dignae memoriae viro Matathias, I MACHAB. ii:[2] *Etsi omnes regi[c] Antiocho, id est principi tyranno, obediunt[d], ut[e] discedat unusquisque a servitute patrum suorum et consenserint mandatis ejus, ego*
10 *et fratres mei et filii mei obediemus legi patrum nostrorum. Propitius nobis sit Deus, non est nobis[f] relinquere legem et justitias Dei. Non audiemus verba regis, transgredientes legis nostrae mandata, ut eamus altera via.*

Neque etiam paucis de victoria desperandum est, dummodo tamen ad Dominum toto corde convertantur, quia scriptum est, I MACHAB.
15 ii:[3] *Non est differentia in conspectu Dei caeli, liberare in multis et in paucis, quia non in multitudine exercitus est victoria, sed de caelo est fortitudo.* Et I REG. iiii:[4] *Non est Deo difficile salvare vel in[g] multitudine vel in paucis.* Et iterum II PARAL. xiiii:[5] *Domine, non est apud te ulla distantia, utrum in paucis auxilieris, aut in pluribus.* Quae etiam multae veteris
20 testamenti comprobant historiae. Unde qui amore justitiae, persecutionis periculo, perseveranter se subiciunt in Domino confidentes de duobus alterum sperare habent: Aut quia in hoc tempore gratiose liberabuntur ab inimicis in die, quem constituit Dominus, aut multo melius secundum apostolum HEB. xi,[6] *non suscipientes temporalem*
25 *redemptionem, ut meliorem invenirent resurrectionem,* quibus sine dubio

---

[a] apparerent *T H*   [b] reliquis *M*   [c] rei *T*   [d] obediant *V*   [e] et *M V*   [f] add. utile *H*
[g] om. *M*

---

[1] *Job* 12, 16–18.
[2] *I Machab.* 2, 19–22.
[3] *I Machab.* 3, 18–19.
[4] *I Reg.* 14, 6.*
[5] *II Paral.* 14, 11.
[6] *Hebr.* 11, 35.

A DEFENSE OF APOSTOLIC OBEDIENCE

Yet let them not trust in their own strength, but in the Lord only, *with whom are strength and wisdom; the deceived and the deceiver are his. He leads counselors away stripped, and judges he makes fools. He looses the bonds of kings, and binds a waistcloth on their loins* (JOB 12). Although these assailants may appear more formidable in secular and human terms, and although all the world may offer approval and favor to the rebels, we must say with Mattathias, that man of worthy memory (I MAC-CABEES): *Even if all obey King Antiochus*, that is, the tyrant ruler, *and choose to do his commandments, departing each one from the religion of his fathers, yet I and my sons and my brothers will obey the covenant of our fathers. May God be gracious to us, for we will not abandon the law and righteousness of God. We will not heed the words of the king by turning aside from the commands of our covenant to walk in another road.*

Even a few faithful must not despair of victory, provided, of course, they turn their whole hearts to the Lord, since it is written (I MACCA-BEES 2): *In the sight of the God of heaven there is no difference between victory by many or by few, since it is not on the size of the army that victory depends; strength comes from heaven.* It is written in the book of SAMUEL, chapter 4: *It is easy for God to save by many or by few.* Or again it is recorded in II CHRONICLES, chapter 14: *Lord, for you there is no difference whether few or many require help.* Many events of the Old Testament affirm this. Therefore those who, led by the love of justice, steadfastly submit to the danger of persecution and trust in the Lord have two grounds for hope: they will be rescued providentially from their enemies in this world on the day that the Lord ordains or, even better, in the words of the Apostle (HEBREWS 11): *disdaining temporal release, they will win a better resurrection.* To such, without doubt, *the Lord provides*

215

DEFENSORIUM OBEDIENTIAE APOSTOLICAE

Dominus facit, I COR. x,[1] *cum temptatione proventum, ut possint utiliter sustinere*. De quo sit haec propositio novissima et finalis.

PROPOSITIO DUODECIMA[a]

Quisquis ex Dei caritate pro hujus obedientiae justitia conservanda impugnatus sanguinem fundens moritur, tamquam martyr a Domino
5 coronatur.

Martyr est coram Domino, quicumque amore Dei propter actum virtutis moritur, ut vult beatus THOMAS in SUMMA, ii, ii, quaest. cxxiiii, art. v.[2] Cui consonat illud evangelii MATT. v:[3] *Beati qui persecutionem patiuntur propter justitiam. Est autem justitia omnis virtus*, V
10 ETHICORUM.[4] Hinc multos ecclesia tamquam martyres veneratur, qui non professione[b] fidei, sed alterius virtutis actu mortem susceperunt. Sic beatus Joannes Baptista propter adulterii reprehensionem gladio occubuit. Sic Matthaeus, apostolus et evangelista, quia virginitatis votum matrimonia praetulit, atque Epigeniam Deo sacratam virginem,
15 ab Hirtaci regis copula prohibuit, jussu ejusdem tyranni ferro interemptus est.[5] Sic beatus Hermigildus, cujus supra mentio habita est,[6] quia eucharistiam ab Arriano episcopo accipere recusavit jussu patris sui est extinctus. Sic beatus Thomas Cantuariensis episcopus[c], a tyranno christiano pro libertate ecclesiae, cui cedere indignum judicaverat,
20 martyrio coronatur. Dum itaque homines hujus saeculi variis ex causis, quidam propter[d] perituras[d] divitias, alii propter momentaneas voluptates, alii propter amicorum fidem, alli propter patriae liberationem, alii mundanum propter honorem, alii propter diffamiae repulsionem, alii

---

[a] *add.* ET FINALIS *M V*   [b] pro confessione *T H*   [c] archiepiscopus *T H*
[d-d] perituras propter *M V*

[1] *I Cor.* 10, 13.*
[2] *Summa theol.*, P. II, II, qu. 124, a. 5 (Moos, 2057a–2058b; Parma III, 437).
[3] *Matth.* 5, 10.
[4] Arist., *Opera, Nic. Eth.*, L. V, c. 1, 1129b.
[5] Cf. *Acta sanctorum septembris* (Antwerp, 1757), VI, 196C.
[6] Vide 170.

when the test comes, that they may be able to sustain it properly (I CORIN-THIANS 10). The very last proposition upon these matters follows.

TWELFTH PROPOSITION

Anyone who, led by the love of God, dies violently to defend the justice of this obedience receives a martyr's crown from the Lord.

The Lord regards him as a martyr who, led by the love of God, suffers death for an act of virtue, as ST. THOMAS AQUINAS declares in his SUMMA (II, II, question 124, article 5). The words of the gospel are in agreement (MATTHEW 5): *Blessed are those who have suffered persecution for the cause of justice.* ARISTOTLE asserts (ETHICS, Book V): *Justice is all virtue.* Hence the Church reveres many as martyrs who suffered death, not for an acknowledgment of their faith, but for another sort of virtue. Thus St. John the Baptist died by the sword for condemning adultery. Thus St. Matthew, apostle and evangelist, because he preferred the vow of virginity to marriage and forbade King Hirtacus to wed Ephigenia, a virgin consecrated to God, was slain by the sword upon the order of this tyrant. Thus St. Hermengild, who has been mentioned before, suffered death because he refused to obey the command of his father to receive the Eucharist from an Arian bishop. Thus St. Thomas, Bishop of Canterbury, received the martyr's crown for defending the liberty of the Church against a Christian tyrant, to whom he considered it disgraceful to yield. Therefore when men of this age have faced the danger of death for various reasons, some for riches that vanish, for fleeting pleasures, for the bond of friendship, for the liberation of their homeland, for worldly honor, for their vindication against

propter rem publicam, alii propter honestatem aut quamlibet moralem justitiam periculo corporalem vitam supposuere[a], effeminatus nimium probatur catholicus, qui dum aeterna sibi offertur corona, mortem corporis quam solvere necesse est, timet tempore modico praevenire.
5 Sed magis guadendum est christiano, dum propter justitiam persecutionem patitur, dum ad Christi Domini imitationem sicut amicus singularis, sicut filius electionis suae signo certiore ad palmam sublimemque gloriam vocitatur.

Propter quod apostolus, PHIL. i, ait:[1] *In nullo terreamini ab adver-*
10 *sariis, quae est illis causa perditionis, vobis[b] autem causa salutis, et hoc ideo* [sic!], *quia vobis datum est a Christo, non solum ut in eum credatis, sed ut etiam pro illo patiamini.* Ideoque apostoli a concilio Judaeorum colaphizati, ACT. v,[2] *ibant gaudentes, quia digni inventi sunt pro Christi nomine contumeliam pati.* Hinc beatus JACOBUS ait, JACOB. i:[3]
15 *Omne gaudium existimate, fratres, cum in varias temptationes incideritis, quia beatus vir, qui suffert temptationem, quoniam cum probatus fuerit, accipiet coronam vitae, quam repromisit Dominus diligentibus se.* Quae verba tractans beatus HIERONYMUS, in epistola AD ASELLAM ait:[4] Illos, inquit, apostolus, probatos, et ab his Deum diligi, qui ob
20 nominis ejus causam in temptationibus perstiterunt[c], quibus merito corona promittitur. Illos vero reprobos et nullius vitae praemio dignos quos[d] nulla temptationum causa vexarit. Sed et ipsa quae neminem fallit aeterna veritas, MATT. v, ait:[5] *Beati estis cum vobis maledixerint homines et persecuti vos fuerint, et dixerint omne malum adversus[e] vos*
25 *mentientes propter me, gaudete et exultate, quoniam[f] merces vestra multa est in caelis.*

---

[a] supponere *M V* [b] nobis *M* [c] praestiterunt *M* [d] quas *T H* [e] adversum *T H*
[f] ecclesiae enim *M V*

[1] *Philip.* 1, 28–29.
[2] *Act.* 5, 41.
[3] *Jacob.* 1, 2–12.
[4] Cf. *Epist.* 45 (*PL* 22, 483).
[5] *Matth.* 5, 11–12.

A DEFENSE OF APOSTOLIC OBEDIENCE

slander, for public concerns, and for integrity and other virtues, a Catholic is proven fainthearted indeed, who, when he is offered an immortal crown, fears to hasten slightly the physical death which he must undergo. But the Christian ought rather to rejoice when he suffers persecution for the cause of justice, when he is summoned by a more evident sign to the imitation of Christ his Lord as a special friend and as his chosen son, and when he is summoned to a martyr's crown and sublime glory.

On account of this joy, the Apostle says (PHILIPPIANS 1): *Meet your opponents without so much as a tremor, for this is a sign to them that their doom is sealed, but for you a sign of your salvation, afforded by God himself; for you have been granted the privilege not only of believing in Christ but also of suffering for him.* Therefore the apostles, flogged by order of the council of the Jews (ACTS 5), *went out rejoicing that they had been found worthy to suffer indignity for the sake of the name of Christ.* Hence ST. JAMES declares (JAMES 1): *Count yourselves supremely happy, my brothers, when you face trials of many kinds, for happy is the man who endures trial; for having passed that test, he will receive the crown of life promised to those who love God.* ST. JEROME expounds these words in a letter to Asella. The Apostle says those endure trial and are loved by God who for the sake of his name stand fast in temptations; to these is a crown justly promised. They are indeed reprobate and in no way worthy of the reward of life who are disturbed by no temptation. Moreover he who is the eternal truth which deceives no man declares (MATTHEW 5): *Blessed are you when men revile you and persecute you and utter all kinds of evil against you falsely on my account. Rejoice and be glad, for your reward is great in heaven.*

DEFENSORIUM OBEDIENTIAE APOSTOLICAE

CONCLUSIO[a]

Haec est praedicationis meae summa, haec mea doctrina, quam in causa saepe dicta coram populo exposui. *Haec est et fides mea, hanc in sancta catholica didici ecclesia*, xxiiii, quaest. i, *Haec est*,[1] quam cum beatissimo Hieronymo sanctae romanae sedi humiliter offero. In qua
5 si minus perite, aut parum caute forte positum est, emendari cupio ab eo, qui Petri et sedem tenet et fidem. Si vero haec mea confessio apostolatus sui judicio comprobatur, quicumque me culpare voluerit, se imperitum aut malivolum, aut etiam non catholicum sed haereticum comprobabit. Verum quia nihil tam solidum, quod dubitationem non
10 recipiat, nihil tam claris probationibus deductum, contra quod non possit obici multaque ex verbis legis et scripturae apparenter adduci. *Siquidem multa sunt verba in scripturis divinis*, ait beatus CLEMENS dist. xxxvii, *Relatum*,[2] *quae possunt retrahi ad eum sensum, quem sibi sponte unusquisque praesumpsit.*
15 Idcirco cum his, qui hanc meam confessionem sophistice ad simplicium seductionem impugnare conabuntur, nolo scriptis aut verbo inutiliter replicando contendere. Sed si qui eam ex intentione censuerint impugnandam, cum his paratus sum apostolicae sedis judicium experiri.

Et quoniam sunt plerique a Deo carnali passione caecati, ut apostoli-
20 cam sedem in hac causa suspectam habeant, et quod dictu nefas est, blasphemantes infament, eapropter ut malignantium ora omnimodis obstruantur, et oblatrandi sistat emulatio, quisquis me in his scriptis impie sensisse criminabitur, offero meipsum et haec mea scripta, cujuslibet catholici non suscepti episcopi apostolicae sedis gratiam habentis,
25 aut universitatis cujuspiam, quam causa saepe dicta quantum ad temporale damnum vel lucrum verisimiliter tangere non poterit, justo judicio, etiam de parendo eidem, cautionem sufficientem praestaturus,

---

[a] *om. M V*

[1] c. 14, C. XXIV, qu. 1 (RF I, 970); ibi Hieronymo ascribitur.
[2] c. 14, D. XXXVII (RF I, 139).

220

CONCLUSION

This is a summary of my preaching, this is my teaching, which I have expounded again and again before the people in this issue. *This is my faith, this I taught in the holy Catholic Church* (Cause xxiv, question 1, *Haec est*). This I offer humbly with the most blessed Jerome to the holy Roman see. If this treatise is unskilled or overstated in any respect, I desire to be corrected by him who holds the chair and faith of Peter. If my confession is indeed acknowledged by his apostolic judgment, anyone who attempts to criticize me is acknowledged to be unskilled, ill disposed, or even not Catholic but heretical. I grant that nothing is so solid that it does not admit doubt, nothing concluded from proofs so clear that many things from law and Scripture cannot be speciously cited and suggested against it. ST. CLEMENT declares (distinction xxxvii, *Relatum*): *There are many words in Holy Scripture which can be interpreted according to personal preference and whim.*

Therefore I do not wish to enter into a futile exchange of words or writings with those who will endeavor to attack my confession sophistically in order to mislead simple folk. But if any are of the opinion that my basic premise ought to be assailed, I am prepared to await with them the judgment of the Apostolic See.

Many men, blinded by God and carnal passion, suspect the Apostolic See in this issue, and blasphemously slander it, I am shocked to say. Therefore, in order that the mouths of the wicked may be muzzled and the strife of tongues may cease—including those who accuse me in their writings of distortion in this treatise—I offer myself and my writings to the equitable judgment of any Catholic bishop, not under suspicion, who enjoys the favor of the Apostolic See, or the judgment of any university that this conflict does not involve in probable temporal loss or gain. I will abide by such a decision and I will offer a sufficient pledge of such

221

DEFENSORIUM OBEDIENTIAE APOSTOLICAE

dummodo tamen se ad paria meus impugnator dolo et fraude cessantibus obligabit.

Datum[a] anno Domini millesimoquadringentesimosexagesimosecundo, die vicesimasecunda, mensis octobris, pontificatus sanctissimi in Christo patris et domini nostri[b] Pii, divina providentia papae secundi, anno quinto.

Deo[c] gratias[c].

[a] Datis *M*   [b] *add.* domini *T H*
[c–c] Finis DEFENSORII OBEDIENTIAE APOSTOLICAE *T H*

intent, provided, naturally, that my assailant will bind himself by similar pledges to desist from guile and deceit.

I write this on the twenty-second day in the month of October, in the one thousand four hundred and sixty-second year of our Lord and the fifth year of the pontificate of our most holy father and lord in Christ, Pius II, Pope by divine providence.

Thanks be to God!

EXECRABILIS

Execrabilis et pristinis temporibus inauditus tempestate nostra inolevit abusus, ut a Romano Pontifice, Jesu Christi vicario, cui dictum est in persona beati Petri:[1] *Pasce oves meas, et quodque ligaveris super terram, erit ligatum et in caelis*, nonnulli, spiritu rebellionis imbuti, non
5 sanioris cupiditate judicii, sed commissi evasione peccati, ad futurum concilium provocare praesumant, quod quantum sacris canonibus adversetur, quantumque reipublicae christianae noxium sit, quisquis non ignarus jurium intelligere potest. Namque (ut alia praetereamus, quae huic corruptelae manifestissime refragantur) quis non illud ridi-
10 culum judicaverit, quod ad id appellatur quod nusquam est, neque scitur, quando futurum sit? Pauperes a potentioribus multipliciter opprimuntur, remanent impunita scelera, nutritur adversus Primam Sedem rebellio, libertas delinquendi conceditur, et omnis ecclesiastica disciplina et hierarchicus ordo confunditur.
15 Volentes igitur hoc pestiferum virus a Christi Ecclesia procul pellere,

---

[1] *Joan*, 21, 17; *Matth*. 18, 18.**

EXECRABILIS

A horrible abuse, unheard-of in earlier times, has sprung up in our period. Some men, imbued with a spirit of rebellion and moved not by a desire for sound decisions but rather by a desire to escape the punishment for sin, suppose that they can appeal from the Pope, Vicar of Jesus Christ; from the Pope, to whom in the person of the blessed Peter it was said, *Feed my sheep,* and *whatever you bind on earth will be bound in heaven* —from this pope to a future council. How harmful this is to the Christian republic, as well as how contrary to canon law, anyone who is not ignorant of the law can understand. For, not to mention all the other things which so clearly gainsay this corruption, who would not consider it ridiculous to appeal to something which does not now exist anywhere nor does anyone know when it will exist? The poor are heavily oppressed by the powerful, offenses remain unpunished, rebellion against the first see is encouraged, license for sin is granted, and all ecclesiastical discipline and hierarchical ranking of the Church are turned upside-down.

Desirous, therefore, of banishing this deadly poison from the Church

NOTE: The Latin text is reprinted from *Bullarium diplomatum et privilegiorum sanctorum Romanorum pontificum,* ed. S. Franco and A. Dalmazzo (Turin, 1860), V, 149–150.

225

EXECRABILIS

et ovium nobis commissarum saluti consulere, omnemque materiam
scandali ab ovili nostri Salvatoris arcere, de venerabilium fratrum nostrorum Sanctae Romanae Ecclesiae cardinalium cunctorumque praelatorum ac divini et humani juris interpretum Curiam sequentium consilio
5 et assensu, ac certa nostra scientia, hujusmodi provocationes damnamus,
et tamquam erroneas ac detestabiles reprobamus, cassantes et penitus
annullantes, si quae hactenus taliter interpositae reperiantur, easque,
tamquam inanes ac pestiferas, nullius momenti esse decernimus et
declaramus. Praecipientes deinceps, ut nemo audeat, quovis quaesito
10 colore, ab ordinationibus, sententiis, sive mandatis quibuscumque
nostris ac successorum nostrorum, talem appellationem interponere, aut
interpositae per alium adhaerere, seu eis quomodolibet uti.

Si quis autem contrafecerit, a die publicationis praesentium in Can-
cellaria Apostolica, post duos menses, cujuscumque status, gradus,
15 ordinis vel conditionis fuerit, etiam si imperiali, regali vel pontificali
praefulgeat dignitate, ipso facto sententiam execrationis incurrat, a qua,
nisi per Romanum Pontificem, et in mortis articulo, absolvi non possit.
Universitas vero sive collegium ecclesiastico subjaceat interdicto, et
nihilominus, tam collegia et universitates, quam praedictae et aliae
20 quaecumque personae, eas poenas ac censuras incurrant, quas rei
majestatis et haereticae pravitatis fautores incurrere dignoscuntur.
Tabelliones insuper ac testes, qui hujusmodi actibus interfuerint, et
generaliter qui scienter consilium, auxilium dederint vel favorem talibus
appellantibus, pari poena plectantur.
25 Nulli ergo hominum liceat hanc paginam nostrorum voluntatis,
damnationis, reprobationis, cassationis, annullationis, decreti, declarationis et mandati infringere, vel ei ausu temerario contraire. Si quis
autem hoc attentare praesumpserit, indignationem omnipotentis Dei ac
beatorum Petri et Pauli apostolorum ejus se noverit incursurum.
30 Datum Mantuae, anno Incarnationis dominicae millesimo quadringentesimo sexagesimo[a], decimo quinto kalendas februarii, pontificatus
nostri anno primo.

---

[a] quinquagesimo nono *Magnum Bullarium Romanum.*

226

EXECRABILIS

of Christ, and concerned with the salvation of the sheep committed to us and the protection of the sheepfold of our Savior from all causes of scandal; with the counsel and with the assent drawn from our venerable Fathers of the holy Roman Church, all the cardinals and prelates and all those who interpret divine and human law in accordance with the Curia; and being fully informed: we condemn appeals of this kind, reject them as erroneous and abominable, and declare them to be completely null and void. If any such appeals are found to have heretofore been made we declare and decree them to be of no effect but rather void and injurious. And we lay down that from now on, no one should dare, regardless of his pretext, to make such an appeal from our decisions, be they legal or theological, or from any commands at all from us or our successors, to heed such an appeal made by another, or to make use of these in any fashion whatsoever.

But if anyone—regardless of his status, rank, order, or condition, even if he be distinguished by imperial, regal, or pontifical dignity—should violate this command when two months have expired from the day this bull has been published in the papal chancery, he, by this fact alone, incurs excommunication from which he cannot be absolved except through the Pope and at the time of death. Moreover, a college or university ought to be subject to ecclesiastical mandates, and colleges and universities, no less than the aforesaid persons and any others whosoever, will incur these punishments or censures. In addition, notaries and witnesses who give expert counsel, help, and assistance to those who make such appeals are to be punished with the same punishment.

No one, therefore, is allowed to violate or daringly oppose this, our expression of what is to be desired, condemned, reproved, voided, annulled, decreed, asserted, and commanded. If, however, anyone should be presumptuous enough to attempt this, he should know that he will incur the indignation of almighty God and of his blessed apostles, Peter and Paul.

Promulgated at Mantua in the year of our Lord's incarnation 1460, on the eighteenth day of January, in the first year of our pontificate.

SENTENTIA EXAUCTORATUS CONTRA DIETHERUM, ELECTOREM MOGUNTINUM

Pius episcopus, servus servorum Dei, ad perpetuam rei memoriam.

In apostolicae sedis specula divino consilio constituta duo inter alia praecipua, quae a nobis diligentissime inspici curarique debent, alterum, ut bene merentes condignis praemiis et gratiis prosequamur, alterum, ut
5 divinae legis contemptores, contumaces ac rebelles, qui corrigi et emendari nolunt, congruis poenis ac suppliciis afficiamus. Praemio enim et poena res publica continetur, dum nostri aevi conditio, in quo, qui populo praesunt, non tam praemiandi quam puniendi curam habere oportet, quamvis nec superiorum temporum bonorum numerus malorum

SENTENCE OF DEPOSITION
PROMULGATED AGAINST DIETHER,
THE ELECTOR OF MAINZ

Pius, Bishop, Servant of the Servants of God, for perpetual remembrance.

In the watchtower of the Apostolic See, established by divine intent, there are two matters of particular importance which we ought to consider with the utmost concern: the first, that we bestow suitable rewards and marks of favor upon the well deserving; the second, that we inflict suitable penalties and torments upon those who scorn divine law and those obstinate and rebellious men who oppose correction and chastisement. Indeed, a commonwealth is held together by rewards and penalties. It is the condition of our age—although the number of wicked men does not surpass the number in former, better times—that those who rule the people must be more concerned to chastise than to reward, and that

NOTE: The Latin text is reprinted from Joachim Johann Müller, *Des Heiligen Römischen Reichs Teutscher Nation Reichstag Theatrum, wie selbiges unter Keyser Friedrichs V allerhöchsten Regierung von Anno MCCCCXL bis MCCCCXCIII gestanden* ... (Jena, 1713), II, 31–35.

excesserit, et omnis pontifex inter adversantium insidias atque arma transiverit, perrari quippe boni sunt et prona in malum est natura hominis, quae, si aliquam impunitatem assequitur, tanquam provocata, magis ac magis prolabitur, nec tam venia communi utilitati consulit, 5 quam vindicta, cessant enim peccare homines, ubi severitas delicta compescit, facilitas veniae incentivum delinquendi praebet.

Experti sumus hoc nos in pluribus aliis, sed praecipue in Diethero, qui se Moguntinum electum appellat, quem tanto contumaciorem et rebelliorem invenimus, quanto ei clementiam et benignitatem majorem 10 ostendimus, quemadmodum ex his, quae infra dicemus, cuilibet intelligere licebit, vocavit siquidem superioribus temporibus, cum Mantuam pergeremus ecclesia Moguntina, quemadmodum et metropolitica est, per obitum bonae memoriae Theodorici ultimi ejus archiepiscopi, canonici capitulariter, ut moris est, congregati, ad electionem futuri pastoris 15 procedere volentes, in quosdam arbitros compromisere, qui suo nomine electionem facerent, illi similiter convenientes Dietherum praedictum elegerunt, quamvis, ut postea nobis enotuit, non sine labe et infamia simoniae. Siquidem unus ex arbitris magna vi pecuniae corruptus extitit, cujus vox quarto loco accedens inter septem arbitros causam prae- 20 buit ut Dietherus majorem partem haberet et electus diceretur, qui similiter cum capitulo procuratores et decretum electionis ad nos misit, petens, ut electionem hujusmodi confirmantes de persona sua Moguntinae Ecclesiae provideremus, non attendentes, quanta est Moguntini archiepiscopi apud Germanos auctoritas, et quam conventui Mantuan- 25 ensi, cui tunc praesidebamus, sua praesentia admodum utilis esset, propterea, quae contra Turcorum perfidiam agere intendebamus, Diethero eidem mandavimus, ut ad nos, sicut jura volunt, pro confirmatione sese conferret, quia multa pro Dei honore et salute populi Christiani secum tractaturi eramus, prorogantes veniendi tempus et certissimam 30 suae confirmationis spem facientes, tum ejus promotionem illi ecclesiae utilem putaremus, sed homini pertinaci ac durae cervicis nunquam

every pontiff must chart his course amidst the snares and arms of his adversaries; indeed, the good are exceedingly rare, and human nature is prone to evil. If human nature finds any respite from punishment, it errs more and more, as if encouraged. The general welfare is not defended so much by indulgence as by chastisement; for men cease to sin when severity restrains crime, but lenience offers an incentive to it.

This has been our experience with many other men, but it has been most striking in the case of Diether, who calls himself the elected Archbishop of Mainz, and who has proven even more obstinate and rebellious as we have shown him greater mercy and forbearance—as we will relate later to whomever is entitled to know. In former times when we were involved with the Mantuan enterprise, the church of Mainz announced a convocation. Upon the death of Dietrich of devout memory, the late Archbishop of Mainz, the canons gathered in chapter according to their custom, since Mainz is a metropolitan church, in order to elect their future pastor. They bound themselves to abide by the decision of certain arbiters who would carry out the election in their name. These arbiters, upon assembling, elected the said Diether, although not without the defect and horror of simony. Indeed one of the arbiters was swayed by an enormous bribe; his vote, falling in the fourth place among the seven arbiters, determined that Diether secured the majority and was proclaimed the Archbishop-elect. Diether and likewise the chapter dispatched envoys and the election decree to us, seeking that we confirm such an election and that we provide him to the church of Mainz; they did not consider how great the authority of the Archbishop of Mainz is among the Germans and how very useful his presence would be to the Congress of Mantua, over which we were at that time presiding, because we intended to assail the perfidious Turks. We ordered the said Diether to come to us for his confirmation, as the laws provide, so that we might consider with him many things concerning the honor of God and the security of Christendom. We postponed the time of his appearance and expressed the firmest hope of his confirmation, because we considered his promotion at that time advantageous to that church. But this obstinate,

231

persuaderi potuit, ut ad nos et conventum tam necessarium accedere
vellet, modo corporis infirmitatem, modo pauperiem praetendenti,
quamvis et valitudinem bonam ejus expectaturos nos diceremus, quae
mox consecuta est, et adventum ejus cum parvo comitatu requireremus,
5 tum staret immobile vitiati animi propositum, nec flecti adveniendum
posset, cessimus insectari superiores et ad discipuli voluntatem magistri
descendimus, sperantes vincere in bono malum, et dari capitis opinionem
clementi benignitate mollire, providimus Ecclesiae Moguntinae de sua
persona litterasque provisionis in forma consueta decrevimus, neque
10 enim ea nobis innotuerant, de ipso vitia, quae postea palum emerserunt,
et bonum esse arbitrabamur, quem capitulum moguntinum in pastorem
efflagitasset, procuratores, Dietheri ejus nomine et in animam ejus ea
nobis juraverunt, quae caeteri episcopi Romanis Pontificibus jurare
consueverant, et ultra hoc venturum ipsum personaliter infra annum ad
15 praesentiam nostram, quocumque in loco cum Romana Curia degeremus,
ad quae facienda procuratores praedicti speciale mandatum exhibuerunt.

Credidimus bonis verbis ejusdem Dietheri, qui per litteras et nuntios
ejus optimum se futurum et obedientissimum filium pollicebatur, sed
cum animo sitiendi expectaremus hunc hominem, tanquam sedis
20 apostolicae propugnatorem et Catholicae fidei defensorem, ea curare,
quae pro tutela Christianae religionis in Mantuensi conventu concluse-
ramus, invitare homines suae nationis ad expeditionem contra Turcos
obeundam, ad obediendum in ea re carissimo filio nostro Frederico
Romanorum Imperatori Augusto, ad quem idcirco legatum de latere
25 miseramus ad parandos exercitus, ad solvendas decimas, ac vigesimas et

stiff-necked man could not be persuaded to come to us and this congress which was so important; at one time he claimed physical infirmity, and at another time he claimed poverty, although we declared that we would await his restoration to good health, which shortly came to pass, and that we would require him to come with only a small retinue.[1] When the said Diether remained immovable in his corrupted soul and could not be persuaded to come, we ceased to reproach superiors and turned our attention [to winning] the assent of the master's disciples. Hoping to overcome evil with good and to soften the opinion of this ruler by merciful forbearance, we provided him with the church of Mainz and we promulgated the letters of provision in the accustomed form, for those vices were unknown to us which became public knowledge afterwards. We thought it well [to recognize him] whom the chapter of Mainz had earnestly requested as its pastor. The envoys of Diether swore to us in his name and upon his soul those things which other bishops [of Mainz] were accustomed to swear to the Roman pontiffs. In addition, they swore that he would come to us in person within a year, wherever the Roman Curia was then established. The envoys of the said Diether presented a special written pledge to fulfill this obligation.[2]

We believed the fair words of the said Diether, who promised through his letters and his envoys to be a very good and most obedient son; with soul athirst we waited for this man to concern himself, as a champion of the Apostolic See and defender of the Catholic faith, with those things we had concluded in the Congress of Mantua for the defense of the Christian religion: to summon the men of his nation to undertake an expedition against the Turks, and to summon them to obey in this enterprise our dearly beloved son, Frederick, August Emperor of the Romans, to whom for this reason we had sent a personal legate[3] to raise an army, to levy

---

[1] See p. 255.

[2] See p. 255.

[3] A *legatus de latere* enjoys the highest rank in the papal diplomatic service. Cardinal Bessarion was the legate in this instance.

trigesimas contribuendas et alia praesidia praestanda, homo in reprobum
sensum datus, Dei hostis, et totius gratitudinis inimicus mox cornua
erexit in apostolicam sedem, et matri suae maledicere coepit, latravit
contra nos pluribus modis, legatum nostrum calumniatus est, qui decimas
5 conaretur exigere, quibus copiae contra Turcos armari possent; palamque
dicere non est veritus, nos argentum nationis non fidei defensionem
quaerere, licet nos decimas ipsas non nisi consentiente natione exigi
mandavissemus, et illarum custodiam ac dispensationem in manibus
eorum tradi jussissemus, quos natio ipsa delegisset.

10   Inter haec accidit, ut ad instantiam mercatorum, qui pecunias Apostolicae Sedi debitas sibi mutuo concesserunt, cum jam satisfactionis tempus praeterisset, Dietherus ipse excommunicaretur absque nostra
conscientia, nam id per judices inferiores in forma camerae fieri solet.
Quod ubi ad ejus notitam [sic] pervenit, censuris ecclesiasticis innodatus
15 non quomodo se solveret, et ad communionem fidelium rediret, sed
quomodo magis ac magis se poenis immergeret excogitavit; non recurrit
ad nos, nullam nobis quaerelam fieri curavit, nullum a nobis praesidium,
nullum remedium petiit, sed passim clamans et vociferans contra nos
indigna se pati dicens, et Apostolicam Sedem blasphemans, conficto
20 quodam infamatorio libello ad futurum concilium contra Mantuanam
bullam appellavit, excommunicationem ipso facto, a qua, nisi a nobis,
absolvi non potest, et alias poenas contra reos majestatis, et haereticae

various taxes,[1] and to organize other defenses. This man, given to false understanding, an enemy of God, and a totally ungrateful foe, quickly rose up in rebellion against the Apostolic See and began to curse the Church, his mother. He snarled at us in many ways and insulted our legate who attempted to levy the tithes needed to arm troops against the Turks. He was not ashamed to declare publicly that we sought the wealth of his nation and not the defense of the faith, although we had ordered that these taxes ought to be levied only with the consent of the nation, and although we had commanded that the supervision and administration of these taxes be entrusted to the hands of those whom the nation delegated.[2]

Meanwhile, the time for Diether to discharge the debts he owed to the Apostolic See arrived; he was then excommunicated upon the insistence of the bankers who had discharged his debts. This was done without our knowledge, for such an excommunication is customarily issued by lesser officials, according to the procedure of the Camera.[3] When this excommunication came to his knowledge, although he was implicated in ecclesiastical censures, he did not consider how he might secure absolution and return to the communion of the faithful, but only how he might involve himself in greater and greater penalties. He did not consult us or concern himself to avert our condemnation; he sought no assistance or relief from us. Shouting and bellowing everywhere against us, he declared he had suffered an injustice, and he blasphemed the Apostolic See. In a certain infamous pamphlet he composed, he appealed to a future council against the bull of Mantua,[4] and incurred by this act alone the excommunication that no one can absolve but us and other penalties hurled against traitors and promoters of heretical depravity.[5] Moreover,

---

[1] *Decimae, vigesimae,* and *trigesimae* were papal taxes assessed in extraordinary circumstances such as crusades.

[2] See p. 259.

[3] See p. 261.

[4] See p. 265.

[5] See p. 227.

pravitatis fautores a jure fulminatas incurrens. Nec animo irreverenti, et infrunito satis fuit, primam sedem his modis contempsisse, nisi et divina quoque contemneret, illis se publice immiscens, palam et notorie excommunicatus et in irregularitatem incidens. En, quae reverentia
5 canonum! Quis timor Dei! Quae religionis consideratio! Bis excommunicatus, bis extra ecclesiam factus, non coactus, non jussus, non absolutus, ecclesiam ingreditur et divinis officiis se ingerit et sacrosancta polluere audet.

Nimia est haec contumacia, ac rebellio et argumenta sunt haec
10 hominis de Christiana religione parum bene sentientis, et omnia jura divina, et humana confundentis; quod in Diethero manifestissimum est, quem violasse juramentum suum, nobis praestitum, apertissime constat; namque cum terminus ad nos veniendi, jam semel prorogatus, instaret, non fidei memor, non promissi tenax, non debiti observator,
15 non juramenti cultor, sed excommunicatus, perjurus, irregularis et totius religionis expers atque inimicus, labi tempus praemisit, nec ad nos venit, nec quod venire non posset, se excusavit; quippe qui elevata facie, et arroganti mente nihil se debere Romano praesuli existimat, et fortasse majorem eo se credidit, verbo et opere superbus, et inflatus
20 opinione sua nunc istos, nunc illos hortatus est, ut appellationi suae damnatissimae adhaererent, sperans suam nequitiam tanto magis inultam esse, quanto plures mali consilii consortes inveniret; sed paucissimi ei adhaeserunt, et illi quidam decepti ac circumventi, quorum aliqui, cognita fraude, mox ab eo in ea parte sequestrati sunt, et appellationi
25 renuntiaverunt, seque fideles Romanae Ecclesiae filios declaraverunt, scientes, nihil tam perniciosum esse, quam in errore cognito persistere. Dietherus autem feroci animo et mente perversa quotidie magis ac magis insaniens, quamvis capituli cui adhaesionem extorquere non potuisset, tamen aliarum ecclesiarum capitula, ac praelatos in suam dementiam
30 trahere omni studio nisus est.

236

it was not enough to have defied the primal see in these ways with an irreverent, senseless heart; he also scorned the sacraments, meddling in them publicly—[he, who was] openly and notoriously excommunicated and destitute of all legal rights. Lo, what reverence for canons! What fear of God! What consideration for religion! Twice excommunicated, twice placed outside the church, he enters a church without compulsion to do so, without a command to do so, and without absolution, and interferes with divine worship and dares to defile the sacraments.[1]

This obstinacy is excessive, as is this rebellion. These are the arguments of a man who entertains little respect for the Christian religion and who violates all divine and human laws. It is quite openly known that such conduct is most evident in Diether, who violated his oath, which he swore to us. For when the deadline for his coming to us, extended once already, approached, he, not mindful of the faith, not steadfast to his promise, not discharging his debt and observing his oath, but as an excommunicate, a perjurer, a rebel, an outcast, and a foe of all religion, permitted the deadline to pass and did not come. He did not even offer the excuse that he was unable to come. Indeed, this man of haughty demeanor and arrogant temperament deems that he owes nothing to the Roman pontiff, and perhaps he believes himself greater than he! Insolent in word and deed and swollen with his own importance, he has exhorted various folk to adhere to his most damnable appeal, hoping that this wickedness may remain unpunished as long as he finds colleagues in his evil intent. But very few have adhered to him and some of these have been duped and deceived. Some, when they recognized their error, quickly deserted his faction, retracted their appeal, and declared themselves faithful sons of the Roman Church, for they know that nothing is more pernicious than persisting in recognized error. But Diether, with an insolent spirit and a diseased mind, has daily become increasingly deranged; although he has been unable to obtain the support of his chapter by force, he has sought most ardently to drag the prelates and chapters of other churches into his madness.

---

[1] See p. 267.

SENTENTIA EXAUCTORATUS

Indixerat auctoritate sua nationis conventum apud Francofordiam;
quod sibi ex eo licere affirmat, quia Moguntinus praesul per nationem
Germanicam Romani Imperii archicancellarius existat. Fatemur eum,
qui Moguntinae praesit ecclesiae archicancellarium esse imperii apud
5 Germanos, sed vocare nationem in unum aliquem locum invito Imperatore posse, aut ei licere, nequaquam fatemur; sed ipse vero nimis multa
sibi arrogans, nondum sacris pontificialibus initiatus, nondum episcopus,
non investitutus ab Imperatore, nondum regalia consecutus, adversante
et contradicente Imperatore nationem vocare audet, et conventum
10 tenere, et quamvis dicat ea se idcirco agere, ut nationi et reipublicae
Christianae consulat, quod ad eum non pertinet, nisi quatenus a superioribus mandetur, re tamen vera nihil aliud studebat, quam sibi favores
adversus Apostolicam Sedem in reprobata appellatione sua quaerere.

Haec cum nos accepissemus, nuntios nostros, viros praestantes, ad
15 eum misimus, qui male vadentem retraherent, et in viam reducerent,
monstrarent sibi, quantum a recto tramite discessisset, quantum divinis
legibus adversaretur, quanto in periculo esset, quantum sibi et nationi
suae, et universae Christianitati ejus consilia nocere possent; sed nihil
profuerunt hortamina nostra, multi principes ac praelati eum flectere
20 frustra conati sunt; non audivit genitorem, qui recta monebat, non
consiliariis suis auscultavit, suffraganeum suum, insignem theologum,
qui quantum Apostolicae Sedi quilibet episcopus obnoxius existat, per
sacras litteras fideliter ostendebat, contumeliis prosecutus est; nemo
animum suum potuit immutare, nullum audire nisi se ipsum voluit, et
25 qui prurientes auribus suae cupiditati consona dicerent. Cumque apud
Francofordiam, prohibente Imperatore, congregationem habere non
posset, nam boni cives domino paruerunt, ad Moguntiam conventum

SENTENCE OF DEPOSITION

He called a national diet upon his own authority to meet in Frankfurt; he asserts that he may legally do so because the Archbishop of Mainz is the Archchancellor of the Holy Roman Empire in the German nation. We acknowledge that he who rules the Church of Mainz is the Archchancellor of the Empire among the Germans, but we do not at all acknowledge that he may legally convoke the German nation in any place against the Emperor's will. But this man, who makes such excessive claims for himself, who has never received the sacred prerogatives of the episcopal office, who has not been invested by the Emperor, and who has not acquired the regalia, presumes to convoke the German nation to a diet in defiance and opposition to the Emperor. Although he may say that he does so in order to consider the welfare of the German nation and Christendom, this is not his concern, except when he receives a mandate to do so from his superiors; his real concern is nothing other than to seek support for his damnable appeal against the Apostolic See.

When these matters came to our hearing, we sent our legates, men of distinction, to reclaim this prodigal, to lead him back into the true road, and to inform him how far he had strayed from the true path, how much he opposed divine law, how dangerous his position was, and how harmful his designs were to himself, to his nation, and to all Christendom. But our exhortations proved to be of no avail; many rulers and prelates attempted to dissuade him, to no effect. He did not listen to his father who gave him sound advice; he did not heed his advisers; he heaped scorn upon his suffragan, an illustrious theologian, who faithfully demonstrated through sacred texts to what extent every bishop is subject to the Apostolic See.[1] No one could change his mind; he had no desire to listen to anyone but himself and those who told him what he longed most keenly to hear. When he was unable to hold his diet at Frankfurt because of the Emperor's prohibition—for the good burghers [of that city] obeyed their lord—he transferred it to Mainz and then presumed to preside over it.[2] Although few attended and most of those [who did come came] not

---

[1] This may be a reference to Biel.
[2] See p. 269.

239

transtulit, ibique praesidere praesumpsit, quamvis pauci advenere, quorum magna pars non ut ei auscultaret, sed ut ejus reprimeret audaciam, nec tamen defuere nonnulli, qui ejus insaniae consentirent, inter quos Gregorius Heimburgensis inventus est, quem veriori vocabulo
5 "errorium" appellant, iniquitatis alumnus, quem, quamvis haereticum publice damnatum, excommunicatum ac rebellem Dietherus ipse non ignoraret, ad conventum admisit, et illi palam communicavit, nostris nuntiis, ne id ageret, commonentibus. Sed cur vitet excommunicatus excommunicatum, infidelis infidelem, perjurus perjurum, aut rebellis
10 rebellem, pares cum paribus facile conveniunt, et colligatas inter se gerunt perfidi caudas. Gregorius Sigismundi ex principibus Austriae jam damnati, et excommunicati propter injectas in cardinalem sancti Petri manus, in eo conventu nuntius affuit, dignus domini sui orator, et dignus, quem Dietherus suae perfidiae consortem admitteret.

15 Habitus igitur est conventus Moguntiae multo minor, quam Dietherus speravit, in quo ipse plenus minarum multa contra nos et Imperatorem locutus est, audens os in caelum ponere, et de duobus capitibus vilis ovicula maledicere; et quamvis nuntii nostri magnopere eum hortarentur, ne se hostem Apostolicae Sedi redderet, ne damnatam appellationem
20 prosequetur, ne Imperatori molestus esset, ne Papam impugnaret; intelligeret, se nullam habere causam, cur talia tentaret, persuaderet sibi, omnia, quae honesta essent, facile posse a nobis impetrari, recognosceret statum suum, neque altiora se quaereret, sciret, se quantum ad Romanum Pontificem attineret, ovem esse non pastorem, et quantum ad
25 Imperatorem, vasallum se gerere non dominum, et utrumque sibi

to heed him but to curb his presumption, there were, nevertheless, several persons present who consented to his madness. Among these was Gregor Heimburg, who may be more accurately called "error," disciple of iniquity. Although Diether was not unaware that this man was a publicly condemned heretic, an excommunicate, and a rebel, he admitted him to the assembly and openly consulted him although our nuncios urged him not to do so.[1] But why should one excommunicate avoid another, one infidel another, one perjurer another, and one rebel another? Equals get along easily with equals; scoundrels are joined together by their tails.[2] Gregor attended that assembly as the envoy of Sigismund, one of the princes of Austria, who had been previously condemned and excommunicated for the violent measures he had adopted against the Cardinal of St. Peter's.[3] He is a spokesman worthy of his lord and worthy to be included by Diether in his perfidy.

Therefore the end result of the Mainz Diet was much less than Diether hoped. In this assembly, he uttered many threats against us and the Emperor, daring to defy the heavens and as an outcast from the flock cursed both his overlords, though our nuncios exhorted him most earnestly not to set himself up as a foe of the Apostolic See, not to persist in his condemned appeal, not to antagonize the Emperor, and not to oppose the Pope. [They sought to bring him] to understand that he had no ground to undertake such rash endeavors and to persuade him that any honorable concessions could easily be obtained from us; [they exhorted him] to recognize his position and not to seek higher ones, to understand what pertains to the Roman pontiff, that a sheep is not the shepherd, and what pertains to the Emperor, that a vassal does not conduct himself as

---

[1] See p. 273.

[2] This expression refers to the medieval image of heresy as a hydra. Just as the hydra in legend possessed many heads that were joined in one tail, heresy was viewed as possessing many forms which stemmed ultimately from one source of rebellion. Cf. Heiko A. Oberman, *Forerunners of the Reformation: The Shape of Late Medieval Thought* (New York: Holt, Rinehart & Winston, 1966), pp. 27–32.

[3] See p. 297.

judicem esse, impenderet reverentiam suis superioribus, et dominorum potius clementiam, quam censuram experiri vellet; homo tamen criminosus, et qui odio inextinguibili contra Romanam sedem ardet, nec Imperatoris nomen audire potest, nullis flecti precibus, nullis deterreri
5 comminationibus potuit, quin conceptum contra nos virus evomeret, plura attemptare ausus, quae Apostolicae Sedis, et Romani Imperii juribus mirum in modum adversabantur; sed noverunt prudentes viri, qui aderant, machinamenta ejus, nec manus tantae malignitati dederunt. Finem habuit conventus aliter, quam praeparavit Dietherus; ruunt
10 enim vana consilia, nec temeritatis diuturna est cum prosperitate societas.

Fractus omnino et desertus ab his, in quibus plurimum spei collocaverat Dietherus, paululum immutatus est, vocatisque nostris, tamquam resipere vellet, mendaci et contumeliosissimae appellationi suae renun-
15 ciavit, verum id haud quamquam publice, sed in domo coram paucis, ut quem non tam appellasse, quam appellationem revocasse pudebat, speraverunt tamen nuntii nostri eum in viam velle redire; sed cum interius homines tetigerent, nihil solidi inventum est, perseverabat in austeritate sua, et sibi Romanam sedem cedere dignum arbitrabatur, et
20 tamquam nos ab eo, non ipse a nobis, instrui deberet, arrogantissime loquebatur, non se satisfacturum mercatoribus obtulit, non vitam emendaturum, non juramenta servaturum, aut alia facturum, quae tenetur, sed tamquam nobiscum pacisci vellet, haec atque illa promittebat, si nos sibi, quod ipse cupiebat, promitteremus. Quibus ex rebus
25 animadvertentes incorrigibile cor ejus esse, nec sperandum, quod ad frugem recte vivendi perduci possit, et maxime cum ejus electio, sicut ante diximus, per simoniacam labem celebrata fuerit, de qua nobis postea gravia testimonia sunt exhibita, ex hoc in partibus illis vulgatissimum est, difficile est enim, ut potestas malis artibus acquisita bonis

a lord, and to understand that both are his judges; [they urged him] to give due reverence to his superiors and to test the mercy of his overlords rather than their displeasure. But this wicked man, who burns with an unquenchable hatred against the Roman see, cannot abide the name of the Emperor, cannot be moved by any entreaty or restrained by any threat. He vomits forth his distilled venom against us and has dared many other things which were strikingly opposed to the laws of the Apostolic See and the Holy Roman Empire. But prudent men who were present recognized his stratagems and did not lend support to such malice. This assembly ended in a manner other than Diether hoped; for false intents come to nothing and foolhardiness does not enjoy lasting prosperity.

Diether, wholly crushed and abandoned by those in whom he had placed the highest hopes, for a short time changed his tactics. He summoned our nuncios as if he wished to come to his senses, and retracted his false and most insolent appeal; it must be noted, however, that he did not do so publicly, but privately in the presence of a few, for he was not so ashamed that he had made such an appeal as he was that he withdrew it. Nevertheless, our nuncios hoped that he wished to return to the true path. But when our men examined him more closely, they found that he was not at all sincere. He persisted in his hardened position, deemed that the Roman see ought to yield to him, and spoke with the utmost insolence as if we ought to be instructed by him and not he by us. He did not offer to satisfy his creditors, to amend his life, or to fulfill his vows and other obligations, but he promised us one thing and another if we would promise him what he desired[1]—as if he wished to bargain with us! We realized from these indications that his heart was incorrigible and that we ought not to hope that he could be induced to lead an upright life—particularly because his election, as we have said previously, was conducted under the taint of simony. Weighty evidence concerning this matter has since come to our attention and this is general knowledge in

[1] See p. 271.

moribus administretur. Cumque multae quaerelae ad nos pervenerint de malo ipsius Dietheri regimine, de violentia, qua utitur in subditos, de tyrannide, de rapina, de saevitia, de pluribus aliis excessibus non est visum nobis haec ulterius dissimulare; esset enim nimis periculosum, si 5 Dietherum ipsum in ecclesia non sua praesidere, et sponsam illam immaculatam ulterius in adulteri potestate permitteremus, quod nihil aliud videre posset, quam oves lupo devorandas tradere, et devotum ecclesiae Moguntinae clerum, qui hactenus ab eo corrumpi non potuit, in manu hostis dimittere, qui pro sua libidine vindicatam sumeret, et cum 10 impunita huic tanta rebellio cessisset, facile aliorum animos ad audenda similia traheret.

Eapropter cum manifestissimum sit Dietherum praefatum ad futurum concilium appellasse easque in poenas incidisse, quae in litteris per nos Mantuae editis continentur, juramentumque violasse non solum de 15 veniendo ad nos intra praescriptum tempus, sed etiam de obedientia et reverentia praestanda, qui mandata nostra contempsit, et multa contra nos et statum nostrum molitus est, cum litteras apostolicas accipere neglexerit, cum intra tempus a jure statutum nec se fecerit promoveri, nec prorogati tempus postulaverit, cum excommunicatus ac publice 20 denunciatus divinis se immiscuerit officiis, et irregularitatem incurrerit, atque in censuris sorduerit, ut de haeresi vehementer suspectus videatur, cum eos multis modis persecutus sit, qui se excommunicatum vitare voluerunt, cum multa sibi arrogaverit, quae ei non conveniunt, de Papa et Imperatore judicare praesumens, cum clero et populo suo gravis et 25 injuriosus existat, atque ecclesiam ipsam Moguntinam in spiritualibus et temporalibus male gubernet, et multis incommodis afficiat, sintque haec omnia ita publica atque notoria, ut nulla possint tergiversatione

SENTENCE OF DEPOSITION

those regions; for it is difficult to administer in a worthy manner authority acquired by devious means. Since many complaints have come to us concerning his tyranny, his pillaging, his barbarity, and his many other excesses, it has not seemed possible to leave these matters unnoticed any longer. For it would be far too dangerous for us to permit Diether to rule over the church which is not his and to permit that immaculate bride to remain any longer in the hands of an adulterer. To do so could only be regarded as delivering the sheep over to the wolf to be devoured and consigning into the hands of the enemy the devout clergy of the church of Mainz, whom thus far he has been unable to corrupt and upon whom he may take revenge according to his whim. If such rebellion succeeded in evading punishment, others would be easily drawn to attempt similar things.

Therefore, since it is most manifest that the said Diether has appealed to a future council, has incurred those penalties that are included in the bull we issued at Mantua, and not only has broken his vow to come to us within the time allotted, but also has failed to render us due reverence and obedience; since it is most manifest that he has scorned our mandates, and has attempted many things against us and our authority; since he has neglected to heed apostolic letters; since he has not been elevated within the time appointed by law and has sought no postponement; since, excommunicated and publicly denounced, he has tampered with the administration of the sacraments, has been deprived of the protection of the law, and has turned a deaf ear to censures, so that he seems strongly suspect of heresy; since he has harassed in manifold ways those who have sought to avoid him as an excommunicate; since he has arrogated to himself many prerogatives not his and presumes to judge Pope and Emperor; since he oppresses and endangers his clergy and people, misgoverns the church of Mainz in both spiritual and temporal matters, and inflicts many hardships upon it; since all these things are so blatant and notorious that they may be concealed by no evasion;[1] and although

---

[1] See p. 141.

245

SENTENTIA EXAUCTORATUS

celari, quamvis propter praemissa jam cecidisse a jure suo videri possit, si quod in ecclesia Moguntina, aut ex electione, aut ex provisione nostra praemissis sibi competiit, nihilominus de venerabilium fratrum nostrorum sanctae Romanae Ecclesiae Cardinalium consilio ad majorem cautelam

5 propter hujusmodi tam temerarios ausus, et tam enormia facinora, ipsum dicta ecclesia Moguntina, et omni jure, quod sibi in ea competere posset, privamus et privatum esse declaramus, atque amovemus ab eadem, et ab omni vinculo absolvimus, quo tenerentur eidem capitula, praepositos, scholasticos, custodes, camerarios, cantores, thesaurarios,

10 omnesque ac singulos praelatos, quocumque nomine censeantur, canonicos, pastores, plebanos, vicarios perpetuos ac temporales, altaristas ipsius ecclesiae, ac totius dioecesis Moguntinae, omnes denique ac singulos vasallos, ligios, castrenses ac simplices, officiatosque omnes, cujuscumque status aut conditionis existant; scabinos civitatum ac

15 oppidorum, villarum, fortalitiarumque omnium, burgimagistros, consules, eorumque rectores, quocumque censeantur nomine, et subditos universos ac singulos ejusdem ecclesiae Moguntinae, eidem Diethero in nulla re obedientiae vinculo teneri, et a juramento, si quod ei praestiterunt, liberos et absolutos esse decernentes, ac mandantes eisdem, et

20 eorum cuilibet, sub excommunicationis poena, quem ipso facto contravenientes incurrent, ne de caetero ipsi Diethero aut suis procuratoribus in aliquo respondeant, pareant vel intendant, sed ipsum, tanquam morbidam pecudem, et pestilentem bestiam, ubique devitent. Nulli, ergo omnino hominum liceat, hanc paginam nostrae privationis, declarationis,

25 amotionis, absolutionis, constitutionis, mandati et voluntatis infringere vel ei ausu temerario contraire, si quis autem hoc attemptare praesumserit, indignationem omnipotentis Dei et beatorum Petri et Pauli Apostolorum ejus, se noverit incursurum.

Datum Tiburi anno incarnationis Dominicae MCCCCLXI, xii kalendis

30 septembris, pontificatus nostri anno tertio.

SENTENCE OF DEPOSITION

from these considerations it can be seen that he has already abdicated any right if he claims the church of Mainz as his due on the basis of his election and our provision, notwithstanding, with the advice of our venerable brethren, the cardinals of the holy Roman Church, and for our greater security against such desperate measures and such prodigious crimes, we now depose and declare him to be deposed from the church of Mainz and from every prerogative within that church which he can claim as his due; we remove him from that church and we absolve from all obligations to him chapters, provosts, scholastics, churchwardens, chamberlains, cantors, treasurers, all and sundry prelates whatever their title, canons, pastors, rural priests, vicars perpetual and temporal, acolytes of this church and the entire diocese of Mainz, all and sundry vassals, liege subjects, castellans and lowborn folk, and all officials of whatever rank or dignity, all and sundry stewards of all cities, towns, villages, and strongholds, and all burgermeisters, consuls, and leading men whatever their title, and all and sundry subjects of the said church of Mainz. We declare that these are bound to Diether by no obligation and that they are released and absolved from any oath that they have sworn to him; we enjoin them and their adherents under the pain of the excommunication which they incur by the very act of opposing our mandate, not to respond, yield, or submit to Diether or his henchmen in any respect, but to shun him everywhere as a diseased animal and a pest-ridden beast. Therefore, let absolutely no one nullify the letter of our deposition, declaration, removal, absolution, constitution, mandate, and will, or oppose it with desperate measures. If anyone should attempt to do this, let him know that he will incur the wrath of God Almighty and his blessed apostles, Peter and Paul.

Promulgated at Tivoli in the year of our Lord's incarnation 1461, on the twenty-first day of August, in the third year of our pontificate.

CHURFURSTEN DIETHERS ZU MEINTZ DEFENSIONSSCHRIFT, WIDER DIE ENTSETZUNG SEINES STIFFTS

Allen und iglichen Fürsten, Graven, Herren Prälaten, und der gemeinen Pfaffheyt und Geistlicheit, Rittern und Knechten, Burgern, Dorffern und Gemeynden, enpieten Wir Dither von Gottes Gnaden des Heiligen Stuhls zu Mentze erwelter und und bestetigter, des Heiligen Römischen
5 Reichs durch Germanien Erzcantzler und Kurfürste, unsern fründlichen Dienst, Frintschafft, Gruss und alles Gut, Erwirdigen in Got Vatere, Hochgepornen Fürsten, Wohlgebornen, Edeln, Wirdigen, Strengen, Vesten, Ersamen und Wisen, lieben besundern Frunde, Neven, Vettern, Oheimen, Getruwen und Besundern, yeden nach seinem
10 Gupure.

Nachdem und uff Samstag nechst vergangen, von wegen unsers heiligen Vatters Babst Pii, vor unsern Capitel und Pfaffheit hie zu Menze

THE DEFENSE OF THE ELECTOR DIETHER OF MAINZ AGAINST DEPOSITION FROM HIS SEE

To all and sundry princes, counts, lords, and prelates, to the whole priesthood and clergy, to all knights and menials and to all burghers, villagers, and all others; to all the most venerable in God the Father, the most honorable princes, to all those of noble birth, to all nobles, to all our worthy, valiant, mighty, honored, wise, and most beloved friends, nephews, cousins, uncles, and to all men faithful and true, according to their station, we, Diether, by the grace of God elected and confirmed in the holy see of Mainz and Archchancellor and Elector of the Holy Roman Empire in Germany, offer our best regards, friendship, greetings, and good wishes.

Last Saturday on the behalf of our Holy Father, Pope Pius, several papal bulls were openly published and proclaimed here in Mainz before

---

Note: The German text is reprinted from Joachin Johann Müller, *Des Heiligen Römischen Reichs Teutscher Nation Reichstag Theatrum, wie selbiges unter Keyser Friedrichs V allerhöchsten Regierung von Anno MCCCCXL bis MCCCCXCIII gestanden . . .* (Jena, 1713), II, 38–46.

offentlich verkundet und verlesen wurden sint etlich Pebstlich Bullen, inhaltende, wie derselbe unser heiliger Vater der Pabst, nach Rate siner Bruder, der Cardinäle, uns unsers Stiffts zu Menze entsazt und Grav Adolfen von Nassaw, Domherrn des vermelten unsers Stiffts, damyt
5 versehen haben, deshalben, dass wir mit der Symonien Unstätigkeit besprenget, meyneidiger, offenbar verkundigter, gebanneter, Verachter der Geboter des Stuhls zu Rome, irregularis und von Kezery mercklich vermerckt sint, auch suhst fast viel ungeburliches Vornemens wider sin Heyligkeit, und unsern Herrn den Keyser, er uns beschuldiget, wir
10 gehandelt und begangen soolen haben, ernstlichen dabey an unsern Capitel und Pfaffheit, und auch alle unserer Amtlute, Dyener, Unterdanen und andere uns verwandt gesynnende, uns fürbasser zu mygen, nicht mehr zugewarten, sunder den benanten Graf Adulffen voreinen Herrn unsers Stifts zu halten, Sie auch damit aller irer Verpflichtunge,
15 Eyde und Gelobten, die sie uns verhafft sint, entbindet und erlöset, als er vermeynet usw. wie solichs dann die Päbstlichen Bullen mit fernerm Innhalt begriffen.

Uff das nu meniglich versteen und gewissen möge, dass uns an solicher Bezihnige und Schuldigunge ungütlich beschicht, wir der Dinge ganz
20 unschuldig sin, uns dergleichen gegen dem Stule zu Rome, sin Heiligkeyt und unserm Herrn dem Keyser, noch auch suhst yemands anders nicht gehalten han, und auch ungern thun und halten wolten, anders dann eynen frummen Christlichen Fursten wohlgezemet. So thun wir daruf die Underrichtunge nachgerurt, die wir bitten, durch Got und der
25 Gerechtigkeit willen, mit unverdrossener Gedult zuvernemen, auch nach Notdurfft zubetrachten und zubedencken.

Erstmals, als unser Heyliger Vater der Pabst vermeynt, wir mit der Symonien Unfledigkeit befleckt sin sollen, deshalben, dass, nach unser Erwelunge, als yem zu wissen wurden sy, eyner uss den sieben Kiesern,
30 mit mercklichen Gelde corrumpiert, mit seiner Stimme der vierden Stede ursache, dass wir den meistentheile unserer Erwelunge gehabt, und Erwelter geheysen möchten werden, geben haben sollen.

THE DEFENSE OF DIETHER

our chapter and clergy; these bulls declare that the same, our Holy
Father, the Pope, with the advice of his brethren, the cardinals, has
deposed us from our see of Mainz and has provided to our see Graf
Adolf von Nassau, canon of the said see for the following reasons: that we
are stained with the fault of simony; that we are notorious perjurers,
openly proclaimed excommunicates, despisers of the mandates of the
Roman see, outcasts of the law, and heretics. These bulls accuse us of
other almost innumerable unlawful intents against His Holiness and our
lord, the Emperor, and declare that we ought to have proceeded and
acted seriously to persuade our chapter, our clergy, as well as all our
officials, ministers, subjects, and others with whom we are involved,
that they should no longer patiently serve us, but should henceforth
regard the said Graf Adolf as the lord of our see. These bulls release and
absolve all the above from all obligations, oaths, and vows that they have
sworn to us—as our Holy Father imagines. Such then is the content of
the papal bulls.[1]

Now we proceed so that all may know and understand that we are
unjustly accused in such charges and allegations, that we are entirely
innocent in these matters, and that likewise we have never acted otherwise than befits a devout Christian prince nor have intended to act or
proceed unjustly against the Roman see, His Holiness, our lord, the
Emperor, or anyone else. Thus we regard the matters with which we are
concerned, and seek by the support of God and justice to consider them
with untiring patience and to pursue the examination and investigation
that the charges demand.

In the first place, our Holy Father, the Pope, contends that we are
defiled with the filth of simony because it came to his knowledge after
our election that one of the seven arbiters, swayed by an enormous bribe,
gave us his vote, which was the fourth, and which assured us that we
possessed the majority for our election and that we were declared the
Archbishop-elect.[2]

---

[1] See p. 247.
[2] See p. 231.

DIETHERS DEFENSIONSSCHRIFT

Daruff ist unsre Antwort, dass uns an solicher Schuldigunge gantz
ungütlich und unrecht geschicht, auch mit Warheit nimmer bibracht
werden soll, noch möge, dann wir wissen uns des ganz unschuldig, auch
mit der Warheyt, ob und wo sichs begeben und not sin wurt, nach
5 Geburnisse zu Recht wohl zu verantworten und unschuldig zu machen.
Sint auch sunder Zwifel, so der vierdte, davon unser heiliger Vater der
Babst meldet, des von yem oder yemands anders zu Rede gesetzt oder
der Beschuldigunge suhst innen wurden, er wisse das nach Notturfft
siner Eren und Gelympf auch wohl zu verantworten, und sich zu ent-
10 schuldigen, wie recht ist. So ist auch nicht davor zuhalten, dass es
fürzunemen not gewesst wer, einen aus den sieben Kiesern zu cor-
rumpiren, angesehen dass unser Capitel, darinne wir, auch der benant
Graf Adolf, mit und bey gewest sin, alle Umstende dardurch destomyner
einiche Symonien oder andere ungebürliche Tadt und Suchunge, zu
15 Verhinderunge der eynträchtigen Wale, in dieselbe Wale fallen möchte,
nach Notturft versorgt, und soliche Wale uff sieben Dumherren des
Capitels die Zyt gesezt han, in der Meynunge, welcher usser uns von den
sieben, oder den mereren Deyle eyntrechtig gekorn und erwelt würde,
den vor einen Herrn des Stiffts zuhalten usw.
20 Nachdem Wir nu von den sieben einträchtiglich und myt eyner
eynmütigen Stimme und Wale erwelt wurden sin, als dass das Decret
und Brieff, und auch Handel derselben unserer eyntrechtigen und
eynmüthigen Erwelung, darzu wir uns des ziehen, clerlich zuversteen
gibt, besagt und innhat; so wurdet unbillig unserer Wale zugelegt, dass
25 die nicht ufrichtig, sunder durch Symonien und Liebunge wes vierden,
durch Gebunge mercklichs Gelds erkobert und erlägt sin soll. Darzu ist
es auch zu versehlich, were unsere Wale durch Befleckunge der Symonien
des vierdten oder yemandts andershalber unrecht bescheen, unser
heiliger Vater, der Pabst, hette darinne, nachdem und yem die Symon-
30 ische beschehen, als er schreipt, zu wissen gethan wurden seyn, solle
getragen, und die mit nicht zugelassen, sunder eynen andern nach
synen Gefallen damyt versehen, dass nu von syner Heyligkeit nicht
beschehen, sunder das Decret unserer Erwelunge yem durch unser und
unsers Capitels Botschafft umb Erlangunge willen unserer Bestetunge

252

THE DEFENSE OF DIETHER

This is our answer. We are accused in such an allegation with the utmost injustice and error, and this cannot and ought not ever to be alleged with any basis in truth, because we know our complete innocence and because we are prepared for the truth to go anywhere any time, if necessary, to defend and argue our innocence according to the obligations of law. It is also beyond doubt that the fourth arbiter to whom our Holy Father, the Pope, refers—this man or anyone else called to account or otherwise accused—knows how to defend rightly and rectify his good name and honor, if necessary. It must not be supposed that there was any need to attempt to bribe one of the seven arbiters, since our chapter, in which Graf Adolf and we were members, had necessarily provided for all contingencies, including simony or any other illegal act or attempt that might arise in this election as an obstacle to a harmonious election; our chapter at this time appointed seven canons to carry out the election, intending to regard as the occupant of the see the one of us who would be harmoniously chosen and elected by the seven arbiters or the majority of us.

Thereafter we were harmoniously elected by the seven in a unanimous vote and election; moreover, the election decree and letter includes, declares, and explains clearly the procedure of the said harmonious and unanimous election by which we were elected. Thus it is unjust to assert that our election was attained and won through simony and bribery of the fourth arbiter by an enormous sum of money. It is also quite likely, had our election been accomplished illegally under the shadow of bribery of the fourth arbiter or anyone else, that our Holy Father, the Pope, when such simony had come to his knowledge as he writes, would not have tolerated or permitted such an election, but would have appointed another of his own choosing. But His Holiness did not do this; instead, he acknowledged and accepted the decree of our election sent to him through

zugesant, unverworffen, anund uffgenommen wurden ist, und ist auch
der Besesse unsers Stiffts mit syner Zugehorunge uns als eyme einmüti-
gen Erwelten desselben unsers Stiffts gegeben, synt auch also darinne
gefurt und gesazt von unserm Capitel, daby und mit der egenant Graff
5 Adolff gewest ist, und in denselben unsern Stifft kummen, nicht heimlich,
verborgenlich oder betränglich, auch nicht durch einige Gabe noch suhst
eynicherley anderer unbilliche Wege oder Gedinge, dadurch Wir in der
Symonien Befleckunge desselben unsers Ingangs zum Stifft oder eincher
anderer Sachen halber in eynche Wise gefallen oder befleckt vermergt
10 solten oder möchten sie oder werden, es were denn des Geldes halber,
das wir syner Heyligkeit vor unser Pallium geben, bezalt und ussgericht
han, desselben Geldes halber Wir doch destomynner bekümmernisse
hätten ussgeben und bezalt haben, auch destomynner dardurch Symonien begangen vermeynten, hielten und halten, diwil das den alten
15 gewönlichen Tax und Saze unsers Stiffts ergrift. So ferne unser heyliger
Vater der Pabst es darby verbliben lassen, und uns damit nicht höger
zubelestigen understanden hette.

Als dann unser heyliger Vater, der Pabst, vorbasser meldet, wie er
nach Ersuchunge unserer Bestetunge begert habe, uns personlich zu
20 yem gein Mantua nach solicher Bestetunge zufügen, des uns nyemandts
habe überraten mögen, ist nicht sunder, als Wir unser Capitel zu der
Zyt als Wir unsern Stifft, wie vorsteet, erwelt wurden, und kummen sin,
haben Wir unser Botschafft mit dem Decret unserer Erwelunge zu sin
Heyligkeit gein Mantua geschicket, yem dasselbe Decret tun fürbringen,
25 und demütiglich um die Bestetunge, als eyn Gehorsamer, bitten und
ersuchen lassen, hat syn Heyligkeit, als uns von derselben unsern und
unsers Capitels Botschafft verkundet ward, an sy gesinnen und zuschri-
ben personlich zu yem gein Mantua nach der Bestetigunge zufügen, sin
Heyligkeit wolle sich darinne gegen uns gnediclich und willig erzeigen,
30 bewiessen und halten. Nu weren wir des also zuthun gewest ganz willig
und begierig, hette uns daran nicht verhindert mercklich tödlich
Kranckheit unsers Libs, damyt wir der Zyt, alsdann kuntlichen ist, und
sich auch warlich so und wann das Not würde sin, erfunden solte, be-
laden und beheftet gewist sint.

the legation of our chapter dispatched to attain our confirmation; he granted us the possession of our see with its prerogatives as a unanimously elected archbishop of our see. We were invested and installed in our see by our chapter, which includes the aforesaid Graf Adolf. We entered our see not secretly, furtively, or fraudulently; not through any bribe or any other illicit means or conditions; thus we should not be considered, could not be considered, and are not considered to have fallen under the shadow of simony in our accession to this see or in any other matter in any respect. But for the money that we were forced to pay, disburse, and give to His Holiness for our pallium, we considered, believed, and do believe that for this payment and expenditure we would have incurred no less sorrow than the crime of simony, because this involves the ancient traditional taxes and prerogatives of our see. Until now our Holy Father, the Pope, had left these taxes and prerogatives intact and had not attempted to burden us more heavily.

Our Holy Father, the Pope, moreover, declares that he demanded when we sought confirmation that we come to him in person at Mantua for such confirmation. We could consult no one;[1] but at the time we were elected—as we have related—and entered our see, we dispatched our legation with the decree of our election to His Holiness in Mantua to deliver to him the said decree and to request humbly and beseech, as an obedient son, the confirmation. His Holiness, when he learned of the legation sent by us and our chapter, declared that he would show us his good will and favor, if they promised and pledged in writing that we would come to him in person in Mantua to seek our confirmation. We were entirely willing and eager to do so, had we not been prevented by a mortal illness of our body with which we were afflicted and oppressed at that time—this is widely known and could easily be established as true if there were need to do so.

---

[1] See p. 233.

DIETHERS DEFENSIONSSCHRIFT

Aber, nachdem syner Heyligkeyt Gesinnen und Anmuthen an unser Botschaft die Zyt nach dem Pallio zu ym geschickt gewest ist, dass sie sich vor uns verpflichten solten, dass wir hinfüre kein Versammlunge unserer Mitkurfürsten, auch etlicher anderer Puncte mere, hinfüro
5 gehalten, uns doch als einen Erzbischoff unsers Stiffts zu Menze, und einen Dechant unserer Mitkurfürsten, durch Verpflichtunge und Gepürlichkeit gepüren und zusteende zuthun ist, nicht thun noch fürnemen solten, mag nicht unmerglichs sonder verstentlich Under-richtunge thun und geben, uff was Meynunge sin Heyligkeyt unser
10 Zukunfft und Bysin by yem zuhaben begerig gewest ist, und als unser Bottschafft solichs, nachdem und sie das von unsern wegen inzugeen nicht in Bevehle hatten, das auch in sich selbs uns billich zemlich und gepurlich sin inzugeen nicht zuerfynden möchtent, ist yen von syner Heyligkeyt uns das Pallium zugeben geweigert und verhalten wurden,
15 wir haben dannoch nicht abgelassen sunder ander Werbe unsere Bot-schafft, als der Gehorsamer, zu syner Heyligkeit geschicket, und aber um die Bestetunge demüticlichen thun bitten und ersuchen lassen, auch desmahls unser Bestettunge und Pallium von yem erlanget, uf Massen nachgerurt, dasselbe Pallium uns unser Botschafft auch also bracht hat,
20 wir also mit gebürlicher Gezierden, als sich geheischt, uffgenummenen und entpfangen, und nochmals hinter uns in unser Gewalt ligende und uns in dem als auch in andern, nach unsern und unsers Stiffts Gelegen-heit und Vermögende, nicht anders dann gepurlich gehalten han.

Als sin Heyligkeit dann furter berürt, dass wir meyneidig sollen sin,
25 dardurch, dass unser Botschafft, die wir zu yem nach solichem Pallio geschickt, in unsern Namen und Seele yem geschworen sollen han, was andre Bischoffe dem Bapste gewönlichen gepflogen hetten zu schweren, und darüber, dass wir personlich binnen Jars Frist vor yem erschienen solten, und als er, dem Zusagen nach, unserer Zukunfft also gewartet
30 habe, und sorgen helffen, dass das zu Schirmunge und Hanthabunge des Christenglaubens zu Mantua beschlossen were, zu erinnern unsere Lute zu dem Zugk wider den Torcken, zu tulgen in den Dingen dem Keiser, darzu er siner Päbstlichen Legaten geschicket habe, den Zugk zumachen, auch zubezaln den Zehenden Pfennig, den zwanzigsten und

THE DEFENSE OF DIETHER

But afterwards, His Holiness determined to propose to our legation, which had been dispatched to him for the pallium, that they should pledge themselves in our behalf that we should henceforth convene no assembly of our fellow Electors and observe several other conditions which, as the Archbishop of our see of Mainz and the Dean of our fellow Electors, according to our obligations and honor, it is dishonorable and unpermissible for us to fulfill. [Our legation] could not act without being fully informed as to the reason His Holiness was eager to have us come and be present at his court. Since our legates did not possess authorization from us to enter into such matters, matters in which we also could not involve ourselves justly, honorably, or legitimately, His Holiness refused and declined to grant them our pallium. Nevertheless, we did not desist from other attempts, but, as an obedient son, dispatched another legation to His Holiness to request and beseech humbly the confirmation. This time our legation secured the confirmation and pallium from him in the following manner: they received the said pallium in due ceremonial form as required and obligated us in a manner clearly not illegal for what lay within our power and what accorded with our circumstances and resources and those of our see.

His Holiness further declares that we are perjurers because our legation, which we dispatched to him for the pallium, is supposed to have sworn to him in our name and upon our soul those things that other bishops [of Mainz] were bound by custom to swear to the Pope and that we would appear before him in person within a year's time.[1] According to his account, he awaited our coming and support for what had been resolved at Mantua for the defense and maintenance of the Christian faith.[2] He expected us to summon our nation to an expedition against the Turks, to obey in this enterprise the Emperor to whom he has sent his legates to prepare for this expedition, to levy various taxes, and to

---

[1] See p. 233.
[2] See p. 233.

den dreisigsten zugeben und andere Hölff zuthun, sollen wir dem Pebstlichen Stul, unser Mutter, des mit widerwertigen Worten widersetzig würden sin, und sinen Pebstlichen Legaten das betrogen haben usw.

5 Antworten wir, wes unser Botschafft in unsern Namen und Sele, siner Heyligkeit gesworen haben, zupflegen des, das andere Bischoffe gewonlich zusweren gepflogen haben zuthun, haben wir gehalten, und sint dem nachkummen ufrichtig, und getruwen, so das zuverhörunge und an den Tag kommen würde, sich nicht anders erfünden soll, denn uf das,
10 dass wir personlich zu syner Heyligkeit nicht kommen sint, ist kuntlich und merglich, dass wir das erstmals mercklicher Kranckheit halber unsers Lybs, darnach der mercklichen Kriegsleuffte halber die füro und sithero vorhanten gewest, und noch vor Augen sint, uns, unsre Lande und Lüde trefflich beürrende, mit nicht haben thun konnen noch mögen,
15 und das sunder gross mercklich Ursach zuthun, noch auch frevelich nicht verhalten han, was auch durch sinen bebstlichen Legaten zu Fürderung und zü Vollbrengunge des Christlichen Herzogs wider den Torcken, nach Rate anderer unser Mitkurfürsten anderer Fürsten, Herren und Steten des Richs, als es sich wol billich geheischen hette
20 und geburet, beslossen ist und were. Hat an uns durch die unsern, die wir ye zur Zyt trefflich darzu und bey das nach aller Notturft helffen zu handeln geschicket und gehabt haben, nye erwonden.

Aber dass es zu Beschliessunge des zehnden, zwentzigsten und dreisigsten, den sin Bebstlicher Legate mit ungestümmigen Fürnehmen,
25 schweren Drauworten, grossen Mandat und Process understunde inzubrengen, von der Teuschen Nation, die des Uffezunge nicht verwilliget hatten, davon dann nicht alleyn durch uns, sondern alle andre unsere Mitkurfürsten, Fürsten und Herren, die des in Sendboten auf dem Dage zu Wiene, darumbe dahin vorgenummen, uf eyn Meynunge dieselben
30 Rete sich des vertragen hatten, umb willen sich sollichs syns Bepstlichen Legaten Vollfarunge zuversorgen appelirt wurden ist. Es mögen auch die Worte uff die Meynunge, dass unser heiliger Vater der Pabst das Geld und Gut der Dutschen Nation und nicht des Glaubens Hanthabunge suche, geret wurden sin, auch villicht noch geredet werden. Aber es ist

258

organize various defenses;[1] but we supposedly became rebellious against the Apostolic See, our mother, opposing it with harsh words, and deceived the papal legates.[2]

We answer that our legation swore to His Holiness in our name and upon our soul to observe those things that other bishops have been bound by custom to swear. We have observed these things and stand before posterity upright and true. Any investigation would reveal only that we have not come to His Holiness in person. It is quite generally known that we have been unable to come, at first because of a grave illness of our body, and later because of the grave state of war that existed and still exists and severely afflicts our lands and our subjects. We, with the counsel of our fellow Electors and the other princes, lords, and cities of the Empire, have not wrongly opposed the proposals of the papal legates for the furtherance and fulfillment of the Christian expedition against the Turks; we have not opposed what they have justly promised and conceded. We have never ceased to support this [expedition]; we did so through our representatives, whom we dispatched expressly to support this and to proceed according to the dictates of necessity.

But when, in regard to the approval of the various taxes, his legate attempted with fierce determination, several verbal threats, and judicial orders to exact from the German nation taxes it had not authorized, not only we, but all our fellow Electors, princes, and lords who had sent representatives to the Vienna Diet to consider these matters,[3] agreed and determined, upon the advice of our spokesman, to draw up an appeal against his legate's conduct. These words may or may not have been spoken by our representative: "Our Holy Father, the Pope, seeks the wealth and resources of the German nation and not the defense of the

---

[1] See pp. 233–235.
[2] See p. 235.
[3] See Introduction, pp. 22–23.

nicht durch uns, als er schribt, gescheen noch gered wurden, dass auch
sin Heyligkeit sinem Bebstlichen Legaten die Ufsetzunge des zehenden
Pfennigs usw. nicht dann mit Bewilligunge der Nation zuheyschen, und
die in der Nation Behaltenisse der, die sie darzu geben würden, stellen,
5 solte bevolhen han, syn wir nicht wider, aber dem ist also von dem
Bebstlichen Legaten nicht nachkummen, sunder vast beweglich und
ernstlichen von yem gegen der Nation, die usszubrengen, understanden,
und die Nation dardurch beweget wurden, des Mittel und Wege eyner
Uffhaltunge zusuchen, und fürzunemen, uf masse vorgerurt usw.
10   Fürter als er setzt, so als wir nach verschehener Zyt der Bezalunge
des Gelds den Banckerern und Kauflüden zuthun, das wir dem Stule zu
Rome pflichtig gewest sin, und die Banckierer uns gelühen haben, von
iren wegen excommuniciert und verbannet solten wurden syn, nicht
sollen gedacht haben, uns des zuentbenden und zu Gemeinschafft der
15 Glaubigen zukeren, sunder ie merer und mer in die Poene zu vertiefen,
des auch nicht zu ym gepflagen, und uns gein yem nicht erclaget noch
eyniche Hülff gebeten, sunder uns suhst von syner Heyligkeit beclaget
und den Stule zu Rome mit unser Clage beschemet sollen han usw.
      Antworten wir, es möge sin, solten und wolten unsere Botschafft das
20 Pallium von dannen han, sie haben sich über das, das sie von uns zu
bevelhe hatten darvor, darvor ob es anders nach unsers Stiffts Gelegenheyt nicht bedacht, noch betracht wolt werden, mynner zynemen,
zugeben die alte gewönlich Tax und Saze unsers Stiffts, verpflichten und
begeben müsen, den Bankierern darvor zugeben ein Geld by drifach als
25 Hochlaufende, als die alte gewönliche Tax gewest ist. So nu wir und
unser Stifft mit merglichen sweren Kriegsleufften die Zyt überfallen
gewest sint, die dann vor und nach lange Zyt geweret han, und noch für
Augen sint, darüber wir und unser Stifft merglich grosse Cost und
Zerunge und Ussgeben gehabt und gethen han, und deshalben in grosse
30 Schult, des doch wir nicht Ursache gewest, kummen, und besunder in
solich gross merglich Beschwerunge bracht wurden sin, dass wir solichs
so stattlich, sunder ferrer Beschwerunge unsers Stiffts, als das kuntlich
und offenbare am Dage ligt, nit haben können noch mögen ussgerichten.

260

THE DEFENSE OF DIETHER

Christian faith." But we have not opposed in word or deed, as he writes, the levy of the various taxes which His Holiness commanded his legate to exact only with the consent of this nation and through the collectors that this nation would select for this purpose.[1] However, the legate has not complied with this command, but has most ardently and most zealously attempted to exact these taxes from the nation. The nation, troubled by this attempt, sought and adopted the means of resistance we have just mentioned.

Moreover, he contends that we—after the time elapsed for paying to certain bankers and merchants the debt that we owed to the Roman see, the sum that the bankers had loaned to us, and we, upon their insistence, supposedly were excommunicated—did not consider how we might secure absolution and return to the communion of the faithful, but involved ourselves in greater and greater penalties. We did not turn again to him or seek any assistance or relief from him, but supposedly only complained against His Holiness and insulted the Roman see with our complaints.[2]

We answer that it may be that our envoys, wishing to receive the pallium from him, were forced to obligate themselves and yield more than our instructions enjoined—our instructions forbade them to consider or weigh, much less accept, anything contrary to the usage of our see, and instructed them to offer the old customary taxes and fees of our see. But they were forced to pledge to the bankers a sum of money nearly three times the present maximum, the old customary tax. Now we and our see are involved in quite serious warfare, which has raged for a long time and is still raging. This warfare has inflicted upon us and our see enormous expense, loss, and sacrifice; we have incurred large debts that are not our doing. We have been forced into such staggering debt that we are unable to discharge such an enormous additional burden upon our see—this is open and public knowledge.

---

[1] See p. 235.
[2] See p. 235.

DIETHERS DEFENSIONSSCHRIFT

So wir dann also viel des Geltes, als unsers Stiffts Vermogen, auch die
alte gewönlich Tax und Saze unsers Stiffts gewest ist, bezalt und gegeben
han, und das unser heyliger Vater der Pabst nicht genügig wolte syn,
sunder wir, von syner Heyligkeit wegen, über unser und unsers Stiffts
5 Vermögen unterstanden wurden sint mit Bannen und Processen zubesweren, hat unser und unsers Stiffts Notturfft nicht unbillich erfurdert,
uns des mit gebürlichen Wegen und Mitteln versorgen und ufzuhalten,
und uns des davon als beschwert beruffen und appellirt, doch nicht
anders dann zurecht, meynen auch darum, nachden und nyemants
10 über Vermögede zugeben durch Recht pflichtig ist, noch getrungen
sulle werden, daran nicht unrecht, sunder Recht gethan han, denn solte
das sin, dass man die Pallia derer Ertzbischoffe und Bischoffe durch
Ersteigunge über ir alt gewönlich Tax und Satze so hochlich und merglich
brengen solte, were und würde in kurzen zukünftigen Zeyten, als uns
15 nicht zwifelt, merglich wol prüfen mag, zu Sterunge und zu Vergeng-
licheyt aller Stifft brengen, dass billich das nicht zu loben ist. Wir
wissen auch von keiner Verkundunge einigs Bannes, darinne wir behaft
sint, oder sin sollen, uns ist auch nochmals kein Verkündunge einichs
Bannes zu Augen kummen, oder vorgehalten worden, sint auch des
20 von niemands ersucht, denn so viel wir des von Fluckmern binnen Zyt
unserer Appellierunge gehört mögen han, das uns doch, derselben
Appellirunge halber, durch Recht billich nicht bannen noch belestigen
solle noch mag, und dwil wir unser Appellirunge nicht anders dann
beschwert und betrenget über Vermögunge, zu Verhörunge der Sachen
25 zu Recht gethan, auch deshalben nicht anders dann Rechts begert han,
getruwen wir darumbe nicht bennyg, auch des Stuls zu Rome Gepotere
Verachter zusin.

Als fürter unser heyliger Vater der Pabst vermeynt, darumbe dass wir
uns mit einem erdichten beschemten Libell an eyn zukünftig Concilium
30 wider die Mantuanische Bulle und Geseze berufen haben, sollen wir mit
der Gethat in die Pöne des Päbstlichen Bannes, und in andere Pöne, die
wider die Verlezunge der obersten Gewaltsame in den Rechten gegründet,
gefallen, desshalben von Kezery heftiglichen vermergt sin, usw.

Ist unsere Antwort: wiewohl das ist, dass unser heiliger Vater der

THE DEFENSE OF DIETHER

Thereupon we paid and disbursed a sum of money in accord with the resources and the old customary taxes and fees of our see; our Holy Father, the Pope, was unwilling to be content with this. Moreover, we were afflicted with bans and legal proceedings because His Holiness attempted to tax us in excess of our resources and those of our see. Our poverty and that of our see has not unjustly required us to act and to resist in a fitting manner. We protested and appealed against our burden, in a manner entirely correct, because we believe that no one is bound in law to pay taxes that exceed his resources and that no one can be compelled to do so. Thus we have acted not unjustly, but justly, because, if it should happen that the pallium fees of [all] archbishops and bishops were thus steeply and enormously increased over the old customary fees, we have no doubt that in short order the ruin and collapse of every see would follow—a prospect justly undesired. Furthermore, we are not aware of any published ban in which we are implicated, or said to be implicated; no published ban has come to our knowledge and we have received no ban nor has anyone inflicted one upon us, although we have heard many rumors of such a ban since we have appealed. Nevertheless, for this appeal, we should not and could not by the law be justly excommunicated or molested. Because, oppressed and burdened beyond our resources, we made our appeal in due legal form for an investigation of these matters and because we have demanded nothing more than justice, we believe that we are therefore not excommunicated and that we are not proscribed slanderers of the Roman see.

Our Holy Father, the Pope, further contends that, because we have appealed in an infamous treatise we composed to a future council against the laws and the bull of Mantua, we have incurred by this act the penalties of papal excommunication and the other penalties involved in the laws against lèse-majesté, and are therefore strongly suspect of heresy.[1]

This is our answer. It is true that our Holy Father, the Pope, has made

---

[1] See p. 235.

DIETHERS DEFENSIONSSCHRIFT

Pabst zu Mantua ein Geseze gemacht hat, inhaltende dass nyemand
fürbasser von einem Pabst an ein zukünftig concilium appelliren soll,
bey der Pöne Verlezung der obersten Gewaltsamen. Aber so solichs
nicht allein ein Land oder Nation, sunder die Nationes gemeiniglich der
5 Cristenheit berurrende, und auch von den one Indrag von eyme yeden
Beschwerten soliche Appellirunge gebruchet, und nu das sunder der
aller Bewilligunge abgestalt, auch von den allen, die egerurt Constitutie
nich gewilliget noch ufgenommen oder zugelassen, das auch wider alle
Götlich, natürliche und geordnete Weher und Recht, das einem yeden
10 Beschwerten von Got und Recht zugebruchen erlaupt, auch billich
erleubet, gegunnet und gestattet werden soll, ist. So gedruwen wir
darumb und besunder, dwil wir soliche Appellirunge nicht one dreflich
Ursache, sunder merglicher verterplicher Beschwerunge halber, gein uns
und unsern Stifft fürzunemen understanden ist, gethan ist, keynerley
15 Kezerey begangen han, als wir auch ungern tun, ader uns des anders
halten wolten, dann einem Cristlichen, frummen Fürsten und Christen-
menschen, der wir auch sin, und biss an unser Ende zuverbliben, und
zuversterben vermeynen, wol gezemet und gepürt, dann solte das sin,
dass sich nyemand von Beschwerunge eyns Pabsts an ein künftig
20 gemeine Concilium beruffen solte, so möchte ein Pabst mit und gein
einem yeden handeln und fürnemen, wes seins Willens were oder sin
würde, und des möchte sich alsdann nyemants erweren noch ufgehalten,
auch nicht vertragen sin noch verliben, was Last oder Beschwerde das
einem yeden Beschwerten tun und bringen möchte, mag meniglich wol
25 prüfen. Dass wir nu um deswillen, dass wir uns der Appellirunge vorge-
melt, als beschwert vom Pabst, gebrucht haben, und yezund aber in
diesen merglichen und treflichen grossen Sachen und Beschwerunge
wider uns unverschult auch unerfurdert, unverhört und unerwonnen,
alles Rechten wider uns geweltiglich unterstanden, fürzunem ist, aber
30 gebrochen wirden, vor einem Ketzer geschuldiget und gehalten werden
solten, getruwen wir zu Got dem Allmechtigen Bessers, auch von menniglich nicht gelobt noch gebillicht werden solle.

Fürbasser, als unser heyliger Vater der Pabst meldet, dass wir uns als
ein verbannter Ingangs der Kirchen und der heyligen Ampt, der Messe

264

THE DEFENSE OF DIETHER

a law at Mantua declaring that no one should appeal from a pope to a future council under the penalties incurred for lèse-majesté. Such a law which concerns not one land or nation, but all the nations of Christendom, declares that none may make such an appeal for any wrong without detriment; moreover, this bull has been wickedly fabricated without any approval—it has not been approved, accepted, or permitted by anyone. This bull is contrary to all divine and natural law and all ordered right and custom that permits anyone who has been wronged to have recourse to God and the law—such recourse is justly permitted, granted, and conceded. Therefore we believe, especially because we have not ventured or made such an appeal without sufficient reason, but because of the ruinous oppression brought against us and our see, that we have done nothing that is heretical and that we would do such a thing unwillingly. We only wish to be regarded as becomes and befits a devout Christian prince and Christian man, which we trust ourselves to be, to remain until our end, and so to die. Should it come to pass that no one should appeal from the oppression of a pope to a future general council, a pope could deal with everyone according to his whim and no one could defend himself or resist. This could neither be endured nor tolerated; all would experience what burdensome oppression this would bring to anyone who had been wronged. Now for this reason, oppressed by the Pope, we have had recourse to the aforesaid appeal; in these weighty and most significant matters and hardships, force has been ventured against us contrary to all law, without cause, without need, without evidence, and without result. We will suffer defeat before we will be accused and charged with heresy; we trust for a better judgment from God Almighty and [we trust] that everyone will not praise and approve [this action of the Pope].

Furthermore, our Holy Father, the Pope, declares that we, supposedly excommunicated, have undertaken to enter churches and tamper with

und Gezyde zugebruchen underziehen, und dardurch in die Irregularität
verfallen sin sollen usw.

Antworten wir und getruwen zu Gotte, nachdem wir uns, als betrengt
und beschwert, durch den Pabst von syner Heyligkeit zu Verhörunge
5 der Sachen zu Recht beruffen, und auch uf den Grundt des Rechten, und
damit bevestet und versorget hatten, uns auch binnen Zyt der Appellirunge oder auch dafür nye kein Process des Bannes zuhanden kommen,
noch verkundet wurden ist, dass wir darumbe in die Irregularität nicht
verfallen, noch damit in ichts beflekt oder vermergt sin sollen, noch auch
10 dafür gehalten werden.

Fürbasser, als unser heyliger Vater der Pabst meldet, und uns zu
verunglimpfigen vil Lästerlichs begangen zuzühet, und uffmisset und
unter andern hochanzühet, wie wir etwe viel umb Zufall und Adhäsien
unser Appellation ersucht, und angeruffen sollen han usw. Were nun von
15 siner Heyligkeit bedacht unser und unsers Stiffts Notturft und Gelegenheyt, auch dass wir als ein Gehorsamer den alten gewönlichen Tax und
Satze bezalt, auch dass wir überdas, dass nyemants über Vermögen und
Billicheyt pflichtig ist, noch getrungen werden soll, von syner Heyligkeit
wegen unterstanden worden sin, zubesweren und deshalber nicht von
20 eigenem Willen, sunder durch Notturft unsers Stiffts, als das kuntlich
und offenbare vor Augen gewest und noch ist, als beschwert und genottrenget, und doch nicht anders dann zu Recht appelliren haben müssen,
so zwifelt uns nicht, sin Heyligkeit hette uns umb Ersuchunge willen,
Adhesien, und Bekrefftigunge unsers appellirens, so heftiglichen nicht
25 angezogen, und destominner darinne verdacht, angesehen daz die
Notwere eynen yeden zurecht erlaupt ist, und sin soll.

Alsdann syn Heyligkeit fürter anziehet von des vorgenummen Tags
wegen geyn Franckfurt, wir one Wissen und Erleubunge unsers Herrn
des Keysers vorgenummen sollen han usw.

30 Ist unser Antwort. Dass wir solichen Tag durch Beschliessunge
etlicher unser Mitkurfürsten, auch andrer des Richs Fürsten, und

THE DEFENSE OF DIETHER

the holy office, the mass, and sacred worship, and that we supposedly have thus lost all legal rights.[1]

We answer. We trust in God that since we, oppressed and wronged, have validly appealed from His Holiness, the Pope, [to a general council] for an investigation of these matters, and upon the basis of laws have consolidated and secured our position so that while our appeal is pending no excommunication proceeding can be brought against us or be published, we, therefore, have not lost all legal rights, have not incurred the accusation and suspicion of heresy, and cannot be regarded as a heretic.

Furthermore, our Holy Father, the Pope, declares that we supposedly have involved and implicated ourselves in blasphemous slander, and he stresses among other things that we have sought and invoked the support and adherence of many others for our appeal.[2] If His Holiness had considered our impoverished situation and that of our see; and if he had considered that we as an obedient son have paid the old customary taxes and fees and that, because no one is obligated or compelled [to pay taxes] beyond his resources and what equity prescribes, and because His Holiness has undertaken to oppress us, therefore we, not by our own desire, but for the poverty of our see, which was and still is quite openly known to be oppressed and impoverished, have been obligated by right to appeal; [if he had considered these things] we do not doubt that His Holiness would not have so bluntly rejected us and our quest to win support and adherence for our appeal, much less condemned it, since self-defense rightly permits such an appeal.

His Holiness, moreover, contends that we supposedly convoked a diet in Frankfurt without the knowledge and consent of our lord, the Emperor.[3]

This is our answer. We legitimately assembled this diet upon the decision of several fellow Electors, other princes of the Empire, and several

---

[1] See p. 237.
[2] See p. 237.
[3] See p. 239.

267

etlicher Fürsten Botschafft, uff Forme und Masse, das durch sie und uns beschlossen ist, ussgeschreben, das billiche gethan, auch wie mit denselben unsern Mitkurfürsten des unserm Herrn den Keyser Verkündung gethan han, in Hoffnunge syn Keiserlich Majestät daselbst erschenen

5 solte sin, oder syn Sendboten darzugeschickt haben, zuhelffen ratschlagen, wie dem Riche, das lange Zyt in manicherhande Wise in Irrunge mit ungepürlichem Zugriffen, Rauben und Brennen, und Veheden und Gebrechung aller Gericht und Recht ungeprucht gestanden ist, als es leider noch steet und ist, sich auch mit ferer und tiefer Beflec-

10 tunge inrisset, nach Notturft möcht versehen, und der Cristlicher gemeyner Herzogk destobass gefurdert werden, zwifeln auch ganz nicht, wo derselbe Tag nach sinem Usschriben besucht und volngangen were, es solte Dutschland nicht unschedelich gewest, sunder fruchtberlich erschussen sin. Denn als syn Heyligkeit anzühet, dass uns nicht

15 zusteet, der Nation und Gemeynen Nuze der Christenheit zuversehen, es enwere uns denn von den Obersten geboten wurden usw. weren wir begerig zusehen, dass solichs von yem zu beginnen angefangen und auch vollnbracht wurde, es were auch der gemein Cristenheit und insunderheyt unsern Dutschen Nation vorlängst gewest groiss not

20 und nodter dann ye, solte Sie anders etwas lenger in Macht verliben und nicht so gar Unversehunge halber zergenglich werden. Aber, dass dadurch wir von unsers Stiffts und Amtes wegen nicht begeren und handeln solten, dass daz uns von wegen unsers Stiffts, als eynem Kurfürsten und einem Dechant der Kurfürsten, zuthunde zustet und

25 verpflicht sint, getruwen wir von niemants gepillicht solle werden.

Und als unser Heyliger Vater der Pabst fürbasser setzet, wie er unser obgedachten Hendel halber sin Botschafft zu uns geschickt habe, die uns in ungebürlicher Stat und Leben, alles eigen Heupt, und niemants Rats fulgende funden, und mit etweviel nachfulgenden Worten, wir

30 wider Rat syner Sendbotten gered und gehandelt sollen haben, uns in viel Wege zuberungelympfen.

Ist unsere Antwort: haben syne Heiligkeit soliche syne Sendboten zu uns gesant, der masse von uns fürbracht, ist ye die Meynunge des Abschieds zuthun von uns nicht gewest, denn als syn Sendboten uf den

THE DEFENSE OF DIETHER

representatives, in accord with the form and procedure upon which we decided. We and our fellow Electors informed our lord, the Emperor, in the hope that His Imperial Majesty would attend or send his representatives to assist us in our deliberations to provide better for the general Christian expedition and to provide for the distressed Empire, which has long suffered in a multitude of ways from lawless assault, pillaging, burning, and strife, and from the absence of all judicial procedure and law—a condition which unfortunately still prevails, and its poison spreads deeper and wider. We have no doubt that had this diet assembled and fulfilled its task after its convocation, it would not have been to Germany's detriment but would have borne much fruit. His Holiness alleges that it is not our concern to consider the general welfare of our nation and Christendom, except when we receive a mandate from our superiors.[1] We were anxious to see the Emperor begin and bring to an end such a diet. All Christendom and particularly the German nation before long will become more and more impoverished than ever, if such superiors remain any longer in power and their neglect proves more than temporary. But we hope that no one will say that we should not seek to exercise the prerogatives of our see and office and to do what we are bound and obligated to do in the rule of our see as an Elector and as the Dean of the Electors.

Our Holy Father, the Pope, furthermore declares that, informed of these matters, he sent his legates to us and they found us in a lawless way of life, following our own will and heeding the advice of no one; at some length, he declares that we supposedly proceeded and spoke against the advice of his nuncios, and he insults us in many ways.[2]

This is our answer. It was never our understanding from our discussions with his nuncios that His Holiness had sent them to proceed against us, since they declared in effect to us at the most recent diet held on

---

[1] See p. 239.
[2] See p. 239.

nechstgehalten Dage Trinitatis zu Menze mit uns geredet haben, uf
Meynunge, wie sin Heyligkeit etwas Beschwerde in solichen unsern
appelliren haben sollen, und dass wir darumbe die abstellen wolten, so
wolten sie syner Heyligkeit schriben, und ungezwifelt sin, er sulte ein
5 solichs von uns zu guten Danck ufnemen, mit furtfaren gegen uns, biss
uf ir Zukunfft zu yem verhalten, und alsdenn so wolten sie syner Heyligkeit unser und unsers Stiffts anligende Notturft und Beschwerde voll-
kummenlich sagen, uns auch yem in allen gehorsam erbitten, und die
Dinge by yem unser Bottschafft, die wir darumbe auch thun solten, und
10 uns von yem syner Heyligkeit annemyg genant worden, zum getru-
welichsten helffen werben und fürbrengen, und sich mit solichen Fliss
bearweiten, dass Sie nicht zwifelten, uns einen gnedigen Pabst zuerlangen, und dass sin Heyligkeit uns diss egerurten ungegebenen Gelts,
nach unser und unsers Stiffts Notturft, gnedige Verlassunge thun, oder
15 des eyn teyle abstellen, oder zum minsten zu des Bezalunge lenger
gerumere Ziele und Frist geben solte, des sie suhst selber in der vorgenummen Appellirunge besteen und beharren würden, mit nicht
zuerlangen truweten.
   Wir haben uns solicher derselben syner Sendboten glauplich gute
20 Rede und Zusage getroist und verlassen, und uns daruf der egerurten
Appellirunge in irem Bywessen geüssert, und abgestalt. Alles in der
Meynunge, dass uns von syner Heyligkeit, syner Sendboten zusagen
nach, des Gelts Verlassunge beschehen, oder des eynsteyls Abstellunge
getan, oder aber zu des Bezalunge lengere Frist, nach uns und unsers
25 Stiffts Notturfft, gegeben, und darüber von syner Heyligkeit uff uns
nicht vollfaren werden solte, und als wir daruff unser Botschafft, nach
Rate syner Sendboten, syner Heiligkeit genemig zu yem geschickt hann,
die Dinge, wie vorsteet, by yeme zu bearbeiten, hat sin Heyligkeit,
über unser ussgegeben Gelt, wie yem nach alter gewönlicher Tax und
30 Satze unsers Stiffts vor das Pallium bezalt han, auch über unser Abstellunge unserer Appellation und syner egerürten Sendeboten gleüplich
zusagen, diese Bullen egerurt über uns ussgeen verkunden lassen, dass
sin Heylichkeit uns, der vorgemelten Puncte halber, nach Rathe siner
Cardinale, unsers Stiffts entsatzt und den genanten Graf Adolfen damit

270

THE DEFENSE OF DIETHER

Trinity Sunday at Mainz[1] that His Holiness had been somewhat offended by our appeal and that if we would therefore withdraw it, they would write to His Holiness [in our behalf], and they were quite certain that he would graciously receive our withdrawal and would defer proceedings against us until their return. [His nuncios also declared that] they would fully inform His Holiness of our extreme poverty and distress and that of our see; that we should offer in all obedience to fulfill the things our legation had promised in our behalf; and that they would most ardently seek to obtain and secure the acceptance of His Holiness. [They declared that] they would work so ardently in our behalf that they did not doubt but that they would obtain the Pope's favor, and that His Holiness would graciously cancel the unpaid debt due to our poverty and that of our see, would cancel part of it, or at least would grant us more time for payment; [they declared that] they could not obtain [these concessions] if we persisted and continued to advance the aforesaid appeal.[2]

We confidently placed our trust in the good words and promises of the nuncios and in their presence withdrew and renounced the aforesaid appeal. We did this, led by our poverty and that of our see, on the basis of our understanding of the promises of the nuncios on behalf of His Holiness to cancel our debt, or to secure the cancellation of part of it, or to grant us a longer time for payment. Moreover, [we believed] that His Holiness would not proceed against us. Yet when we dispatched in due form our legation, following the advice of his nuncios, to pursue the foregoing matters, His Holiness, despite the payment we disbursed for the pallium in accordance with the old customary taxes and fees of our see, despite our withdrawal of our appeal, and despite the glowing promises of his nuncios, caused the aforesaid bull to be promulgated against us. [In this bull,] His Holiness for the foregoing reasons deposed us from our see, with the advice of his cardinals, and provided the said Graf Adolf to it.[3] Led by the words and promises of his nuncios, we did not at

---

[1] See Introduction, p. 29.
[2] See p. 243.
[3] See pp. 245–247.

271

versehen soll han, des wir uns, dem Abescheyde und Zusage syner egemelten Sendeboten nach, zu syner Heyligkeit mit nicht versehen
hetten, noch wartende gewest sint, indem dass wir unser ussgefertigten
Botschafft egerurt nochmals darum by syner Heyligkeit, und noch kein
5 Antwort von den entfangen haben, und auch alles unerfordert und
unerclärt, und auch unverhört und unerwonnen alles rechten, wir ye
getruwen in keinen Rechten billig, möglich oder recht sy. Wir haben
auch die Zyt Gregorien Heynburg zu dem Dage gein Menze zukummen
nicht verbotet, auch nach yem nicht geschicket, noch uns synes Rats
10 oder Wesens nicht geprucht, meinen auch, dass syn Sendeboten solichs uf
demselbigen Dage nicht anders erfunden haben.

Und als syn Heyligkeit am letzten setzet, und vorwendet etweviel
Puncte ungepurlicher Thete und Hendel, syner Heyligkeit von uns voyr
begangen haben, vorkummen sin sollen, als von bösem unsern Regiment,
15 gewaltiger Gebruchunge in unser Unterthan, von Tyranny, von Reubery
und grymmigen Vornemen, und anderer Puncte halber obgerurt, der
sin Heyligkeit uns, Inhalt der Pebstlichen Bullen begangen, beschuldiget,
und zu merglicher Verungelympfunge vast hoch anzühet, haben syn
Heyligkeit uns unser Kirchen und Stiffts priviret, declarirt und entsatz,
20 darzu aller Geistlichkeyt und Unterthanen unser Stiffts uns fürter nicht
mer zugewarten, gebotten, Sie auch von iren Eyden und Gelobeden des
entbunden, wie das ir beslosse der egerurten Bullen solichs vollenkum-
miglicher begrifft.

Antworten wir. Wir getruwen zu Gott, weren wir der Schuldigung
25 vorgeheyschen und verhört wurden, oder möchten der noch verhört
werden und zu Antwort kummen wir wolten darzu mit der Warheit
geben haben soliche erbere Antwort, und uns der Dinge so vollen-
kummiglich, gnuglich ufrichtiglich warlich und erberlich entschuldiget
und verantwortet haben, auch uns nochmals, so wir verhört solten
30 werden, entschuldiget und verantwortet haben, dass meniglich prüfen,
mercken finden und erkennen soll unsere Unschuld.

Und obe wir joch der Dinge aller, und dannoch merere hynüber begangen hetten, und schuldig weren, des wir doch nit sin, und uns, wie vorsteet,
nach unser Eren und Wirden Notturfft ungezwifelt wol unschuldig

272

all anticipate or expect His Holiness to act in this manner. Because we have dispatched the aforesaid legation to His Holiness again in this matter and have yet to receive a reply, and because [we have been condemned] without a summons, without examination, without evidence, and without sentence, contrary to all law, we trust that this cannot be approved by any law or possibly be just. We did not forbid Gregor Heimburg to attend the diet at Mainz, but we did not send for him and did not avail ourselves of his counsel or presence;[1] it is our opinion that his nuncios at this diet did not find the matter to be otherwise.

His Holiness finally offers and presents several examples of our lawless acts and conduct that supposedly have come to his knowledge; he also alludes to our wicked rule, our armed oppression of our subjects, our tyranny, our pillage, our savage harassment, and the other acts of which he accuses us in the papal bulls, and he slanders us most outrageously.[2] For these reasons His Holiness has declared us removed and deposed from our church and see; moreover, he has enjoined all the clergy and the subjects of our see to serve us no longer and he has released them from their vows and obligations[3]—the contents of the aforesaid bulls fully deal with these matters.

We answer. We trust in God that had we been summoned upon this charge and heard or had we been permitted to be heard and to respond, we would have given with the truth [of these matters] a most convincing rebuttal and quite completely, competently, uprightly, truthfully, and honorably defended ourselves and responded in these matters; we could still do so, if we could be heard, defended, and permitted to respond, so that all would be bound to discover, perceive, recognize, and acknowledge our innocence.

If indeed we were guilty of all these charges and had committed even more crimes than these, which we certainly did not commit, we could [still] proceed, as we have, quite innocently and with undoubted justice

---

[1] See p. 241.
[2] See p. 245.
[3] See p. 247.

zurecht machen mogen, nachdem denn unser heiliger Vater der Pabst, von Got und des Römischen Stuhls wegen, darzu geordnet und bewedempt, auch in Craft der Pflicht, den er dem Römischen Stule und syner Pebstlichen Wirde verwant, und nach Usswisunge götlicher und
5 menschlicher Recht vorzunemen, zuvorteyln. So solt sin Heyligkeit bas geyn uns mit dem Rechten und nit mit der That zuthunde und erstanden und gethan han, und uff, auch wider und über uns, uns der Dinge ganz unersucht, unerfurdert, auch unerclagt, unerhört, und unerwunnen aller Gericht und Recht, besunder auch in unsern Abwessen, diwil die
10 Schuldigunge uns zu hefftlich unsere Wirde Eren und Gelympf berürnde und antreffen ist, nicht vollnfarn und unterstanden haben, uns one Recht und sunder alle Gerichtsordenunge solicher masse zu priviren und zuentsetzen, und uns an unsern Wirden, Eren, und Gelympf, so gar unverschuld, aller Gericht und Recht unerkant, zuletzen, auch syn
15 Bebstlich Gewalsamen und Oberkeyt deshalben gegen uns usserhalber Rechts nicht gepruct haben. So und dwil aber solichs, von syner Heyligkeit wegen, gegen uns anders dann zu Recht, wie fürsteet, fürgenummen wurden ist, alles usserhalber aller Gerichtordenunge und Rechts, und auch über das, dass wir syner Heyligkeit unser Gelt vor das
20 Pallium nach der gewönlichen Tax und Saze unsers Stiffts gegeben, und bezalt han, Syn Heyligkeit das auch also von uns bezalt entpfangen und genummen hat, getruwen wir zu Got, dass uns durch Recht solich schwerlich fürnemen nicht bynden, belestigen noch behefften könne, soll, noch möge, auch von menniglichen darvor nicht anders dann uns
25 zu Unschuld vorgenummen sy, verstanden und gehalten worden.

Nachdem auch wir mit eintrechtiger Wale zu unsern Stifft kummen, auch in Beywessen des genanten Graf Adolfs darinne gesatzt sint, denn auch Jare und Dag, und aber Jare und Dag, und dannoch lenger one Anlangunge und Ansprach desselben von Nassawe une menniglichs
30 geruwelich besessen, regiert, gebrucht und ingehabt, Syn Heyligkeit auch uns sin Pallium ubersant, das Gelt davor, nach alter gewönlicher Tax und Saze unsers Stiffts, von uns genummen hat, wir und unser Stifft in fürder Bezalunge nach vorberurter Gelegenheyt in Vermogen nicht gewest sint, noch gehabt, auch in allen unsern fürnemen das

THE DEFENSE OF DIETHER

according to our honor, office, and need, because our Holy Father, the Pope, with regard to God and the Roman see in which he is ordained and consecrated, and with regard to the fulfillment of his obligation to the Roman see and his papal office, likewise outrageously proceeds contrary to divine and human law. Thus His Holiness ought to have proceeded and acted against us with law and not with force; he should not have dared to make charges entirely without substantiation, without a summons, without examination, without evidence, and without sentence, contrary to all law and justice, particularly [because this was done] in our absence and because these charges concern and involve too deeply our office, honor, and reputation; he should not have deposed and dismissed us in such a manner contrary to law and completely without due juridical order; he should not have assailed our office, honor, and reputation, indeed our innocence, in a manner quite unknown to law and justice; and he should not have employed his papal authority and power against us thus contrary to law. But because His Holiness has proceeded against us in a manner other than legal, as has been shown, and contrary to all juridical order and law, because we have paid and dispatched our debt to His Holiness for the pallium in accord with the customary taxes and fees of our see, and because His Holiness has received and accepted our payment, we trust in God that such oppression cannot, ought not, and may not legally bind, trouble, or afflict us, and that all men in this matter will consider, recognize, and regard us as innocent.

Accordingly we entered our see with a harmonious election and were installed therein in the presence of the said Graf Adolf. Furthermore, we peacefully possessed, ruled, enjoyed, and filled that see for a year and a day, and for a still longer period of time without encountering opposition from the said Adolf von Nassau or anyone else. His Holiness sent us the pallium and accepted our payment in accord with the old customary taxes and fees of our see. It was not in our power or that of our see, nor did we possess the resources, to pay more, on account of the situation which we have described previously. In all our actions—the debt out-

usssteende Gelt, das appelliren und anders wir von syner Heyligkeit
beschuldiget werden, nicht anders dann zu Recht gethan und fürgenummen han, deshalber auch Rechts begert und gesucht han, und noch
nicht anders zusuchen und fürzunemen begeren, wie recht ist. So zwifelt
5 uns nicht, menniglich verstehe wol, wes darüber von syner Heyligkeit
gegen uns begangen und fürgenummen ist, und von yem und andern
ferrer zuthunde understanden und gethan würde, dass solichs were und
ist gethan mit der That der Gewalt und Unrecht, und destoviel merer
unrechter, auch destomynner von meniglichen zu billichen und zuloben.
10 Sich ist auch darüber nicht unbillich zubefremden, so und dwil der
benant Graf Adolf, also wol als wir, und die andern, die zu der Zyt unser
Erwelunge unsers Capitels waren, einen Liplichen Eyd zu Got und den
Heiligen gesworn hat, welicher usser uns die Zyt unsers Capitels von den
sieben Dumherren der Wale gesazt und gegeben, eintrechtiglich erwelt
15 wurde, dass wir andern all des Capittels, samt den Kiesern, den also
erwelt vor einen Herrn und Erzbischoff des Stiffts zu Menze ufnehmen,
halten und haben, dem auch getruwen Bistand, yen daby zuhalten,
thun solten, dass darüber der benant Graff Adolff in Vergesse des
egemelten sins hochgelopten, duren gesworn Eyds zu Got und den
20 Heiligen durch eynen vermessem Schien der Bebstlichen Versehung,
Gebots Erlösunge und Entpindunge desselben sins Eyds, als er vermeint,
unbillich und erstehet und vorhat, sich des vorgerurten unsers Stiffts
zuunderziehen und anzunemen, und uns des zuentweltigen, aller Gericht
und Recht unerwonnen und unentsatzt, auch demselben unsern Stifft
25 zu grosser merglicher und wantlichen Zuentrennunge, Zurissunge und
Schaden, des er billicher Vermyder und Vorkummer, nachdem er unsern
Stifft gewant ist, ist, sin soll, dann Ursacher oder Furderer.

Es ist darzu wol selzum und sich mer dann zuvil zuverwundern von den
Ihenen, die uns und unserm Stifft von Eynunge, Bintnisse und Lehunge
30 wegen, mit Eyden und Globden verpflicht und gewant sint, in vergesse
aller irer Verpflichtunge egerurt, alles unbewarter Dinge, auch unofge-
sagt irer Verpflichtunge, und gantz unbesorget dazu auch unbeschriben,
unerfurdert, unersucht, auch unverhört und unerfolget alles Rechten,
und ohne alle Vehede, uff eyn vermessen Schyn und Behelff des

standing, our appeal, and our other acts which His Holiness condemns—
we have proceeded and acted only justly. Therefore we have sought and
desired justice and have not desired to seek or to strive after anything
that is not just. Thus we do not doubt that all clearly understand that
what His Holiness has undertaken and perpetrated against us, and furthermore what he and others attempted to do and would have done
[against us], was and is done with coercion and injustice; it is therefore so
much more unjust and so much less to be approved and praised by anyone. Therefore this cannot be unknown because the said Graf Adolf,
as well as we and the others who were members of our chapter at the
time of our election, swore a bodily oath to God and the saints that all
the chapter, including the Electors, should accept, recognize, and
regard the one harmoniously elected and chosen by seven canons of our
chapter as our lord and Archbishop of the See of Mainz and that all should
lend him loyal support. [It cannot be unknown] that the said Graf
Adolf, forgetting his aforesaid oath sworn solemnly and openly to God
and the saints, through the audacious pretext of papal provision, release
from authority, and dispensation from his oath, unjustly imagines,
protests, and contends that he assumes and claims our aforesaid see and
that he ousts us—this is contrary and opposed to all law and justice. He
ought more justly to be the defender and guardian of our see—as is and
ought to be his duty—than the promoter and instigator of such ruinous
schism and misfortune for our see.

It is therefore quite astounding and very strange that those who are
bound and obligated to us and our see by oaths and vows of feudal contract, alliance, and obligation, most unexpectedly forgetful of these
obligations, not released from them, entirely oblivious to them, without
any authorization, without substantiation, without legal procedure,
without evidence, contrary to all law, without any cause for enmity,
rely upon an audacious pretext and the support of papal decree and

DIETHERS DEFENSIONSSCHRIFT

Pebstlichen Gebots und Usschribens, Erlösunge und Entpündunge irer
Eyde, als sie vermeinten, so sie doch wol wissen und yen kuntlich ist,
dass wir des vom Pabst zu recht nye vorgeheischen, verhört noch er-
wonnen sin, unterstent und fürhant, Hulff und Volge wieder uns zu-
5 thunde, auch thunt, und samt demselben Graff Adolffen und irer An-
henger, unsern würdigen Stifft, alles unverschuldigeter Dinge jemerlich
zurissen, zubeschedigen, zubestoren, und zuergenglich zumachen, und
auch Lant und Lude in soliche merglich Ufrure, gross Blutvergiessen
und Verderben zubringen, und wir sin unzwifelich solicher Handel,
10 Fürnemen und Geschicke an uns und unserm Stifft obberurter Wise
begangen sollen, von allen erbern State, auch allen unsern Unterthanen,
und zu uns und unsern Stifft verwandt, edeln und unedeln, und suhst
meniglichen der Sachen unverwand, nit gebillicht, gemögelicht noch
gelopt, sunder wider Got und die Gerechtigkeit und wider alle Erberkeit
15 vorgenummen sin, vermergt werden. Dann solte solich Vornemen in
diesen Landen ufersteen, dass man einen so schwerlich, sunder alle
Gerichtsordenunge und Recht, syner Wirden, Eren und Gelympf, unerhört, unerwonnen, berauben und entsetzen, und denjhenen, der
darzu furdert, syner Gelobde und Eyde und aller Verpflichtunge ent-
20 pinden, were nyemand sicher, auch anzwifel wider den Glauben, Truwe
Erberkeit, und wider alle Recht, und darumbe mit nicht zudulden
solich Entpündunge und Erlösunge der Eyde und Gelobden, nach
Gelegenheyt und Gestalt der Sachen egerurt, were auch gegen allen
erbern Stat nit unbillich, etwas vast erschrecklich derselben Worte der
25 Entpundunge soliche Eyde würden dann von unserm heyligen Vater
dem Pabst mit den angehengt, und zugegeben die Worte, welcher uns
und unsern Stifft verwant sich getrosten wolte, gegen uns und unsern
Stifft meyneidig zuwerden, der solte Graf Adolffen wider uns zuhelffen
syner Eyde und Gelobde ledig und entpunden sin, suhst mag ist nach
30 aller Verhandelunge und ergangener Sache nicht wohl gesin, noch
gebillicht werden, es mögen yen auch diejene, die das gern sehen und
haben wolten, und uns entsaz, ein solichs durch solichen vermessen
Schin understeen, zu Erschönunge irer Eyde und Gelobede vorzunemen,
auch das gegen den in iren Gedencken inwendig sie ansehen, das gemein

THE DEFENSE OF DIETHER

proclamation [to claim] that they are absolved and released from their oaths. They certainly realize and are aware that we have never been legally summoned, heard, or convicted by the Pope; yet they undertake and attempt to win help and support against us and, together with the said Graf Adolf and his adherents, lamentably rend, molest, destroy, and trouble our honored see without any justification and cause great disorder, bloodshed, and lawlessness within our land among our people. We have no doubt that such action, behavior, and conduct undertaken against us and our see as just declared should not be approved, supported, or commended by any honorable men, whatever their rank, by any of our subjects and those bound to us and our see, by any nobles and commoners, or by any men not involved in these matters, but should be regarded as contrary to all honor and opposed to God and justice. When it comes to pass in this land that one is so outrageously, without all juridical process and justice, without a hearing or a conviction, robbed and deprived of his office, honor, and reputation, and the rival advanced against him, released from all his vows, oaths, and obligations, no one is safe! Without a doubt this is opposed to good faith and honor and contrary to all law, and in the described situation, all honorable men rightly would not tolerate such absolution and release from oaths and obligations; moreover, the words of release from such an oath [would appear] almost monstrous. Then the words declared and decreed by our Holy Father, the Pope, by which he led us and our see to entertain hope, become perjury against us and our see, should he assist Graf Adolf against us by releasing him from his oaths and obligations. This, however, would be contrary to all due process and correct order, and could not be approved. Thus those who eagerly desire to depose us and to undertake this, claiming so audaciously that they have freed themselves from their vows and obligations, could [just as easily abandon] Adolf and apply to

279

Sprichwort, das man pfleget zu sagen, were one das gern danzt, dem ist lichtlich zu pfiffen.

Aber wer suhst mit seinen Eren, Eyden und Gelympfen nicht gern geschertzt wil han, auch nicht gern hette noch vertragen wolte sin, des 5 verkerlichen Nachreden, als es denn hie wol sin und bescheen mögte, der möchte des solichs Gebots und Entpindunge halber, von unserm heiligen Vater dem Pabst, wie vorsteet, verkundet und ussgegangen, wol und mässig geen, angesehen, dass das mit Fugen, Eren und Gelympf von nyemand zu recht verantwort mag werden, und so nu wir und unser 10 Stifft so merglich und schwerlich wieder alle Geburde und Billicheyt ohberurten zu belestigen unterstanden sint und werdent, werden wir genottrenget, uns dargegen und wider nicht unbillich, nach aller unser Notdurft, der Gegen- und Notweren zugebruchen.

Bitten darumbe allermenniglich, so wir innerlichst, gütlichst unde 15 früntlichst können sollen und mögen, uns heruff verantwurt haben, auch wo sichs begeben, ire des Rede, Sage oder Verkündunge vornemen oder hören werdent, und not sin würdet, biss uff uns zuverantwurten, denn ire und meniglich unser, der Dinge halber, zu gebürlicher, rechtlicher Verhörunge und Verantworten, auch an gebürlichen Enden und Stetten 20 fürzukommen, vollmechtif sin sollent, und darumbe herüber, zu Hülff der Gerechtigkeit, wieder uns unsern Stifft unserm Wiederteyle kein Hülff, Fulge noch Zulegunge thun, als wir uch allesampt, und besundere zusampt der Billicheyt, des obgerürten ungepürlichs Fürnemens halber, an uns begangen ist, und würdet wol getruwen, wollen wir gegen uch und 25 uwer yeden insunderheit früntlich gern verschulden, und gegen den unsern mit Gnaden in allem Guten nicht vergessen. Geben in unser Stat Menze an Dornstage nach Michaelis, Anno usw. Sexagesimo primo.

THE DEFENSE OF DIETHER

him the common proverb: it is easy to pipe to him who dances gladly without a piper.

Furthermore, he who does not trifle lightly with his own reputation, honor, or good name could not eagerly or indifferently receive this unwelcome slander—since such it most certainly proved to be—and could not find tolerable the mandate and absolution promulgated and decreed by our Holy Father, the Pope, as mentioned previously. No one would justify this with right, honor, and justice. Since we and our see are so remarkably and grievously oppressed contrary to all measure and justice, we are compelled not unjustly to defend ourselves against this wrong according to our need.

Therefore, since we have justified ourselves in this matter as earnestly, acceptably, and cordially as possible, we implore all men, when it befalls them to hear or encounter this report or desire and when the need arises, to defend us, since all men should be most ready to accept our very fitting and just defense and justification in this matter [and to pursue it] to an appropriate end and conclusion. Thus in the cause of justice none should lend support, assistance, or aid to those who oppose us and our see. Since we are quite confident in you in all respects, particularly that of justice, with regard to the lawless undertaking that has been launched against us, we will gladly be indebted to you and all your subjects and we will not forget to seek most graciously every benefit for our subjects. Decreed in our city of Mainz on the Thursday after Michaelmas in the year 1461.[1]

---

[1] 29 September 1461.

REPLICA THEODORI LAELII
EPISCOPI FELTRENSIS,
PRO PIO PAPA II
ET SEDE ROMANA, AD
SCRIPTUM GREGORII HEIMBURG

Oblatrantem te, Gregori, adversus Christum Domini ore sacrilego, et impiis vocibus obstrepentem, Pius Pontifex Maximus jure contempsit; non quod garrulitati tuae atque blasphemiae disertissimus virorum respondere non posset, sed quia aeterni Pastoris, cujus vices gerit, qui
5 cum malediceretur non maledicebat, cum pateretur, non comminabatur, imitandum humilitatis exemplum putavit. Meminerat quippe et Christum Dominum a Pharisaeis, quorum tu perfidiam imitaris, crebris conviciis lacessitum, et nunc *voracem*,[1] nunc *vini potatorem*,[2] nunc *Samariten et daemoniacum*[3] appellatum, et patientiae ipsius documenta suscipiens
10 illud dominicum arcano volvebat in pectore: *Non est servus major domino*

---

[1] *Matth.* 11, 19.
[2] *Matth.* 11, 19.
[3] *Joan.* 8, 48.

REPLY WRITTEN
BY TEODORO LAELIO,
BISHOP OF FELTRE
IN DEFENSE OF POPE PIUS II
AND THE ROMAN SEE AGAINST
A WORK OF GREGOR HEIMBURG

Pius, the Supreme Pontiff, justly ignored you, Gregor, when you blasphemously snarled at the Lord's anointed and when you cried out against him impiously. This was not because this most eloquent of men could not respond to your babbling and blasphemy, but because he thought that he ought to follow the example of the Eternal Shepherd, in whose stead he rules, who did not curse when he was cursed and did not utter threats when he was threatened. Indeed, he remembered that Christ the Lord was repeatedly insulted by the Pharisees, whose perfidy you imitate, and called on one occasion *a glutton*, on another *a wine-bibber*, and on still another *a Samaritan and a man possessed by a demon*; mindful of these lessons of forbearance, he pondered deep in his heart the words of the Lord: *A servant is not greater than his master nor a pupil greater*

NOTE: The Latin text is reprinted from Marquard Freher and Burchard Struve, *Rerum Germanicarum scriptores varii, qui res in Germania & imperio sub Friderico III, Maximiliano I. Impp. memorabiliter gestas illo aevo litteris prodiderunt* (Strasbourg, 1717), II, 214–228.

283

suo, nec discipulus eo qui misit illum. Quoniam si Patrem familias Beelze-
bub vocaverunt, quanto magis domesticos ejus.[1] Sic ille non quod tu mere-
baris, sed quid se deceret, attendit. Verum et plurimi et magno atque
excellenti ingenio viri tuis blasphemiis respondere potuissent, si vel ad
5 illos maledicta illa sacrilega pervenissent, vel ineptissimum, atque
perditissimum hominem coinquinationis et maculae voluptatibus
fluentem, et tanquam bestiam inter luxum semper epulasque sudantem,
dignum responso putavissent, quorum plerique insaniam indicente,
atque juxta Sapientis eloquium in ore stulti esse baculum contumeliae
10 agnoscentes, illud ex SAPIENTE proferebant:[2] *Noli respondere stulto*
secundum stultitiam suam, ne forte similis fias ei.

Ineptum sane existimabant congredi tecum, cum nec docere indoci-
bilem, nec reducere pertinacem, nec cohibere furentem posse confi-
derent. Ac talia cogitantes errantem perfidum hactenus silentio
15 contempsere. Sed cum patientia illorum abutens contra lenitatem odio et
adversus Pontificis mansuetudinem furore et insania bacchari coepisses,
et blasphemiarum tuarum exempla per Italiam Germaniamque dis-
pergere, me unum ex pusillis Curiae et Apostolicae Sedis ministris
domus Dei zelus accendit, ut diutius me continere non possem, quin
20 volantia jam paene toto orbe jacula falsitatis, clypeo veritatis exciperem.
Verebar enim, ne si nullus tuis calumniis responderet, jam patientia
diffidentiae inciperet imputari, ut vel saltem injustae damnationis tuae
Apostolica Sedes videretur crimen agnoscere. Licet enim apud ipsius
sedis pontificem justi judicii conscientia sola sufficeret, non incongruum
25 tamen visum est, et reliquis, si qui forte quasi de injusto anathemate tuo

---

[1] *Matth.* 10, 24–25.**
[2] *Prov.* 26, 4.

284

than him who sent him. For if the master has been called Beelzebub, how much more his household. Thus he considers not what you deserve but what becomes himself. Granted, many men of outstanding ability could have responded to your blasphemies if those sacrilegious and accursed words had come to their knowledge, and if they had thought there was any use in responding to a man so absurd and incorrigible in his faults and filthy pursuits, a man debauched in foul pleasures and continually sweating like an animal between debauchery and gluttony. Several of these men, recognizing this madness, and understanding with the wise man that eloquence is a source of reproach in the mouth of a fool, uttered the wise words of the wise man: *Answer not a fool according to his folly, lest you become like him yourself.*

They sensibly considered it foolish to contend with you since they believed it impossible to teach the unteachable, to win back one so obstinate, or to restrain a madman. For such reasons they have silently ignored until now this wicked man who has gone astray. But because you abuse their patience and have begun to rant hatefully, furiously, and insanely against the forbearance and clemency of the Pope and to dispatch copies of your blasphemies throughout Italy and Germany, zeal for the house of God incites me, one of the more insignificant servants of the Curia and the Apostolic See, so that I can no longer contain myself, but must intercept with the shield of truth the arrows of falsehood that are flying almost everywhere.[1] For I feared that if no one responded to your slanders, patience might be mistaken for indifference, or at least the Apostolic See would seem to acknowledge the weight of your unjust condemnation. For although the inner conviction of the pontiff of that see that his verdict was just would suffice, it nevertheless did not seem amiss to render proper justification to those who might perchance be offended and think your condemnation to be unjust. Thus at one time Gelasius[2]

---

[1] See p. 71.
[2] Gelasius I (492–496) defended Roman primacy against Acacius, the Patriarch of Constantinople, and Anastasius, the Byzantine Emperor.

viderentur offensi, congrue satisfacere. Sic quondam Gelasius ac Nicolaus sanctissimi dissertissimique pontifices, alter de Achatii, alter de Photii pseudoepiscoporum damnatione, Anastasio Michaelique principibus et orientalibus populis tomos scribentes satisfecerunt.

5 In quo genere illud aureum Pii Pontificis flumen eloquentiae omnes facile superasset, nisi illum vel indignitas tua, vel criminis evidentia, vel forsan remaledicendi apud quosdam suspicio retraxissent. Movit nos praeterea et Catholicae fidei ratio, contra quam cum multa in ipsis tuis blasphemiis haeretice impieque prolata legissem, et scandalo et periculo
10 verebar amplius esse silentium, ac proinde populare quasi apud Christianos tuendae fidei officium arbitrabar. Nam etsi cetera crimina silentio praeteriri queant, hoc tamen in fide si fiat, et scandalum et periculum generat. Licet apud te casso labore desudem, apud ceteros tamen, quos tuis blasphemiis forsan concitasti, atque impia et maledicta seminando
15 tui erroris comites effecisti, speramus Deo propitio aliquid profuturos. Nam qui per errorem moti sunt tuo mendacio fallente, facilius veritatem admittent ratione cogente.

Respondebimus ergo, licet incompositis verbis, veniam a legentibus rudioris stili facile praesumentes; quoniam contra impias blasphemias
20 justitia ac fidei patrocinium suscepturi non nitori sermonis, sed veritati studemus. Ante tamen quam tuis maledictis respondeam, abs te postulare libet, doctorum eximie et jurisconsultorum dissertissime, qui tibi utriusque juris scientiam vendicas, et—ut tuis verbis utar[1]—*qui te quicquid ratio et industria praecipuum habet, et quidquid tradunt utriusque*

---

[1] *Gregorii Heimburg Appellatio a Papa . . . ad Concilium Futurum* in Frehero et Struvio, *Rerum Germanicarum Scriptores varii . . .* (Strasbourg, 1717), II, 213.*

REPLY BY TEODORO LAELIO

and Nicholas,[1] most holy and most eloquent pontiffs, justified their actions in treatises sent to the rulers, Anastasius and Michael, concerning the condemnation in one case of Acacius and in the other of Photius, both false bishops.

The golden stream of Pope Pius' eloquence would easily have surpassed all others in this literary genre, but your unworthiness, the manifest nature of your crime, or perhaps the suspicion that might be aroused among some if he answered such abuse in the same vein restrained him. Moreover, concern for the Catholic faith has moved me [to write], since I have read the many blasphemies that you have included and that you have advanced heretically and impiously against it;[2] for I feared that silence would prove to be a far greater scandal and danger, and therefore deemed it my public responsibility to defend the faith among Christians. For although other crimes can be passed by in silence, to do so in matters that concern the faith begets scandal and danger. Even though my efforts may be wasted upon you, nevertheless let us hope they may have with God's help some profit for those whom you perhaps have swayed by your blasphemies or have made partakers of your error by sowing your impious and accursed words. For those who were moved through error when deceived by your lies will more easily admit the truth when impelled by reason.

Therefore I will respond, although with disordered words, certainly assuming forbearance from my readers for my somewhat unfinished style; for I concern myself with taking up the defense of justice and the faith against his wicked blasphemies, not by means of the eloquence of my discourse, but by its truth. Nevertheless, before I respond to your evil words, permit me to ask you something, most learned of doctors and most eloquent of jurists, who claims to know both civil and canon law and who boasts that *he has learned whatever application and understanding may*

---

[1] Nicholas I (858–867) in 863 deposed and excommunicated Photius, who had been elected Patriarch of Constantinople uncanonically. Emperor Michael III reigned from 842 to 867.

[2] See p. 71.

juris instituta, percepisse gloriaris; hoc ne in legibus aut canonibus, aut in moralibus disciplinis didicisti, ut contra pontificem summum, ecclesiae caput et principem, et miserae animae tuae episcopum atque pastorem, vel quomodolibet laesus inveheres? Hominum perditissime, quis un-
5 quam haereticorum, qui a Romana damnati sunt sede, in illius antistitem talia maledicta congessit? Lege Nestorium, Macedonium, Eutychen, Coelestinum atque Pelagium, Macarium atque Dioscorum, et caeteras haereticorum pestes, quis unquam tam turpiter ora laxavit? Qui licet damnationem suam graviter tulerint, tamen a talibus blasphemiis
10 temperarunt.

Unus inventus est Dioscorus, qui pro eo solo, quod anathema in sanctum et venerabilem Leonem ausus est, in Chalcedonensi synodo sive ulla fuit restitutione damnatus. Cujus praesumptionem ob hoc potissimum sancti patres detestati sunt, quia ponens os in coelum et lingua
15 ejus transeunte super terram, inferior majorem injuriis lacessere ausus est. Et hoc noscens Concilii fuisse statutum, adhuc Conciliorum audes mentionem facere, nec revereris illorum pro minori culpa censuram. Miserrime hominum, non te terruit evangelica illa tuba,[1] *quod qui scandalizaverit unum ex pusillis illis minimis, qui in me credunt, expedit*
20 *ei, ut suspendatur mola asinaria in collo ejus, et demergatur in profundum.* Quod si scandalizandi unumquemque pusillum in Christum credentem

---

[1] *Matth.* 18, 6.

attain and whatever the teachings of civil and canon law declare. Have you learned in the laws, in the canons, or in moral doctrine to assail in any manner whatever the Supreme Pontiff, the head and ruler of the church and the bishop and pastor of your wretched soul? Most wicked man, what heretic condemned by the Roman see ever showered such foul insults upon that bishop? Consider Nestorius,[1] Macedonius,[2] Eutyches,[3] Celestinus,[4] Pelagius,[5] Macarius,[6] and Dioscorus,[7] and other pestilential heretics; did any of these ever speak more shamefully? Although they seriously invited their own damnation, nevertheless they restrained themselves from such blasphemies.

Only one of these is your equal: Dioscorus, who, because he dared on his own initiative to promulgate an anathema against the holy and venerable Leo, was condemned by the Council of Chalcedon without any hope of restitution. The Holy Fathers detested this presumption most vehemently because, defying the heavens and permitting his tongue to run loose upon the earth, the subordinate dared to assail his superior with insults. Although you are aware that this was the statute of a council, you continue to refer audaciously to councils and do not respect their condemnation for faults less grievous than yours. Most wretched of men, does not Christ, the Evangelical Trumpet, terrify you? *If a man is a cause of stumbling to the least of these little ones who have faith in me, it would be better for him to have a millstone hung round his neck, and be drowned in the depths [of the sea.]* If such a punishment is meted out to anyone who is a cause of stumbling to any little one who believes in Christ,

---

[1] Nestorius (381–c. 451) was the founder of the Nestorian heresy.

[2] Macedonius (fl. 350), Patriarch of Constantinople, was deposed by the synod of Constantinople for Trinitarian errors in 360.

[3] Eutyches (b. c. 378), presbyter of Constantinople, was definitively condemned at the Council of Chalcedon in 451.

[4] Laelio probably alludes to Coelestius, a contemporary and associate of Pelagius.

[5] Pelagius (d. c. 420), a British monk, was the classical founder of the Pelagian heresy.

[6] Macarius was the author of a mystical treatise condemned at the Council of Chalcedon in 451.

[7] Dioscorus (fl. 345), Patriarch of Antioch, was condemned at Chalcedon as a partisan of he Monophysite heresy.

talem vindictam comminatur; qua ultione plectendus eris, qui totum corpus scandalizas ecclesiae, qui ecclesiarum omnium patrem et pastorem, haereticum, garrulum, insanum, et quicquid turpitudinis tuae immunditiaeque foetor ingerit, in illum causaris? Nec mirum quidem, 5 quoniam non potest nisi spurce loqui, qui consuevit spurca committere. *Ex abundantia enim cordis os loquitur, et malus homo de malo cordis thesauro non potest nisi mala proferre.*[1] An vero quanti sacrilegii sit principi populi maledicere, ex lege discere non potuisti, quae maledictio aeterna morte condemnat.[2] Cujus verba non modo in Romani, sed 10 omnium episcoporum injunctione solemni, inter ipsa sacra terribiliter intonantur, pronuntiante episcopo et conformantibus ceteris:[3] *Qui male dixerit tibi, sit ille maledictus, et qui benedixit, ipse benedictionibus repleatur.*

Quod si de probis non de reprobis principibus ac sacerdotibus dictum 15 esse contendis, audias Paulum apostolorum, qui cum jussu principis sacerdotum injuste caesus, illi divinam ultionem precaretur, atque astantes dicerent:[4] *Summum sacerdotem Dei maledicis?* Mox territus lege divina se purgans ait:[5] *Nesciebam, fratres, quia princeps esset sacerdotum. Scriptum est enim, "Principem populi tui non maledices."* An forte juste 20 homini iniquo, sacrilego, et contra legem agenti se maledixisse contendit, et non potius errati veniam petiit, et nefas principi sacerdotum maledicere legis auctoritate professus est? Sed quid ego Paulum memoro? Ipse Dominus noster Jesus Christus, summus sacerdos, rex et judex, usque ad passionis suae diem non solum bonis et piis, sed etiam indignis 25 et reprobis detulit sacerdotibus, quamvis illi nec timorem Dei, nec agnitionem Christi servassent. Ut enim alia omittamus, ipse subditus passioni cum alapam accepisset, et ei diceretur:[6] *Sic respondes pontifici?*

---

[1] *Matth.* 9, 33.
[2] Cf. *Exod.* 22, 28.
[3] *Gen.* 27, 29.
[4] *Act.* 23, 4.
[5] *Act.* 23, 5.
[6] *Joan.* 18, 22.

how will you be chastised who are a cause of stumbling to the whole body of the church and who term the father and pastor of all churches a heretic, a prattler, and a fool? What will be the effect on him when the stench of your filthy squalor and wickedness reaches him? Such vituperation is not surprising, since one can speak only foully when he has been accustomed to do foul deeds. *For the mouth speaks out of the abundance of the heart and a wicked man cannot produce other than evil from the wicked treasure of his heart.* Could you not learn from the law that condemns such curses with eternal death what sacrilege it is to curse the ruler of your people? These words are intoned fearfully not only in the solemn injunction of the Roman bishop but of all bishops in the liturgy of ordination when the bishop declares and the others present join in: *Who curses you, let him be accursed, and he who blesses you, let him abound with blessings.*

But if you argue that this is said of upright rulers and priests, and not of wicked ones, consider the apostle Paul, when he was wrongly struck upon the high priest's order; he called for divine retribution, and those who stood by asked: *Would you curse God's high priest?* Then, fearing the divine law, he excused himself saying: *I did not know, brethren, that he was the high priest; for it is written: "You shall not curse the ruler of your people."* Perchance you contend that he justly cursed this wicked, sacrilegious man and transgressor of the law, that he only sought forgiveness for his error, and that he professed to curse the unjustice of the high priest by the authority of the law. But I need not recall only Paul. Our Lord himself, Jesus Christ, our high priest, our king and judge, until the day of his Passion paid deference not only to good, devout priests but also to unworthy, wicked ones, although they did not observe the fear of God or the knowledge of Christ. [I shall give but one example,] omitting other instances: Christ was submissive to his Passion when he was smitten upon the cheek, and when asked, *Is that how you answer the high priest?*

291

nihil contumeliose in personam locutus est, quem sciebat esse sacrilegum, sed magis innocentiam suam tutatus est, dicens:[1] *Si male locutus sum, testimonium perhibe de malo; si autem bene, cur me caedis?* Quod idem beato CYPRIANO teste et canone attestante[2] factum est, ut humili-
5 tatis et patientiae ipsius haberemus exemplum. *Docuit enim sacerdotes veros plenius honorandos, dum ipse circa falsos talis extiterit.*

At vero Gregorius contra legem se asserens injuste communione dejectum, non solum in verba contumeliae injuriaeque prorupit, sed famosum libellum totam scandalizantem ecclesiam blasphemans
10 evomuit; nec illi satis est deliquisse, nisi de malitia gloriabundus exem- plaris congreget, et publice legenda dispergat. Leges civiles, quarum se professorem vaniloquus temerator gloriatur, eum qui libellum famosum in injuriam alicujus ediderit, vel ab alio editum non celaverit, capitali sententia damnant.[3] Et tamen audet leges appellare, qui tam sacrilege
15 committit in legem. Praevaricator legis legem attende, quoniam non in unumquemque privatum, sed Dei vicarium atque legatum gregis domi- nici directorem, ecclesiarum omnium patrem,[4] sed et miserae animae tuae et cunctorum fidelium episcopum atque pastorem parricidali furore baccharis, lingua interficis, maledictis discerpis, blasphemiis
20 laceras, et quantum ad reatum tuum attinet, tanquam truculentus homicida transfodis ac jugulas. Homicidam recte appellaverim, cum ex canone tria homicidiorum genera,[5] et poenam eorum parilem cognos- camus; inter quae detractores linguis proximos confodientes constat esse deterrima.
25 Impudentissime hominum, non te divina terruerunt exempla, cum legas Mariam sororem Aaron, quae prima post transitum maris rubri in tympano hymnum cantare meruerat,[6] eo quod murmurasset in Moysen,

---

[1] *Joan.* 18, 23.
[2] c. 25, D. XCIII (RF I, 329).
[3] Non invenitur.
[4] Cf. Caspar Schatzgeyer, *Apologia status fratrum ordinis minorum de observantia* (Nurem- berg, 1516), f. Bii[v].
[5] Cf. *de poen.*, D. I, c. 24 (RF I, 1164).
[6] *Exod.* 14, 20–21.

REPLY BY TEODORO LAELIO

he said nothing insolent to one whom he knew to be wicked; rather he preserved his innocence, saying: *If I have spoken wrongly, bear witness to the wrong; but if I have spoken rightly, why do you strike me?* ST. CYPRIAN and canon law bear witness that he said this in order to give us a perfect example of humility and patience. *For he taught that true priests must be honored even when they are surrounded with false ones.*

But in fact Gregor, unlawfully claiming that he was unjustly ousted from the Church, not only burst into words of abuse and insult, but blasphemously vomited forth an infamous treatise that is a scandal to the entire Church. He is not content to have sinned, but exultantly assembles copies of his roguery and dispatches them to be read publicly. The civil law of which this boastful transgressor brags that he is a professor condemns to death the man who produces an infamous treatise to the detriment of anyone or who does not conceal such a work. Yet he who so sacrilegiously violates the law dares to appeal to the laws. Violator of the law, consider the law, since you do not rage in murderous fury against just anyone, but against the vicar and legate of God, the guardian of the Lord's flock, and the father of all churches, and against the bishop and pastor of your miserable soul and of all the faithful. You slay him with your tongue; you rend him with your foul words; you mutilate him with your blasphemies; and as concerns your accursed state, like a savage murderer you stab and slay him. I have correctly termed you a murderer, since canon law acknowledges three sorts of murder and equivalent forms of chastisement; it is well established that the worst of these involves those slanderers who stab their fellows with their tongues.[1]

Most shameless of men, do not scriptural examples terrify you? You read that Miriam, the sister of Aaron, who after the Red Sea crossing first worthily sang a hymn with a timbrel, because she murmured against

---

[1] See p. 185.

lepra fuisse percussam.[1] Ecce tu non solum murmurasti, sed publice blasphemasti, certe non Moysen—qui et ipse inter sacerdotes inscribitur, PSALMISTA testante atque dicente[2] *Moyses et Aaron in sacerdotibus ejus*—sed Moyse non merito, sed auctoritate majorem. Oziam audisti 5 pro eo, quod sacerdotes contemnens sacrorum praesumptor extiterit, simili plaga percussum esse.[3] Bethleemiticos pueros ob derisionem prophetae morte damnatos.[4] Ecce autem plusquam Moyses aut aliquis prophetarum, quem tu impie blasphemas, nisi forte mentitus sit BER- NARDUS, Doctor illustris, qui Eugeniam Papam ad considerationem 10 suae auctoritatis adducens, atque ostendens, qualem in Dei ecclesia Romanus pontifex personam gerat:[5] *Attende*, inquit, *quis sit et quam videlicet pro tempore in ecclesia Dei personam geras. Sacerdos magnus es, summus pontifex, princeps episcoporum, tu heres apostolorum, tu primatu Abel, gubernatione Noah, patriarchatu Abraham, ordine Melchisedech,* 15 *dignitate Aaron, auctoritate Moyses, judicatu Samuel, potestate Petrus, unctione Christus. Tu es cui claves traditae, cui oves creditae sunt.*

Hunc ergo perfidissime blasphemare non veritus es; saltem illud considerasses arcanum, quod in EPISTOLA CLEMENTIS habetur quae alias Petri dicitur, in ordinatione Clementis, cujus plurima in 20 decretis et Conciliorum gestis propter auctoritatem habentur excerpta, ubi claviger regni coelestis Clementem sibi ordinans successorem, post- quam illius ecclesiastici principatus ministerium multis verbis extulerat, cunctos fideles quanta reverentia illum observare, quo timore revereri quo affectu complecti deberent, admonuit. Ubi inter reliqua:[6] *Vos,* 25 inquit, *fratres et conservi mei, huic, qui praesidet vobis, in omnibus obedire*

---

[1] *Num.* 12.
[2] *Psal.* 98, 6.
[3] *II Paral.* 26, 16–21.
[4] *II Reg.* 2, 23–24.
[5] *De consideratione*, L. II, c. 8 (*PL* 182, 751C).
[6] Cf. c. 1, D. XCIII (RF I, 320).

REPLY BY TEODORO LAELIO

Moses, was afflicted with leprosy. Yet you have not only murmured, but you have publicly blasphemed, not Moses assuredly—who is included among the priests, as the PSALMIST bears witness when he declares: *Moses and Aaron were among his priests*—assuredly not Moses, but one who possesses greater authority. You have heard that Uzziah was smitten with a similar disease because he scorned the priests. The children of Bethlehem were condemned to death because they derided the prophet. But more than Moses or any of the prophets whom you impiously blaspheme, you perchance impugn the authority of ST. BERNARD, an illustrious doctor, who prompted Pope Eugenius to realize his authority and made manifest what authority in the Church of God the Roman bears in his person:[1] *Consider who you are, namely what authority in the Church of God in this world you bear in your person. You are the high priest and the supreme pontiff. You are the prince of bishops and the heir of the apostles. By your primacy, you are Abel; by your office as helmsman, Noah; by your patriarchate, Abraham; by your orders, Melchizedech; by your dignity, Aaron; by your authority, Moses; by your judicial power, Samuel; by your jurisdiction, Peter; and by your anointment, Christ. You are the one to whom the keys have been given and the sheep entrusted.* You have not been hesitant to blaspheme perfidiously against this. At least you might have reflected upon that mysterious passage that occurs in the EPISTLE OF CLEMENT, elsewhere assigned to Peter, which concerns the ordination of Clement. Because of its authority, many extracts of this citation appear in the decrees and acts of councils; in this citation, the Keeper of the keys of the kingdom of heaven, in ordaining Clement to be his successor, after he had extolled at length the office of that ecclesiastical principate, admonished all the faithful to honor him with the utmost reverence, to revere him with the utmost respect, and to embrace him with the utmost affection. Among other things, he said:[2] *You, my brethren and fellow servants, must obey this one who rules*

---

[1] See p. 93.
[2] See p. 189.

oportet, atque summo studio niti, ut omni erga eum vinculo amoris innexi,
plenissimo erga eum inhaereatis affectu. Rursus si inimicus fuerit Clemens
iste alicui, pro actibus suis, nolite vos expectare, ut ipse vobis dicat: Illi
nolite amici esse, sed prudenter observare debetis, et voluntati ejus absque
5 *commonitione obsecundare.* Et paulo post in tui similes maledictionem
terribilem comminatur, quae tuae iniquitatis merito jam interiora tua
intravit, ut subter te scateat:[1] *Scientes,* inquit, *quod si quis hunc contri-*
staverit, Christum, qui ei credidit cathedram, non recipit; et tanquam qui
Christum non suscepit, non suscipietur in regnum caelorum. Et iterum
10 terribilius insonat:[2] *Quicumque contristaverit doctorem veritatis, peccat in*
Christum, et patrem omnium exacerbat Deum, propter quod et vita carebit.
Haec tu inde excerpta in canonibus legere debuisses.

    Verum non uno tantum blasphemiae sacrilegio contentus, ne aliquid
intentatum relinqueres, etiam in alterum monarchiam maledicta
15 depromis, Caesarem vaecordiae ignaviaeque condemnas, ut utramque
potestatem, quibus principaliter hic mundus regitur, blasphemares,
senatum quoque ecclesiae, videlicet cardinalium coetum, tanquam
consilii expertem et temerarium,[3] tu totius orbis censor notas et arguis;
in unum, contra quem commissum nefarium sacrilegium defendis, plus
20 ceteris debaccharis, et virum sanctissimum, vita et religione, doctrina
et integritate incomparabilem, cardinalem S. Petri ad vincula, infamia
conaris aspergere. Et cum nihil comperias, quo innocentiam vitae
etiam inimicis percognitam offuscare queas, tu omnium factiosissimus
et procacissimus ipsum modo factionis, modo procacitatis accusas.[4] O,
25 linguam maledicam et radicitus praecidendam! Nonne licet cum propheta clamare:[5] *Disperdat Dominus labia dolosa, et linguam magnilo-*
quam. Nempe ex illis es, *qui dixerunt: Linguam nostram magnificabimus,*

---

[1] Pseudo-Clem., *Epist.* 1 (*PL* 130, 26A–B).
[2] c. 12, C. XI, qu. 3 (RF I, 643).
[3] Cf. *Appellatio*, Frehero et Struvio, II, 212.
[4] Cf. *Appellatio*, Frehero et Struvio, II, 214.
[5] *Psal.* 11, 4.

REPLY BY TEODORO LAELIO

over you in all things and strive most zealously so that you are bound to him by every bond of love and so that you cling to him with the deepest affection. If Clement spurns anyone on account of his actions, do not wait for him to tell you to avoid the friendship of that man. On the contrary, you ought to note his will and support it without an express command. Shortly thereafter, he threatens your sort with the curse that has already, [as punishment] for your wickedness, entered your bowels and now wells forth from within you: *They know that if anyone wrongs him, that man does not receive Christ who entrusted this see to him; and since he does not receive Christ, he will not be received into the kingdom of heaven.* Elsewhere he thunders more terribly: *Anyone who wrongs him who teaches the truth sins against the truth and provokes the wrath of God, and therefore will not attain life.* You must have read these extracts in the canons.

You have not been content with only the sacrilege of blasphemy, lest you leave anything untried; you utter foul words against the other realm and condemn the Emperor for folly and sloth. Thus you blaspheme both powers which regally rule this world and you, critic of everything, term and declare the senate of the Church, namely, the company of cardinals, to be unadvised and destitute of understanding. You wildly rage against one more than others; you defend an abominable sacrilege committed against him. You seek to bring into disrepute a man of most holy life and piety, incomparable in learning and integrity, the Cardinal of St. Peter-in-chains.[1] And since you are unable to find anything with which you may blacken the uprightness of his life, which is well known even to his enemies, you, who are the most seditious and impudent of all, accuse him of sedition and impudence. Oh, your tongue is accursed and worthy to be torn out by the roots! May I not cry out with the prophet: *May the Lord cut off all flattering lips, the tongue that makes great boasts.* Without question you are among those *who have said, "With our*

---

[1] Nicholas of Cusa (1401–1464).

labia nostra a nobis sunt.[1] Quibus noster Dominus vere inquit:[2] *Tu ex illis es inflatus sensu carnis, nullum in terris agnoscens caput, qui ordinatas a Deo potestates blasphemare te putas impune.*

Ceterum ne putes, me execrationibus blasphemiarum tuarum detrec-
5 tare pugnam, et manum non audere conferre, vel tuos inextricabiles nodos non posse dissolvere, ecce jam ad singula festinat oratio. Postquam noster Demosthenes altius quaedam de vi consilii experte ac mode-rate exorsus,[3] cava verba in modum vesicarum tumentia buccis ebuc-cinavit inflatis, primum accusationis caput intendit, questus *se contra*
10 *divinam et humanam legem non vocatum damnatum.*[4] Quod indignum facinus esse proclamans exempla producit primi parentis et Cain,[5] quorum alter propter praevaricationem, alter propter homicidium non nisi vocati damnati fuere. Subdens ipsum Deum, cui aperta sunt omnia, ut nos a praecipitante sententiae temeritate compesceret, Sodomos prius
15 perdere noluisse, quam eorum scelera manifeste cognosceret.[6] Sicque trifaria exemplorum compage, quasi phalange quadam aciem struit. Verum nos invalidam struem uno possemus arietis ictu concutere, et paria referendo exemplorum silvam obicere.

Sed ut ex multis pauca proferamus, Moysen legimus comperto populi
20 scelere, quod palam contra Deum commissum erat, nulla accusatione vel cognitione praevia vindicasse, et immane idolatriae crimen plurima populi strage expiasse.[7] Phinees accepimus ultionem non praemissa sententia, cum agentes contra legem et edictum ante prolatum propria manu transfoderet.[8] Novimus Eliam sacerdotes Balaam prius ad suppli-
25 cium quam ad judicium produxisse.[9] Eundem scimus Ochoziae regis

---

[1] *Psal.* 11, 5.
[2] *Colos.* 2, 18–19.**
[3] *Appellatio*, Frehero et Struvio, II, 211.
[4] *Appellatio*, Frehero et Struvio, II, 211.
[5] *Gen.* 2–4; *Appellatio*, Frehero et Struvio, II, 211.
[6] *Gen.* 18–19; *Appellatio*, Frehero et Struvio, II, 211.
[7] *Exod.* 32.
[8] *Num.* 25.
[9] *III Reg.* 18, 40.

REPLY BY TEODORO LAELIO

tongue we will prevail, our lips are with us." To such our Lord truly said: *You, puffed up without reason by your carnal mind, are among those who think that they may safely blaspheme the powers ordained by God.*

Lest you think that I refuse to do battle with your abominable blasphemies, that I dare not put my hand to this business, and that I cannot untie your inextricable knots, I hasten to a more detailed consideration. After our Demosthenes has begun more loudly with some words about force devoid and unrestrained by understanding, and has trumpeted forth empty words with puffed-up cheeks like swollen bladders, he introduces his first accusation, lamenting that *he has been condemned contrary to divine and human law without a hearing.* Crying out that this is an intolerable action, he advances the examples of the father of the human race and Cain; he contends that the former, who was condemned for lying, and the latter, who was condemned for murder, were condemned only after a hearing. He adds that God himself, to whom all things are known, in order to restrain us from hasty and rash judicial decisions, did not wish to destroy the Sodomites before he was openly acquainted with their crimes. Thus with three examples he draws up his battle order. But we can smash this weak barricade with one blow of our battering-ram and oppose it with a forest of similar examples.[1]

But to choose a few instances from the many, we read that Moses, when he learned of the crime that the people had openly committed against God, chastised them with no previous accusation or inquiry and atoned for the people's monstrous crime of idolatry with enormous slaughter. We learn that Phinehas, when certain people transgressed an edict of the law, and when no preceding judicial decision was pronounced, stabbed the evildoers with his own hand. We know that Elijah led the priests of Baal to chastisement before he led them to judgment. We also

---

[1] For similar examples in the *Defensorium*, see pp. 131–137.

299

nuntios igne de caelo impetrato cremasse.[1] Par zelus in scripturis
Eleazari commendatur.[2] Et ut ad recentiora veniamus, constat Petrum
apostolorum principem mox prolato mendacio Ananiam et Saphiram
morte mulctasse.[3] Paulum vero coapostolum ejus Cliniam magum
5 resistentem Spiritui Sancto subita caecitate damnasse.[4] Et ut efficacius
aliquid proferamus, apostolus absens corpore, spiritu praesens, Corin-
thium excommunicavit, tradens in interitum carnis, ut salvus fieret
spiritus,[5] nullus adhibitus strepitus fori, nullus judiciarius ordo, nulla
tela judicii.

10 Numquid prophetae Domini, numquid apostoli perperam aliquid
egerunt? Numquid praecones legis legem transgressi sunt, vel nuntii
potuerunt his, quae a Spiritu Sancto edocti erant, adversa docere?
Sunt ergo judicia Domini vera, justificata in semetipsa;[6] quoniam ea
quae ulta et vindicata praescripsimus, ita clara et aperta erant, ut ad
15 tenorem ceterorum et aedificationem nascentis ecclesiae plectenda
magis quam discutienda viderentur. Hoc est quod canones saepe pro-
clamant:[7] *Quod nota est manifesta inquisitione non indigent.* Talibus
sanctionibus referti sunt codices; et tu id simulas ignorare!

Satis ad excommunicationem tuam AMBROSII in epistolae Pauli
20 sufficiebat auctoritas, dicentis:[8] *Licet judicis non sit sine accusatione*
damnare, quia Dominus Judam, cum fur esset, non ejecit; apostolus tamen
cognito Corinthi opere, eum de coetu fraternitatis ejecit. Omnes enim scie-
bant crimen ejus, publice novercam loco uxoris habebat; in qua re nec opus
erat testibus, nec aliqua tergiversatione tegi poterat crimen. Vides quantum
25 inter occultum, quale Judae fuit, et manifestum quale Corinthi, crimen
intersit. An vero inficiari poteris crimen tuum non fuisse notorium, qui

---

[1] *IV Reg.* 1.
[2] *I Mac.* 6, 42–47.
[3] *Act.* 5, 1–11.
[4] *Act.* 13, 6–11.
[5] *I Cor.* 5, 3–5.**
[6] *Psal.* 18, 10.
[7] Cf. e.g. c. 61, X (2,28) (RF II, 437–438); c. 5, X (2,28) (RF II, 411).
[8] *Comm. in epist. I ad Cor.,* c. 5 (*PL* 17, 219A–B).**

REPLY BY TEODORO LAELIO

know that he burned the messengers of King Ahaziah with fire called down from heaven. The equal zeal of Eleazar is also commended in the Scriptures. To come to more recent matters, it is well known that Peter, the chief of the apostles, as soon as the lie of Ananias and Sapphira was known, put them to death. Assuredly Paul, his fellow apostle, inflicted instantaneous blindness upon the magician Elymas who resisted the Holy Spirit. To make this even clearer the apostle, absent in body but present in spirit, excommunicated the Corinthian and delivered him over for the destruction of the flesh, that his spirit might be saved. In this instance, there is no clamor stirred up about a trial, nothing about juridical due process, and nothing about the instruments of judgment.

Did the prophets of the Lord or the apostles do something wrong? Did the heralds of the law transgress the law, or could those messengers who were instructed by the Holy Spirit teach anything opposed to it? *Therefore the judgments of the Lord are true, and righteous altogether.* For those chastisements and punishments we have cited were so clear and obvious that, for the defense of others and the edification of the early church, they appear to chastise rather than to discuss. This is what the canons often proclaim:[1] *Notorious and manifest matters do not require an investigation.* The law codes are filled with such decrees. And you pretend that you do not know this!

For your excommunication, the authority of ST. AMBROSE suffices when he wrote upon the epistle of Paul: *Although a judge may not condemn without condemnation, because the Lord did not oust Judas because he was a thief, nevertheless when the apostle learned of the deed of the Corinthian he ousted him from the brotherhood. For all knew of his crime, that he had openly taken his stepmother as his wife. There was no need of witnesses in such a matter; such a crime could not be ignored.* You must see the great difference between the secret crime of Judas and the manifest crime of the Corinthian. Can you actually deny that your crime was notorious?

---

[1] See p. 137.

palam criminosum et sacrilegum Sigismundum in crimen confovebas,
qui in elusionem ecclesiasticae districtionis damnatam appellationem
emiseras, qui eam ipsam per urbes, oppida, plateas et vicos palam jacti-
tabas. Nec vero calumnieris, id non permanentis facti fuisse notorium.
5 Non enim distat evidentia facti ab eo, qui in publico opere, et quidem
participatione continua criminis suum etiam reatum publice confitetur,
et—quod deterius est—daemonum imitando duritiem jure factum esse
contendit, quod publicis sanctionibus noverit esse damnatum. Verum ut
intelligas te omnino non sapere, et vix prima legum et canonum rudi-
10 menta gustasse, intellige quae vel omnino nescis vel te scire dissimulas.

Inter modernos veteresque juris interpretes fuit saepe tractatum, an
in re notoria, de qua canones loquuntur, sit praemittenda citatio. In
quo quidem inter notorium et manifestum juris et notorium facti
distinxerunt? Omnes tamen in eam sententiam conveniunt, ut si tale sit
15 factum et tam manifestum, ut nulla ad ejus probationem indagine opus
esse videatur, nec possit aliqua tergiversatione celari, contra quod nec
ulla competere possit defensio, quia id criminosus agat, quod jam
constat esse damnatum, nullam exigi citationem. Pro quo expressi
canones allegantur, quos tu nisi inscitiam tuam fateri volueris, ipse
20 comperies. Rursus et id convenit inter eos, quod ubi apud judicem et in
judicis conspectu delinquitur, potest is quidem id mox damnare, ac
plectere delinquentem minime citatum. At in te quis negare potest
utrumque concurrere, qui non solum factum damnatum vetitae appellationis palam admiseras, verum in judicem et judicis praesentiam plus
25 quam notorie deliqueras, qui in pontificis curia funestas schedulas
appellationum in basilicarum foribus platearumque porticibus appendi
curaveras?

Verum ne tibi inter opinionum varietatem contentionis relinquatur

REPLY BY TEODORO LAELIO

You have openly encouraged Sigismund in his slander and sacrilege; you have issued a damnable appeal to escape the Church's chastisement; and you have openly published this appeal through cities and towns and through the streets and public squares. You certainly do not falsely allege that such repeated conduct was not notorious! For the evidence of such action is close at hand against one who in his public conduct indeed openly professes his guilt by continual involvement, and contends—which is far worse—that in imitating the insensibility of the demons his conduct is just, when he knows that it is condemned by well-known decrees. Thus you may clearly perceive that you are utterly ignorant and have scarcely broached the rudiments of canon law; you may perceive what you certainly do not know or pretend that you know.

Modern and ancient interpreters of the law have often considered whether a summons is necessary in a notorious matter such as the canons discuss. On this subject some have distinguished between a crime that is notorious and manifest from the viewpoint of the law and one that is notorious from the viewpoint of the crime. Nevertheless, all share this opinion: if such a crime is so well known that there seems to be no need of an investigation to establish clear proof, that it can be no longer ignored, and that no defense can competently be made against it for this would be slanderous, no summons is necessary, because it is well established that the crime is already condemned. In support of this, many canons may be offered; and even you will acknowledge this, unless you wish to confess your ignorance. Again they agree that when a crime is committed near the judge or in his presence, he can certainly quickly condemn it and chastise the criminal without recourse to a summons. And who can deny that both these accepted legal principles are applicable to you? You have not only openly confessed the condemned crime of a forbidden appeal, but have committed this crime most notoriously, near the judge, and in his presence; you have troubled yourself to post wretched copies of your appeal in the papal Curia, on the doors of the basilicas, and at the entrances of the marketplaces.

But lest you still find some opportunity for controversy in the variety

303

occasio, aliud tuae garrulitati responsum opponamus, quod te scio torvo oculo et elato supercilio auditurum. Disce, miser, inter principalem et privatum multum distare judicandi potestatem. Formam judiciorum ceteris esse praefixam ad temeraria coercenda judicia. Principem vero
5 legibus solutum formae non subici; atque proinde quicquid censeatur in aliis, tamen libere atque intrepide confitendum processum atque sententiam pontificis summi in notoriis absque citatione valere; praesertim ubi notorietas ipsa resurgit ex his, quae acta sunt coram eo. Haec non nostra, sed probatissimorum juris consultorum verba sunt, quorum in
10 scholis et judiciis gravissima fuit auctoritas atque sententia.

Attende simile aliquid in jure scripto; reperies testamentum, quod exactam scrupulosamque solemnitatem exigit, ex principis praesentia sine ulla observatione vires assumere, propter principalem praesentiam cuncta supplentem, quae formae a lege introductae non subditur. Ex
15 hac quidem auctoritate Gelasius Papa Sillanos in jus non vocatos, ob notorium proprii antistitis parricidium damnavit. Innocentius III electionem Philippi ad imperium, Henrici persecutoris ecclesiae stirpe progeniti, licet non citati, ob notorium defectum jure dicit improbatam. Innocentius IV clericos, qui Frederico fatali ecclesiae hosti adhaeserant.
20 Clemens IV auctores caedis Silvani episcopi, et idem eos, qui Conradino paruerunt, anathematis mucrone et temporalium mulctatione damnavit;

REPLY BY TEODORO LAELIO

of opinions on this subject, let us offer another answer to your babbling nonsense. I know that you will listen to this with glaring eye and raised eyebrow. Learn, wretch, that there is a great discrepancy between the prerogative of a sovereign and that of a subject to judge. This form of judgment [without a summons] was suppressed in others in order to prevent rash judgments. Assuredly because the ruler is not bound by the law, he is not subject to this suppression; therefore, although it may be condemned in others, it must be acknowledged that the procedure and decision of the Supreme Pontiff is valid in notorious crimes without a summons. This is particularly true where this notoriety is occasioned by crimes committed in his presence. These are not our words, but the words of the best jurists, whose authority and opinions are most respected in the universities and in the courts of law. Consider something similar in written law. You will find that a will that requires precise, scrupulous formality receives full validity from the presence of the ruler without any official procedure; from the presence of the ruler all is supplied that is needed to fulfill the requirements of the law. By this authority Pope Gelasius condemned the inhabitants of Bruttium for the notorious murder of their bishop without recourse to a legal summons.[1] Innocent III nullified, on account of a notorious legal defect, the imperial election of Philip, member of the house of Henry, the persecutor of the Church, although he did not summon him.[2] Innocent IV condemned those clerics who had supported Frederick, the Church's mortal enemy.[3] Clement IV condemned those who murdered Bishop Sylvanus and those who obeyed Conradin [punishing them] with anathema and the loss of temporal

---

[1] Gelasius I (492–296). This incident is comparable to the one suggested in a canon that appears in *PL* 59, 141–142.

[2] Innocent III (1198–1216), after long hesitation, in March 1201 declared his open support for the anti-emperor, Otto von Brunswick, and his opposition to the elected emperor, Philip von Suabia, brother of the deceased emperor, Henry VI (1190–1197).

[3] Innocent IV (1243–1254) promulgated this sentence against Frederick II at the Council of Lyons on 17 July 1245.

sicut nos vel ex canonibus, vel ex pontificum gestis agnovimus, quae si
quis curiosius perscrutetur, exempla plura reperiet. Scio te inclamaturum,
et more quo soles cuncta censere, dicturum, ad adulationem pontificum
ista praescripta. Verum quis loquacitati tuae plura tribuet, quam
5 probatissimis jurisconsultis?

At nunc missa omnia priora faciamus. Tu qui tibi utriusque juris
vendicas principatum, tuam aliquando inscitiam—ne dicam ruditatem—
agnosce, atque intellige, te aristas tantum in studiis messuisse. Nonne
intelligis permagni referre, an de crimine contra quempiam inquiratur,
10 ut damnetur, vel tantum declaretur, aliquem sub facto damnatum in
poenam a jure aut statuto promulgatam incidisse. Non enim aliquid
novi facit, qui declarat, non damnat, non pronuntiat, sed aliquem in
poenam jam legis constitutione irrogatam incidisse denuntiat. In quo
casu constat non exigi citationem, cum non sententiam ferre, sed magis
15 sententiam a jure latam judex exsequi videatur. Quod usque adeo tenuere
doctores, ut censuerint excommunicatum sive monitioni subditum eo
casu, quo a jure vel statuto excommunicatus apparet non incurrere
poenam a canonibus inflictam. Hoc juris interpretes constanter affir-
mant, quos si forte non legeris tuam ignorantiam fateare; si vero legisti,
20 dolum atque perfidiam confiteri necesse est, qui generalibus vulgatisque
etiam apud pueros divini testimonii exemplis odium et invidiam Romano
pontifici concitare voluisti.

Jam igitur, obtrectator, absolve te ab hoc nexu, si potes. Pridem
fuerat generali constitutione sancitum, et quidem aequissime, ut infra
25 subdemus:[1] *Ne quis in elusionem ecclesiasticae censurae ad futurum*

---

[1] Cf. *Execrabilis*, 224.

REPLY BY TEODORO LAELIO

goods.[1] We offer these instances drawn from the canons and the acts of the popes; if anyone examines these canons more closely, he will find many examples.[2] I know that you will cry out aloud in the manner in which you are accustomed to condemn everything and will say that these instances are intended to adulate the Papacy. But who will grant more respect to your prattling than to the most distinguished jurists?

Let us now leave aside our former considerations. You, who claim the first place for yourself in civil and canon law, perceive and recognize for once your lack of knowledge—or I should say, your ignorance. You have garnered so much chaff in your studies. Do you not recognize that very great jurists determine whether one seeks to condemn a man for a crime or to declare that the man condemned in the crime has incurred the penalty established by law and statute? For he who declares does nothing new; he does not condemn, he does not give a verdict, but he declares that someone has incurred the penalty already inflicted on the basis of existing law. In this matter it is well established that a summons is not necessary, since the judge does not render a verdict but rather carries out the verdict. The doctors have long held that they might condemn one excommunicated or one subject to admonition when, apparently excommunicated by law or statute, he does not incur the penalty inflicted by the canons. The interpreters of the law invariably affirm this. If perchance you have not read them, you confess your ignorance; but if you have read them, you must acknowledge your fraud and treachery. You wished to arouse hatred and ill will against the Roman Pontiff by general examples of scriptural evidence that are commonly even known to school boys.

Now then, slanderer, free yourself from this knot if you can. Long ago this was established in a general constitution, indeed most equitably, and we repeat: *Let no one appeal to a future council to evade ecclesiastical*

---

[1] Clement IV (1265–1268) pronounced the anathema against Conradin on 18 November 1267.

[2] See p. 143–145.

concilium, sub poena anathematis et laesae majestatis, appellaret. Appellasti, et quidem notorie, et appellationem etiam palam non tam insinuare quam inculcare curasti. Declarat te pontifex pro eo, quod damnatum jam facinus admisisti, in spirituales ac temporales poenas a lege

5 inflictas incidisse. Quid habes, quod conqueraris? Quid quod detesteris, quid quod inclames divina et humana jura violata? Te non citatum, ob illa quae non solum publice confiteris, sed tumentibus buccis in coetu principum te fecisse gloriaris. Satis superque, satis te blasphemiae et procacitatis arguimus, et objectam divini juris violati calumniam con-

10 futavimus utriusque testamenti exemplis. Ostendimus facinorosos homines pro manifestis criminibus sine ullo judiciario ordine potuisse damnari et probavimus delictum tuum omnibus fuisse notorium in conspectu summi judicis et contemptum Apostolicae Majestatis admissum; ab eo prolatum esse judicium, qui supra jus constitutus, juris

15 ordini et formae non subditur. Postremo, non ab homine neque per hominem, sed ex lege et per legem, merito tuae iniquitatis te fuisse damnatum. Superest, ut reliquas invectivarum tuarum partes percurrentes, non solum procacem te atque maledicum, sed etiam haereticum et infidelem, ex ipsis tuis sermonibus convincamus.

20 Prosequamur igitur reliqua, et ne nos carpendi studio aliquid confingere suspicetur, ipsa prout locutus es, verba proponamus.[1] *Quam tenuem,* inquit, *telam exorsus, quam debilem texit rationem, quaeso videte. Salvator, inquit,*[2] *noster Petrum apostolorum principem ad gubernationem ecclesiae substituit, et cetera. Quis ignorat omnibus apostolis a Jesu esse*

25 *praeceptum,*[3] *tu eant in orbem praedicaturi fidem. baptismum et salutem? Quis nescit passim omnibus esse promissum,*[4] *ligatum in caelis quod ipsi ligarent in terris, et solutum esse quod solverent? Sed quod Cephae singulariter dictum est:*[5] *Tibi dabo claves coelorum. Hoc ait HIERONYMUS esse*

---

[1] *Appellatio,* Frehero et Struvio, II, 211.
[2] Cf. *Execrabilis,* 224.
[3] Cf. *Matth.* 28, 19–20.
[4] Cf. *Matth.* 18, 18.
[5] *Matth.* 16, 19.

REPLY BY TEODORO LAELIO

censures under the pain of anathema and high-treason. You have appealed, and quite notoriously; you have also troubled yourself not so much to win us over to your appeal as to thrust it upon us. The Pope declares that because you have admitted a crime already condemned you have incurred the spiritual and temporal penalties inflicted by the law. What right do you have to complain? Why do you detest this? Why do you cry out that divine and human laws are broken? [You were condemned] without a summons for actions which you not only acknowledge publicly but even boast of with swollen cheeks in the assembly of princes. We have convicted you decisively and more than decisively of blasphemy and impudence, and we have refuted conclusively your pretended argument that divine law was being transgressed, which you advanced with examples from both the Old and New Testaments. We have demonstrated that wicked men could be condemned for manifest crimes with no observance of due legal process, and we have proven that your crime was notorious to all and that you have stated your contempt for His Apostolic Majesty in the presence of the Supreme Judge. He who has pronounced judgment upon you is established above the law and is not subject to the order and procedure of the law. Finally, you were justly condemned for your iniquity not by a man or through a man but by the law and through the law. Now, referring rapidly to the other parts of your invective, we will convict you not only as an insolent scoundrel and a blasphemer, but also as a heretic and an infidel by your own words.

Let us proceed, therefore, to these matters, and lest anyone suspect us of inventing something in order to slander you, let us give your words just as you spoke them: *Consider carefully what a thin web you have begun to weave and what frail reasons you have devised. You say that our Savior instituted Peter, the first of the apostles, to the rule of the Church. Who does not know that all the apostles were instructed by Jesus to go into the world to preach the faith, baptism, and salvation? Who does not know that he promised them all indiscriminately that whatever they might bind upon earth would be bound in heaven and whatever they might loose upon earth would be loosed in heaven. But he did say to Peter individually: "I will give you the keys of the kingdom of heaven." JEROME says that this was*

factum,[1] *ut schismatis tolleretur occasio. Et AMBROSIUS in suo pastorali dicit:*[2] *Quod nedum Petro trina rogatione interrogato, an amaret, ac trina responsione subsequente, amare se teste ipso interrogatore Jesu, traditas sibi esse claves, sed omnibus ipsis contraditas, apostolosque post ascensionem*
5 *Domini convenisse, ac Petrum sibi principem constituisse, et Antiochiae in cathedra collocasse referuntur.*[3] *Nihil tamen de potestate universis apostolis a salvatore data, ipsorum omnium universali missione diminuerunt. Ergo et hodie exorat ecclesia Catholica sese per apostolos ipsos continua protectione custodiri, quos salvator ipse vicarios tanti operis constituit praeesse pastores.*
10 *Horum legitimos successores constat esse universalia Concilia, christianae fidei fundamenta, quae pontificum actiones pro tempore saluberrimis doctrinis instruxerunt, errores emendarunt. De quibus summus ille pontifex Gregorius scribit:*[4] *"Quisquis illa destruere tentaret, seipsum destruit." Sed quorsum haec? Eo certe pertingunt, ut convellatur illa superstitio, in qua*
15 *Pius Papa factionibus cardinalis Cusani astruit Concilium supra Papam non esse, dum dicit—ut ejus verbis utar—ad futurum concilium appellari non posse,*[5] *quod supra Christi vicarium esse nequit. Videte ergo, quam vim consilii exsortem Papa inferre tentavit. Nam si omnes apostoli sunt missi a Domino Jesu, dicente illis: Ite in orbem, quodcumque ligaveritis et cetera,*
20 *quos constat postea conciliariter congregatos, ac ipsum Cepham in messem Domini misisse, quis dubitat Concilia sacra vicem Christi gerere, quae coetui apostolico successisse comprobantur, siquidem orbis major est urbe.*[6]

Haec sunt illius portenta verborum. Miror profecto, cum apud Aure-

---

[1] *Adversus Jovinianum,* L. I, c. 26 (*PL* 23, 258).
[2] Cf. *Apol. prophetae David,* c. 9 (*PL* 14, 911–912).
[3] Cf. *Act.* 15, 22–29.**
[4] c. 2, D. XV (RF I, 35–36).
[5] Cf. *Execrabilis,* 224; et *Infructuosos palmites* (2 Nov. 1460) in G. B. Picotti, "La Pubblicazione e i primi effetti della 'Execrabilis' di Pio II," *Archivio della R. Società di Storia Patria* (Rome, 1914), 51–52.
[6] Hieronymo, *Epist.* 146 (*CSEL* 56, 310); Joannes Parisiensis: "Et quod orbis major est urbe et papa, concilium majus est papa solo," *De papali et regia potestate* (1302), ed. M. Goldast, *Monarchia seu Romani imperii,* II, 399.

REPLY BY TEODORO LAELIO

done so that the opportunity for schism might not present itself. AMBROSE
says in his Sermons that when Peter was asked three times whether he loved
Christ and had responded three times, he bore witness that he loved Jesus,
but that the keys were not given to him since they were entrusted to all. It is
recorded that after the Lord's ascension the apostles assembled, elected Peter
as their head, and established him in the See of Antioch. Nevertheless, the
worldwide mission of all the apostles did not diminish the authority given
them all by the Savior. Therefore, the Catholic Church still prays to be pre-
served by the continual protection of the apostles, those pastors whom the
Savior himself established as his vicars to direct such a great enterprise. It is
well established that their legitimate successors are the universal councils,
foundations of the Christian faith, which have informed, according to the
circumstances, the actions of popes with most sound teaching, that they might
mend their errors. Concerning councils, the Supreme Pontiff Gregory
writes: "He who would attempt to destroy these, destroys himself." But what
is the point of all this? They make this point at least: the superstition must
be rooted out which Pope Pius offered the faction of Cardinal Cusa when he
declared that a Council is not above the Pope and—to use his words—
declared that one cannot appeal to a future council because it cannot be
superior to the Vicar of Christ. See, thus, how the Pope has attempted to
employ force destitute of understanding. For if all the apostles were sent
forth by the Lord when he enjoined them "to go into the world" and "what-
ever you will bind," and so forth; and if, as is well known, the apostles later
assembled as a council and dispatched Cephas into the Lord's harvest; who
may doubt that sacred councils rule in the place of Christ—sacred councils
which are acknowledged to have succeeded the company of apostles? For
the world is larger than Rome.

This is the tenor of his words. I wonder, indeed—since I read in

lium Augustinum legerim, nullam falsam esse doctrinam, quae non
aliqua vera permisceat, Gregorium in tantam prolapsum esse vesaniam,
ut brevi verborum serie paene quasi plura expresserit vitia, quam verba
sicut quisque facile percipere potest. In ipso namque sermonis hujus
5 exordio pariter apostolis ecclesiam fuisse commissam, ex missionis,
baptismi ac praedicationis communione conjectat, ipsosque in tradi-
tione clavium parem potestatem accepisse profitetur. Tum vero ob hoc
uni singulariter claves esse permissas, ut *schismatis tollatur occasio*,[1]
apostolum Petrum apostolica et humana institutione cathedram et
10 praelationem accepisse. Et ne dubium relinqueretur ex praemissis
primatum Petri negasse, etiam veterum haereticorum ab arcanis usque
depromptum de missione Petri argumentum inducit, innuens majorem
misso esse mittentem. Inde transvolans ad alia, ut quem singulis aequa-
verat apostolis, in unum collectis ostenderet fuisse minorem, *universalia*
15 *Concilia*—ut ineptiis suis utar[2]—*apostolorum* dicit *legitimos successores*.
Quorum auctoritatem extollens tria plane infert ridicula: concilia
christianae fidei fundamenta pontificum actiones instruxisse et errata
correxisse, eadem vicem Christi gerere, et ab illo potestatem accipere, ac
propterea Petro illiusque successoribus superiora esse contendit.
20 Sequamur ordinem propositionum suarum, veniam—ut opiniamur—
a legentibus impetraturi, si paulo altius principia repetentes, sermonem
longius protendamus. Necesse est enim, ut vana procacitas, quae sibi
non legum et canonum, sed omnium divinarum atque humanarum rerum arrogat sapientiam, non divinis solum atque humanis testimoniis,
25 sed ex ipsis quoque naturae principiis revincatur, ut juxta apostolum *se*
evanuisse in cogitationibus suis et obscuratum insipiens cor ejus agnoscat,
qui cum dixerit se sapientem, stultum se factum intelligat.[3] Credere te,
Gregori, arbitramur ecclesiam Christi, quae in hoc mundo peregrinatur

---

[1] *Adversus Jovinianum*, L. I, c. 26 (*PL* 23, 258).
[2] *Appellatio.* Frehero et Struvio, II, 211.
[3] *Rom.* 1, 21–22.**

REPLY BY TEODORO LAELIO

Aurelius Augustine that there is no false teaching which does not include something true—that Gregor has fallen into such insanity that in this brief passage he mouths almost as many errors as he does words. Anyone can easily perceive this. For at the outset of this treatise, he conjectures that the Church was committed equally to the apostles on the basis of their common mission, baptism, and preaching, and professes that they received equal authority in the commission of the keys. Yet you concede that the keys were given to an individual for one reason —that *the opportunity for schism might be removed;* you also concede that the apostle Peter received his see and leadership through apostolic and human establishment. Lest it might appear doubtful from the foregoing that you have denied the primacy of Peter, you draw upon the mysteries of the ancient heretics, including your argument on the commission of St. Peter, when you contend that the one who sends is greater than him who is sent. From this Gregor passes quickly to other things. In order that he may demonstrate that what he bestowed equally to each apostle was less than what he bestowed upon them all, he says— if I may use his foolish words—that *the universal councils are their legitimate successors.* In praising their authority, he advances three obviously absurd assertions: he contends that councils are the foundations of the Christian faith that have informed the actions of popes and have corrected their errors; that councils rule in Christ's stead and have received their authority from him; and that, therefore, councils are superior to Peter and his successors.

Let us follow the development of his propositions. I must, I suppose, ask forbearance from my readers if in repeating certain principles mentioned above, I extend somewhat the length of my treatise. Groundless impudence which claims to possess not only the knowledge of the laws and canons, but also the knowledge of all things divine and human, is necessarily contradicted not only by divine and human authority, but also by the very principles of nature. Therefore the apostle says that *their thinking has ended in futility, their foolish heart is darkened, and they boast of their wisdom, but they have made fools of themselves.* I suppose, Gregor, that you believe that the Church of Christ, which sojourns as a stranger

ex fide vivens, aliquo ordine esse distinctam utpote ab eo constitutam, cujus perfecta sunt opera, quique hanc legem naturae indidit, ut infima summis, summa infimis per media copulentur, qui ordinem caelis ac terris dedit.

5 Nam cum dicat apostolus:[1] Quae a Deo sunt esse ordinata, aut ecclesiam ex Deo non esse, aut ab illo ordinatam esse oportet; praesertim cum illam Spiritus Sanctus vocet in CANTICIS:[2] Castrorum aciem ordinatam, et superiori hierarchiae dicatur exemplata divinitus, in qua —ut scribit Gregorius[3]—caelestium militiarum exempla nos instruunt, 10 quia dum sunt angeli et archangeli, liquet non esse aequales, sed ordine et potestate discretos. Nec enim universitas posset alia ratione subsistere, nisi hujusmodi magnus eam talis, qua totum corpus sanum sit, et quaeque organa suis fungantur officiis, differentiae ordo servaret. Porro, si ordinem non diffiteris, magis ex naturae principiis, quibus 15 tamen per omnia non in uno solo, quod praeoptas, non solum ex divina institutione, sed ex ipsis quoque naturae principiis, cujusvis politiae recto regimine unum caput, unius ecclesiastici corporis, unum principem sanctae civitatis, unum monarcham ecclesiasticae hierarchiae, unum pastorem dominici gregis atque ovilis in terris fateare necesse est.

20 Nam cum omnis ordo sit multorum in gradibus differentium, et id ipsum sit secundum praelationem et subjectionem, ad unum tantum deveniri necesse est, in quo finis statusque consistat, ut evitetur infinitas, quem supremum in ecclesia principem atque rectorem esse constat, in quo et ex quo totius ecclesiae potestas et status. *Ubi enim unitas, ibi* 25 *perfectio;*[4] reliqui numeri perfectionem non habent, sed divisiones ab unitate recedentes. Porro ut AURELIUS AUGUSTINUS ait:[5] *Multis praeponitur unum. Non enim a multis unum, sed multa ab uno.* Ceterum nemo tam iniquus existimator esse potest, ut regimen ecclesiae minus

---

[1] *Rom.* 13, 1.
[2] *Cant.* 6, 3.
[3] Cf. *Hom. 34 in evang.*, c. 7–14 (*PL* 76, 1249D–1255D).
[4] Bernardi, *De consideratione*, L. II, c. 8 (*PL* 182, 752A).
[5] *Serm.* 105, c. 2 (*PL* 38, 617).

in this world sustained by faith, is distinguished by some order since it was established by him whose works are perfect, who imposed this law of nature and who ordered the heavens and the earth so that the creatures that are lowest are bound to the highest and the creatures that are highest are bound to the lowest by the creatures that are intermediate.

For this is true, because the apostle says that since existing authority is ordered by God, the Church must either not be from God or be ordered by him, and [this is also] particularly [true] because the Holy Spirit calls the Church in the SONG OF SOLOMON *an army drawn up in battle array*. It is said—GREGORY writes thus—that this is exemplified by providence in the heavenly hierarchy, and the example of the celestial host so instructs us, since there are angels and archangels who are manifestly not equal but separated in rank and authority. For the universe could not endure unless a great ordered diversity, such as that by which the whole body is sound and each organ fulfills its function, preserved it. Moreover, if you do not deny order, you must acknowledge—not from the phenomena of nature, which you may prefer, which do not extend as a single origin through all things, but from the very principles of nature—that the correct rule of any polity requires one head of the ecclesiastical body, one ruler of the holy city, one absolute ruler of the ecclesiastical hierarchy, and one pastor of the Lord's flock and sheepfold upon earth.

For since every order includes many degrees of disparity ordered according to superiority and inferiority, it must reach one point at which its end and nature are fulfilled in order to avoid infinity; therefore it is well established that there is a supreme head and ruler in the Church, in whom and from whom exists the authority and nature of the whole Church. *For where there is unity, there is perfection;* plurality does not possess perfection, but only divisions receding from unity. Moreover, as AURELIUS AUGUSTINE declares: *One is set above many. For the one does not originate in the many, but the many in the one.* Besides, none can be so unjust in his judgment that he believes that the rule of the Church

315

ordinatum esse credat, quam naturae; cum gratia supergrediatur
superetque naturam. Quod si in his, quae a natura sunt, omne regimen
naturale ad unum dirigitur principale, quod regit, ut in corpore multa
membra varietate compacta unius capitis sumunt influxum, et de fonte
5 uno rivi plurimi defluunt, et multi arboris rami ad unum stipitem
reducuntur, et multi stipites una radice figuntur, et inferioris corporis
motus uno primo mobili movetur et regitur, quis non credat ecclesiam
diversis gradibus in unum Christi corpus unitam, uno in terris capite
gubernari?[1] Praesertim cum dicat propheta:[2] *Congregabuntur filii*
10 *Judae et filii Israel pariter, ut ponant sibi caput unum.* Probat autem ratio
finis, qui pax est, et unitas subditorum, quae quidem nisi ab uno et per
unum consistere recte non posset. Ad hoc enim divina providentia
gradus et ordines constituit esse distinctos, ut ex reverentia inferioris
ad caput vera concordia fieret, et ex diversitate contextio, et recte
15 officiorum gereretur administratio singulorum.

Quod etiam philosophorum princeps in METAPHYSICIS recognovit,
dicens:[3] *Entia nolle male disponi. Pluralitatem principatuum malam.*
Necessario igitur unum principem esse fatendum. *Natura enim princi-*
piorum amat singularitatem, ut beatus AUGUSTINUS ait:[4] Ita ut
20 ipsius singularis principatus bonum etiam quibusdam ingerat anim-
antibus, ut in apibus unus principetur. Et sicut beatus quoque
HIERONYMUS ait:[5] *grues unam sequuntur ordine literario.* Hoc nobis
repraesentat ad Moysen de figura caelestis hierarchiae divina praeceptio
dicens:[6] *Omnia fac secundum exemplar tibi in monte monstratum.* Et visio
25 Joannis in APOCALYPSI revelata, qui *civitatem sanctam Jerusalem*
novam descendentem de caelo se vidisse perhibuit,[7] quam figuram clarus

---

[1] Cf. c. 18, C. XXIV, qu. 1 (RF I, 972)*; Cypriani, *De unitate ecclesiae*, c. 5 (*PL* 4, 501A–
502B).
[2] *Osee* 1, 11.
[3] Cf. Aristoteles, *Opera*, *Metaphys.*, L. XI, c. 1, 1059b.
[4] *De nuptiis et concupiscientia*, L. I, c. 9 (*PL* 44, 419).
[5] *Epist.* 125, c. 15 (*PL* 22, 1080); Plinii, *Hist. Nat.*, L. X, c. 32.
[6] *Exod.* 25, 40.
[7] *Apoc.* 21, 2.

is less ordered than the rule of nature, since grace surpasses and over-
comes nature. If in the phenomena of nature every principle of nature is
directed to one origin which governs it, so that in the body many members
in their appointed diversity are influenced by one head, many streams
flow from one spring, the many branches of a tree arise in one trunk, and
many trunks are grounded in one root, and the movement of an inferior
body is moved and governed by one prime mover, who may not believe
that the Church in its various ranks is united in the one body of Christ
and that it is ruled by one head on earth? This is especially so since the
prophet declares: *The sons of Judah and the sons of Israel shall be gathered
together, and they shall appoint for themselves one head.* The nature of her
end, which is peace, and the unity of her subjects, which could not
rightly fulfill itself unless in and through one source, demonstrates this.
For divine providence established distinct ranks and orders so that true
harmony might arise from the deference of the inferior to the head, so
that union might arise from diversity, and so that the administration of
the individual offices might be correctly directed.

The prince of philosophers also recognized this in his METAPHY-
SICS, stating: *Entities oppose incorrect order. The plurality of sovereign-
ties is evil.* Therefore, the necessity of one ruler must be acknowledged.
As ST. AUGUSTINE says: *Nature delights in one common rule.* Thus the
good of the rule of one is apparent in certain living creatures: one bee
rules over the bees. As ST. JEROME also declares: *The cranes fly after
one of their number in the shape of the letter V.* The divine precept to Moses
concerning the figure of the celestial hierarchy reveals this to us: *Make
them all after the pattern which was shown you on the mountain.* The apoc-
alyptic vision of John in the book of REVELATION supports this;
John declared that *he saw the holy city, the new Jerusalem, coming down*

ille doctor Claraevallis abbas eximius BERNARDUS exponit, dicens:[1] *Non vilis putanda est forma terrestris Jerusalem, quae formam habet a caelo, ut sicut ibi seraphin et cherubin et ceteri ordines sub uno capite Deo, ita et hic patriarchae, archiepiscopi et reliqui sub uno summo pontifice.*

5 Hoc denique ratio unitatis insinuat, ut unius corporis unum caput necessario praedicetur. Nam si secundum apostolum *unum corpus multi sumus,*[2] et unam esse ecclesiam Spiritus Sancti in CANTICIS,[3] consequens est, quod beatus ac facundissimus martyr CYPRIANUS ait, cujus verba tuam de parilitate apostolorum haeresin transfodiunt atque
10 confundunt:[4] *Inquit Dominus ad Petrum:*[5] *Ego dico tibi, quia tu es Petrus, et super hanc petram aedificabo ecclesiam meam. Super unum aedificabo ecclesiam. Et quamvis omnibus apostolis post resurrectionem parem potestatem tribuat, dicens:*[6] *Sicut me misit pater, et ego mitto vos, accipite Spiritum Sanctum, tamen ut unitatem manifestaret, unitatis*
15 *ejusdem originem ab uno incipientem sua auctoritate disposuit. Et post pauca:*[7] *Exordium ab unitate proficiscitur, ut ecclesia Christi una monstretur, quoniam unam ecclesiam Spiritus Sanctus in CANTICO CANTICORUM ex persona Christi designat, et dicit:*[8] *Una est columba mea, perfecta mea, una est matris suae filia, electa genitricis.* Hoc denique Christi
20 institutio nobis insinuat, qui velut pastor bonus oves errantes collecturus advenerat, et unitatem nobis ostendens de divina auctoritate venientem, ait:[9] *Ego et pater* secundum divinitatem *unum sumus.* Ad quam unitatem redigens ecclesiam suam, dicit:[10] *Erit unum ovile et unus pastor.* Qui cum in tantum dilexisset ecclesiam, ut propter nimiam charitatem

---

[1] *De consideratione*, L. III, c. 18 (*PL* 182, 768D–769A).*
[2] *I Cor.* 10, 17.
[3] Cf. *Cant.* 6, 8.
[4] *De unitate ecclesiae*, c. 4 (*PL* 4, 498B–500A).
[5] *Matth.* 16, 18.
[6] *Joan.* 20, 21.
[7] *De unitate ecclesiae*, c. 4 (*PL* 4, 500A).
[8] *Cant.* 6, 8.*
[9] *Joan.* 10, 30.
[10] *Joan.* 10, 16.*

REPLY BY TEODORO LAELIO

love beyond measure he shed his blood [for her]. Even concerning the
Synagogue, he declared through ISAIAH: *What more was there to do for
my vineyard that I have not done?* He would certainly have deserted her,
if, having ascended to the Father and having withdrawn his bodily
presence from his faithful, he had not appointed another who might rule
the Church Universal in his stead, since he visibly concerned himself
with fulfilling all the duties of a ruler. Therefore lest the Church should
lack any advantage, he entrusted the care of her to Peter, the first of the
apostles, that he might strengthen his brothers in the Christian religion
by the steadfastness of his own faith. For this reason, Christ, before his
Passion, in committing his flock to him, declared: *Feed my sheep.* ST.
BERNARD, celebrated doctor of the Church, expounded these words in
a distinguished work, DE CONSIDERATIONE, which he wrote to
Pope Eugenius:[1] *There are indeed other gatekeepers of heaven, and there
are other shepherds of the flock; but you are in both respects more glorious and
exceptional than they "in as much as you have inherited a title superior to
theirs." They have assigned to them particular portions of the flock, but you
have been given charge of all the sheep. You are the one shepherd not only of
the sheep, but of all the shepherds. Do you wish to know how I prove this?
"If you love me, Peter, feed my sheep." To what sheep did Christ refer?
Was it to the people of this or that city, of this or that region or kingdom?
"My sheep," the Lord said. Who does not see clearly that Christ instead of
designating some sheep of the flock, rather assigned the whole flock? There
can be no exception where there is no distinction. And probably the other
disciples were present when the Lord committed all the sheep to the care of
one alone, and thus commended unity to all in one flock and one shepherd,
according to the text: "There is but one who is my dove, my beautiful one, my
perfect one."* He shortly continues: *Thus it is that the other apostles, who
understood this mystery, each received the charge of a particular community.
Therefore, James, "who was reputed to be a pillar of the Church," was
content with Jerusalem alone, yielding the Church Universal to Peter. Very*

---

[1] See p. 93.

fratris defuncti,"[1] *ubi occisus est ille; nam dictus est "frater Domini."*[2]
Petro cedente Domini fratre, quis se alter ingerat Petri praerogativae?
Ergo, juxta canones tuos, alii in partem sollicitudinis, tu in plenitudinem
vocatus es potestatis. Aliorum potestas certis arctatur limitibus, tua ex-
5 *tenditur et in ipsos, qui super alios potestatem acceperunt.* Audis igitur,
quae doctor eximius loquitur, ex quo discere potuisti, Petri potestatem
a caeteris apostolis et universitate et praelatione discretam; cum illi
singulis, iste universis plebibus et ipsis quoque apostolis, quos ex ovibus
Christi, et Petro commendatas fuisse nemo ambigit, praelatus extiterit.
10 Scio te frontem contracturum, et—sicut assoles—nos Horatiano sale
decisurum atque dicturum:[3] *Trojanum gemino bellum ordiris ab ovo.*

Sed tua nos coegit impudentia, qui coruscante evangelio, et totiens in
consortibus tuis damnatis haereticis, singularem Petri in universalem
ecclesiam potestatem diffitentibus, tu eandem palam ingerere et refu-
15 tare curasti.

Audi igitur vel invitus, quos praedictus doctor ex evangelio typos
annectit, quos recensendos existimo, quo magis confutetur tua insania.
Accipe—inquam—illud, quod nihilominus id ipsum confirmatur:[4]
Discipuli navigabant, et Dominus apparebat in littore, quodque jucundius
20 *erat in corpore redivivo.* "Sciens Petrus quia Dominus est, in mare se misit,"[5]
et sic venit ad ipsum, aliis navigio pervenientibus. Quid istud? Nempe
signum singulorum pontificatus Petri, per quod non navim unam, ut ceteri
quisque suam, sed saeculum ipsum susceperit gubernandum. Mare enim

---

[1] *Gal.* 2, 9.
[2] *Matth.* 22, 24.
[3] *Ars poetica*, Loeb Classical Library, vol. 194 (Cambridge, Mass.: Harvard University Press, 1955), p. 462, l. 147.
[4] *De consideratione*, L. II, c. 8 (*PL* 182, 752B–C).
[5] *Joan.* 21, 7.

REPLY BY TEODORO LAELIO

appropriately was James appointed to the see where Christ was slain in order to "raise up children for his brother"; for he is called "the brother of the Lord." If even the Lord's brother yielded to Peter's prerogative, what other disciple may claim it? Therefore, according to your own canons, while the other bishops are called to a share in the Church's pastorate, you are invested with the plenitude of power. Their authority is confined within certain limits, but yours extends itself even to them that have received power over others. Give ear therefore to what the distinguished doctor says. From this you could learn that the authority of Peter was distinguished from the authority of the other apostles in universality and primacy; since the apostles were placed over particular communities, but Peter was placed over all communities and even over the apostles, no one doubts that all the sheep of Christ were entrusted to Peter and that he is primate. I know that you will wrinkle your forehead and, as you are accustomed, will pelt us with Horatian salt, saying:[1] *You begin the Trojan War from twin eggs.*

But your impudence compels us to go on. You, brandishing the Gospel as often as your comrades, the condemned heretics, who deny the sole authority of Peter over the Church Universal, trouble yourself to assail and deny this openly.

Heed therefore, even if reluctantly, the types which the aforesaid doctor draws from the gospel; I suppose I must review this so that your madness may be conclusively refuted. Learn, I say, what nevertheless demonstrates itself: *When the disciples were fishing and the Lord appeared to them upon the shore, this was all the more joyous because it was after the Lord's resurrection. "When Simon Peter realized that it was the Lord, he plunged into the sea" and so reached him, the others following in the ship. What could this mean but that it is a sign of the pontificate of Peter over all the others and that he assumed not the rule of one ship, as the other apostles did, but the rule of the whole world? For the sea is the world and the ships*

---

[1] The beautiful Helen, whose abduction by Paris, son of the King of Troy, caused the Trojan War, was in legend hatched from an egg laid by Leda or Nemesis.

saeculum, et naves ecclesiae. Inde est, quam altera vice instar Domini
gradientis super aquas,[1] *unicum se Christi vicarium designavit, qui non uni*
populo, sed cunctis praeesse debet. "*Siquidem aquae multae populi multi.*"[2]
Ita cum quisque ceterorum habeat suam, tibi una commissa est grandissima
5 *navis, facta ex omnibus, ipsa universalis ecclesia, toto orbe diffusa.*

Cum igitur superiorum omnium ratio deducta concludat singularem
Petri in universalem ecclesiam potestatem, quae et in naturis ostenditur,
in caelo exemplificatur, in operibus typice demonstratur, et in toto
corpore mystico observatur, et in lege divina ac evangelio commendatur.
10 Tu tamen, virorum acutissime, ausus es quibusdam verborum strophis
illam parilem ceteris apostolis judicare, atque ex humana magis quam
divina institutione, vel ab apostolis sine imminutione propriae potestatis,
vel consensu ecclesiae in remedium schismatis, attributam asserere,
illud in tui erroris argumentum adducens, quod *caeteris* quoque *apostolis*
15 *claves*—ut tuis utar verbis—*contraditae fuerint.*[3] Ad quod licet per superiora monstraverim, ita reliquis traditas claves, ut tamen Petro prae
omnibus et pro omnibus ante tradiderit, ita a se petra Petri nomen
indicens, et in illo hujus muneris sacramentum imponens, ut non nisi
per Petrum velut a capite in eos sit derivata potestas, eaque non univer-
20 saliter sed certis coartata limitibus, trium tamen sanctorum patrum
super ea re visum est tibi explicare sententias, ut eorum mentes aedifi-
cent, quos forte verborum tuorum virus infecit.

Possemus quidem infinita congerere; sed cui pauca non sufficiunt, nec
multa proficiunt. Primus igitur excitetur beatus martyr ANACLETUS,

---

[1] *Matth.* 14, 29.
[2] *Apoc.* 17, 15.**
[3] *Appellatio,* Frehero et Struvio, II, 211.

are the [individual] churches. Thus when, on another occasion, Peter walked upon the waves with his Lord, he revealed himself to be the one Vicar of Christ who must rule not any one people, but all peoples. "The many waves are the many peoples." Thus although each of the other bishops has his own ship, the largest ship of all is entrusted to you. Your ship is the Church Universal, made up of all the particular churches and extending throughout the world.[1]

Therefore the nature of all the above instances argues the sole authority of Peter over the Church Universal: this is revealed in nature; this is exemplified in heaven; this is shown figuratively in God's works; this is observed in the whole mystical body; and this is commended in divine law and in the gospel. Yet you, the most acute of men, have dared by several verbal tricks to declare the authority of Peter equal to that of the other apostles and to assert that the authority given to Peter was given by human rather than divine institution, by the apostles, without detriment to their own authority and with the approval of the Church, as a remedy for schisms. You argue in support of your error that *the keys* —if I may use your words—*were entrusted to all the apostles.* Although I have demonstrated above that the keys were given to the other apostles, that nevertheless Christ previously committed them to Peter before all and for the benefit of all, that Christ named him Peter for himself, the Rock, and that he imposed this sacramental office upon him so that no authority might be conferred upon the others but through Peter as from the head, and so that such authority might not be universal but be restricted by certain bounds; [although I have demonstrated these things,] I think that I should set forth the opinions of three holy Fathers upon this matter so that they may instruct the minds of those whom the venom of your words has perhaps infected.

We could certainly assemble an infinite number of such citations; but for one for whom a few do not suffice, many are of no avail. Therefore the first cited is the blessed martyr ANACLETUS, contemporary

---

[1] See pp. 92–94.

vicinus apostolorum, atque ipsius Petri successor, qui tuae respondens insaniae, in decretali epistola ita praefatur:[1] *Sacrosancta Romana ecclesia et Apostolica non ab apostolis sed ab ipso salvatore primatum obtinuit, sicut beato apostolo dixit:*[2] *"Tu es Petrus."* Et post aliqua:[3]

5 *Inter beatos apostolos quaedam fuit discretio potestatis, et licet omnes essent apostoli, Petro tamen concessum est a Domino. Et ipsi inter se voluerunt id ipsum, ut reliquis omnibus praeesset apostolis, et Cephas, id est, caput et principium teneret apostolatus.*

Exsurgat et canonis lator, veritatis praeco LEO PAPA, in canone

10 dicens:[4] *Ita Dominus noster Jesus Christus humani generis salvator, instituit, ut veritas, quae antea legis et prophetarum praeconio continebatur, per apostolicam tubam in salutem universitatis exiret, sicut scriptum est:*[5] *"In omnem terram exivit sonus eorum et in fines terrae verba eorum."* Sed *hujus muneris sacramentum ita Dominus ad omnium apostolorum officium*

15 *pertinere voluit, ut in beatissimo Petro apostolorum omnium summum principatum collocaret, ut ab ipso quasi quodam capite dona sua velut in corpus omne diffunderet, ut exsortem se ministerii intelligeret esse divini, qui ausus fuisset a Petri soliditate recedere. Hunc enim in consortium individuae unitatis assumptum, quod erat ipse, Dominus voluit nominari*

20 *dicendo:*[6] *"Tu es Petrus, et super hanc petram aedificabo ecclesiam meam," ut aeterni templi aedificatio mirabili munere gratiae Dei in Petri soliditate existeret. Hanc ecclesiam sua etiam corroborans firmitate, ut illam nec humana temeritas posset apetere, nec portae inferi contra illam praevalerent.*

Et continuo, quasi Gregorium haereticum et blasphemum spiritu

25 praevidens, adjecit:[7] *Verum hanc petrae istius sacratissimam firmitatem Deo, ut diximus, aedificante, constructam, nimis impia vult praesumptione*

---

[1] c. 2, D. XXII (RF I, 73–74).
[2] *Matth.* 16, 18.
[3] c. 2, D. XXII (RF I, 73–74).
[4] c. 7, D. XIX (RF I, 62).
[5] *Psal.* 18, 5.
[6] *Matth.* 16, 18.
[7] c. 7, D. XIX (RF I, 62).

326

of the apostles and successor of Peter's successor, who in response to your madness thus declares in a decretal:[1] *The most holy and apostolic Roman Church obtained its primacy not from the apostles, but from the Lord, our Savior, when he said to the blessed apostle: "You are Peter."* He shortly continues: *There was a certain inequality in authority among the holy apostles—though all were apostles. Nevertheless, the apostles concurred in the Lord's grant to Peter to rank above them all and to hold primacy among them—indeed Cephas signifies "head."*

POPE LEO, legislator and herald of the truth, comes forth in the canon to say:[2] *Thus our Lord Jesus Christ, the Savior of mankind, instituted that the truth, which previously was confined to the proclamation of the law and the prophets, might go forth through the apostles' trumpet blast for the salvation of all men, as it is written: "Their voice goes out through all the earth and their words to the end of the world." The Lord wished this sacramental office to be the concern of all the apostles, but he has placed the principal burden upon the most blessed Peter, chief of all the apostles. From Peter, as from the head, he wishes his gifts to flow into all the body. Therefore anyone who dares to withdraw from the solid rock of Peter may understand that he has no part in the divine ministry. The Lord wished Peter's true function to be expressed, namely, his assumption into this bond of profound unity, when he said: "You are Peter, and on this rock I will build my church," so that the eternal temple might be built by the wonderful gift of God's grace upon the solid rock of Peter. He strengthened his Church to such a degree that neither human rashness could assail it nor the gates of Hell prevail against it.* And immediately he adds as if he foresaw Gregor, heretical and blasphemous in spirit: *But a man seeks in wicked arrogance to attack the most holy authority of the rock, erected, as we have said, by God,*

----

[1] See p. 94.
[2] See p. 104.

violare, quisquis ejus potestatem tentat infringere, id, quod accepit a veteri-
bus, non sequendo. Clangat nunc tuba evangelii, tuba—inquam—sacer-
dotalis, qua clangente sicut olim muri Jericho, ita Nestoriana atque
Eutychiana propugnacula corruerunt. Magnus ille LEO, quem Chalce-
5 donensis synodus columnam fidei, oecumenicum atque apostolicum
acclamavit, cujus auctoritati canon tantum attribuit, ut si quis ejus
dicta usque ad iotam scrutari voluerit, et non in omnibus reverenter
receperit, anathema sit; is ergo in sermone de ordinatione sua de primatu
Petri sic loquitur:[1] *Utile ac dignum est, ad beatissimi apostoli Petri*
10 *gloriam contemplandam aciem mentis attollere, qui ab ipso omnium*
chrismatum fonte tam copiosis est irrigationibus inundatus, ut cum multa
solus acceperit, nihil in quemquam sine illius participatione transierit. Et
iterum in eadem:[2] *De toto mundo unus Petrus eligitur, qui et universarum*
gentium vocationi, et omnibus apostolis, cunctisque ecclesiae partibus
15 *praeponatur; ut quamvis in populo Dei multi sacerdotes sunt, multique*
pastores, omnes tamen regat Petrus, quos principaliter regit Christus.
Magnum et mirabile, huic viro consortium potentiae suae tribuit divina
dignatio, ut sic quod cum eo commune ceteris voluit esse principibus,
numquam nisi per ipsum dedit, quicumque aliis non negavit. Et post
20 pauca:[3] *"Ego dico tibi, quia tu es Petrus"; hoc est, sicut tibi pater meus*
manifestavit divinitatem meam, ita et ego tibi notam facio excellentiam tuam;
quia tu es Petrus, id est, cum ego sim immobilis petra, ego "lapis angularis,
qui facio utraque unum,"[4] ego fundamentum praeter quod nemo potest aliud
ponere; tum tu quoque petra es, quia mea virtute solidaris, ut quae mihi
25 *potestate sunt propria, sint tibi participatione communia. Et alibi:[5] "Tibi*
dabo claves regni caelorum, et quaecumque ligaveris" et cetera.[6] Transivit
quidem et in alios apostolos jus potestatis istius, et ad omnes ecclesiae

---

[1] *Serm.* 4, c. 2 (*PL* 54, 149B).
[2] *PL* 54, 149C–150A.
[3] *PL* 54, 150B.
[4] *Ephes.* 2, 14 et 20.**
[5] c. 3 (*PL* 54, 151A).
[6] *Matth.* 16, 19.

when he attempts to infringe its power, not following ancient tradition.
The evangelical trumpet is now sounding, sounding, I say, as the priestly
trumpet that brought down the walls of Jericho and overcame the
Nestorian and Eutychian defenses. LEO THE GREAT, whom the Council
of Chalcedon acclaimed as a pillar of the faith, as being ecumenical
and apostolic and one to whom the canon law assigned such authority
that if any man wished to question the smallest detail of his pronouncements or did not receive them respectfully, he was anathema, thus
writes in his own ordination sermon concerning the primacy of Peter:
*It is advantageous and worthwhile to elevate one's thoughts to the considera-
tion of the glory of the most blessed Apostle, who was flooded by the source of
all benediction with such abundant streams of grace that, although he alone
received many things, nothing fell to another in which he did not share.* He
adds: *In the whole world only Peter was called to be the head of all the chosen
people, all the apostles, and all parts of the Church. Although among the
people of God there are many priests and many pastors, yet Peter rules all
whom Christ reigns over in his rule. It is significant and wonderful that
divine majesty bestows a partnership in its power upon this man so that what
he willed to be shared by other rulers, and whatever he did not deny to others,
he never bestowed except through this man.* He continues: *"I say to you,"
that is, as my Father revealed to you my divinity, so I will make known to
you your preeminence, "that you are Peter"; that is because I am the rock
which cannot be moved, because I am "the cornerstone which makes both
one," and because I am the only foundation which can be laid. You are a
rock, because you are established by my strength so that you may participate
fully in my authority.* He goes on: *"I will give you the keys of the kingdom
of heaven; what you will bind,"* and so forth. He certainly entrusted the
exercise of this authority to the other apostles and addressed this declaration

REPLICA THEODORI LAELII

principes decreti hujus constitutio commigravit. Sed non frustra uni commendatur, quod omnibus intimatur. Petro ideo singulariter hoc creditur, quia cunctis ecclesiae rectoribus Petri forma proponitur.

Quid ergo hoc testimonio firmius, quid hac assertione stabilius esse
5 potest? Et post haec tanta testimonia non erubescit insaniens paritatem in apostolis potestatis atque jurisdictionis asserere, et in augmentum sui erroris etiam impia veterum haereticorum argumenta non veretur congerere. Sic enim in superioribus dixit:[1] *Apostolos conciliariter congregatos, et ipsum Cepham in messem Domini transmisisse*, quasi superio-
10 ritatem ex missionis authoritate pronuntians. Hoc idem pronuntians argumentabatur impius Arius, adstruens in divinis personis inaequalitatem subesse, pro eo quod Filius et Spiritus Sanctus mitti dicuntur. Ignorabat quippe, quod tu quoque ignoras, aut ignorare te simulas, triplicem missionis modum vel secundum authoritatis imperium, prout
15 dominus servum emittit, vel secundum originem, prout florem arbor producit—ex quo sensu missio licet sublimius atque ineffabilius dicitur in divinis—vel secundum consilium, prout consiliarii regem mittere dicuntur ad bellum, cum tamen cunctorum ipse sit dominus. Adjicere nos possumus missionem secundum amorem. His duobus extremis modis
20 Samariam ab apostolis missus est Petrus, consilio quidem illorum atque suasu et amore eorum, ad quos mittebatur impulsus, cum inter apostolos majori auctoritate atque miraculorum gratia coruscaret. Haec quidem dicimus damnantes sermones tuos; neque enim aliam Petri in messem Domini legimus missionem. Nam si forte Roman Petrum ex Antiochia a
25 reliquis apostolis asseris transmissum fuisse, quam te continuo mendacii falsitatisque convincat Eusebius Caesariensis HISTORIAE ECCLESIASTICAE scriptor illustris, Marcellus Papa ac martyr insignis, et magnus ille Leo, vir authoritatis incomparabilis, qui divina revelatione et Dei instinctu ad oppugnandum Simonem Magum testantur esse profectum.
30   Sic namque secundo ECCLESIASTICAE HISTORIAE libro testatur:[2]

---

[1] *Appellatio*, Frehero et Struvio, II, 211; *Act.* 8, 14.
[2] c. 14 (*PG* 20, 171A).

330

REPLY BY TEODORO LAELIO

to all the rulers of the Church. But what is shared by all is not entrusted to one without reason. This authority is entrusted to Peter alone so that the person of Peter may stand above all rulers of the Church.

Therefore what can be firmer than this witness? What can be more certain than this affirmation? After such witnesses as these this madman is not ashamed to assert equality of authority and jurisdiction for the apostles; he is not afraid to compound his error by assembling the ungodly arguments of the ancient heretics. For he stated above: *The apostles assembled as a council and sent Cephas into the Lord's harvest,* as if to declare their superiority from the authority of the mission. The ungodly Arius argued in the same way, inferring inequality in the persons of the Trinity because the Son and the Holy Spirit are said to be sent forth. He apparently did not know and you do not know or pretend you do not know that "mission" has a three-fold meaning: that of the authority of command, as a master dispatches his servant; that of origin, as a tree sends forth its blossoms—in this sense, although far more sublimely and ineffably, "mission" is applied to the Trinity; and that of advice, as advisers are said to send their king to war although he is the lord of them all. We can add "mission" in the sense of love. In these last two senses, Peter was sent to Samaria by the apostles; indeed, impelled by their advice, persuasion, and love, he was sent because he shone among the apostles by his greater authority and power to work miracles. I say this to condemn your words; for I do not read that Peter was again sent into the Lord's harvest. If perchance you assert that Peter was transferred from Antioch to Rome by the other apostles, Eusebius of Caesarea, the illustrious author of the ECCLESIASTICAL HISTORY, immediately convicts you of a lie and a falsehood, as do Pope Marcellus, a renowned martyr, and Leo the Great, a man of incomparable authority. These bear witness by divine revelation and the inspiration of God that this was done to oppose Simon the Magician.

For this EUSEBIUS bears witness in the second book of the ECCLE-SIASTICAL HISTORY: *In the reign of the Emperor Claudius divine*

REPLICA THEODORI LAELII

In ipsis Claudii temporibus divinam clementiam probatissimum omnium
apostolorum et maximum fidei magnificentia meritoque virtutis principem,
Petrum ad urbem Roman velut adversum humani generis perniciem com-
munem deduxisse. MARCELLUS quoque beatissimus, scribens universis

5 episcopis per Antiochiae constitutis provinciam, in haec verba consentit:[1] *Rogamus vos, dilectissimi, ut non aliud doceatis, quam quod a beato*
Petro et a reliquis apostolis accepistis. Ipse enim est caput totius ecclesiae,
cujus sedes primitus apud vos fuit, quae postea jubente Domino Romam
translata est. LEO quoque ad Petrum dirigens sermonem ita testatur:[2]

10 *Jam Antiochenam ecclesiam, ubi primum christiani nominis dignitas*
exorta,[3] fundaveras, jam Pontum, Galatiam, Cappadociam, Asiam atque
Bithyniam legibus evangelicae praedicationis impleveras; nec aut dubius
de proventu operum, aut de spatio tuae ignarus aetatis, trophaeum crucis
Christi Romanis arcibus inferebas. Quodque *divinis praeparationibus*

15 *anteibant et honor potestatis et gloria passionis,* merito dixit,[4] divina prae-
ordinatione id ante fuisse statutum, in quantum per ISAIAM antea
fuerat prophetatum, urbem Roman orbis caput jugo Christi per apostolorum Petri et Pauli praedicationem subigendam. Sic enim prophetaverat:[5]
Civitatem sublimem humiliabit et conculcabit eam pes pauperum, scilicet

20 Christi, *et egenorum,* id est apostolorum Petri et Pauli, ut sacri exposuere
doctores.[6] Cui sententiae adstipulatur et beatus AMBROSIUS doctor,
divinitus institutum fuisse confirmans,[7] *ut in urbe Romana, quae caput*
obtinet nationum, uno die et sub uno persecutore apostolorum principes
paterentur, et ubi erat caput superstitionis, illic caput quiesceret sanctitatis;

25 *et ubi gentilium principes habitabant, illic ecclesiae principes morarentur.*

Vides ergo, qui aliis obiciebas, *tenuem telam esse contextam,*[8] te nec

---

[1] c. 15, C. XXIV, qu. 1 (RF I, 970).
[2] *Serm.* 82, c. 5 (*PL* 54, 425A–B).
[3] Cf. *Act.* 11, 26.
[4] c. 5 (*PL* 54, 425B).
[5] *Isai.* 26, 5–6.
[6] *Biblie iampridem renovate* . . . , V, f. 49ʳ.
[7] c. 37, C. II, qu. 7 (RF I, 494).
[8] *Appellatio,* Frehero et Struvio, II, 211.

REPLY BY TEODORO LAELIO

mercy led the most excellent of the apostles, preeminent in the greatness of his faith and courage, Peter, to the city of Rome to oppose this common foe of mankind. The most blessed MARCELLUS writing to all the bishops in the province of Antioch also agreed in these words: *We beseech you, dearly beloved, to teach nothing other than that teaching you received from Peter and the other apostles. For he is the head of the whole Church, whose primal see was among you before it was transferred to Rome by the Lord's command.* LEO, addressing a sermon to Peter, declares: *You had already founded the church of Antioch, where first the glory of the Christian name arose; you had already filled Pontus, Galatia, Cappadocia, Asia, and Bithynia with the precepts of the gospel. Without a doubt about the successful outcome of your work and fully aware of your short life-span, you bore the victorious cross of Christ into the citadel of Rome.* LEO rightly said that *the honor of Peter's authority and the glory of his martyrdom went before him by divine preparation* for it was established by divine predestination, before it came to pass, because it had already been foretold through ISAIAH that the city of Rome, the capital of the world, would bow itself to the yoke of Christ through the preaching of the apostles Peter and Paul. For he prophesied: *He will humble the lofty city, and the feet of the poor* (that is, Christ), *and the feet of the needy* (that is, the apostles Peter and Paul) *will trample it;* this is the exposition of the holy doctors. The blessed doctor AMBROSE is in accord with this opinion, affirming that it was divinely ordained *that in the city of Rome, the capital of the nations, the princes of the apostles might suffer martyrdom one day under one persecutor, so that the seat of holiness might rest where the seat of superstition had been and so that the rulers of the Church might dwell where the rulers of the Gentiles had lived.*

Thus you, who protest to others that they have woven a thin web,

tenuem quidem vanissimis argumentationibus texere potuisse, sed cum adhuc ordiretur, praecisam esse. Somniasti namque Petrum conciliariter fuisse transmissum, cum in apostolico concilio Petrus primus sententiam tulisse legatur, nec ipsum ab apostolis et senioribus tunc convenientibus
5 Antiochiam missum, sed Barnabam et Silam sacra APOSTOLORUM ACTUUM testetur historia.[1] Ex Chrysippi aut Theophrasti te credo acumine argumenta talia mutuatum, ex quo genere illud dici potest, ut arguas ecclesiam non uni capiti, sed omnibus pariter apostolis fuisse commissam, pro eo quod *hodie usque oret ecclesia eorum protectione*
10 *defendi.*[2]

Quod si ita est, nullum ordinem mansionum, nullam graduum differentiam arguamus in caelis; cum ecclesia per singulas horas in communi commemoratione Dominum deprecetur, *ut quorum merita recolit, eorum sentiat patrocinia.*[3]

15 Ergo jam stella a stella non differet in claritate, et falsa diversitas mansionum in caelo in evangelio repromittitur.[4] Illud vero qualis impudentiae, ut beatum Petrum ab apostolis principem constitutum sine propriae imminutione potestatis asseveret, ex ipso constitutionis verbo Petri primatum ex apostolica magis quam divina institutione
20 manasse significat, ac si coetus aliquis aut collegium praelatum sibi praeficeret.

Improbissime haereticorum, quis ista te docuit? Cum omnes vere evangelii textus apostolorum electione, inter quos Petrus non vocatione, sed dignitate dictus est primus, usque ad ascensum Domini salvatoris,
25 Petri principatum aut promissum, aut figuratum, aut redditum eloquatur, ubi omnium cura immediate committitur:[5] *Pasce oves meas.* Quo verbo, ut beatus CHRYSOSTOMUS scribit, signanter expressit:[6] *Loco*

---

[1] Cf. *Act.* 15, 22–23.
[2] *Appellatio*, Frehero et Struvio, II, 211.
[3] Cf. "In natali apostolorum," in *Missale Aquileia* (Venice, 1519), 251.
[4] Cf. *Joan.* 14, 2.
[5] *Joan.* 21, 15.
[6] Cf. *De sacerdotio*, L. II, c. 2 (*PG* 48, 633).

REPLY BY TEODORO LAELIO

have not even been able to weave a thin one with your completely ground-less contentions; your web was broken before you began to spin. For you foolishly think that Peter was transferred by a council, since he is first read to have received a judgment in the council of the apostles; but the ACTS OF THE APOSTLES bear witness that Barnabas and Silas, and not Peter, were sent to Antioch by the assembled apostles and elders. I believe that you have shrewdly borrowed such arguments from Chrysip-pus[1] or Theophrastus.[2] It can be said that you assert that the Church was not committed to one head, but equally to all the apostles, on this basis: *The Church still prays to be preserved by their protection.*

If this is so, one can assert no order of mansions and no distinction of rank in the heavens although the Church in the hours prays to the Lord in the commons *to experience the protection of their renewed merits.*

Thus one heavenly body would not differ from another in brightness, and disparity of mansions would be falsely promised in the gospel. What impudence would assert that St. Peter was constituted as their ruler without detriment to the authority of the apostles, and would declare from the very words of the commission of Peter that his primacy originated in apostolic rather than divine institution, as if any group or corporate body were choosing its head!

Most shameless of heretics, who taught you these things? Truly every text of the gospel expresses the primacy of Peter either in promise, in figure, or in token from the choosing of the apostles—among whom Peter was regarded as the first, not by calling, but by authority—until the ascension of our Lord, the Savior, when he directly entrusted the pastor-ate of all to Peter: *Feed my sheep.* In these words, as ST. CHRYSOSTOM

---

[1] Greek Stoic philosopher of the 3rd century B.C.
[2] Greek philosopher of the late 4th century B.C.; disciple of Aristotle.

335

mei praepositus, et caput esto fratrum tuorum. Nonne haeresim tuam disertissime Nicolaus confutat in canone dicens:[1] *Non quaelibet terrena sapientia, sed illud verbum, quo constructum est caelum et terra, per quod omnia condita sunt elementa, Romanam fundavit ecclesiam. Cujus privi-*
5 *legium ab ipso summo capite ecclesiarum traditum, qui auferre conatur, hic procul dubio in haeresim labitur.* Et eadem de conciliis, a quibus quidam temere praelationem ecclesiae Romanae concessam asseverabant, testatur beatus PELAGIUS dicens:[2] *Quamvis universae per orbem catholice institutae ecclesiae unius thalamus Christi sunt, tamen sancta*
10 *Romana ecclesia catholica apostolica apostolica nullis synodicis constitutis ceteris ecclesiis praelata est, sed evangelica voce Domini et salvatoris prima-tum obtinuit.*

Patet igitur, apostolos non instituisse Petri primatum, sed dominicae atque evangelicae institutionis, quam noverant executos, illi humiliter
15 detulisse. Sicut beatus ANACLETUS in canone:[3] *Licet,* inquit *omnes essent apostoli, Petro tamen concessum est a Domino, et ipsi inter se voluerunt idipsum, ut reliquis omnibus praeesset apostolis.* Notandum vero, quam fallaciter beati Hieronymi testimonium inducat, ut asserat uni ad schisma submovendum singulariter claves ecclesiae permissas, id
20 est, quasi haec sola fuerit divini altitudo consilii, Petrum praeficere, ut scandala submoveret. Non illi satis est haereticum esse, nisi probatissimo omnium Catholicorum tractatorum similem notam, infligat. Audi, miser, quid HIERONYMUS sentiat, hoc nempe quod ceteri, et quod ex illius auctoritate GLOSSA ORDINARIA scribit super MATTHAEUM:[4]
25 *Specialiter Petro claves concessit, ut ad unitatem nos invitaret. Ideo enim principem apostolorum constituit, ut ecclesia haberet unum principalem Christi vicarium, ad quem diversa Christi membra recurrerent, si forte inter se dissentirent. Quod si diversa forent in ecclesia capita, unitatis vincula*

---

[1] c. 1, D. XXII (RF I, 73).
[2] c. 3, D. XXI (RF I, 70).
[3] c. 2, D. XXII (RF I, 74).
[4] Cf. *Adversus Jovinianum,* I, c. 26 (*PL* 23, 258); *Biblie iampridem renovate* . . . , V, f. 42ᵛ–53ʳ.

REPLY BY TEODORO LAELIO

writes, Christ expresses himself figuratively: *Rule in my stead and be a father to your brothers.* POPE NICHOLAS most eloquently refutes your heresy in canon law:[1] *No earthly wisdom, but the Word which made heaven and earth and established all the elements founded the Roman church. He who attempts to remove the prerogative bestowed upon the Roman church by the supreme head of all the churches without doubt falls into heresy.* Some have asserted the same for the councils, rashly declaring that the councils conferred primacy upon the Roman church; to these ST. PELAGIUS[2] declares: *Although all churches universally established throughout the world are the one marriage bed of Christ, nevertheless the holy catholic and apostolic Roman Church was not elevated by any other churches established by a council, but received its primacy from the words of our Lord and Savior.*

It is evident, therefore, that the apostles did not institute the primacy of Peter, but carried out and humbly deferred to the Lord's commission which they acknowledged. As ST. ANACLETUS states in the canon:[3] *Although all were apostles, nevertheless they concurred in the Lord's grant to Peter to rank above them all.* It must certainly be observed how deceptively he employs the authority of St. Jerome to assert that the keys of the church were permitted to one alone in order to prevent schisms, in other words, as if this were the whole extent of divine wisdom: to elevate Peter in order to prevent scandals. If that were not heretical enough, he imposes the same blemish upon the most excellent of all Catholic writers. Listen, wretch, to what JEROME thinks, certainly what others declare, and what the GLOSSA ORDINARIA upon his authority writes upon MATTHEW: *He specifically committed the keys to Peter to call us to unity. For he instituted the ruler of the apostles so that the Church might possess one ruling vicar of Christ to whom the various members of Christ might recur if perchance dissension arose among them. But if there were various heads in the Church, the bonds of unity would be broken.*

---

[1] See p. 97.
[2] This canon is attributed to Gelasius I (492–496).
[3] See p. 95.

rumperentur. Nonne et tibi videtur, et unitatis causam, et fidei conven-
ientiam, et in vicariatu Christi plenitudinem potestatis et mystici
corporis caput contra caput schismatis brevi verborum serie conjunxisse ?
Si id tibi non sufficit, et Hieronymi de primatu Petri vis plenius nosse
5 sententiam, ex aliis mutuare codicibus. Sed videbis in COMMENTARIIS
SUPER MATTHEUM dicentem:[1] *Simonem propter fidem in petram
Christum, Petri sortitum esse vocabulum, ac secundum metaphorum illi
dictum:*[2] *"Aedificabo ecclesiam meam."* In quo manifeste primatus ipsius
super totam ecclesiam designatur. Intuere eundem scribentem ad
10 Terentium, DE VERA CIRCUMCISIONE,[3] et novi testamenti patres
patribus veteribus comparantem, Petrum apostolum Abrahae prae-
ferentem, ut *sicut illi generatio large promittitur, ita huic generatio pascenda
traditur; et cum ab illo justificando procedant, in hoc justificatio fundatur.*
Et multa percurrens, *Petrum dominici gregis pastorem, ecclesiae funda-*
15 *mentum, apostolorum verticem* clarissime profitetur.[4] Lege rursus,
haeretice, quemadmodum apud Petri successorem Damasum fidem
exponat.[5] *Ego,* inquit, *nullum primum nisi Petrum sequens, beatitudini
tuae, id est, cathedrae Petri communicando consortio, super illam petram
fundatam ecclesiam scio. Quicumque extra hanc domum agnum comederit
20 prophanus est a lege.* Iterum cum in libro VIRORUM ILLUSTRIUM
tantum auctoritatis Petro attribueret, ut ab eo consummatum evangelium esse testetur:[6] *Scripsit,* inquit, *Marcus evangelium Romanis, rogatus
a fratribus, quod cum Petrus audisset, probavit, et ecclesiae legendum sua
auctoritate dedit.* Ad quod Clementis etiam Papae inducit testimonium.
25 Audi denique illum ad Augustinum de capitulo ad Galatas[7] differentem,

---

[1] L. III, c. 16 (*PL* 26, 121D–122A).
[2] *Matth.* 16, 18.
[3] c. 17 (*PL* 30, 211A).
[4] Cf. D. 1, c. 54 (RF I, 198); non invenitur in Ambrosio, sed in Maximo Taurinensis, *Hom.* 54 (*PL* 57, 353).
[5] *Epist.* 15, c. 2 (*PL* 22, 355); c. 25, C. XXIV (RF I, 976).
[6] c. 8 (*PL* 23, 654).
[7] Cf. *Comm. in Gal.,* L. I, c. 2 (*PL* 26, 357B–C).

REPLY BY TEODORO LAELIO

Does it not appear to you that the basis of unity, the harmony of the faith, and the fullness of authority were joined in this short passage in the vicariate of Christ that opposes the head of schism as the head of the mystical body? If this is not sufficient evidence for you, and you wish to know the judgment of Jerome on the primacy of Peter more fully, consult other texts. But you will see that he says in his COMMENTARY ON MATTHEW: *Simon was given the name of Peter for his faith in the rock, Christ; Christ addressed him figuratively: "I will build my church."* In these words his primacy over the entire Church is clearly indicated. Consider the same author writing to Terentius, ON THE TRUE CIRCUMCISION, where he compares the Fathers of the New Testament with the patriarchs and places the apostle Peter before Abraham: *As Abraham is promised many offspring, to Peter these offspring are given to pasture; from the former they set forth to righteousness, in the latter they are established in righteousness.* To mention several texts in passing, he most clearly affirms that Peter is *the Pastor of the Lord's flock, the foundation of the Church and the head of the apostles.* Read again, heretic, how he expounds the faith to Damasus, the successor of Peter:[1] *As I seek no reward but Christ, so I join in supporting your blessedness, that is, the chair of Peter. I know that the Church is built upon this rock. Whoever will eat the lamb outside this house is an outcast from the law.* Again in his book of ILLUSTRIOUS MEN he ascribed so much authority to Peter that he declares that the gospel was completed by him: *Mark wrote his gospel for the Romans in response to the request of the brethren; when Peter heard of it, he approved it and gave it to the Church to read upon his own authority.* He even adduces the support of Pope Clement[2] for this. Listen finally to this:

---

[1] See p. 89.
[2] Jerome alludes to Clement of Alexandria, not Clement of Rome.

tantum Petro tribuere, ut super illo:[1] *Ascendi autem secundum revelationem et exposui eis evangelium*, dicat Paulum hisce ipsis verbis ostendere, non habuisse securitatem evangelii praedicandi, nisi Petri et eorum, qui cum eo erant, fuisset sententia roboratum. Talia legens aut audiens de
5 fine [sic] catholico, desine haereticorum prosecutioni tuae participationis inferre calumniam. Quae est enim societas lucis et tenebrarum, conventio Christi ad Belial, quae pars fidelis tecum,[2] hominum perfidissime? Alterum rectius Hieronymum pro simili errore Constantiae damnatum allegare debueras, si tibi credi volebas. Nam de beatissimo viro,
10 quod minus recte de ecclesiae institutione senserit, refugiunt aures Catholicorum audire.

Et quoniam beato quoque Ambrosio similem tentasti inferre calumniam, cum illum pastorali dixisse refers:[3] *omnibus apostolis claves una fuisse contraditas*, disce, miser, illum ita affirmare claves apostolis pariter
15 esse contraditas, ut tamen intelligat Petrum prae omnibus et pro omnibus claves regni caelorum accepisse; ut et unitas et praelatio demonstraretur in Petro. Quod ex ipsius scriptis in pluribus licet cognoscere, quibus illum fundamentum ecclesiae, totius dominici gregis pastorem esse commemorat Christianitatis compagem molemque contineat. Cogis
20 nos de multis pauca proferre. Illustris ille doctor in COMMENTARIIS SUPER LUCAM exponens eum locum, in quo Dominus in naviculam Petri conscendisse perhibetur.[4] *Non turbatur*, inquit, *navis quae Petrum habet; turbatur illa quae Judam habet*. Et post pauca:[5] *Quemadmodum enim turbari poterit, cui praeerat is, in quo fundamentum ecclesiae est*. Et
25 deinde illius primatum in agnitione ac determinatione fidei attollens, ait:[6] *Denique et aliis imperatur, ut laxent retia in capturam. Soli tamen Petro dicitur*:[7] *"dux in altum,"* hoc est, *in profundum disputationum*.

---

[1] *Gal*. 2, 2.*
[2] Cf. *II Cor*. 6, 14–15.
[3] *Appellatio*, Frehero et Struvio, II, 211.
[4] *Expos. in Lucam*, L. IV (*CCh* 14, 132; *PL* 15, 1717D).
[5] *CCh* 14, 132; *PL* 15, 1718A.
[6] *Ibid*.
[7] *Luc*. 5, 4.

REPLY BY TEODORO LAELIO

Jerome revered Peter so highly that when he writes to Augustine upon the passage in GALATIANS, *I went up because it had been revealed that I should do so; I laid before them the gospel,* he says that Paul indicates by these words that he could not have preached the gospel confidently without the support of the knowledge of Peter and those who were with him. Read there and heed these teachings on the Catholic faith and cease the effrontery of your association with heretics. For what fellowship has light with darkness? What accord has Christ with Belial? What has a believer in common with you, most wicked of men? You ought to mention more carefully that Jerome was condemned for a similar error at Constance, if you wish to be believed.[1] For the ears of Catholics shun hearing that that most blessed man expressed a view less than correct upon the institution of the Church.

You have attempted to misconstrue Ambrose in a similar fashion, since you allege that he declared in his Sermons that *one key was entrusted to all the apostles.* Understand, wretch, that he does affirm that the keys were entrusted equally to all the apostles, but he also declares that Peter received the keys of the kingdom of heaven before all and for all so that the unity and primacy in Peter might be made manifest. His many writings acknowledge that he regarded him as the foundation of the Church and the pastor of the Lord's whole flock; his primacy is figuratively described in the command of the ship that is entrusted to him— the ship that includes the power and authority of the whole body of Christendom. That illustrious doctor in his COMMENTARY ON LUKE in expounding the passage in which the Lord is said to have entered Peter's boat, declared: *The ship is not troubled that carries Peter, but the ship that carries Judas is troubled.* He goes on: *For how could it be troubled since it is ruled by Peter in whom is the foundation of the Church?* Then bringing himself to Peter's primacy in the recognition and determination of doctrine, he declares: *Finally he orders the others to let down their nets for a catch. Yet he says to Peter only: "Put into the deep,"* in other

---

[1] The allusion is to Jerome of Prague who was burned in Constance on 30 May 1416.

341

REPLICA THEODORI LAELII

Quid enim tam altum, quam altitudinem divinitatis videre, id est, scire
Dei filium et professionem divinae generationis assumere? Idem quoque de
apostolorum principibus Petro et Paulo, quod emineant inter universos
apostolos et peculiari quadam virtute praecellant, satis evidens profert
5 et omnibus notum testimonium, in quorum martyrio Romanae ecclesiae
primatum ac singularem indicat dignitatem, uno loco illos occubuisse
perhibens,[1] *ne alteri Roma deesset, atque in urbe quae principatum et caput*
obtinet nationum, ut illic caput quiesceret sanctitatis. Et reliqua leguntur in
canone, quae principatum Apostolicae Sedis insinuant. De cujus princi-
10 patus mystica in evangelio figura alio loco sic loquitur:[2] *Est aliud*
piscandi genus, quo genere solum Petrum Dominus piscari jubet, dicens:[3]
Mitte hamum, et eum piscem, qui primum ascenderit, tolle. Ubi satis
aperte demonstrat per hamum intelligi jurisdictionem, qua Petrus
praefuit universis. Denique ut nulla tibi relinquatur tergiversandi
15 occasio, ac fatearis AMBROSIUM publice esse testatum, Petrum totius
fuisse gregis pastorem, qui firmamentum sit ecclesiae institutum, et non
unius tantum partis, sed totius Christianitatis velut mystici corporis
compagem molemque continere, audimini hunc ipsum in HOMILIA
apertius protestantem:[4] *Majorem,* inquit, *gratiam Petrus reperit, post-*
20 *quam fidem se perdidisse deflevit. Tanquam bonus enim pastor tuendum*
gregem accepit; ut is, qui sibi ante infirmus fuerat, fieret omnibus firma-
mentum, et qui interrogationis tentatione nutaverat, ceteros fidei stabilitate
fundaret. Denique pro soliditate elevationis ecclesiarum petra dicitur, eo
quod prius in nationibus fidei fundamenta posuerit, et tanquam saxum
25 *immobile totius corporis Christianitatis compagem molemque contineat.*
Desine haereticorum more truncata verba proferendo, tanti praesulis
calumniari sententias. Desine fidei ipsius puritati inferre calumniam;
cujus omnes sententiae—beato teste Hieronymo[5]—fidei ecclesiae, et

---

[1] c. 37, C. II, qu. 7 (RF I, 494).
[2] *Expos. in Lucam,* L. IV (*CCh* 14, 132; *PL* 15, 1718C); c. 8, C. XXIV, qu. 1 (RF I, 969).
[3] *Matth.* 17, 26.
[4] D. 1, c. 54 (RF I, 198); non invenitur in Ambrosio, sed in Maximo Taurinensis, *Hom.*
54 (*PL* 57, 353).
[5] Cf. *Comm. in epist. ad Gal.,* L. I, c. 2 (*PL* 26, 362).

words, into the depth of disputations. For what is so profound as to see the profundity of divinity, that is, to know the son of God and to receive the profession of divine generation? AMBROSE also pronounces most satisfactorily in a declaration known to all on the rulers of the apostles, Peter and Paul, who stand out among all the apostles and surpass the others by their singular virtue, and proclaim the primacy and singular glory of the Roman church in their martyrdom, declaring that they perished in Rome *lest Rome should be deprived of this distinction and that the seat of holiness might rest in the city that attained dominion and sway over the nations.* And other texts are found in the canon which support the primacy of the Apostolic See. Concerning the mystical expression of this primacy, AMBROSE speaks thus elsewhere: *There is another manner of fishing, the manner in which the Lord enjoins Peter to fish, saying: "Cast a hook [in the lake] and take the first fish that comes up."* This clearly indicates that the hook signifies the jurisdiction by which Peter rules over all. Finally, to leave you no opportunity for evasion and to bring you to acknowledge that AMBROSE openly declared that Peter was the pastor of the whole flock and was the instituted bulwark of the Church, and that Peter possesses the power and authority of not only a portion, but all of Christendom as over the mystical body, listen to what he declares to me more openly in a certain sermon: *Peter discovered greater grace after he wept that he had betrayed the faith. For as a good shepherd he received the flock to protect it, so that he who was previously weak might establish others in the firmness of his faith. Finally he is declared the rock of the churches for the solidity of his support, since he first laid the foundations of the faith among the nations and was an immovable rock that comprised the power and authority of the whole body of Christendom.* Stop citing words wrenched out of context in the fashion of the heretics and assailing the decisions of such a prelate. Stop assailing the purity of his faith whose every decision is a firm pillar of the faith of the Church and of all virtue, as JEROME

omnium virtutum firmae sunt columnae. Possem et aliorem sanctorum
patrum testimonia infinita cogerere. Sed nimis praeposterum videretur,
in re tam perspicua, quam totus orbis profitetur et noscit, quasi in recenti
controversia exquirere testimonia, ut cum secundum humanas leges
5 triginta annis praescribatur, primatus Petri post tot saecula disputatione
temeraria ventiletur. At Hieronymi et Ambrosii non alia de causa sub-
jecimus, nisi ut eorum rectam catholicamque sententiam proferentes, ad
tuae pravitatis robur de illorum auctoritate tibi non blandiereris, et
simpliciores quosque eorum consideratione non falleres.

10   Liquet igitur, te orientalibus atque Bohemicis venenis imbutum talia
protulisse, quae Petri primatum ejusque super omnem ecclesiam principatum negarunt. Qui quidem error tam detestabilis atque gravis est, ut
eos sanctus doctor Thomas de Aquino[1] illis haereticis comparaverit, qui
Spiritum Sanctum negant a Patre Filioque procedere. Quoniam sicut
15 Christus Dei Filius ecclesiam suam consecrat et consignat Spiritu Sancto,
quasi suo charactere et sigillo, ita Christi vicarius suo primatu universalem ecclesiam, tanquam fidelis minister. Nec mirum quidem. Tales enim
gravissimum schismatis reatum incurrunt, cujus tam immanis est culpa,
ut—Augustino et Cypriano testibus[2]—illam nec eleemosyna redimere,
20 nec baptismus abluere, nec pro Christi nomine sanguis effusus valeat
expiare. Hanc igitur tuam, quam sub verborum praestigiis contra
primatum Petri declarasti sententiam, ex venenis orientalis erroris
procedentem, quidam ante te apud occiduas partes astruere conati sunt.
Marsilius Patavinus et Johannes de Janduno, non veriti dicere, *aposto-*
25 *lorum principem Petrum, nec plus auctoritatis accepisse, nec pro reliquis*
apostolis caput ecclesiae divinitus institutum.[3] Hi quidem a Joanne XXII
pontifice justo anathemate damnati sunt. Sed et Johannem Wickliff, et
sectatorem ejus haereseos, Johannem Huss, eadem disseminantes magna
Constantiensis synodus condemnavit. Tu vero post damnationem eorum

---

[1] Cf. *Contra errores Graecorum*, c. 32 (Parma XV, 256).
[2] Cf. c. 29, C. XXIV, qu. 1 (RF I, 977); c. 31, C. XXIV, qu. 1 (RF I, 977–978).
[3] Cf. Marsilius de Padua, *Defensor pacis*, ed. C. W. Previté-Orton (Cambridge, England, 1928), Dictio II, c. 28, §5, 435.

REPLY BY TEODORO LAELIO

bears witness. I could assemble an endless number of such testimonies by the other holy Fathers. But is would be quite absurd in a matter so clear, which the whole world knows and acknowledges, to investigate opinions in recent controversy and to disturb the primacy of Peter after so many centuries with imprudent disputation, although such opposition may be prescribed in human laws during these last thirty years. I do not offer other statements concerning this matter in addition to Jerome and Ambrose, except to note their orthodox Catholic opinion; I offer them in order that you may not delude yourself as to the strength of your perversion on the basis of their authority and that you may not deceive more simple folk with such allusions.

It is therefore evident that you have made declarations imbued with the poison of the Bohemians and the Greeks who deny the primacy of Peter and his dominion over the whole Church. Indeed such an error is so detestable and serious that the holy doctor THOMAS AQUINAS compared those who professed it to those heretics who deny that the Holy Spirit proceeds from the Father and the Son. For as Christ, the Son of God, consecrates his Church and seals it with the Holy Spirit, as with his own mark and seal, so the Vicar of Christ in his primacy rules over the Church Universal as the faithful minister of Christ. This is certainly not surprising. For the assailants of Peter incur the most serious charge of schism, whose guilt is so enormous that alms cannot redeem it, baptism cannot absolve it, and even blood shed for the name of Christ cannot expiate it—as AUGUSTINE and CYPRIAN declare. Some before you have attempted to affirm in the West the opinion you declared in sly words against the primacy of Peter, an opinion which proceeds from the venom of Greek error. MARSILIUS OF PADUA and JOHN OF JANDUN were not ashamed to declare that *Peter, the first of the apostles, did not receive more authority than the other apostles and was not divinely instituted as the head of the Church before the other apostles.* These scoundrels were condemned by the just anathema of Pope John XXII. Moreover, the great Council of Constance condemned John Wyclif and his follower in heresy, John Huss, for spreading the same opinion. You assuredly attempt to renew their heresy after their condemnation and to

eandem haeresim instaurare moliris, et Catholicorum principum auribus
inculcare. Mirum profecto est te, quorum actus imitaris, eorum exitus
non perhorrescere. Quid ergo restat, nisi, ut sancti illi beatissimique
pontifices excitentur, Felix atque Gelasius, haereticorum expugnatores
5 acerrimi, quorum alter si viveret, nunc contra te ut quondam contra
Achatium inclamaret:[1] *Gregorius non est factus erroris novi inventor, sed*
veteris imitator, atque ideo non est necesse, ut adversus eum nova sententia
prodeat, sed vetus tantummodo renovetur. Quicumque enim in haeresim
semel damnatam labitur, ejus damnationi se involvit. Alter vero te per-
10 petui anathematis mucrone feriret ac diceret:[2] *Habeto cum his, quos*
libenter amplecteris, portionem, non cum honore et communione Catholica;
nec non etiam a fidelium numero segregatus, sublatum tibi nomen, et inimi-
cus Christianae religionis agnosce, Sancti Spiritus judicio et apostolica
auctoritate damnatus, numquam ab anathematis vinculis excipiendus.

---

[1] Cf. *Epist.* 4 (*PL* 59, 28); c. 1, C. XXIV, qu. 1 (RF I, 966).
[2] Felice, *Epist.* 6 (*PL* 58, 923C–D).

force it into the ears of Catholic rulers. It is certainly astounding that you, who imitate their deeds, do not tremble at their end. Nothing therefore remains but to cite those holy and most blessed popes, Felix and Gelasius, most zealous foes of heretics; if the one was alive, he would now cry out against you as he once did against Acacius: *Gregor has not become the discoverer of new error, but the imitator of old error; therefore it is not necessary to issue a new judgment against him, but only to renew an old one. For anyone who falls into a heresy previously condemned includes himself in its condemnation.* The other would certainly smite you with the sword of everlasting anathema, and would say: *Share the lot of those whom you freely embrace and not the honor and communion of the Catholic Church. Likewise realize that you are separated from the number of the faithful; that you receive the name of an enemy of the Christian religion; that you are condemned by the judgment of the Holy Spirit and apostolic authority; and that you are never released from the bonds of this anathema.*

ENCYCLICA, AD OPEM ADOLFO, PRO POSSESSIONE ECCLESIAE MOGUNTINAE NANCISCENDA, PRAESTANDAM

Pius episcopus, servus servorum Dei, universis et singulis carissimis in Christo filiis, Romanorum imperatori et regibus, ac venerabilibus fratribus nostris patriarchis, archiepiscopis, episcopis, aliisque ecclesiarum et monasteriorum praelatis, saecularibus, et ordinum quorum-
5 cumque regularibus, necnon dilectis filiis nobilibus viris, principibus electoribus, ducibus, marchionibus, comitibus, baronibus, nobilibus, militaribus, et quibuscumque communitatibus civitatum, oppidorum et locorum quomodolibet, ubilibet constitutis, salutem et apostolicam benedictionem.
10 Cum omnes reges et principes Christianae religionis Romano Pontifice ut ipsius religionis pastori et capiti obedientiam et reverentiam impendere consuerint, condecens est, ut etiam adversus protervorum audaciam, qui, claves ecclesiae contemnentes, et aliunde quam per

ENCYCLICAL SEEKING SUPPORT FOR ADOLF VON NASSAU IN SECURING POSSESSION OF THE CHURCH OF MAINZ

Pius, Bishop, Servant of the Servants of God. Health and our apostolic benediction to all our dearly beloved sons in Christ, to the Emperor of the Romans and all rulers, to our venerable brethren, the patriarchs, the archbishops, bishops, and to other prelates of churches and monasteries, to secular clerics and regular clerics of every monastic order, and likewise to our beloved sons of the nobility, the Prince Electors, dukes, margraves, counts, barons, nobles, knights, and to all the ruling bodies of cities, towns, and other places however and wherever constituted.

Since all kings and rulers of Christendom are accustomed to lend obedience and reverence to the Roman pontiff as the pastor and head of the Christian religion, it is only fitting that they lend support and assistance freely to this pontiff and to the Emperor of the Romans struggling

NOTE: The Latin text is reprinted from Ferdinand de Gudenus, *Codex diplomaticus anecdotorum, res Moguntinas, Francicas, Trevirenses, Hassiacas, finitimorumque regionum, necnon ius Germanicum et S.R.I. historiam vel maxime illustrantium* (Frankfurt and Leipzig, 1758), IV, 350–353.

AD OPEM ADOLFO

ostium ingredi satagentes, ecclesiarum metropolitanarum regimina, contra ipsius pontificis voluntatem, armis invadunt, tanquam adversus fures et latrones, eidem pontifici et Romanorum imperatori pro justicia certanti, subsidia et opem libenter impendant.

5 Dudum siquidem, cum iniquitatis filium Dietherum de Isenberg, Moguntinensi ecclesia pastore carente eidem ecclesiae in archiepiscopum et pastorem, ut electum justis ac juratis conditionibus praefecissemus; demum cognito, ipsum Dietherum, ob non promotionem seu consecrationem infra juris terminum, ab omni jure ad dictam ecclesiam cecidisse, 10 atque etiam perjurio et excommunicationis ac aliarum censurarum ecclesiasticarum contemptu, nec non irregularitate, et contra nos et sedem praefatam rebellione, ac aliis gravibus morbis et excessibus notorie laborare, propter quae omnia indignus quidem, ut ipsi ecclesiae et tanto populo praeficeretur, censendus erat, habito super hoc cum 15 venerabilibus fratribus nostris sanctae Romanae ecclesiae cardinalibus tractatu et deliberatione matura, de eorum consilio et assensu, juxta formam juris procedendo dictum Dietherum praefata ecclesia, et omni jure quod sibi in illa vel ad eam competere posset, auctoritate apostolica privatum declaravimus, privavimusque et ab illa realiter amovimus, 20 ipsumque a vinculo, quo dictae ecclesiae tenebatur, absolvimus. Decrevimusque capitula, praepositos, decanos, scholasticos, custodes, camerarios, cantores, thesaurarios, omnesque et singulos praelatos, quocumque nomine censerentur canonicos, vicarios perpetuos et temporales, altaristas ipsius ecclesiae et totius diocesis Moguntinae, omnes 25 denique vasallos, ligios, castrenses, ac simplices officiatos, scabinos civitatum et oppidorum, villarum, fortiliciorumque omnium, burgimagistros, consules eorumque rectores, quocumque censeantur nomine, ac subditos universos et singulos [etc.] . . . dicto Diethero in nulla re obedientiae vinculo teneri, et a juramento, si quod ei praestiterant, 30 liberos et absolutos esse. Mandavimusque ipsis [etc.] . . . ne de cetero dicto Diethero [etc.] . . . aut ejus procuratoribus in aliquo parerent vel responderent, sed eum tanquam morbidam pecudem et pestilentem bestiam devitarent.

350

for justice as against thieves and robbers, even against the impudence of the wicked who, despising the keys of the Church and striving to enter the fold over the wall and not through the gate, usurp with force the rule of metropolitan churches against the will of the pontiff.

Recently, because we appointed Diether von Isenburg, son of iniquity, to the church of Mainz, which lacked a pastor, as the Archbishop-elect and pastor of this church upon just, sworn conditions; because we finally realized that Diether, because he was not elevated or consecrated within the term [established] in law, had fallen from every right to the said church; because Diether was notoriously involved in perjury, in scorn for his excommunication and other ecclesiastical censures, in rebellion against us and the aforesaid see, and in other serious disorders and excesses: it was determined at last that it was assuredly intolerable that such a man should rule over this church and so many souls. After we had conducted a full discussion and consultation upon this matter with our venerable brethren, the cardinals of the holy Roman Church, and with their advice and consent, following due legal procedure, we deposed and declared him to be deposed by the apostolic authority from the aforesaid church and from every prerogative within that church which he enjoyed or could claim as his due; and we removed him in effect from that church and released him from the bond which united him to the said church. We decreed that chapters, provosts, deans, scholastics, chamberlains, cantors, treasurers, all and sundry prelates, canons whatever their title, vicars perpetual and temporal, acolytes of the Church and the entire diocese of Mainz, all vassals, liege subjects, castellans and low-born officials and stewards of cities, towns, villages, and strongholds, and all burgermeisters, consuls, and leading men whatever their title, and all and sundry subjects [etc.] . . . were bound to the said Diether by no obligation and that they were released and absolved from any oath that they had sworn to him. We enjoined them [etc.] . . . not to respond or submit to the said Diether [etc.] . . . or his henchmen in any respect, but to shun him as a diseased animal and a pest-ridden beast.[1]

---

[1] See p. 247.

AD OPEM ADOLFO

Postmodum vero ipsi ecclesiae Moguntinae de persona dilecti filii
Adolfi de Nassau, tunc dictae ecclesiae canonici, de comitum genere
procreati, de eorundem fratrum consilio providimus, ipsumque illi
providimus in archiepiscopum et pastorem, prout in variis nostris super
5 his confectis litteris plenius continetur.

Verum cum ipse Dietherus in reprobum sensum datus, ac ut fur et
latro aliunde quam per ostium intrare satagens, suffultus praesidio
nobilis viri Frederici, Comitis Palatini Rheni, et aliorum complicum et
adhaerentium suorum, praefatam ecclesiam vi et armis invadere adorsus
10 esset. Et tam ipse quam dictus Comes Palatini et complices atque adhaerentes, verum et legitimum dictae ecclesiae sponsum Adolfum
electum praefatum persequi, dictaeque ecclesiae oppida et loca alia,
quae poterant, occupare, et plurima bella in diocesi Moguntina im-
miscere, et varia mala et homicidia perpetrare non cessarent; carissimus
15 in Christo filius noster Fredericus, Romanorum imperator Augustus,
misertus conditionis dictae ecclesiae Moguntinae, eamque quoad posset
ab oppressionibus relevare volens, mandavit principibus et communitatibus sibi subjectis nationis Germanicae quibuscumque, ut praefato
Adolfo electo in assequenda et conservanda possessione dictae ecclesiae
20 [etc.] . . . auxilio essent, atque injunxit.

Nos igitur attendentes, quam pernicioso exemplo in eadem Christiana
religione sit, patere alicui aditum vi et armis ad pontificales dignitates; et
eum, cui per successorem beati Petri animarum cura et regimen com-
mitti debet, usurpare potentia, quod ejus demerita consequi non per-
25 mittunt; ac huic morbo tamquam pestifero et nocivo, et tyrannicam
haeresim sapienti, non solum per Romanum pontificem et imperatorem,
sed etiam per quoscumque alios principes et praelatos dignum esse ut
occurratur, non immerito existimantes. Vos reges [etc.] . . . ac alios
principes hortamur et obsecramus, archiepiscopis vero et episcopis, ac
30 ducibus, marchionibus [etc.] . . . quibus per praefatum imperatorem id

IN SUPPORT OF ADOLF

Thereafter with the advice of our brethren we provided the church of Mainz with the person of our beloved son, Adolf von Nassau, then a canon of the said church, who stems from a line of counts; we provided him as her archbishop and pastor, as is more fully elaborated in our various letters which deal with these matters.[1]

Indeed because this Diether, given up to false understanding and supported by the assistance of the nobleman, Frederick, Count Palatine of the Rhine, and his other confederates and adherents, as a thief and a robber who strives to enter over the wall and not through the gate, has dared to usurp the aforesaid church by the force of arms, and because both he and the said Count Palatine, as well as their confederates and adherents, have not ceased to assail the aforesaid Adolf, the true, the rightful, and the elected spouse of the said church, to occupy walled towns and places belonging to the said church to the extent of their power, to launch assaults upon the diocese of Mainz, and to commit various crimes and homicides, our dearly beloved son in Christ, Frederick, August Emperor of the Romans, moved to pity by the plight of the said church of Mainz and wishing to rescue it from oppression to the extent of his power, ordered and enjoined all rulers and cities subject to himself in the German nation to assist the aforesaid Adolf, the Archbishop-elect, in securing and maintaining possession of the said church [etc.].

We therefore realized what a pernicious example to the Christian religion it would be to permit such a man access by the force of arms to archiepiscopal rank and to permit him, who ought to receive his pastorate and rule over souls from the successor of St. Peter, to usurp authority to which his sins do not entitle him; and not only the Roman pontiff and the Emperor, but all other rulers and prelates have considered it proper to oppose this diseased man, this noxious pest-ridden person who openly displays his tyranny and heresy. We exhort, beseech, and enjoin you kings [etc.] . . . and other rulers, and we strictly admonish you archbishops, bishops, dukes, and margraves [etc.] . . . who were ordered and

---

[1] See Introduction, p. 30.

AD OPEM ADOLFO

mandatum et injunctum est, seu mandari et injungi continget, sub
poenis, quibusdam monitorialibus litteris nostris, quae sub data sexto
idus januarii pontificatus nostri anno quarto expeditae fuerunt, contentis
districte praecipiendo mandamus, ut eidem electo Adolfo in assequenda
5 et obtinenda possessione dictae ecclesiae Moguntinae omnem opem vobis
possibilem, ac auxilium, consilium et favorem contra Comitem Palatinum
et Dietherum complicesque et adhaerentes praefatas juxta mandatum
imperiale praedictum impendatis, Comitemque Palatinum et Dietherum
et praedictos ab eorum nefariis conatibus quoad vobis possibile fuerit
10 arceatis, ac praeceptis et mandatis praefati imperatoris quoad hoc
efficaciter parere studeatis, ut per hujusmodi obsequia, quae pro justicia
Sedi et Moguntinae ecclesiae impenderitis, non solum ipsius sedis
benivolentiam et gratiam, sed etiam ab eo, qui beatitudinem patientibus
persecutionem propter justiciam repromisit,[1] perennis vitae praemium
15 consequi valeatis.

Datum Romae apud Sanctum Petrum, anno incarnationis dominicae
MCCCCLXII, kalendis maii, pontificatus nostri anno quarto.

---

[1] Cf. *Matth*. 5, 10.

354

enjoined, or will be ordered and enjoined, by the aforesaid Emperor, under the threat of chastisement included in certain of our letters of admonition dispatched on the eighth day of January in the fourth year of our pontificate,[1] to offer all support, assistance, advice, and good will possible to Adolf, the Archbishop-elect, in accordance with the aforesaid imperial decree, in opposing the Count Palatine, Diether, and their aforesaid accomplices and adherents and in procuring and obtaining possession of the said church of Mainz; to thwart the Count Palatine, Diether, and their aforesaid henchmen in their impious endeavors to the extent of your ability; and to apply yourselves in carrying out the precepts and commands of the aforesaid Emperor to the extent of your power. Any services of this sort that you contribute for the sake of righteousness to the Apostolic See and the church of Mainz will earn you not only the good will and favor of this see, but even the reward of life everlasting from him who promised his blessing to those who are persecuted for righteousness' sake.

Promulgated at Rome in St. Peter's in the year of our Lord's incarnation 1462, on the first day of May in the fourth of our pontificate.

––––––––

[1] See Introduction, pp. 34–35.

IN MINORIBUS AGENTES
EXCERPTA

His auctoribus, unam ecclesiam Catholicam et Apostolicam esse
didicimus matrem omnium fidelium, extra quam non invenitur salus;
sponsam Christi immaculatam, in qua omnes qui militant finem sibi
proponunt vitam aeternam. Idcirco enim in ecclesia militanti laborant
5 homines, et cum daemonibus tamquam hostibus pugnant, ut pacem
tandem assequantur, et cum Jesu magistro ac legifero suo in caelesti
Hierusalem triumphare ac regnare possint. Hic finis christiano proponitur, huc omnes ecclesiae militantis conatus, omnes leges, omnes regulae
tendunt; quoniam ecclesia quidam exercitus est Deo militans, *terribilis ut*
10 *castorum acies ordinata* dicitur,[1] uni procul dubio imperatori subjecta, ad
cujus nutum cuncta referuntur. Cumque pius ac maximus et optimus
Deus in suo sanguine fundaverit ecclesiam, eamque voluerit ad finem
usque saeculi perdurare, quis non dixerit in ea id regimen institutum
esse, quod optimum censetur? At vero, inter genera gubernationum,

---

[1] *Cant.* 6, 9.

356

EXCERPT FROM
IN MINORIBUS AGENTES

From these origins we learned that the one catholic and apostolic Church is the mother of all the faithful, outside of which there is no salvation, for she is the immaculate bride of Christ in whom all who strive to the end attain eternal life. For men struggle in the Church militant and do battle with demons as with her foes in order that they may at last attain peace and reign in triumph with Jesus, her master and law-giver, in the heavenly Jerusalem. This end is placed before the Christian; to this all endeavors, all laws, and all rules of the Church militant strive. Because the Church is an army waging war for God, it is said to be *terrible as an army drawn up in battle array*; without doubt she is subject to one ruler to whose will all matters are referred. Because the holy, omnipotent, and all-righteous God founded the Church in his own blood and willed her to endure until the end of time, who will not say that he established in her the rule which he considered the best? Certainly it is

NOTE: The Latin text is reprinted from *Bullarium diplomatum et privilegiorum sanctorum Romanorum pontificum*, ed. S. Franco and A. Dalmazzo (Turin, 1860), V, 178–180.

357

communis philosophorum sententia est praestare monarchiam, et Romani, quorum toto micuit orbe dignitas, quamvis, ejectis regibus, duos annuos consules elegerunt, et modo tribunos addidere, modo alios magistratus invenere, in adversis tamen casibus bellisque gravioribus ad
5 unum aliquem recurrerunt, virtute et auctoritate praestantem, quem dictatorem appellaverunt, cujus dicto non liceret adversari; et quamquam dictaturam ab initio temporaneam instituerunt, in Julio tamen et successoribus ejus perpetua effecta est. Nec umquam Romana res admirabilior aut celsior fuit quam sub Augusto Caesare, quando, jam
10 clausis Jani portis, totus fere orbis sub unius hominis gubernatione quievit. Quo tempore natus mundi salvator, monarchicum regimen ceteris praetulisse videtur gubernationibus. Idem probat totius fere orbis consuetudo, cujus maximam partem gubernant reges, sive christianos intueamur sive barbaros. Et quamvis civitates aliquot reperiantur,
15 quae, cum maxime serviant, liberas sese vocitant, sine rege viventes, non possunt tamen effugere, quin unum praeferant aliis, eique tamquam capiti pro tempore obediant. Quid plura? Caelestis aula nos admonet. Quid illa pulchrius? Quid ordinatius? Quid majus aut durabilius? Quid melius aut beatius? Quamvis in ea et angelorum diversi sint ordines, et
20 sanctorum spirituum innumerabiles chori, unus est tamen omnium rex aeternus Deus, qui condidit universa, et nihil negligit eorum quae condidit, cujus filius unigenitus Christus Jesus, cum pro nostra salute venisset in hunc mundum, servili accepta forma, ecclesiam, de qua loquimur, in cruce patiens, suo sanguine acquisivit, et in ea usque in
25 diem ascensionis corporaliter praesedit, et tamquam dux verus et imperator cuncta in finem suum direxit. Et cum ascendisset in caelum,

the consensus among philosophers that monarchy surpasses all other forms of government. Although the Romans, whose glory dazzled the whole world, chose two consuls annually after they expelled their kings, and at one time added tribunes and at another devised other magistracies, nevertheless in periods of crisis and in more serious wars they reverted to the rule of one who excelled in capacity and authority, whom they termed a dictator; no one was permitted to oppose his command. Although the Romans instituted this dictatorship at opportune times from the beginning of their history, nevertheless, with Julius [Caesar] and his successors this institution became permanent. The state of Rome was never more worthy of awe or more glorious than under Augustus Caesar, when, with the gates of war closed, almost the whole earth was at peace under the rule of one man. At this time the Savior of the world was born; thus he appears to have preferred the rule of a monarch over all other forms of rule. The custom of most of the earth confirms this, since kings rule most of the earth whether we consider Christians or barbarians. Although certain cities are found that call themselves free, though those are particularly enslaved that live without a king, nevertheless they cannot escape elevating one above the other citizens and obeying him as their ruler according to circumstances. What more need be said? The celestial host admonishes us. What could be more beautiful than that? What could be more ordered? What could be greater and more enduring? What could be better or more blessed? Although there are different orders of angels in the angelic host and innumerable choirs of holy spirits, nevertheless there is one eternal king of them all, the God who created all things and neglects nothing which he created.[1] His Son, the only-begotten Jesus Christ, when he came into this world for our salvation, assumed the form of a servant, and suffering upon the cross, secured the Church of which we speak with his own blood; he ruled over it in the flesh until the day of his ascension and as a good leader or general directed all things to their proper ends. When he ascended into heaven, he left the

---

[1] See p. 315.

IN MINORIBUS AGENTES

eum indubitanter sui gregis pastorem reliquit, cui dixerat: *Pasce oves meas, et tibi dabo claves regni caelorum.*[1] Neque enim dixit et non fecit, qui solus est verax. Grex Christi ecclesia est. Pastor primus ipse Christus fuit, et *pastor bonus, qui posuit animam suam pro ovibus suis.*[2] Secundus
5 pastor Petrus extitit, ab ipso Domino institutus atque omni potestate donatus, quae ad bene regendum commissas oves necessaria ducitur; alioquin Christus, qui sapientia Patris est, et omnino sapienter agit ecclesiae suae haud sufficienter providisset, quod est nefarium asserere. Et quamvis plures per orbem ecclesiae institutae fuerint et plures
10 episcopi, id est plures greges et ovilia plura et pastores plures; omnes tamen sub uno pastore et in uno grege atque ovili continebantur, sicut et hodie continentur, quia unus est Christi thalamus, una sponsa, unum ovile et unus pastor, et omnium episcoporum unus episcopus Romanus praesul, beati Petri successor et Jesu Christi vicarius. Petrus enim in
15 Antiochia primum sedit, deinde Romam venit, unde cum persecutionem fugiens vellet abire, a Domino prohibitus est, et hic glorioso martyrio vitam finivit, successore Clemente substituto; atque ita in hanc usque diem servatum est, ut qui Romae sederit antistes, rite institutus per legitimum electionis tramitem, tamquam Aaron vocatus a Domino, hunc
20 omnes christianae plebes, omnes populi, omnes reges, omnes clerici, omnes episcopi, tamquam Jesu Christi vicarium et beati Petri successorem, universalis eccelsiae caput ac rectorem et ducem, venerati sunt. Inter quos plurimi pro Christi nomine asperrimos perpessi cruciatus et morte mulctati, coronam martyrii susceperunt; plurimi confessores
25 egregii, vita, moribus et doctrina fulgentes, quamvis sine sanguinis effusione, non tamen sine periculis et labore ac voluntate parata, pro conservanda sacri evangelii auctoritate moriendi, ad caelestem gloriam pervenere, ut Gregorii, Damasi, Leonis, Innocentii, Bonifacii, Benedicti

---

[1] *Joan.* 21, 15–17; *Matth.* 16, 19.
[2] *Joan.* 10, 11.*

pastorate of his flock clearly to him to whom he said: *Feed my sheep,*
and *I will give you the keys of the kingdom of heaven.* For he who alone is
truth did not declare and then not accomplish what he had declared.
The Church is the flock of Christ. Christ himself was her first shepherd,
the good shepherd who laid down his life for his sheep. Peter was her second
shepherd, instituted by the Lord himself and endowed with all authority
that is considered necessary to rule well the sheep entrusted to him;
otherwise Christ, who is the wisdom of the Father and does all things
wisely, did not provide adequately for his church; but to assert this is
wicked. Although many churches were established throughout the world,
and these are numerous, that is, there are many flocks, many sheepfolds,
and many shepherds, nevertheless all were included then, as they are
included today, under one shepherd and in one flock and sheepfold. For
there is one marriage bed of Christ, one bride, one sheepfold, and one
shepherd, and there is one bishop over all bishops, the Roman Pontiff,
the successor of St. Peter and the Vicar of Jesus Christ.[1] For Peter first
ruled in Antioch and then came to Rome; and when he desired to leave
that city to flee persecution, he was not permitted to do so by the Lord.
Here he ended his life in a glorious martyrdom, after appointing Clement
as his successor. Thus it is observed until this day that he who occupies
the See of Rome, he who has been duly instituted through the legal
procedure of election and who has been called as Aaron by the Lord, is
venerated by all Christian peoples, all races, all kings, all clergy, and all
bishops as the Vicar of Jesus Christ, the successor of St. Peter and the
head, leader, and ruler of the Church Universal. Many of these bishops
suffered the most savage torments for the name of Christ and underwent
death to receive the crown of martyrdom; so, also, many illustrious confessors who were conspicuous in their life, deeds, and teaching—although they died without suffering a violent death—nevertheless with
peril, struggle, and fixed purpose, defended the authority of the Holy
Gospel and attained celestial glory, as the names of Gregory, Damasus,

---

[1] See pp. 73–75.

et alia nomina, inter quae tertius claruit Eugenius, ex monasterio sancti Anastasii ad summum sacerdotium evocatus, ad quem divus BERNAR-DUS monachorum pater, non minus doctrinae fulgore quam vitae sanctimonia illustris, inter multa, hujusmodi verba conscripsit:[1] *Inda-*
5 *gemus*, inquit, *adhuc diligentius quid sis, quam geras videlicet personam pro tempore in ecclesia Dei. Tu es sacerdos magnus, summus pontifex, tu princeps episcoporum, tu haeres apostolorum, tu primatu Abel, gubernatu Noe, patriarchatu Abraham, ordine Melchisedech, dignitate Aaron, auctoritate Moyses, judicatu Samuel, potestate Petrus, unctione Christus.*
10 *Tu es, cui claves traditae, cui oves creditae sunt. Sunt et alii quidem caeli janitores et gregum pastores, sed tu "tanto gloriosius quanto et differentius, utrumque prae illis nomen haereditasti."[2] Habent illi assignatos sibi greges singuli singulos, tibi universi crediti uni sumus. Nec modo ovium, sed et pastorum tu unus omnium pastor.* Haec BERNARDUS ad Eugenium III
15 scribit, cui supremam et omnimodam in ecclesia potestatem concedit. Quod ille de tertio testatur Eugenio, hoc nos de quarto et omnibus aliis Romanis Pontificibus profitemur, quia dignitatis est auctoritas. Liquet igitur unum in ecclesia caput esse et unum principem, quia pax populi ex uno rectore dependet, et pluralitas principum discordiam parit.
20 Christus ecclesiae suae in ultimo testamento pacem reliquit, et pacem multis verbis commendavit. Dedit ergo et regimen pacis amicum, id est monarchicum, sub beato Petro et successoribus ejus administrari cuncta praecipiens, clavibus illi commissis et cura gregis damandata.

---

[1] *De consideratione*, L. II, c. 8 (*PL* 182, 751C–D).
[2] *Hebr.* 1, 4.

IN MINORIBUS AGENTES

Leo, Innocent, Boniface, Benedict, and others [bear witness]. Among these shone Eugenius III, summoned to the supreme pontificate from the monastery of St. Anastasius, to whom the divine BERNARD, father of monks, illustrious no less for the renown of his teaching than for the holiness of his life, wrote words of this sort, among many others:[1] *Let us now examine more carefully who you are, namely what authority in the Church of God in this world you bear in your person. You are the high priest and the supreme pontiff. You are the prince of bishops and the heir of the apostles. By your primacy, you are Abel; by your office as helmsman, Noah; by your patriarchate, Abraham; by your orders, Melchizedech; by your dignity, Aaron; by your authority, Moses; by your judicial power, Samuel; by your jurisdiction, Peter; and by your anointment, Christ. You are the one to whom the keys have been given and the sheep entrusted. There are indeed other gatekeepers of heaven, and there are other shepherds of the flock; but you are in both respects more glorious and exceptional than they "in as much as you have inherited a title superior to theirs." They have assigned to them particular portions of the flock, but you have been given charge of all the sheep. You are the one shepherd not only of the sheep, but of all the shepherds.* BERNARD writes these words to Eugenius III to whom he grants the supreme authority in the Church in every respect. What Bernard declared for Eugenius III we acknowledge for Eugenius IV and all other Roman pontiffs: that their authority springs from the dignity of their office. It is evident therefore that there is one head and ruler in the Church because the peace of the people depends upon one ruler and the plurality of rulers breeds discord. Christ bequeathed peace to his Church in his last testament and commended peace with many words. Therefore he gave it the form of rule that fosters peace, that is, monarchy, ordering all things to be administered under St. Peter and his successors, when he gave Peter the keys and entrusted the care of his flock to him. We, to whom authority has been given to convoke and dissolve general councils, declare these things concerning the power and

---

[1] See p. 93.

363

IN MINORIBUS AGENTES

Haec nos de Romani pontificis auctoritate et potestate sentimus, cui et congregare generalia concilia et dissolvere datum est. Qui, etsi filius est propter regenerationem, propter dignitatem tamen pater habetur; et sicuti filiationis causa venerari debet ecclesiam tamquam matrem, ita et
5 praelationis causa praefertur ei, ut pastor gregi, princeps populo, rector familiae. Cum his et generalis concilii auctoritatem et potestatem complectimur, quemadmodum et aevo nostro Constantiae, dum ibi fuit synodus universalis, declaratum definitumque est. Veneramur enim Constantiense concilium et cuncta quae praedecessoribus approbata,
10 inter quae nullum invenimus umquam fuisse ratum, quod, stante Romano indubitato praesule, absque ipsius auctoritate convenerit; quia non est corpus ecclesiae sine capite, et omnis ex capite defluit in membra potestas. Haec nostra sententia est, filii; haec credimus et profitemur; haec jam senes et in apostolatus apice constituti pro veritate
15 asserimus.

Si quae vel vobis vel aliis conscripsimus aliquando, quae huic doctrinae repugnent, illa, tamquam erronea et juvenilis animi parum pensata judicia, revocamus atque omnino respuimus.

Datum Romae apud Sanctum Petrum, sexto kalendas maii, anno
20 millesimo quadringentesimo sexagesimo tertio.

authority of the Roman pontiff. Although the Pope is a son because of his rebirth [in baptism], nevertheless he is esteemed as a father because of his dignity; because this father ought to be revered as the Church our mother, so the source of primacy is set over the Church, as a shepherd is set over a flock, a ruler over a people, and a head over a household. With these authorities, we recognize the power and authority of a general council as it was declared and defined in our age at Constance, when the ecumenical council was there assembled. For we revere the Council of Constance and all councils that were approved by our predecessors; we have never heard of an approved council that assembled without papal authority when[1] there was an unquestioned Roman pontiff[1]; the body of the Church is not without a head and all power flows from the head into the members. This is our position, our sons; this we believe and this we acknowledge; this we assert, already aged and established at the summit of the Apostolate to defend the truth.

If we have ever written to you or to others things that are opposed to this teaching, we reject and retract these as the erroneous and lightly pondered judgments of an adolescent mind.

Promulgated at Rome in St. Peter's on the twenty-sixth day of April in the year 1463.

[1-1] This important qualification allows for the views of that party in Conciliarism which regards the superiority of the Council over the Pope as obtaining 'in case of emergency' such as, e.g., schism.

INDEX OF
SCRIPTURAL QUOTATIONS

INDEX OF SCRIPTURAL QUOTATIONS

INDEX OF SCRIPTURAL QUOTATIONS

INDEX OF SCRIPTURAL QUOTATIONS

INDEX OF SCRIPTURAL QUOTATIONS

GENERAL INDEX

GENERAL INDEX

Aachen, city of, 30

Aaron, 134, 136, 292, 294, 362

Abel, 92, 294, 362

Abihu, 134

Abimelech, 134

Abraham, 92, 134, 294, 338, 362

Absalom, 150

Abyron, 108

Acacius, 285, 286, 346

Acceptatio (Pragmatic Sanction of Mainz), 10, 12, 13

Achan, 134

Acta sanctorum, 216

Adam, 130, 132

Adolf, Graf von Nassau-Wiesbaden, Archbishop of Mainz: and election of Diether, 252, 254; oath of fealty of to Diether, 274, 276, 278; administration of in Thuringia, 18; provision of as archbishop, 30–31, 42, 66, 122, 154, 250, 270, 276; coronation of, 32; response of German princes to, 33–35, 352, 354; response of University of Heidelberg to, 36, 154; defeat of at Seckenheim, 37; and capture of Mainz, 38–39; and settlement of Zeilsheim, 40; mentioned, 5, 17, 58, 156

Agathon, Pope, 96

Ahaziah, King, 44, 300

Ailly, Pierre d', 50

Albert, Archduke, 41

Albert Achilles, Margrave and Elector of Brandenburg, 13, 21, 23, 24, 29, 34

Alexander II, Pope, 169

Alexander III, Pope, 163

Amalekites, 136

Ambrose, 84, 96, 176, 190, 332, 344;
Apol. prophetae David, 310;
Comm. in epist. I ad Cor., 300;
De officiis, 176, 180, 196;
De paradiso, 208;
Expos. in Lucam, 340, 342

GENERAL INDEX

Anacletus, Pope, 84, 94, 178, 184, 324, 326, 336

Ananias, 44, 300

Anastasius, Emperor, 285, 286

Anastasius, Pope, 182

Andreas, Joannes, 126

Annates, 10, 12, 13, 21, 22, 23, 24, 30, 31, 33, 40. *See also* Indulgences; Pope, provisions of; Tithes

Anterus, Pope, 184, 186

Antioch, 330, 332, 334, 360

Antiochus, King, 214

Anti-trinitarianism, 46

Apostolic See: defense of rights of, 12, 232; rebellion against, 16, 35, 44, 104, 130, 188, 200, 206, 234, 240, 250, 258; obedience to, 36, 66, 70, 102, 110, 154, 190, 238, 274, 354; submission to, 41, 98; and authority of the Church, 51, 53; foundation of, 80; decrees of, 96, 100, 106, 108, 112, 210, 242; judgment of, 220; appeal against, 238; primacy of, 342; mentioned, 148, 150, 152, 228, 260, 284. *See also* Curia, Roman

Appollinarius of Laodicea, 101

Aquinas, Thomas:
    Contra errores Graecorum, 344;
    In scripto sententiarum, 170, 186;
    Summa theologica, 100, 180, 216

Archchancellor of Germany, 20, 21, 238, 248

Arians, 48

Aristotle, 335;
    Ethica Nicomachea, 124, 140, 216;
    Metaphysica, 316;
    Physica, 140

Arius, 330

Asella, 218

Asia, 332

Aubenas, Roger, 9, 15

Augustine, 49, 50, 51, 84, 158, 164, 180, 184, 196, 200, 338, 344;
    Confessiones, 110;
    Contra epistolam Manichei quam vocant fundamenti, 75;
    Contra Faustum Manich., 80, 118, 208;
    De baptismo contra Donatistas, 162;
    De civitate Dei, 150, 180;
    De diversis quaestiones LXXXIII, 82;
    De doctrina christiana, 100;
    De duabus animabus, 208;
    De mendacio, 202;
    De nuptiis et concupiscientia, 316;
    Enarrationes in Psalmos, 172, 190;
    Epistolae, 176, 178, 186, 192, 316;
    Retractationes, 3;
    Sermones, 112, 114–116, 190, 314;
    Tractatus in Joannis evangelium, 158, 164, 166

Augustine, Hermits of St., 8

Augustus Caesar, 358

Aurelius Augustine, 312, 314

Austin convents, 8

Austria, duke of, 32

Baalphegor, 136

Bamberg, Bishop of, 32

Barnabus, 334

Basel: Council of, 3, 5, 7, 10, 11, 12, 13, 14, 15, 17, 23, 24, 42, 43, 53; University of, 5

Basil:
    Regulae brevius tractatae, 116, 192

Bavaria, duke of, 32

Bede, the Venerable, 106, 150

Beheim, Michel:
    Reimchronik, 34

Benedict, 360

GENERAL INDEX

GENERAL INDEX

84, 86, 90, 94, 96, 102, 110, 112, 320, 322, 328, 338, 340, 342, 362, 364; excommunication from, 162, 168, 210; defense of, 170, 172, 174, 204; mentioned, 104, 148, 188, 213, 292, 330, 332, 334, 358

Cistercians, 152

Claudius, Emperor, 332

Clement, 84, 184, 188, 220, 294;
    Epistola, 294

Clement IV, Pope, 44, 304, 307

Clement of Alexandria, 339

Cochlaeus, Johann:
    De authoritate ecclesiae et scripturae (1524), 54

Coelestine, 288

Collation of benefices, 8, 12, 13, 146. *See also* Expectative graces; Pope, provisions of; Reservations

College of Cardinals, *see* Cardinals, Sacred College of

Cologne: cathedral chapter of, 18; city of, 30, 128; Elector of, 9; University of, 3, 14

Conciliarism, 3, 6, 7, 10, 11, 12, 14, 20, 24, 27, 30, 42, 43, 48, 49, 50, 52, 53, 95, 365. *See also* Council, general

Concordat of Bologna, 6

Concordat of Vienna, *see* Vienna, Concordat of

Congregatio fidelium, 48

Congress of Mantua, *see* Mantua, Congress of

Conradin, 304, 307

Constance: Council of, 7, 12, 14, 24, 42, 43, 48, 51, 340, 344, 364; See of, 54

Constantine, 196–198

Constantius, 196, 198

Corbi, 136

Coronation, imperial, 9

Corpus Juris Canonici:

Decretum Gratiani, Pars I:
c. 54, D. I: 338, 342;
c. 2, D. VIII: 110;
c. 11, D. IX: 116;
c. 3, D. XI: 86;
c. 9, D. XI: 80;
c. 2, D. XII: 102;
c. 2, D. XV: 76, 310;
c. 1, D. XIX: 100;
c. 2, D. XIX: 96;
c. 3, D. XIX: 106;
c. 5, D. XIX: 102;
c. 6, D. XIX: 100;
c. 7, D. XIX: 86, 104, 116, 326;
p. 1, D. XXI: 86;
c. 2, D. XXI: 86;
c. 3, D. XXI: 86, 336;
c. 9, D. XXI: 144;
c. 1, D. XXII: 86, 96, 336;
c. 2, D. XXII: 86, 94, 326, 336;
c. 6, D. XXXII: 170;
c. 14, D. XXXVII: 220;
c. 1, D. XLIII: 202;
c. 2, D. LXXV: 126;
c. 2, D. LXXX: 86;
c. 15, D. LXXXI: 104;
c. 3, D. LXXXIII: 182;
c. 3, D. LXXXVI: 182;
c. 21, D. LXXXVI: 176;
c. 1, D. XCIII: 188, 294;
c. 3, D. XCIII: 98;
c. 25, D. XCIII: 292;
c. 1, D. C: 126;
c. 8, D. C: 106;

Decretum Gratiani, Pars II:
c. 30, C. I, qu. 1: 164;
c. 32, C. I, qu. 1: 162;
c. 34, C. I, qu. 1: 164;
c. 61, C. I, qu. 1: 164;
c. 77, C. I, qu. 1: 162;
c. 84, C. I, qu. 1: 164;

GENERAL INDEX

GENERAL INDEX

GENERAL INDEX

GENERAL INDEX

GENERAL INDEX

Pastor, Ludwig, 8, 14, 15

Patarines, 48

Paul, 44, 98, 136, 246, 290, 300, 332, 340, 342

Paulinus, Bishop of Antioch, 100

Pelagians, 48

Pelagius, 288

Pelagius, Pope, 81, 336

Penance, 41, 168

Peter: power of the keys of, 47, 308, 328, 336, 340; as embodiment of unity in Church, 48, 92, 318, 340; papal succession to primacy of, 49, 88, 90, 94, 96, 124, 326, 338, 352, 360; primacy of over apostles, 51, 82, 310, 312, 320, 326, 330, 332, 334; primacy of over Church, 52, 80, 84, 86, 94, 104, 120, 294, 308, 322, 324, 328, 340, 342, 344, 362; mentioned, 48, 188, 246, 294, 300

Peter Lombard:

Sent., 186

Pfaffenrachtung, 34

Pfedersheim, 22

Philip, Duke of Burgundy, 37

Philip, Graf of Katzelnbogen, 33, 38

Philip von Swabia, 304

Phinehas, 136, 298

Photius, 286

Piben, Bishop of, 8

Piccolomini, Aeneas Sylvius, *see* Pius II

Picotti, G. B., 4, 5, 6, 26, 41, 310

Pilate, 198

Pisa: Council of (1409), 7; Council of (1511), 3

Pius II, Pope: orator at Council of Basel, 3; as Aeneas Sylvius Piccolomini, 3, 8, 11, 13–14; and *Execrabilis*, 3–7, 27, 43, 224; and Congress of Mantua and confirmation of Diether, 20, 22; relations with German princes, 23, 28, 29, 348; deposition and excommunication of

Diether, 16, 31, 34, 66, 122, 248; provision of Adolf, 31, 66; struggle against Diether and allies, 37, 44; struggle against Sigismund and Gregor Heimburg, 17, 25, 27, 41, 48, 310; favor to Gabriel Biel, 66, 68; mentioned, 18, 19, 20, 45, 46, 47, 54, 58, 222, 282, 286;

Commentaries, 18, 19, 20, 29, 30, 31, 44

Plenitudo potestatis, 42, 52, 92, 95, 322

Pliny:

Hist. Nat., 316

Podiebrad, George, King of Bohemia, 23, 28, 41

Pontus, 332

Pope: absolution by, 40, 41; better informed, appeal to a, 25, 26, 32, 33, 36, 109, 148; bankers of, 21, 22, 234, 260; monarchy of, 3, 28, 47; primacy of, 6, 41, 47, 49, 51, 294, 322, 342, 344, 362, 364; provisions of, 25, 31, 122, 232, 276. *See also* Collation of benefices; Expectative graces; Reservations

Post, R. R., 55

Power of the keys, 47, 49, 92, 96, 132, 294, 308, 312, 324, 328, 336, 340, 360, 362

Pragmatic Sanction of Bourges, 4, 10, 15

Pragmatic Sanction of Mainz, *see Acceptatio*

Prierias, Sylvester:

In praesumptuosas Martini Lutheri (1517), 54

Primate of Germany (archbishop of Mainz), 20

Pseudo-Augustine:

De fide ad Petrum, 78

Pseudo-Chrysostom:

Hom. in Mattheum, 200, 206

Pseudo-Clement:

Epist., 296

Pseudo-Gelasius, 113

GENERAL INDEX

GENERAL INDEX

Timothy, 136, 138

Tithes, 9, 11, 12, 29; and crusade, 15, 20, 22, 23, 24, 29, 30, 234. *See also* Annates; Indulgences

Tivoli, 246

Tower of Babel, 42, 132

Trent: Bishop of, 8; Council of, 17

Trier: cathedral chapter of, 18; Elector of, 9

Trieste, Bishop of, 8

Trojan War, 322

Tübingen, University of, 59

Ugonius Matthias:
    De conciliis, 6

Ullmann, Karl, 14

Ulric, Graf of Württemberg, 30, 34, 37

Unam Sanctam, 5

Urban II, Pope, 168, 192

Utrecht, See of, 54

Uzziah, 294

Venice, 5, 41

Ventanius, Bishop, 204

Verden, Bishopric of, 20

Vicar of Christ, 43, 44, 46, 49, 90, 98, 110, 114, 210, 224, 292, 310, 336, 344, 360

Vienna: Corcordat of (17 February 1448), 12–13, 14, 15, 16, 25; Reichstag (September 1460), 22, 23, 258; University of, 14

Vio, Thomas de, *see* Cajetan

Vitalis, Bishop of Antioch, 100

Voigt, George, 10, 13, 14, 21, 25, 26, 28, 35, 36, 37, 38, 39, 41, 44

Volprecht von Ders, 21

Wadding, Luke, 186

Werner, Johann, von Flassland, 29, 30, 31

Wernheim, 33

William, Duke of Saxony, 32, 34

Wismair, Leonard, 25

Wittelsbach, 28, 39

Worms: Bishop of, 32; diet of (1521), 7

Wrede, Adolf, 7

Würzburg, Bishop of, 32

Wyclif, John, 46, 48, 344

Zamometič, Andrea, Archbishop of Gran, 5

Zeilsheim, 40

Zimri, 136

Zur, 136

387